CHILTON BOOK COMPANY

REPAIR & TUNE-UP GUIDE

OMNI HORIZON RAMPAGE 1978-86

All U.S. and Canadian models of DODGE Omni, Miser, 024, Charger 2.2 • PLYMOUTH Horizon, Miser, TC3, TC3 Tourismo, Rampage

President LAWRENCE A. FORNASIERI
Vice President and General Manager JOHN P. KUSHNERICK
Executive editor KERRY A. FREEMAN, S.A.E.
Senior Editor RICHARD J. RIVELE, S.A.E.
Editor RONALD T. WEBB

CHILTON BOOK COMPANY
Radnor, Pennsylvania
19089

SAFETY NOTICE

Proper service and repair procedures are vital to the safe, reliable operation of all motor vehicles, as well as the personal safety of those performing repairs. This book outlines procedures for servicing and repairing vehicles using safe, effective methods. The procedures contain many NOTES, CAUTIONS and WARNINGS which should be followed along with standard safety procedures to eliminate the possibility of personal injury or improper service which could damage the vehicle or compromise its safety.

It is important to note that repair procedures and techniques, tools and parts for servicing motor vehicles, as well as the skill and experience of the individual performing the work vary widely. It is not possible to anticipate all of the conceivable ways or conditions under which vehicles may be serviced, or to provide cautions as to all of the possible hazards that may result. Standard and accepted safety precautions and equipment should be used when handling toxic or flammable fluids, and safety goggles or other protection should be used during cutting, grinding, chiseling, prying, or any other process that can cause material removal or projectiles.

Some procedures require the use of tools specially designed for a specific purpose. Before substituting another tool or procedure, you must be completely satisfied that neither your personal safety, nor the performance of the vehicle will be endangered.

Although information in this guide is based on industry sources and is as complete as possible at the time of publication, the possibility exists that the manufacturer made later changes which could not be included here. While striving for total accuracy, Chilton Book Company cannot assume responsibility for any errors, changes, or omissions that may occur in the compilation of this data.

PART NUMBERS

Part numbers listed in this reference are not recommendations by Chilton for any product by brand name. They are references that can be used with interchange manuals and aftermarket supplier catalogs to locate each brand supplier's discrete part number.

SPECIAL TOOLS

Special tools are recommended by many vehicle manufacturers to perform specific jobs. Use has been kept to a minimum in this guide, but, where absolutely necessary, special tools are referred to in the text by the part number of the tool manufacturer. These tools can be purchased, under the appropriate part number from Miller Special Tools, Division of Utica Tool Company, Inc., 32615 Park Lane, Garden City, Michigan 48135 or an equivalent tool can be purchased locally from a tool supplier or parts outlet. Before substituting any tool for the one recommended, read the SAFETY NOTICE at the top of this page.

ACKNOWLEDGMENTS

The Chilton Book Company expresses its appreciation to the Chrysler Corporation, Dodge and Plymouth Divisions, Detroit, Michigan for their generous assistance.

629.287
CH1

Copyright © 1987 by Chilton Book Company
All Rights Reserved
Published in Radnor, Pennsylvania 19089 by Chilton Book Company

Manufactured in the United States of America
1234567890   6543210987

Chilton's Repair & Tune-Up Guide: Omni/Horizon/Rampage 1978–86
ISBN 0-8019-7685-5 pbk.
Library of Congress Catalog Card No. 85-47985

CONTENTS

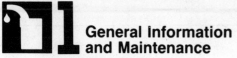

Quick Reference Specifications For Your Vehicle

Fill in this chart with the most commonly used specifications for your vehicle. Specifications can be found in Chapters 1 through 3 or on the tune-up decal under the hood of the vehicle.

 Tune-Up

Firing Order_____

Spark Plugs:

    Type_____

    Gap (in.)_____

Torque (ft. lbs.)_____

Idle Speed (rpm)_____

Ignition Timing (°)_____

    Vacuum or Electronic Advance (Connected/Disconnected)_____

Valve Clearance (in.)

    Intake_____   Exhaust_____

Capacities

Engine Oil Type (API Rating)_____

    With Filter Change (qts)_____

    Without Filter Change (qts)_____

Cooling System (qts)_____

Manual Transmission (pts)_____

    Type_____

Automatic Transmission (pts)_____

    Type_____

Front Differential (pts)_____

    Type_____

Rear Differential (pts)_____

    Type_____

Transfer Case (pts)_____

    Type_____

FREQUENTLY REPLACED PARTS

Use these spaces to record the part numbers of frequently replaced parts.

PCV VALVE	OIL FILTER	AIR FILTER	FUEL FILTER
Type_____	Type_____	Type_____	Type_____
Part No._____	Part No._____	Part No._____	Part No._____

General Information and Maintenance

HOW TO USE THIS BOOK

Chilton's Repair & Tune-Up Guide is intended to help you learn more about the inner workings of your vehicle and save you money on its upkeep and operation.

The first two chapters will be the most used, since they contain maintenance and tune-up information and procedures. Studies have shown that a properly tuned and maintained car can get at least 10% better gas milage than an out-of-tune car. The other chapters deal with the more complex systems of your car. Operating systems from engine through brakes are covered to the extent that the average do-it-yourselfer becomes mechanically involved. This book will not explain such things as rebuilding the differential for the simple reason that the expertise required and the investment in special tools make this task uneconomical. It will give you detailed instructions to help you change your own brake pads and shoes, tune-up the engine, and do many more jobs that will save you money, give you personal satisfaction, and help you avoid expensive problems.

A secondary purpose of this book is a reference for owners who want to understand their car and/or their mechanics better. In this case, no tools at all are required.

Before removing any bolts, read through the entire procedure. This will give you the overall view of what tools and supplies will be required. There is nothing more frustrating than having to walk to the bus stop on Monday morning because you were short one bolt on Sunday afternoon. So read ahead and plan ahead. Each operation should be approached logically and all procedures thoroughly understood before attempting any work.

All chapters contain adjustments, maintenance, removal and installation procedures, and repair or overhaul procedures. When repair is not considered practical, we tell you how to remove the part and then how to install the new or rebuilt replacement. In this way, you at least save the labor costs. Backyard repair of such components as the alternator is just not practical.

Two basic mechanic's rules should be mentioned here. One, whenever the left side of the car or engine is referred to, it is meant to specify the driver's side of the car. Conversely, the right side of the car means the passenger's side. Secondly, most screws and bolts are removed by turning counterclockwise, and tightened by turning clockwise.

Safety is always the most important rule. Constantly be aware of the dangers involved in working on an automobile and taking the proper precautions. (See the section in this chapter "Servicing Your Vehicle Safely" and the SAFETY NOTICE on the acknowledgement page.)

Pay attention to the instructions provided. There are 3 common mistakes in mechanical work:

1. Incorrect order of assembly, disassembly or adjustment. When taking something apart or putting it together, doing things in the wrong order usually just costs you extra time; however, it CAN break something. Read the entire procedure before beginning disassembly. Do everything in the order in which the instructions say you should do it, even if you can't immediately see a reason for it. When you're taking apart something that is very intricate (for example, a carburetor), you might want to draw a picture of how it looks when assembled at one point in order to make sure you get everything back in its proper position. (We will supply exploded views whenever possible.) When making adjustments, especially tune-up adjustments, do them in order; often, one adjustment affects another, and you cannot expect even satisfactory results unless each adjust-

ment is made only when it cannot be changed by any other.

2. Overtorquing (or undertorquing). While it is more common for overtorquing to cause damage, undertorquing can cause a fastener to vibrate loose causing serious damage. Especially when dealing with aluminum parts, pay attention to torque specifications and utilize a torque wrench in assembly. If a torque figure is not available, remember that if you are using the right tool to do the job, you will probably not have to strain yourself to get a fastener tight enough. The pitch of most threads is so slight that the tension you put on the wrench will be multiplied many, many times in actual force on what you are tightening. A good example of how critical torque is can be seen in the case of spark plug installation, especially where you are putting the plug into an aluminum cylinder head. Too little torque can fail to crush the gasket, causing leakage of combustion gases and consequent overheating of the plug and engine parts. Too much torque can damage the threads, or distort the plug, which changes the spark gap.

There are many commercial products available for ensuring that fasteners won't come loose, even if they are not torqued just right (a very common brand is "Loctite®"). If you're worried about getting something together tight enough to hold, but loose enough to avoid mechanical damage during assembly, one of these products might offer substantial insurance. Read the label on the package and make sure the product is compatible with the materials, fluids, etc. involved before choosing one.

3. Crossthreading. This occurs when a part such as a bolt is screwed into a nut or casting at the wrong angle and forced. Crossthreading is more likely to occur if access is difficult. It helps to clean and lubricate fasteners, and to start threading with the part to be installed going straight in. Then, start the bolt, spark plug, etc. with your fingers. If you encounter resistance, unscrew the part and start over again at a different angle until it can be inserted and turned several turns without much effort. Keep in mind that many parts, especially spark plugs, use tapered threads so that gentle turning will automatically bring the part you're threading to the proper angle if you don't force it or resist a change in angle. Don't put a wrench on the part until it's been turned a couple of turns by hand. If you suddenly encounter resistance, and the part has not seated fully, don't force it. Pull it back out and make sure it's clean and threading properly.

Always take your time and be patient; once you have some experience, working on your car will become an enjoyable hobby.

TOOLS AND EQUIPMENT

Naturally, without the proper tools and equipment it is impossible to properly service your vehicle. It would be impossible to catalog each tool that you would need to perform each or any operation in this book. It would also be unwise for the amateur to rush out and buy an expensive set of tools on the theory that he may need one or more of them at sometime.

The best approach is to proceed slowly, gathering together a good quality set of those tools that are used most frequently. Don't be misled by the low cost of bargain tools. It is far better to spend a little more for better quality. Forged wrenches, 10 or 12 point sockets and fine tooth ratchets are by far preferable to their less expensive counterparts. As any good mechanic can tell you, there are few worse experiences than trying to work on a car or truck with bad tools. Your monetary savings will be far outweighted by frustration and mangled knuckles.

Begin accumulating those tools that are used most frequently; those associated with routine maintenance and tune-up.

In addition to the normal assortment of screwdrivers and pliers you should have the following tools for routine maintenance jobs (your Omni or Horizon uses both SAE and metric fasteners):

1. SAE/Metric wrenches—sockets and combination open end/box end wrenches in sizes from ⅛ in. (3 mm) to ¾ in. (19 mm); and a spark plug socket (¹³⁄₁₆).

If possible, buy various length socket drive extensions. One break in this department is that the metric sockets available in the U.S. will all fit the ratchet handles and extensions you may already have (¼, ⅜, and ½ in. drive).

2. Jackstands—for support;
3. Oil filter wrench;
4. Oil filler spout—for pouring oil;
5. Grease gun—for chassis lubrication;
6. Hydrometer—for checking the battery;
7. A container for draining oil;
8. Many rags for wiping up the inevitable mess.

In addition to the above items there are several others that are not absolutely necessary, but handy to have around. These include oil dry, a transmission funnel and the usual supply of lubricants, antifreeze and fluids, although these can be purchased as needed. This is a basic list for routine maintenance, but only your personal needs and desire can accurately determine your list of tools.

The second list of tools is for tune-ups. While the tools involved here are slightly more sophisticated, they need not be outrageously ex-

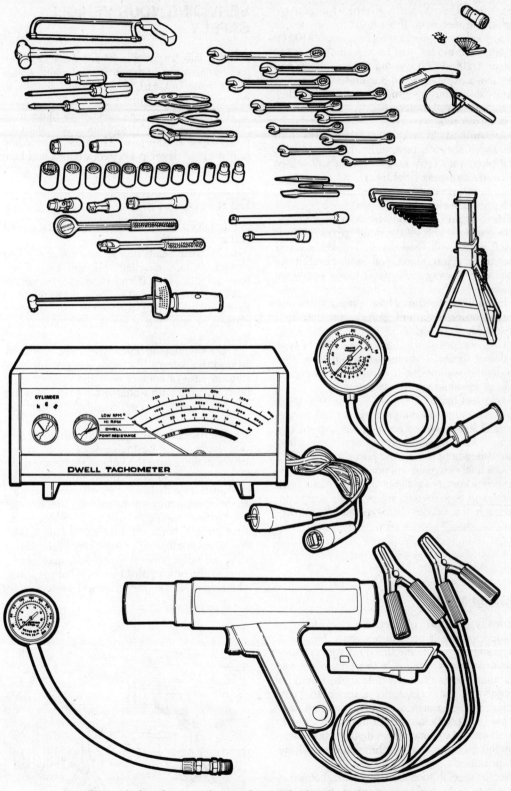

The majority of automotive service can be handled with these tools

pensive. There are several inexpensive tach/dwell meters on the market that are every bit as good for the average mechanic as a $100.00 professional model. Just be sure that it goes to a least 1,200–1,500 rpm on the tach scale and that it works on 4, 6 and 8 cylinder engines. A basic list of tune-up equipment could include:

1. Tach-dwell meter;
2. Spark plug wrench;
3. Timing light (a DC light that works from the car's battery is best, although an AC light that plugs into 110V house current will suffice at some sacrifice in brightness);
4. Wire spark plug gauge/adjusting tools;
5. Set of feeler blades.

Here again, be guided by your own needs. A feeler blade will set the point gap as easily as dwell meter will read dwell, but slightly less accurately. And since you will need a tachometer anyway . . . well, make your own decision.

In addition to these basic tools, there are several other tools and gauges you may find useful. These include:

1. A compression gauge. The screw-in type is slower to use, but eliminates the possibility of a faulty reading due to escaping pressure;
2. A manifold vacuum gauge;
3. A test light;
4. An induction meter. This is used for determining whether or not there is current in a wire. These are handy for use if a wire is broken somewhere in a wiring harness.

As a final note, you will probably find a torque wrench necessary for all but the most basic work. The beam type models are perfectly adequate, although the newer click type are more precise.

Special Tools

Normally, the use of special factory tools is avoided for repair procedures, since these are not readily available for the do-it-yourself mechanic. When it is possible to perform the job with more commonly available tools, it will be pointed out, but occasionally, a special tool was designed to perform a specific function and should be used. Before substituting another tool, you should be convinced that neither your safety nor the performance of the vehicle will be compromised.

Some special tools are available commercially from major tool manufacturers. Others can be purchased from Miller Special Tools; Division of Utica Tool Company, 32615 Park Lane, Garden City, Michigan 48135.

SERVICING YOUR VEHICLE SAFELY

It is virtually impossible to anticipate all of the hazards involved with automotive maintenance and service but care and common sense will prevent most accidents.

The rules of safety for mechanics range from "don't smoke around gasoline," to "use the proper tool for the job." The trick to avoiding injuries is to develop safe work habits and take every possible precaution.

Do's

• Do keep a fire extinguisher and first aid kit within easy reach.

• Do wear safety glasses or goggles when cutting, drilling, grinding or prying, even if you have 20-20 vision. If you wear glasses for the sake of vision, then they should be made of hardened glass that can serve also as safety glasses, or wear safety goggles over your regular glasses.

• Do shield your eyes whenever you work around the battery. Batteries contain sulphuric acid; in case of contact with the eyes or skin, flush the area with water or a mixture of water and baking soda and get medical attention immediately.

• Do use safety stands for any undercar service. Jacks are for raising vehicles; safety stands are for making sure the vehicle stays raised until you want it to come down. Whenever the vehicle is raised, block the wheels remaining on the ground and set the parking brake.

• Do use adequate ventilation when working with any chemicals. Like carbon monoxide, the asbestos dust resulting from brake lining wear can be poisonous in sufficient quantities.

• Do disconnect the negative battery cable when working on the electrical system. The

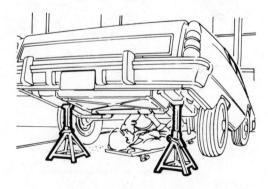

Always use jackstands when working under the car

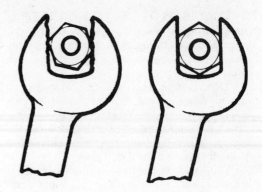

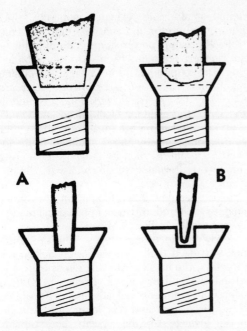

Screwdrivers should be kept in good condition to prevent injury

Use the correct size wrench and position it properly on the flats of the nut or bolt

• Do properly maintain your tools. Loose hammerheads, mushroomed punches and chisels, frayed or poorly grounded electrical cords, excessively worn screwdrivers, spread wrenches (open end), cracked sockets, slipping ratchets, or faulty droplight sockets can cause accidents.

• Do use the proper size and type of tool for the job being done.

• Do when possible, pull on a wrench handle rather than push on it, and adjust your stance to prevent a fall.

• Do be sure that adjustable wrenches are tightly adjusted on the nut or bolt and pulled so that the face is on the side of the fixed jaw.

• Do select a wrench or socket that fits the nut or bolt. The wrench or socket should sit straight, not cocked.

• Do strike squarely with a hammer—avoid glancing blows.

• Do set the parking brake and block the drive wheels if the work requires that the engine be running.

Don'ts

• Don't run an engine in a garage or anywhere else without proper ventilation—EVER! Carbon monoxide is poisonous; it takes a long time to leave the human body and you can build up a deadly supply of it in your system by simply breathing in a little every day. You may not realize you are slowly poisoning yourself. Always use power vents, windows, fans or open the garage doors.

• Don't work around moving parts while wearing a necktie or other loose clothing. Short sleeves are much safer than long, loose sleeves and hard-toed shoes with neoprene soles protect your toes and give a better grip on slippery surfaces. Jewelry such as watches, fancy belt buckles, beads or body adornment of any kind is not safe working around a car. Long hair should be hidden under a hat or cap.

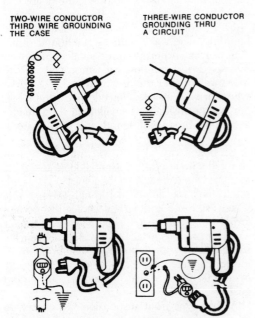

TWO-WIRE CONDUCTOR THIRD WIRE GROUNDING THE CASE

THREE-WIRE CONDUCTOR GROUNDING THRU A CIRCUIT

THREE-WIRE CONDUCTOR ONE WIRE TO A GROUND

THREE-WIRE CONDUCTOR GROUNDING THRU AN ADAPTER PLUG

Power tools should always be properly grounded

primary ignition system can contain up to 40,000 volts.

• Do follow manufacturer's directions whenever working with potentially hazardous materials. Both brake fluid and antifreeze are poisonous if taken internally.

• Don't use pockets for toolboxes. A fall or bump can drive a screwdriver deep into your body. Even a wiping cloth hanging from the back pocket can wrap around a spinning shaft or fan.

• Don't smoke when working around gasoline, cleaning solvent or other flammable material.

• Don't smoke when working around the battery. When the battery is being charged, it gives off explosive hydrogen gas.

• Don't use gasoline to wash your hands; there are excellent soaps available. Gasoline may contain lead, and lead can enter the body through a cut, accumulating in the body until you are very ill. Gasoline also removes all the natural oils from the skin so that bone dry hands will suck up oil and grease.

• Don't service the air conditioning system unless you are equipped with the necessary tools and training. The refrigerant, R-12, is extremely cold and when exposed to the air, will instantly freeze any surface it comes in contact with, including your eyes. Although the refrigerant is normally non-toxic, R-12 becomes a deadly poisonous gas in the presence of an open flame. One good whiff of the vapors from burning refrigerant can be fatal.

HISTORY

In designing the Omni and Horizon models, Chrysler didn't replace a car as much as design a brand new, efficiency-sized car for the U.S. market. The goal was to design a car with outstanding roominess, good handling characteristics, good fuel economy and flexibility of use.

According to chassis and body development studies the new car would be based on those criteria:

• a fuel-efficient 4-cylinder engine
• base weight less than 2,100 pounds
• overall length less than 165 inches
• overall width less than 66 inches
• front wheel drive.

The starting point was a fuel-efficient, 4-cylinder engine, the first 4-cylinder engine to power a domestic Chrysler Corporation passenger car in 45 years. The last 4-cylinder powered Chrysler Corporation passenger car was the 1932 Plymouth.

The base engine is a 1.7 liter power-plant purchased from Volkswagenwerk AG in the form of an assembled cylinder block and cylinder head. The unit is shipped in special containers to the Trenton engine plant, where samples of each shipment are tested on a dynomometer and completely torn down during a complete quality control inspection. The other compo-

nents—intake and exhaust manifolds, fuel pump, carburetor and controls, emission controls, alternator, power steering pump, clutch, air cleaner, ignition system—are all obtained from U.S. suppliers and installed at the engine plant. Since the Omni and Horizon models are Chrysler's first metric designed models built in the U.S., the cylinder block, head and crankshaft are built to metric measurements. Other components, mostly those obtained from domestic suppliers, such as the power steering pump or alternator retain inch-size dimensions.

In 1981, a new 2.2L (135 cu. in.) 4-cylinder engine was introduced as an option on all models except the fuel-efficient Miser.

Early in the design stages, Chrysler engineers realized that even with their design parameters, the luggage carrying needs of people hadn't changed that much. Front wheel drive offered the dimensional advantages to obtain the desired front and rear legroom with a superior luggage carrying capacity, and still stay within the design criteria. The lower floor, made possible by front wheel drive eliminating the driveshaft "tunnel," resulted in extra inches that could be devoted to a luggage area.

Front wheel drive also gave advantages in handling. The car was more stable and didn't drift during cornering; directional stability was increased and traction was improved due to more weight over the driving wheels. The front wheel drive transaxle allowed the car to be bigger on the inside and smaller on the outside, to achieve the overall length and width parameters.

Emphasis was also put on minimal weight coupled with a solid, substantial look, to appeal to those who were used to larger cars. The solid, stable look was achieved through the use of a wider "stance," and careful choice of line and form, the proper degree of curvature to the door and the proportion of body panels. Extensive use of strong, but lightweight, components allowed the final product to weight in at slightly over 2000 pounds, just under the 2100 pound goal.

A strut-type front suspension was chosen to keep weight to a minimum yet provide the best possible handling and ride qualities. The objective was to eliminate the harsh, choppy ride often associated with small cars, through the use of anti-sway bar, soft oval rubber pivot bushings, non-concentric coil springs and well balanced front and rear systems.

The actual design of the cars began in April of 1975, after preliminary planning had settled the issues of length, width, wheel base and configuration. More than 16 different exterior concepts were wind tunnel tested to determine their aerodynamic behavior. The results refined the 4-door hatchback configuration to obtain the minimum aerodynamic drag. Design improvements were translated in half-scale, plastic models before producing a total of 84 prototypes that would log over 6,000,000 test miles. The final result, "Job Number One," rolled off the Belvidere assembly line on November 21, 1977.

Popularity of Dodge Omni and Plymouth Horizon in their first full year in the marketplace, achieved a new production record for Chrysler Corporation's Belvidere assembly plant. In calender year 1978, 288,236 cars were built and sold. Demand was so great that the plant capacity was increased from the initial 960 cars per day to the present rate of almost 1,200 per day.

In 1979 the Plymouth Horizon TC3 and Dodge Omni 024 were introduced. The sporty, 2-door hatchback design had all the basic ingredients that made the 4-door version a success, in addition to a low profile, 2+2 sport look. The aerodynamically styled 024 and TC3 are about 8 inches longer and almost 2½ inches lower than their sedan counterparts.

In 1982 the 024 Charger and the TC3 Turismo performance version were introduced. The Charger and Turismo body styles were refined versions of the original 024 and TC3 models, with added features such as mellow-tuned exhaust, simulated hood scoop and fender exhaust vents. Also included on these models are bold nameplate graphics, rear spoiler and raised white letter tires.

Also an E-Type sedan was added to both the Dodge and Plymouth line. In addition to all the standard features on the other sedans, the E-Type is equipped with Europeon style black-out moldings and mirrors. Also a console and a rallye style instrument cluster is included.

Probably the most radical model introduced in this body style in 1982 was the Dodge Rampage pickup truck which was the first front-wheel drive pickup to be built by a member of Detroits "Big Three." Introduced in both the Sport and High-Line trim packages they share many of the same components with the other Omni/Horizon models. The major difference is in the rear suspension, where the other Omni/Horizon models have rear coil over strut type shocks and independent trailing arms the pickup model has conventional rear shocks, leaf springs and a tubular rear axle in order to support the additional rear weight capacity required in a pickup.

For the 1983 model year Plymouth added a pickup to their model line called the Scamp. This model shared comparable features to the Dodge Rampage pickup introduced the previous year.

Introduced in mid-1983 was the aggressive styled Dodge Shelby Charger. Built to be a high performance "image car" with its high output 2.2 liter engine and five-speed transmission. Its designer, Carol Shelby, that's right, the same man who brought us the 0-100 and back to zero in ten seconds AC Cobra, and the famous Shelby Mustang once again proved that he could come up with a high performance car that would be popular in the 80's.

Introduced in 1984 is the new high output 2.2-liter engine putting out an impressive 110 horsepower, standard in the Dodge Shelby Charger and optional in the other models.

SERIAL NUMBER IDENTIFICATION

Vehicle (VIN)

The vehicle identification number (VIN) is located on a plate attached to the upper left-hand corner of the instrument panel visible through the windshield. The complete VIN is also on the Safety Certification label located on the rear facing of the driver's door. An abbreviated form of the VIN is also stamped on a pad on the engine and on the transaxle housing.

All 1978–80 VIN's contain 13 digits coded to reveal the following information:
- 1st digit—Car line
- 2nd digit—Series

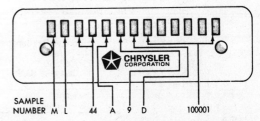

Sample 1978–80 VIN plate (Visible through windshield)

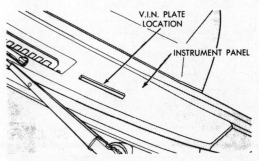

VIN plate location

1978–80 Vehicle Identification Plate Interpretation

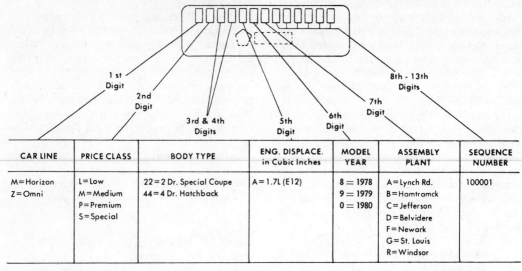

CAR LINE	PRICE CLASS	BODY TYPE	ENG. DISPLACE. in Cubic Inches	MODEL YEAR	ASSEMBLY PLANT	SEQUENCE NUMBER
M=Horizon Z=Omni	L=Low M=Medium P=Premium S=Special	22=2 Dr. Special Coupe 44=4 Dr. Hatchback	A=1.7L (E12)	8 = 1978 9 = 1979 0 = 1980	A=Lynch Rd. B=Hamtramck C=Jefferson D=Belvidere F=Newark G=St. Louis R=Windsor	100001

NOTE: A derivative of the Vehicle Identification Number is also stamped on all Production
Installed Engines and Transmissions; e.g.:

8
Model Year

A
Assembly Plant

100001
Vehicle Sequence Number

1981 and Later Vehicle Identification Plate Interpretation

POSITION	CODE OPTIONS			INTERPRETATION
1	1 = U.S. 2 = Canada	3 = Mexico J = Japan		Country of Origin
2	B = Dodge C = Chrysler	P = Plymouth		Make
3	3 = Passenger Car 7 = Truck			Type of Vehicle
4	B = Manual Seat Belts D = 1-3000 Lbs. GVW			Passenger Safety System
5	C = LeBaron D = Aries E = 600 T = New Yorker D = Lancer	L = Caravelle (Canada) M = Horizon P = Reliant J = Caravelle (U.S.)	V = 600 Z = Omni A = V Daytona A = C Laser C = LeBaron GTS	Line
6	1 = Economy 2 = Low	4 = High 5 = Premium	6 = Special	Series
7	1 = 2 Dr. Sedan 2 = 2 Dr. Specialty Hardtop 3 = 2 Dr. Hardtop 4 = 2 Dr. Hatchback	5 = 2 Dr. Convertible 6 = 4 Dr. Sedan 8 = 4 Dr. Hatchback 9 = 4 Dr. Wagon		Body Style
8	A = 1.6L C = 2.2L	D = 2.2L EFI E = 2.2L Turbo	G = 2.6L	Engine
9*	(1 thru 9, 0 or X)			Check Digit
10	F = 1985			Model Year
11	C = Jefferson D = Belvidere F = Newark G = St. Louis 1	K = Pillette Rd. N = Sterling R = Windsor	T = Toluca W = Clairpointe X = St. Louis 2	Assembly Plant
2 thru 17	(6 Digits)			Sequence Number

*Digit in position 9 is used for VIN verification

- 3rd and 4th digit—Body type
- 5th digit—Engine displacement
- 6th digit—Model year
- 7th digit—Assembly plant
- Last 6 digits—Sequential vehicle serial number

All 1981 and later VIN's contain 17 digits coded to reveal the following information:

- 1st digit—Country of Origin
- 2nd digit—Make
- 3rd digit—Type of Vehicle
- 4th digit—Pass Safety System
- 5th digit—Model Type
- 6th digit—Series
- 7th digit—Body Style
- 8th digit—Engine
- 9th digit—Check Digit
- 10th digit—Model Year
- 11th digit—Assembly Plant
- 12th thru 17th digit—Sequence Number

Engine

The engine identification numbers on the 1.6 and 1.7 liter engines are stamped on a pad on the engine block just above the fuel pump. The

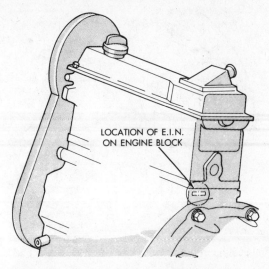

Engine identification number—2.2 liter engine

2.2 liter engine has its number stamped on a pad just above the bellhousing.

Transaxle

The manual transaxle serial number is stamped on a metal pad on top of the transaxle, just above the timing window.

The automatic transaxle serial number is stamped on a metal pad located just above the oil pan at the rear of the transaxle.

Body Code Plate

The body code plate contains important information about your particular car which is usually needed for any correspondence with the factory. The plate is located on the left front fender side shield, on the left side of the upper radiator support or on the wheel housing.

The information on the plate is coded in 6 rows of digits and is read from left to right.

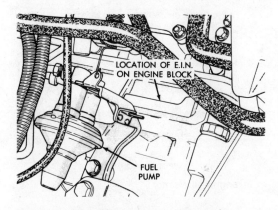

Engine identification number—1.6 liter engine

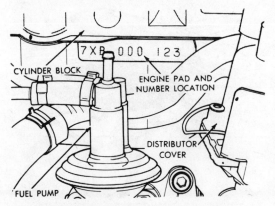

Engine identification number—1.7 liter engine

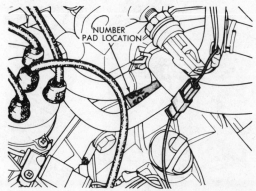

The manual transaxle number is stamped on a pad

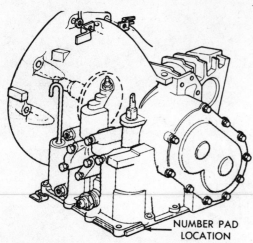

NUMBER PAD
LOCATION

Location of the automatic transaxle number pad

ROUTINE MAINTENANCE

Air Cleaner

1.7L

The carburetor air cleaner should be replaced every 30,000 miles under normal use. If the car is driven continuously in extremely dirty, dusty or sandy areas, the interval should be cut in half.

1. Remove the 2 wing nuts and unsnap the retaining clips.
2. Remove the air cleaner cover with the filter attached.
3. If the hoses come off, note their location for reinstallation.
4. Unscrew the wing nut on the bottom of the filter element and remove the filter.
5. Install a new filter and replace the wing nut.

6. Reinstall the cover and hand-tighten the wing nuts.
7. Snap the retaining clips into place.

1.6 AND 2.2L

1. Remove the three wing nuts that retain the air cleaner cover, remove the cover and lift out the element.
2. Install the new element.
3. Position the cover while aligning the three hold-down clips while allowing the two carburetor and one support bracket studs to protrude through each stud hole in the cover.
4. Install a wing nut on each of the carburetor studs first, and torque them to 14 in. lb.
5. Install the third wing nut on the support bracket stud and torque it to 14 in. lb.

NOTE: *It is important to follow this sequence to avoid air leaks due to air cleaner body distortion.*

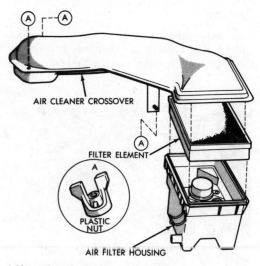

AIR CLEANER CROSSOVER

FILTER ELEMENT

A

PLASTIC NUT

AIR FILTER HOUSING

1.6L engine air cleaner

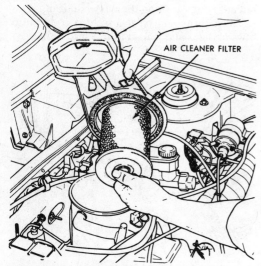

AIR CLEANER FILTER

Replacing the 1.7L air cleaner

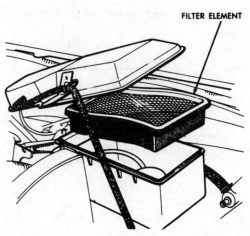

FILTER ELEMENT

2.2L engine air cleaner

PCV Valve

Omnis and Horizons are equipped with a closed crankcase ventilation system. The PCV valve is located in a line running between the cylinder head cover and the air cleaner.

This valve must be kept clean for optimum engine performance and fuel economy. The PCV valve should be inspected every 15,000 miles and replaced every 30,000 miles. In extremely dusty conditions or if the car is subjected to extensive idling or short trip operation, the interval should be halved.

PCV VALVE INSPECTION

There are 2 ways to check the PCV valve. If a valve fails either test, replace it with a new one.

Engine Idling

1. Remove the PCV valve from the rubber grommet in the cylinder head cover.
2. If the valve is not plugged, a hissing noise will be heard and a strong vacuum will be felt when you cover the valve with your finger.

Engine Stopped

1. Remove the PCV valve from the rubber grommet in the cylinder head cover.
2. Shake the valve; a clicking noise should be plainly audible if the valve is free.

PCV VALVE CONNECTING LINE INSPECTION

After a new PCV valve is installed, perform the test under "Engine Idling." If a strong vacuum is not felt, replace or clean the ventilation line and clean the passage in the lower part of the carburetor. The carburetor does not have to be disassembled.

1. Remove the connecting line and either replace it or clean the line in combustion chamber conditioner or a similar solvent. The hose should not remain in solvent more than ½ hour and should be allowed to air dry until thoroughly dry.

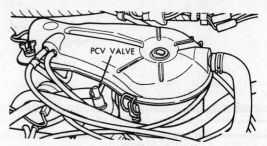

Location of PCV valve—1.7L engine

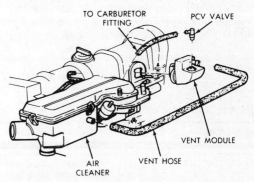

PCV system—2.2L engine

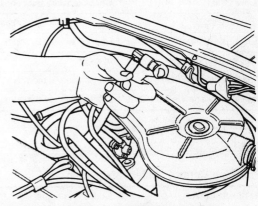

Checking for vacuum at PCV valve—typical

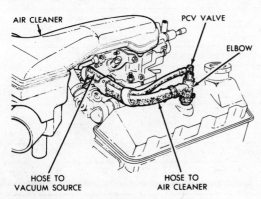

PVC system—1.6L engine

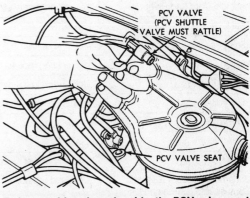

To be considered serviceable, the PCV valve must rattle when shaken

2. Remove the carburetor. Turn a ¼ in. drill through the passage by hand to dislodge any solid particles, then blow the passage clean. If necessary, use a smaller drill so that no metal is dislodged.

3. Reinstall the carburetor, connect the line and PCV valve and repeat the PCV valve test under "Engine Idling."

Evaporative Canister

The charcoal canister is a feature on all models to store fuel vapors that evaporate from the fuel tank and carburetor bowl. Note that on some fuel bowls, the vent to the evaporative canister is capped since the fuel bowl is vented internally.

The only service is to replace the canister filter every 30,000 miles, if the car is driven in particularly dusty areas. Otherwise, no service is necessary.

All hoses used with this system should be inspected periodically and replaced if cracked or leaking. These hoses are of special fuel resistant material and must be replaced with the same type and quality. The OEM (Original Equipment Manufactured) clamps are "Keystone" type and will be destroyed when they are removed. Replacement types should be aircraft type screw clamps if the original equip-

Maintenance Intervals

General Maintenance			Miles—in thousands					
			7.5	15	22.5	30	37.5	45
Brake Linings	Inspect front brakes					•		•
	Inspect rear brakes						•	
*Cooling System	First drain, flush and refill at 24 months	or					•	
	Subsequent drain, flush and refill every 12 months	or						•
	Check and service system every 12 months	or		•		•		•
*Drive Belts	Check tension and condition		•	•	•	•	•	•
*Engine Oil	Change every 12 months	or	•	•	•	•	•	•
*Engine Oil Filter	Change every 12 months	or	•		•		•	
Rear Wheel Bearings	Inspect	or				•		
Clutch Pedal Free Play	Adjust every 6 months	or	•	•	•	•	•	•
Steering Linkage Tie Rod Ends	Lubricate every 6 months	or				•		

* Also an emission control service.

Emission Control System Maintenance			Miles—in thousands					
			7.5	15	22.5	30	37.5	45
Automatic Choke	Check and adjust					•		•
Carburetor Choke Shaft	Apply solvent every six months	or	•	•	•	•	•	•
Carburetor Air Filter	Replace	at					•	
Fast Idle Cam and Pivot Pin	Apply solvent every six months	or	•	•	•	•	•	•
Fuel Filter	Replace	at	•		•		•	
Idle Speed Air-Fuel Mixture	Check and adjust	at				•		•
Ignition Cables	Check and replace as required at time of spark replacement							
Ignition Timing	Check and adjust if necessary					•		•
PCV Valve	Check and adjust if necessary					•		•
PCV Valve	Replace					•		
Spark Plugs	Replace				•		•	•
Valve Lash	Check and adjust if necessary	at			•		•	•
Underhood Rubber & Plastic Components (Emission Hoses)	Inspect and replace	at			•		•	•

Inspect and Service should also be performed any time a malfunction is observed or suspected.

Severe Service Maintenance

Miles—in thousands

Severe Service Maintenance			3	6	9	12	15	18	21	24	27	30	33	36	39	42	45	48
Brake Linings	Inspect	Front		•		•		•		•		•		•		•		•
		Rear				•				•				•				•
Change Oil	Change every 3 months	or	•	•	•	•	•	•	•	•	•	•	•	•	•	•	•	•
Engine Oil Filter	Change at initial oil change and every second oil change thereafter		•		•		•		•		•		•		•		•	
Rear Wheel Bearings	Inspect and Relubricate whenever drums are removed to inspect or service brakes or every				•			•			•			•			•	
Front Suspension Ball Joints	Inspect at every oil change																	
Steering Linkage Tie Rod Ends	Lubricate every 18 months	or					•					•					•	
Transmission Fluid "Automatic"	Change						•					•					•	
Constant Velocity Universal Joints	Inspect at every oil change																	

*Driving under any of the following operating conditions: Stop and go driving, driving in dusty conditions, extensive idling, frequent short trips, operating at sustained high speeds during hot weather (above + 90°F, + 32°C).

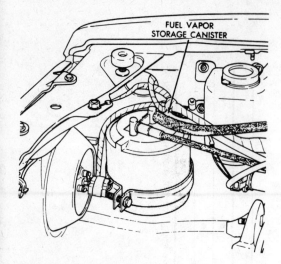

Fuel vapor storage canister

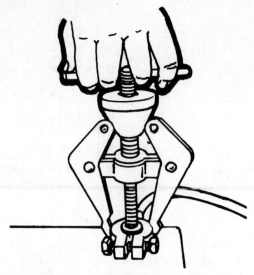

A small puller will easily remove the cable from the terminals

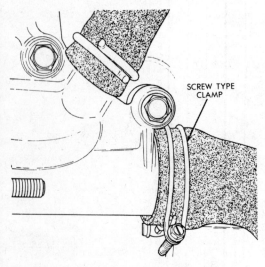

Spring and screw type hose clamps

ment is not available (spring type clamps are not recommended). Position the clamps so that no sharp edges contact adjacent hoses.

Battery

Loose, dirty, or corroded battery terminals are a major cause of "no-start." Every 3 months or so, remove the battery terminals and clean them, giving them a light coating of petroleum jelly when you are finished. This will help to retard corrosion.

Check the battery cables for signs of wear or chafing and replace any cable or terminal that looks marginal. Battery terminals can be easily cleaned and inexpensive terminal cleaning tools are an excellent investment that will pay for themselves many times over. They can usually be purchased from any well-equipped auto store

or parts department. The accumulated white powder and corrosion can be cleaned from the top of the battery with an old toothbrush and a solution of baking soda and water.

Unless you have a "maintenance-free" battery, check the electrolyte level (see Battery under Fluid Level Checks in this chapter) and

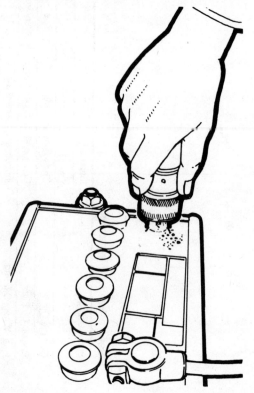

An inexpensive tool easily cleans the battery terminals

Clean the inside of the terminal clamp

check the specific gravity of each cell. Be sure that the vent holes in each cell cap are not blocked by grease or dirt. The vent holes allow hydrogen gas, formed by the chemical reaction in the battery, to escape safely.

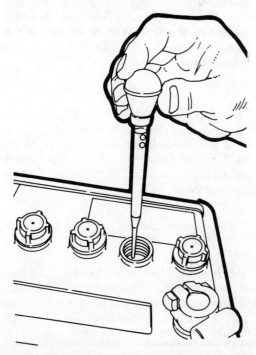

Check the specific gravity of the battery

REPLACEMENT BATTERIES

The cold power rating of a battery measures battery starting performance and provides an approximate relationship between battery size and engine size. The cold power rating of a replacement battery should match or exceed your engine size in cubic inches.

BATTERY FLUID LEVEL

Two types of batteries are used—Standard and Maintenance-Free. Both types are equipped with a Charge-Test Indicator, which is actually a miniature hydrometer built into the filler cap of one cell. The indicator will show green if the battery is above 75–80% fully charged, or dark if the battery needs recharging. Light yellow indicates the battery may be in need of water or replacement.

For standard batteries, check the level of the electrolyte every 2 months—more often on long trips or in extremely hot weather. If necessary add mineral free water to the bottom of the filler well.

At least once a year, check the specific gravity of a standard battery.

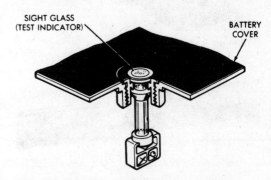

SIGHT GLASS
(TEST INDICATOR)

BATTERY COVER

Test indicator on maintenance free battery

Checking and Adjusting Belt Tension

Your particular car may have as few as one or as many as 4 drive belts for the following accessories: alternator, A/C compressor, power steering pump, water pump, or air pump (California models only).

All Belts Except Alternator Belt

Check the belt tension on any given belt by applying moderate thumb pressure midway in the longest span. The belt should deflect approximately ½ in. If the longest span is not easily accessible, you can also check the shortest span, where the belt should deflect no more than ¼ in. under moderate thumb pressure.

To adjust the tension, loosen the accessory

HOW TO SPOT WORN V-BELTS

V-Belts are vital to efficient engine operation—they drive the fan, water pump and other accessories. They require little maintenance (occasional tightening) but they will not last forever. Slipping or failure of the V-belt will lead to overheating. If your V-belt looks like any of these, it should be replaced.

This belt has deep cracks, which cause it to flex. Too much flexing leads to heat build-up and premature failure. These cracks can be caused by using the belt on a pulley that is too small. Notched belts are available for small diameter pulleys.

Cracking or weathering

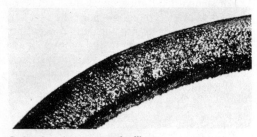

Oil and grease on a belt can cause the belt's rubber compounds to soften and separate from the reinforcing cords that hold the belt together. The belt will first slip, then finally fail altogether.

Softening (grease and oil)

Glazing is caused by a belt that is slipping. A slipping belt can cause a run-down battery, erratic power steering, overheating or poor accessory performance. The more the belt slips, the more glazing will be built up on the surface of the belt. The more the belt is glazed, the more it will slip. If the glazing is light, tighten the belt.

Glazing

The cover of this belt is worn off and is peeling away. The reinforcing cords will begin to wear and the belt will shortly break. When the belt cover wears in spots or has a rough jagged appearance, check the pulley grooves for roughness.

Worn cover

This belt is on the verge of breaking and leaving you stranded. The layers of the belt are separating and the reinforcing cords are exposed. It's just a matter of time before it breaks completely.

Separation

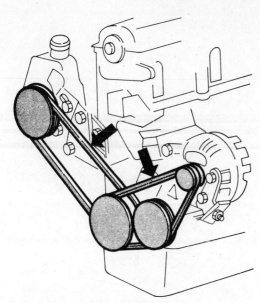

Checking belt tension without A/C

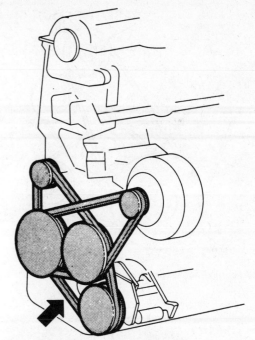

Checking belt tension with AIR pump

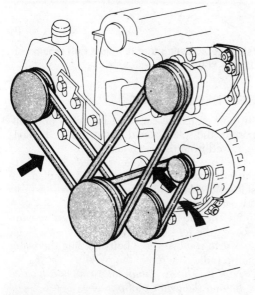

Checking belt tension with A/C

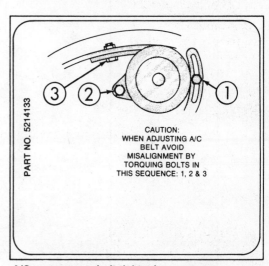

PART NO. 5214133

CAUTION:
WHEN ADJUSTING A/C
BELT AVOID
MISALIGNMENT BY
TORQUING BOLTS IN
THIS SEQUENCE: 1, 2 & 3

A/C compressor bolt tightening sequence

pivot bolt. On A/C compressor loosen all bolts shown on the compressor decal. Insert a ½ in. breaker bar in the accessory tensioning lug and move the accessory until the belt is properly tensioned. Tighten the pivot bolt.

Alternator Belt

Proper belt tension on the alternator belt is critical to proper alternator operation. For ease of adjusting alternator belt tension, a special tool has been developed that is easily fabricated or available from the tool company at about $10. The tool, when used with a torque wrench, assures proper belt tension with greater accessi-

bility. Do not use the thumb pressure method on these belts.

It is essential that belt adjustment be performed from below the vehicle. The splash shield must be removed and on California models with an air pump, removing the horn will ease access to the adjustment bolt.

1. From underneath the vehicle, install a ½ in. drive torque wrench in the adjusting tool. Position the adjusting tool.

2. Loosen the alternator pivot bolt. If you don't do this, you'll break the alternator housing.

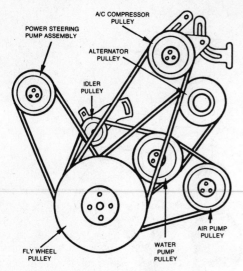

1.7L engine accessory drive belts

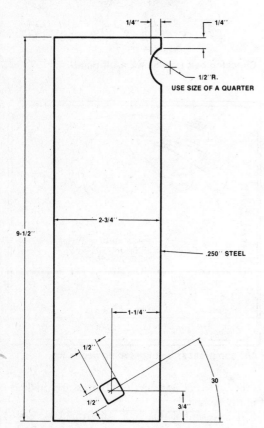

1.7L engine drive belt tension adjusting tool

3. Adjust the belt tension to 70 ft. lbs. (new belt) or 50 ft. lbs. (used belt).

NOTE: *A belt is considered used after 15 minutes of running.*

4. Hold the alternator at the required torque. Tighten the adjusting bolt.

5. Reinstall the horn and splash shield.

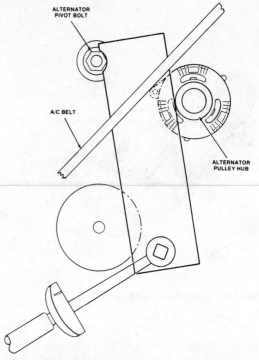

Using the adjusting tool to adjust belt tension on the 1.7L engine

BELT REPLACEMENT

In most cases the car must be raised and supported, the splash shield removed and the horn removed from cars with air pumps.

1. The A/C compressor drive belt is removed first. Loosen the adjusting nut at the slotted bracket and push the compressor to its lowest position.

2. The alternator belt is removed second. Loosen the tension on the belt and use a ¼ in. socket to remove the 3 bolts holding the water pump pulley. Remove the pulley.

NOTE: *The air pump idler pulley is located behind the water pump pulley.*

3. The air pump drive belt is removed next. To remove this belt, the A/C compressor and the alternator belts MUST be removed.

4. The power steering pump drive belt is removed last. It is necessary to remove all other belts, loosen the pump pivot bolt in the slotted bracket and move the pump to its lowest position.

5. New belts are installed in the reverse order. Tension all belts as outlined previously. New belts will usually stretch, so they should be checked after an hour's use.

Hoses

Hoses can be removed or installed with pliers or a screwdriver. Some cars use spring type clamps while others use screw type clamps. If spring type clamps are used, it is recommended to remove these with hose clamp pliers to avoid pinching your fingers.

1. Drain the radiator. If the coolant is less than a year old it can be saved and reused.

NOTE: *Before opening the radiator drain cock to drain the radiator, spray some penetrating solvent around the drain cock to be sure it will open with ease.*

2. Remove the hose clamps.

3. Pull the hose off the fittings on the radiator and engine.

4. Install a new hose. A small amount of soapy water on the inside of the hose end will ease installation.

NOTE: *Radiator hoses should be routed with no kinks and routed as the original. Use of molded hoses is not recommended.*

5. Refill the cooling system and check the level.

Cooling System

The cooling system should be inspected, flushed, and refilled with fresh coolant at the end of the first 2 years and every year thereafter. If the coolant is left in the system too long, it loses its ability to prevent rust and corrosion; if the coolant has too much water, it won't protect against freezing.

The pressure cap should be looked at for signs of age or deterioration. Fan belt and other drive belts should be inspected and adjusted to the proper tension. (See Checking Belt Tension).

Hose clamps should be tightened, and soft or cracked hoses replaced. Damp spots, or accumulations of rust or dye near hoses, water pump or other areas, indicate possible leakage, which must be corrected before filling the system with fresh coolant.

FLUID RECOMMENDATION

If additional coolant is needed, remove the cap from the reserve tank. DO NOT REMOVE THE RADIATOR CAP. Add a 50/50 mix of ethylene glycol coolant and water.

COOLANT LEVEL CHECK

The coolant reserve system provides a quick and easy way to verify proper coolant level. With the engine idling and at normal operating temperature, observe the level of the coolant in the plastic see-through tank. It should be between the minimum and maximum marks.

CHECK THE RADIATOR CAP

While you are checking the coolant level, check the radiator cap for a worn or cracked gasket.

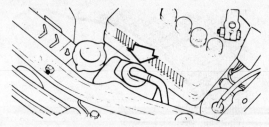

Coolant reserve bottle location

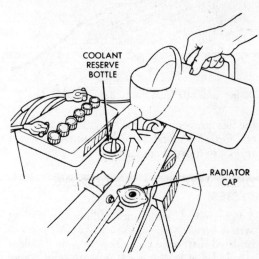

Add coolant to the coolant reserve bottle

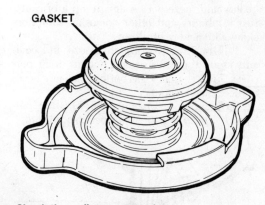

Check the radiator cap gasket

If the cap doesn't seal properly, fluid will be lost and the engine will overheat.

Worn caps should be replaced with a new one.

CLEAN RADIATOR OF DEBRIS

Periodically clean any debris—leaves, paper, insects, etc.—from the radiator fins. Pick the large pieces off by hand. The smaller pieces can be washed away with water pressure from a hose.

Carefully straighten any bent radiator fins with a pair of needle nosed pliers. Be careful—

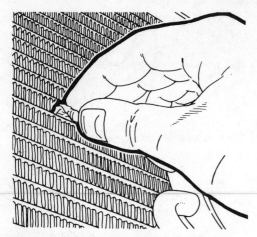

Remove debris from the radiator cooling fins

the fins are very soft. Don't wiggle the fins back and forth too much. Straighten them once and try not to move them again.

DRAIN AND REFILL THE COOLING SYSTEM

Completely draining and refilling the cooling system every year at least will remove accumulated rust, scale and other deposits. Coolant should be at least a 50/50 mixture of ethylene glycol and water for year round use. Use a good quality antifreeze with water pump lubricants, rust inhibitors and other corrosion inhibitors along with acid neutralizers.

1. Drain the existing antifreeze and coolant. Open the radiator and engine drain petcocks, or disconnect the bottom radiator hose, at the radiator outlet.

NOTE: *Before opening the radiator petcock, spray it with some penetrating lubricant.*

Check the anti-freeze protection

2. Close the petcock or re-connect the lower hose and fill the system with water.

3. Add a can of quality radiator flush.

4. Idle the engine until the upper radiator hose gets hot.

5. Drain the system again.

6. Repeat this process until the drained water is clear and free of scale.

7. Close all petcocks and connect all the hoses.

8. If equipped with a coolant recovery system, flush the reservoir with water and leave empty.

9. Determine the capacity of your cooling system (see Capacities specifications). Add a 50/50 mix of quality antifreeze (ethylene glycol) and water to provide the desired protection.

NOTE: *Use a minimum of 50% ethylene glycol anti-freeze and water. This is necessary to provide adequate corrosion protection with aluminum parts.*

10. Run the engine to operating temperature.

11. Stop the engine and check the coolant level.

12. Check the level of protection with an antifreeze tester, replace the cap and check for leaks.

Air Conditioning

AIR-CONDITIONING SAFETY PRECAUTIONS

There are two particular hazards associated with air conditioning systems and they both relate to the refrigerant gas.

First, the refrigerant gas is an extremely cold substance. When exposed to air, it will instantly freeze any surface it comes in contact with, including your eyes. The other hazard relates to fire. Although normally non-toxic, refrigerant gas becomes highly poisonous in the presence of an open flame. One good whiff of the vapor formed by burning refrigerant can be fatal. Keep all forms of fire (including cigarettes) well clear of the air-conditioning system.

Any repair work to an air conditioning system should be left to a professional. Do not, under any circumstances, attempt to loosen or tighten any fittings or perform any work other than that outlined here.

NOTE: *This book contains simple testing procedures for your Omni/Horizon's air conditioning system. More comprehensive testing, diagnosis and service procedures may be found in CHILTON'S GUIDE TO AIR CONDITIONING SERVICE AND REPAIR, book part number 7580, available at your local retailer.*

HOW TO SPOT BAD HOSES

Both the upper and lower radiator hoses are called upon to perform difficult jobs in an inhospitable environment. They are subject to nearly 18 psi at under hood temperatures often over 280°F., and must circulate nearly 7500 gallons of coolant an hour—3 good reasons to have good hoses.

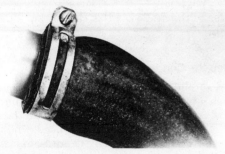

A good test for any hose is to feel it for soft or spongy spots. Frequently these will appear as swollen areas of the hose. The most likely cause is oil soaking. This hose could burst at any time, when hot or under pressure.

Swollen hose

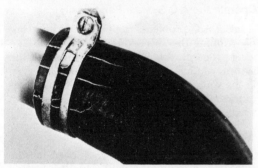

Cracked hoses can usually be seen but feel the hoses to be sure they have not hardened; a prime cause of cracking. This hose has cracked down to the reinforcing cords and could split at any of the cracks.

Cracked hose

Weakened clamps frequently are the cause of hose and cooling system failure. The connection between the pipe and hose has deteriorated enough to allow coolant to escape when the engine is hot.

Frayed hose end (due to weak clamp)

Debris, rust and scale in the cooling system can cause the inside of a hose to weaken. This can usually be felt on the outside of the hose as soft or thinner areas.

Debris in cooling system

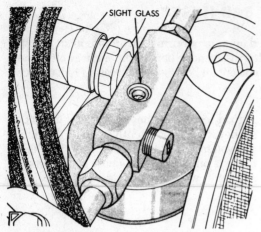

A/C sight glass in the top of the receiver/drier

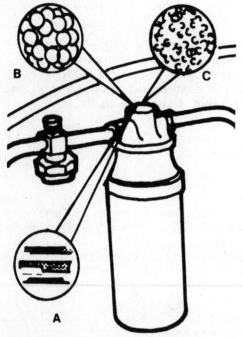

Oil streaks (A), constant bubbles (B) or foam (C) indicate there is not enough refrigerant in the system. Occasional bubbles during initial operation is normal. A clear sight glass indicates a proper charge of refrigerant or no refrigerant at all, which can be determined by the presence of cold air at the outlets in the car. If the glass is clouded with a milky white substance, have the receiver/drier checked professionally

Checking for Oil Leaks

Refrigerant leaks show up as oily areas on the various components because the compressor oil is transported around the entire system along with the refrigerant. Look for oily spots on all the hoses and lines, and especially on the hose and tubing connections. If there are oily de-

posits, the system may have a leak, and you should have it checked by a qualified repairman.

NOTE: *A small area of oil on the front of the compressor is normal and no cause for alarm.*

Check the Compressor Belt

Refer to the section in this chapter on "Drive Belts."

Keep the Condenser Clear

Periodically inspect the front of the condenser for bent fins or foreign material (dirt, bugs, leaves, etc.) If any cooling fins are bent, straighten them carefully with needle nosed pliers. You can remove any debris with a stiff bristle brush or hose.

Operate the A/C System Periodically

A lot of A/C problems can be avoided by simply running the air conditioner at least once a week, regardless of the season. Simply let the system run for at least 5 minutes a week (even in the winter), and you'll keep the internal parts lubricated as well as preventing the hoses from hardening.

Refrigerant Level Check

The first order of business when checking the sight glass is to find the sight glass. It is located in the head of the receiver/drier. Once you've found it, wipe it clean and proceed as follows:

1. With the engine and the air conditioning system running, look for the flow of refrigerant through the sight glass. If the air conditioner is working properly, you'll be able to see a continuous flow of clear refrigerant through the sight glass, with perhaps an occasional bubble at very high temperatures.

2. Cycle the air conditioner on and off to make sure what you are seeing is clear refrigerant. Since the refrigerant is clear, it is possible to mistake a completely discharged system for one that is fully charged. Turn the system off and watch the sight glass. If there is refrigerant in the system, you'll see bubbles during the off cycle. If you observe no bubbles when the system is running, and the air flow from the unit in the car is delivering cold air, everything is OK.

3. If you observe bubbles in the sight glass while the system is operating, the system is low on refrigerant. Have it checked by a professional.

4. Oil streaks in the sight glass are an indication of trouble. Most of the time, if you see oil in the sight glass, it will appear as a series of streaks, although occasionally it may be a solid

stream of oil. In either case, it means that part of the charge has been lost.

Windshield Wipers

Intense heat from the sun, snow and ice, road oils and the chemicals used in windshield washer solvents combine to deteriorate the rubber wiper refills. The refills should be replaced about twice a year or whenever the blades begin to streak or chatter.

WIPER REFILL REPLACEMENT

Normally, if the wipers are not cleaning the windshield properly, only the refill has to be replaced. The blade and arm usually require replacement only in the vent of damage. It is not necessary (except on new Tridon refills) to remove the arm or the blade to replace the refill (rubber part), though you may have to position the arm higher on the glass. You can do this turning the ignition switch on and operating the wipers. When they are positioned where they are accessible, turn the ignition switch off.

There are several types of refills and your vehicle could have any kind, since aftermarket blades and arms may not use exactly the same type refill as the original equipment.

The original equipment wiper elements can be replaced as follows:

1. Lift the wiper arm off the glass.
2. Depress the release lever on the center bridge and remove the blade from the arm.
3. Lift the tab and pinch the end bridge to release it from the center bridge.
4. Slide the end bridge from the wiper blade and the wiper blade from the opposite end bridge.
5. Install a new element and be sure the tab on the end bridge is down to lock the element in place. Check each release point for positive engagement.

Most Trico styles uses a release button that is pushed down to allow the refill to slide out of the yoke jaws. The new refill slides in and locks in place. Some Trico refills are removed by locating where the metal backing strip or the refill is wider. Insert a small screwdriver blade between the frame and metal backing strip. Press down to release the refill from the retaining tab.

The Anco style is unlocked at one end by

Removing original equipment wiper blade and refill

squeezing 2 metal tabs, and the refill is slid out of the frame jaws. When the new refill is installed, the tabs will click into place, locking the refill.

The polycarbonate type is held in place by a locking lever that is pushed downward out of the groove in the arm to free the refill. When the new refill is installed, it will lock in place automatically.

The Tridon refill has a plastic backing strip with a notch about an inch from the end. Hold the blade (frame) on a hard surface so that the frame is tightly bowed. Grip the tip of the backing strip and pull up while twisting counterclockwise. The backing strip will snap out of the retaining tab. Do this for the remaining tabs until the refill is free of the arm. The length of these refills is molded into the end and they should be replaced with identical types.

No matter which type of refill you use, be sure that all of the frame claws engage the refill. Before operating the wipers, be sure that no part of the metal frame is contacting the windshield.

Tires

INFLATION PRESSURE

Tire inflation is the most ignored item of auto maintenance. Gasoline mileage can drop as much as .8% for every 1 pound per square inch (psi) of under inflation.

Two items should be a permanent fixture in every glove compartment; a tire pressure gauge and a tread depth gauge. Check the tire air pressure (including the spare) regularly with a pocket type gauge. Kicking the tires won't tell you a thing, and the gauge on the service station air hose is notoriously inaccurate.

The tire pressures recommended for your car are usually found on the door post or in the owner's manual. Ideally, inflation pressure should be checked when the tires are cool. When the air becomes heated it expands and the pressure increases. Every 10° rise (or drop) in temperature means a difference of 1 psi, which also explains why the tire appears to lose air on a very cold night. When it is impossible to check the tires "cold," allow for pressure build-up due to heat. If the "hot" pressure exceeds the "cold" pressure by more than 15 psi, reduce your speed, load or both. Otherwise internal heat is created in the tire. When the heat approaches the temperature at which the tire was cured, during manufacture, the tread can separate from the body.

CAUTION: *Never counteract excessive pressure build-up by bleeding off air pressure (letting some air out). This will only further raise the tire operating temperature.*

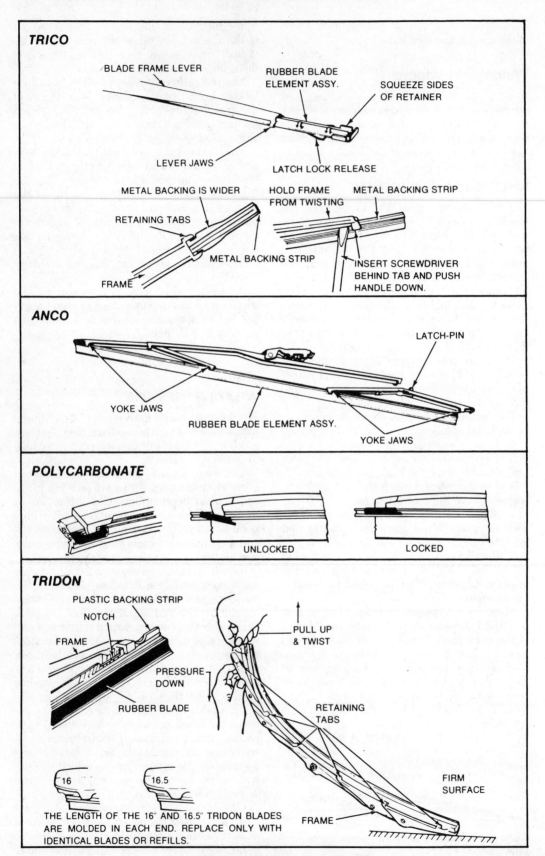

Replacing popular styles of wiper refills

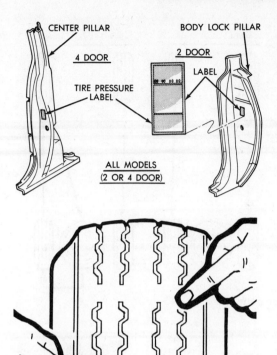

CENTER PILLAR   BODY LOCK PILLAR

4 DOOR   2 DOOR

LABEL

TIRE PRESSURE
LABEL

ALL MODELS
(2 OR 4 DOOR)

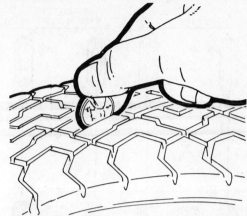

Tread depth can also be roughly checked with a Lincoln head penny. If the top of Lincoln's head is visible, replace the tires

smooth bands across the tire when ¹⁄₁₆″ of tread remains. The appearance of tread wear indicators means that the tires should be replaced. In fact, many states have laws prohibiting the use of tires with less than ¹⁄₁₆″ tread.

You can check your own tread depth with an inexpensive gauge or by using a Lincoln head penny. Slip the Lincoln penny into several tread grooves. If you can see the top of Lincoln's head in 2 adjacent grooves, the tires have less than¹⁄₁₆″ tread left and should be replaced. You can measure snow tires in the same manner by using the "tails" side of the Lincoln penny. If you can see the top of the Lincoln memorial, it's time to replace the snow tires.

Tire wear indicators appear as ¹⁄₂″ wide bands when tread is less than ¹⁄₁₆″

TIRE ROTATION

Tire wear can be equalized by switching the position of the tires about every 6000 miles. Including a conventional spare in the rotation pattern can give up to 20% more tire life.

CAUTION: *Do not include the new "Space-saver®" in the rotation pattern.*

There are certain exceptions to tire rotation, however. Studded snow tires should not be rotated, and radials should be kept on the same side of the car (maintain the same direction of rotation). The belt on radial tires get set in a pattern. If the direction of rotation is reversed, it can cause rough ride and vibration.

NOTE: *When radials or studded snows are taken off the car, mark them, so you can maintain the same direction of rotation.*

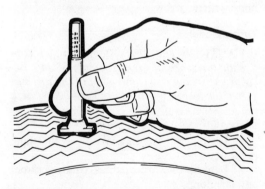

Check tire tread depth with an inexpensive gauge

TIRE STORAGE

Store the tires at proper inflation pressures if they are mounted on wheels. All tires should be kept in a cool, dry place. If they are stored in the garage or basement, do not let them stand on a concrete floor; set them on strips of wood.

Before starting a long trip with lots of luggage, you can add about 2–4 psi to the tires to make them run cooler, but never exceed the maximum inflation pressure on the side of the tire.

TREAD DEPTH

All tires made since 1968, have 8 built-in tread wear indicator bars that show up as ¹⁄₂″ wide

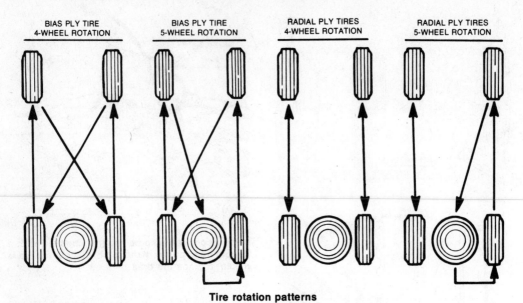

| BIAS PLY TIRE 4-WHEEL ROTATION | BIAS PLY TIRE 5-WHEEL ROTATION | RADIAL PLY TIRES 4-WHEEL ROTATION | RADIAL PLY TIRES 5-WHEEL ROTATION |

Tire rotation patterns

Fuel Filter

1978–79

The fuel filter on 1978–79 models is located behind the fuel inlet of the carburetor. Under normal operating conditions, the filter should be replaced after the first 7500 miles and every 15,000 miles thereafter.

1. Remove the clamp from the rubber hose.
2. Spread some dry rags under the fuel fitting to absorb the inevitable gasoline spillage.
3. Unscrew the fitting and remove the filter.
4. Install a new filter.
5. Install and tighten the fitting.

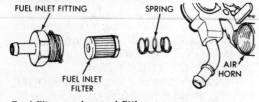

Fuel filter, spring and fitting

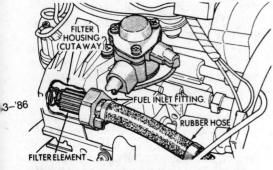

Fuel filter location—typical

6. Connect the fuel line. You may want to use a new screw type clamp that will make future filter replacement easier.
7. Run the engine and check for any leaks.

1980 and Later

The fuel filter on 1980 and later models is located in-line, just above the fuel pump. This filter is the disposable paper element type. The filter is held in place by two squeeze type spring clamps. When installing the new filter, make sure you locate it in the right direction. The direction of flow is usually marked on the filter body with an arrow.

Turbo Models

CAUTION: *The fuel system is under constant pressure of approximately 55 psi. Before servicing any component of the fuel system the fuel system pressure must be released.*

RELEASING FUEL SYSTEM PRESSURE

1. Loosen the gas cap to release fuel tank pressure.
2. Remove the wiring harness connector from any injector.
3. Ground one injector terminal and connect a jumper wire to the second terminal. Touch the jumper wire to the positive battery post for NO longer than 10 seconds. This procedure releases system pressure.

FILTER REMOVAL AND INSTALLATION

1. Release fuel system pressure.
2. Remove the bracket retaining screw and remove the filter from the rail.
3. Loosen the outlet and inlet hose clamps.

Wrap a towel around the filter to absorb any fuel that leaks out of the filter and lines.

4. Remove the hose from the filter and remove the filter.

5. Install the new filter and new clamps between the fuel lines.

6. Tighten the clamps (tighten to 10 in. lbs.). Position the filter on the rail and tighten the mounting screw (75 in. lbs.).

FLUIDS AND LUBRICANTS

Fuel Recommendations

Only gasolines with a 91 Research Octane Number (RON) or an octane value of 87 if using the (R+M)/2 method, should be used. Turbocharged or high performance engines should use premium or super unleaded gasoline with an octane value of 91 using the (R+M)2 method. Unleaded gasoline must be used in cars with a catalytic converter. These cars have specially designed filler necks that prevent the direct insertion of the leaded gasoline pump nozzle.

Avoid the constant use of fuel system cleaning agents. Many of these materials contain highly active solvents that will deteriorate the gasket and diaphragm materials used on Omni and Horizon carburetors.

Engine

OIL RECOMMENDATION

Oils and lubricants are classified and graded according to standards established by the Society of Automotive Engineers (SAE), American Pe-

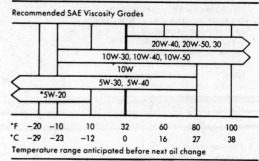

Recommended SAE Viscosity Grades

20W-40, 20W-50, 30
10W-30, 10W-40, 10W-50
10W
5W-30, 5W-40
*5W-20

| °F | -20 | -10 | 10 | 32 | 60 | 80 | 100 |
| °C | -29 | -23 | -12 | 0 | 16 | 27 | 38 |

Temperature range anticipated before next oil change

*SAE 5W-20 Not recommended for sustained high speed vehicle operation.

Oil viscosity chart

troleum Institute (API), and the National Lubricating Grease Institute (NLGI).

Oils are classified by the SAE and API designations, found on the top of the oil can. The SAE grade number indicates the viscosity of engine oils. SAE 10W-40, for example, is a good all-temperature motor oil suitable for use in winter.

The API classification system defines oil performance in terms of usage. Only oils designed for service "SF" should be used. These oils provide sufficient additives to give maximum engine protection.

OIL LEVEL CHECK

The engine oil dipstick is located on the radiator side of the engine. Engine oil level should be checked weekly as a matter of course. Always check the oil with the car on level ground and after the engine has been shut off for about five minutes.

The oil level may read at the top of the Full

Capacities

| Year | Model | Engine Displacement | Crankcase Incl. Filter (qts) | Transmission Pints to Refill after Draining | | Final Drive (pts) | Gasoline Tank (gals) | Cooling System (qts) | |
				Manual	Automatic			W/ AC	W/O AC
'78	All	1.7L	4	2.65	13.0	2.0	13	6.5	8.0
'79	All	1.7L	4	2.65	13.0	2.0	13	6.0	6.0
'80	All	1.7L	4	2.65	13.0	2.0	13	6.0	6.0
'81-'82	All	1.7L	4	2.65	14.5	2.37	13	6.0	6.0
	All	2.2L	4	3.75	15.0	2.37	13	8.7	8.7
'83-'86	All	1.6L	3.5	①	18.0	—	13	6.8	6.8
	All	1.7L	4	①	16.8	—	13	6.0	6.0
	All	2.2L	4 ②	①	18.0	—	13	9.0	9.0

① 4-speed; 3.75
   5-speed; 4.55
② turbo: 5 qts

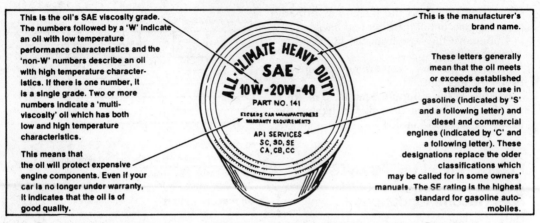

This is the oil's SAE viscosity grade. The numbers followed by a 'W' indicate an oil with low temperature performance characteristics and the 'non-W' numbers describe an oil with high temperature characteristics. If there is one number, it is a single grade. Two or more numbers indicate a 'multi-viscosity' oil which has both low and high temperature characteristics.

This means that the oil will protect expensive engine components. Even if your car is no longer under warranty, it indicates that the oil is of good quality.

This is the manufacturer's brand name.

These letters generally mean that the oil meets or exceeds established standards for use in gasoline (indicated by 'S' and a following letter) and diesel and commercial engines (indicated by 'C' and a following letter). These designations replace the older classifications which may be called for in some owners' manuals. The SF rating is the highest standard for gasoline automobiles.

ALL CLIMATE HEAVY DUTY
SAE
10W-20W-40
PART NO. 141
EXCEEDS CAR MANUFACTURERS
WARRANTY REQUIREMENTS
API SERVICES
SC, SD, SE
CA, CB, CC

The top of the oil can will tell you all you need to know about the oil

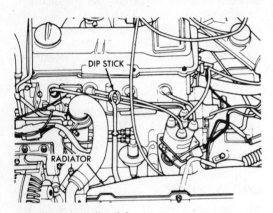

1.7L engine oil dipstick

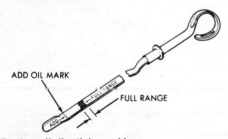

Engine oil dipstick markings

range after the car has been standing for several hours. When the engine is started, the level will drop, due to oil passages filling, but the level should never be allowed to remain below the ADD mark.

1. Remove the dipstick and wipe it clean.
2. Reinsert the dipstick.
3. Remove the dipstick again. The oil level should be between the two marks. The difference between the marks is one quart.
4. Add oil through the capped opening on the top of the valve cover.

CHANGING OIL AND FILTER

Under normal service, the engine oil and filter should be changed every 12 months or 7500

miles, whichever comes first. On turbocharged engines, change the oil and filter every 6 months or 7500 miles, whichever comes first.

Under the following conditions, change the engine oil and filter every 3 months or 3000 miles, whichever comes first:

- Frequent driving in dusty conditions
- Frequent trailer pulling
- Extensive idling
- Frequent short trip driving (less than 10 miles)
- More than 50% operation at sustained high speeds (over 70 mph).

NOTE: *Drain the engine oil when the engine is at normal operating temperature.*

To change the oil, the vehicle should be on a level surface at normal operating temperature. This ensures that you will drain away the foreign matter in the oil, which will not happen if the engine is cold. Oil which is slightly dirty when drained is a good sign. This means that the contaminants are being drained away and not being left behind to form sludge.

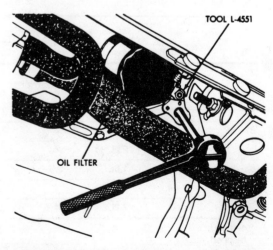

1.7L engine oil filter removal

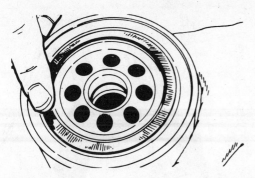

Lubricate the gasket on a new filter with clean engine oil

You should have available some means to support the car, a 13 mm wrench, a filter wrench, 4 quarts of oil (5 if a turbo), a drain pan and some rags.

1. Jack up the front of the car and support it.

2. Position the drain pan under the drain plug, which is located at the rear of the oil pan.

3. Loosen, but do not remove the drain plug. Cover your hand with a heavy rag and slowly unscrew the drain plug. Pushing the plug against the threads in the oil pan will prevent hot oil from running down your arm. As the drain plug comes to the end of the threads, quickly pull it away and allow all of the oil to drain into the pan.

4. When all the oil has drained, replace the drain plug and tighten it.

NOTE: *Be sure to dispose of the old oil in an environmentally safe manner.*

5. Remove the oil filter. It can only be removed with the tools shown, from below the car. Once the filter is loose, cover your hand with a thick rag and spin it off by hand.

NOTE: *On May 29, 1979, the assembly plant began installing 4" diameter oil filters in place of the previously used 3" diameter filters. The 4" filters are the same as those used on other Chrysler vehicles and should be used for service.*

6. Coat the rubber gasket on a new filter with clean engine oil and install the new filter. Tighten it by hand until the gasket contacts the mounting base and then ¾–1 turn further.

7. Refill the engine with 4 quarts (5 if a turbo) of fresh oil of the proper viscosity according to the anticipated temperatures before the next oil change.

NOTE: *It requires 4 quarts of oil (5 if a turbo) to fill the engine regardless of whether the filter was changed or not.*

8. Run the engine for a few minutes and check the oil level.

Manual Transaxle
FLUID RECOMMENDATIONS

The A412 transaxle is a VW design and is the only model to use Hypoid gear lubricant. The A412 transaxle can be easily identified from the Chrysler design models because the starter motor is located on the radiator side of the engine compartment. If it becomes necessary to add or change the fluid to the unit, lubricant conforming to API GL 4 specifications should be used. The recommended SAE grade should be selected from the chart.

All other manual transaxles, A460, A465 and the A525 can be identified by the starter motor being located on the firewall side of the engine compartment. If it becomes necessary to add or change fluid in these units, use only automatic transmission fluid labeled DEXRON II.

Anticipated Temperature Range	Recommended SAE Grade
Above — 10° F.	90, 80W–90, 85W–90
As low as — 30° F.	80W, 80W–90, 85W–90
Below — 30° F.	75W

A412 transaxle lubricant recommendations

LEVEL CHECK

The fluid level in the manual transaxle should be checked twice a year. Maintain the fluid level at the bottom of the filler plug opening.

To check the fluid level, position the car on a level surface and clean the dirt from around the transaxle filler plug. Remove the filler plug. The level should at least reach the bottom of the hole. You can check the level with your finger or a piece of bent wire.

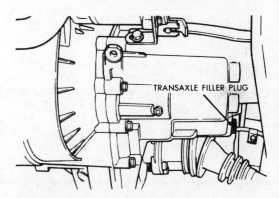

A-412 manual transaxle filler plug

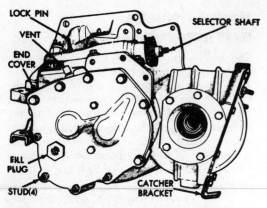

A-460, 465, and 525 manual transaxle filler plug

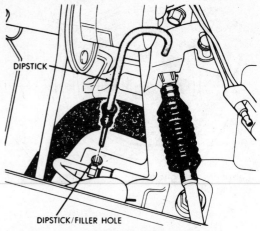

Automatic transaxle dipstick location

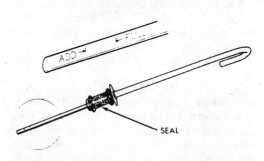

Automatic transaxle dipstick markings

DRAIN AND REFILL

Under normal conditions, the manual transaxle fluid will never need changing. Rare circumstances, such as the fluid becoming contaminated with water will necessitate fluid replacement.

It is relatively easy to change your own transaxle oil. The only equipment required is a drain pan, a wrench to fit the filler and drain plugs, and an oil suction gun. Gear oil and automatic transmission fluid can be purchased in both quart and gallon cans at automotive supply stores.

To change the oil:

1. Jack up the front of the car and support it safely on stands.

2. Slide drain pan under the transaxle.

3. Remove the filler plug and then the drain plug.

4. When the oil has been completely drained, install the drain plug. Tighten to 18 ft. lbs.

5. Using the suction gun, refill the transaxle up to the level of the filler plug.

6. Install and tighten the filler plug.

Automatic Transaxle

FLUID RECOMMENDATIONS

The fluid used in the Omni/Horizon automatic transaxles should be only of the Dexron® or Dexron II® type.

LEVEL CHECK

The automatic transaxle and differential are contained in the same housing, but the units are sealed from each other (1978–82 only). 1983 and later automatic transaxles are filled as one unit. The transmission does not have a conventional filler tube, but is filled through a die-cast opening in the case. The filler hole is plugged during operation by the transmission dipstick.

The fluid level should be checked every 6 months when the engine and transmission fluid are warmed to normal operating temperature.

1. Position the car on a level surface.

2. Idle the engine and engage the parking brake.

3. Shift the lever through each gear momentarily and return the lever to PARK.

4. Remove the dipstick and wipe it clean.

5. Reinsert the dipstick and remove it again. The level should be between the ADD and FULL marks on the dipstick. If necessary, add DEXRON® or DEXRON II® automatic transmission fluid. Do not overfill.

6. While you are checking the fluid level, check the condition of the fluid. The condition of the fluid will often reveal potential problems.

7. If the fluid level is consistently low, suspect a leak. The easiest way is to slip a piece of clean newspaper under the car overnight, but this is not always an accurate indication, since some leaks will occur only when the transmission is operating.

Other leaks can be located by driving the car. Wipe the underside of the transmission clean and drive the car for several miles to bring the fluid temperature to normal. Stop the car, shut off the engine and look for leakage, but

Transmission Fluid Indications

The appearance and odor of the transmission fluid can give valuable clues to the overall condition of the transmission. Always note the appearance of the fluid when you check the fluid level or change the fluid. Rub a small amount of fluid between your fingers to feel for grit and smell the fluid on the dipstick.

If the fluid appears:	It indicates:
Clear and red colored	● Normal operation
Discolored (extremely dark red or brownish) or smells burned	● Band or clutch pack failure, usually caused by an overheated transmission. Hauling very heavy loads with insufficient power or failure to change the fluid, often result in overheating. Do not confuse this appearance with newer fluids that have a darker red color and a strong odor (though not a burned odor).
Foamy or aerated (light in color and full of bubbles)	● The level is too high (gear train is churning oil). ● An internal air leak (air is mixing with the fluid). Have the transmission checked professionally.
Solid residue in the fluid	● Defective bands, clutch pack or bearings. Bits of band material or metal abrasives are clinging to the dipstick. Have the transmission checked professionally.
Varnish coating on the dipstick	● The transmission fluid is overheating.

remember, that where the fluid is located may not be the source of the leak. Airflow around the transmission while the car is moving may carry the fluid to other parts of the car.

8. Reinsert the dipstick and be sure it is properly seated. This is the only seal that prevents water or dirt entering the transmission through the filler opening.

DIFFERENTIAL (AUTOMATIC TRANSAXLE)

1978 thru 1982 automatic transaxles have 2 separate reservoirs that require filling separately. 1983 and later models fill as one unit. Most models have a drain and fill plug in the differential cover; some models will have only a fill plug. Should it become necessary to drain the differential and the cover has only a fill plug, simply remove the cover to drain. A service gasket, should be formed from RTV sealant when the cover is installed. Use a ¹⁄₁₆ in. bead of RTV sealant on the cover.

To check the fluid level, remove the filler plug. The level should be at the bottom of the hole, which can be checked with your finger or a piece of bent wire.

If fluid is needed, use only Dexron® or Dexron II®.

AUTOMATIC TRANSAXLE DRAIN AND REFILL

NOTE: *RTV silicone sealer is used in place of a pan gasket.*

Chrysler recommends no fluid or filter changes during the normal service life of the car. Severe usage requires a fluid and filter change every 15,000 miles. Severe usage is defined as:

a. more than 50% heavy city traffic during 90°F weather.

b. police, taxi or commercial operation or trailer towing.

When changing the fluid, only Dexron or Dexron II fluid should be used. A filter change should be performed at every fluid change.

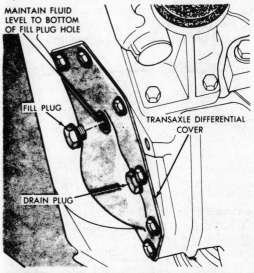

MAINTAIN FLUID LEVEL TO BOTTOM OF FILL PLUG HOLE

FILL PLUG

TRANSAXLE DIFFERENTIAL COVER

DRAIN PLUG

Automatic transaxle differential drain and fill plugs—1978–82 models

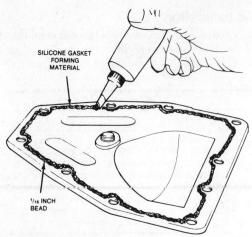

SILICONE GASKET
FORMING
MATERIAL

1/16 INCH
BEAD

Form a silicone gasket as shown

1. Raise the vehicle and support it on jack-stands.

2. Place a large container under the pan, loosen the pan bolts and tap at one corner to break it loose. Drain the fluid.

3. When the fluid is drained remove the pan bolts.

4. Remove the retaining screws and replace the filter. Tighten the screws to 35 inch pounds.

5. Clean the fluid pan, peel off the old RTV silicone sealer and install the pan, using a 1/8 inch bead of new RTV sealer. Always run the sealer bead inside the bolt holes. Tighten the pan bolts to 10–12 ft. lb.

6. Pour four quarts of Dexron® II fluid through the filler tube.

7. Start the engine and idle it for at least 2 minutes. Set the parking brake and move the selector through each position, ending in Park.

8. Add sufficient fluid to bring the level to the FULL mark on the dipstick. The level should be checked in Park, with the engine idling at normal operating temperature.

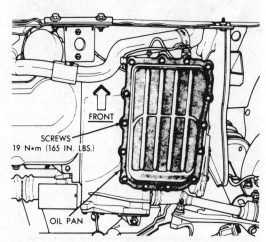

FRONT

SCREWS
19 N•m (165 IN. LBS.)

OIL PAN

Automatic transaxle oil pan

Coolant

See "Cooling System" under Routine Maintenance in this chapter.

Brake Master Cylinder

The brake fluid level should be checked every 6 months.

1. Wipe the area around the master cylinder clean.

2. Remove the master cylinder cap. The fluid level should be within 1/4 in. of the top of the reservoir.

3. If necessary, add brake fluid identified on the container as conforming to DOT 3 specifications.

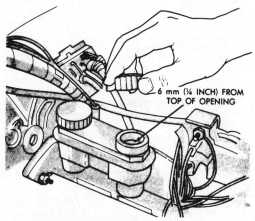

6 mm (1/4 INCH) FROM
TOP OF OPENING

Check master cylinder fluid level

Power Steering Reservoir

The power steering reservoir fluid level should be checked with the engine OFF to prevent accidents. Check the level every 6 months.

1. Position the car on a level surface.

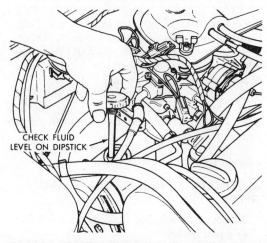

CHECK FLUID
LEVEL ON DIPSTICK

Checking power steering fluid level

2. Wipe the area around the power steering reservoir cap clean and remove the cap.

3. The power steering pump cap has a dipstick attached. Fluid level should be kept at the level indicated on the dipstick.

4. If it is necessary to add fluid, use only MOPAR Power Steering Fluid or the equivalent. DO NOT USE AUTOMATIC TRANSMISSION FLUID.

5. Replace the cap and tighten in place.

Lubricants and Greases

Semi-solid lubricants bear an NLGI designation and are classified as grades 0, 1, 2, 3 or 4. Whenever chassis lubricant is specified, Multi-Purpose grease, NLGI grade 2, EP (Extreme Pressure) is recommended.

Chassis Greasing

Tie-Rod Ends

There are only 2 points on the car that require periodic greasing. The tie-rod end ball joints are semi-permanently lubricated and should be lubricated every 3 years or 30,000 miles, whichever occurs first. These joints should also be inspected whenever the car is serviced for other reasons. Damaged seals should be replaced.

To lubricate the tie-rod end ball joints:

1. Clean the accumulated dirt and grease from the outside of the seal area to permit a close inspection.

2. Clean the grease fitting and surrounding area.

3. Using a grease gun fill the joint with fresh grease.

4. Stop filling when the grease begins to flow freely from the areas at the base of the seal or when the seal begins to balloon.

5. Wipe off the excess grease.

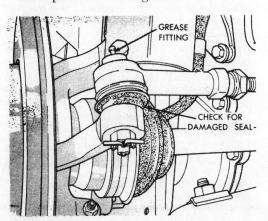

Check the tie-rod end ball joint seals

Steering Shaft Seal

The steering shaft seal where the steering shaft passes through the dash is lubricated at manufacture. If the seal becomes noisy when the steering shaft is turned, it should be relubricated with multi-purpose chassis grease, NLGI Grade 2 EP.

Front Suspension Ball Joints

The 2 lower front suspension ball joints are permanently lubricated at the factory. Inspect the joints whenever the car is serviced for other reasons. Damaged seals should be replaced to prevent leakage of grease.

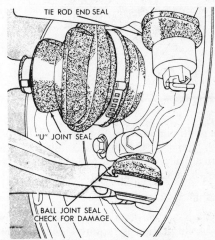

Check ball joints for damaged seals

Clutch Cable

If the clutch cable begins to make odd noises or if the effort to depress the clutch becomes excessive, lubricate the clutch cable ball end with multi-purpose chassis grease NLGI Grade 2 EP.

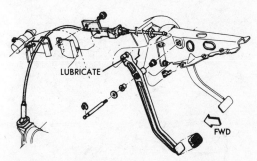

Lubricate the ball end of the clutch cable

Floorshift Control Linkage

The gearshift control linkage should be lubricated whenever the shifting effort becomes excessive or if the linkage exhibits a rattling noise.

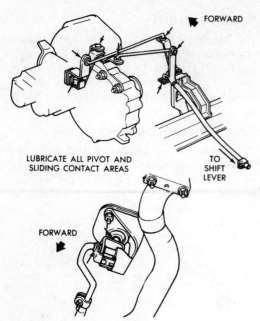

LUBRICATE ALL PIVOT AND SLIDING CONTACT AREAS

FORWARD

TO SHIFT LEVER

FORWARD

Lubricate the floor shift linkage

Use a multi-purpose chassis grease NLGI Grade 2 EP. Remove the unit and lubricate the spherical balls, metal caps and shaft and lubricate each plastic grommet or bushing.

Driveshaft U-Joints

The car has 4 constant velocity U-joints. No periodic lubrication is required, but the joint seals should be inspected for damage or leakage whenever the car is serviced. If damage is found, replace the U-joint boot and seal and fill with fresh grease immediately. Failure to do so will eventually require complete replacement of the constant velocity joint.

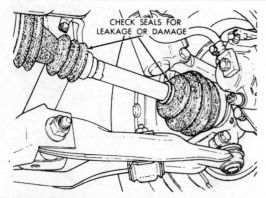

CHECK SEALS FOR LEAKAGE OR DAMAGE

Inspect U-joint seals for leakage

Parts Requiring No Lubrication

Some components are permanently lubricated. Some parts will be adversely affected by lubricants. In particular, rubber bushings should not be lubricated, since it will destroy their frictional characteristics. Parts that should not be lubricated are:

- Alternator bearings
- Drive belts
- Fan idler belt pulley
- Front wheel bearings
- Rubber bushings
- Starter bearings
- Suspension strut bearing
- Throttle cable control
- Throttle linkage
- Water pump bearings

Body Lubrication

Operating mechanisms of the body should be inspected, cleaned and lubricated as necessary. This will provide maximum protection against rust and wear.

Prior to lubricating, wipe the parts clean of dirt and old lubricant. When Lubriplate® is specified, use a smooth, white body lubricant of NLGI Grade 1. When Door-Ease® is specified, use a stainless, wax-type lubricant.

Hood Latch and Release

Apply Lubriplate®, or the equivalent to all pivot and sliding contact areas. Work the lubricant into the lock mechanism. Apply a thin film of the same lubricant to the safety catch.

Body Hinges

These parts should be lubricated with engine oil at the points shown.

Door Check Straps

Apply Lubriplate® or the equivalent whenever the car is serviced.

Lock Cylinders

Pay particular attention to the lock cylinders when the temperature is around the freezing mark. When necessary, apply a thin film of Lubriplate, or the equivalent directly to the key and insert the key in the lock. Work the lock several times and wipe the key dry.

Another alternative is to use a commercial spray that is sprayed directly into the lock to prevent freezing.

Liftgate Prop Pivots and Latch

Lubricate these points with Lubriplate® or the equivalent.

Door Latch, Lock Control Linkage and Window Regulator

To lubricate these parts it is necessary to remove the trim panel. Lubricate all pivot and

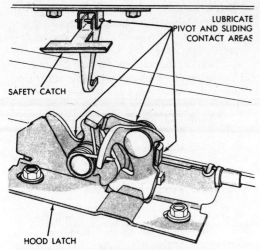

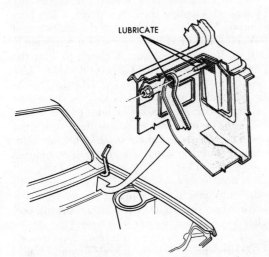

Lubricate the hood latch release

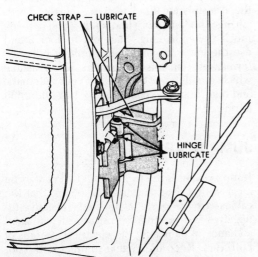

Lubricate the hood hinges

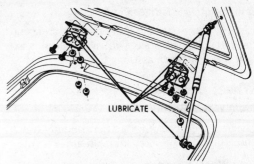

Lubricate the liftgate hinges and prop pivots

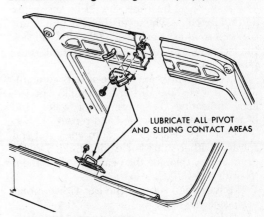

Lubricate the liftgate latch

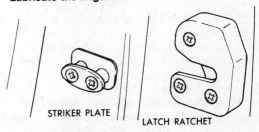

Lubricate the door latches

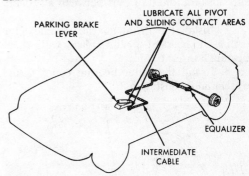

Lubricate the parking brake

sliding contact areas with Lubriplate® or the equivalent.

Parking Brake Mechanism

Lubricate all parking brake sliding and pivot contact areas with Lubriplate® or the equivalent.

Lubricate the door hinge check strap

Door Latch and Striker Plate

Lubricate the striker plate contact area and the ratchet pivot areas with a stainless, wax-type lubricant such as Door Ease®.

Wheel Bearings

Front Wheel Bearings

The front wheel bearings are permanently sealed and require no periodic lubrication.

Rear Wheel Bearings

The rear wheel bearings should be inspected and relubricated whenever the rear brakes are serviced or at least every 30,000 miles. Repack the bearings with high temperature multi-purpose grease.

Check the lubricant to see if it is contaminated. If it contains dirt or has a milky appearance indicating the presence of water, the bearings should be cleaned and repacked.

Clean the bearings in kerosene, mineral spirits or other suitable cleaning fluid. Do not dry them by spinning the bearings. Allow them to air dry.

1. Raise and support the car with the rear wheels off the floor.

2. Remove the wheel grease cap, cotter pin, nut-lock and bearing adjusting nut.

3. Remove the thrust washer and bearing.

4. Remove the drum from the spindle.

5. Thoroughly clean the old lubricant from the bearings and hub cavity. Inspect the bearing rollers for pitting or other signs of wear. Light discoloration is normal.

6. Repack the bearings with high temperature multi-purpose EP grease and add a small amount of new grease to the hub cavity. Be sure to force the lubricant between all rollers in the bearing.

7. Install the drum on the spindle after coating the polished spindle surfaces with wheel bearing lubricant.

8. Install the outer bearing cone, thrust washer and adjusting nut.

9. Tighten the adjusting nut to 20–25 ft. lbs. while rotating the wheel.

10. Back off the adjusting nut to completely release the preload from the bearing.

11. Tighten the adjusting nut finger-tight.

12. Position the nut-lock with one pair of slots in line with the cotter pin hole. Install the cotter pin.

13. Clean and install the grease cap and wheel.

14. Lower the car.

PUSHING AND TOWING

If your car is equipped with a manual transaxle, it may be push started in an extreme emergency, but there is the possibility of damaging bumpers and/or fenders of both cars. Make sure that the bumpers of both cars are evenly matched. Depress the clutch pedal, select Second or Third gear, and switch the ignition On. When the car reaches a speed of approximately 10 or 15 mph, release the clutch to start the engine. DO NOT ATTEMPT TO PUSH START AN AUTOMATIC OMNI OR HORIZON.

Manual transaxle models may be flat-towed short distances. Attach tow lines to the towing eye on the front suspension or the left or right bumper bracket at the rear. Flat-towing automatic transaxle models is not recommended more than 15 miles at more than 30 mph, and this only in an emergency. Cars equipped with the automatic should only be towed from the rear when the front wheels are on towing dollies.

If you plan on towing a trailer, don't exceed 1000 lbs (trailer without brakes). Towing a trailer with an automatic equipped car places an extra load on the transmission and a few items should be made note of here. Make doubly sure that the transmission fluid is at the correct level. Change the fluid more frequently if you're doing much trailer hauling. Start out in 1 or 2 and use the lower ranges when climbing hills. Aftermarket transmission coolers are available which greatly ease the load on your automatic and one should be considered if you often pull a trailer.

JUMP STARTING

Jump starting is the favored method of starting a car with a dead battery. Make sure that the cables are properly connected, negative-to-negative and positive-to-positive, or you stand a chance of damaging the electrical systems of both cars. Keep the engine running in the donor car. If the car still fails to start, call a ga-

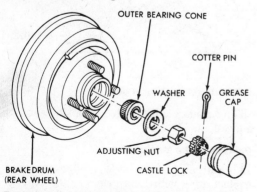

OUTER BEARING CONE

COTTER PIN

WASHER

GREASE CAP

ADJUSTING NUT

CASTLE LOCK

BRAKE DRUM (REAR WHEEL)

Exploded view of rear wheel bearing

JUMP STARTING A DEAD BATTERY

The chemical reaction in a battery produces explosive hydrogen gas. This is the safe way to jump start a dead battery, reducing the chances of an accidental spark that could cause an explosion.

Jump Starting Precautions

1. Be sure both batteries are of the same voltage.
2. Be sure both batteries are of the same polarity (have the same grounded terminal).
3. Be sure the vehicles are not touching.
4. Be sure the vent cap holes are not obstructed.
5. Do not smoke or allow sparks around the battery.
6. In cold weather, check for frozen electrolyte in the battery.
7. Do not allow electrolyte on your skin or clothing.
8. Be sure the electrolyte is not frozen.

Jump Starting Procedure

1. Determine voltages of the two batteries; they must be the same.
2. Bring the starting vehicle close (they must not touch) so that the batteries can be reached easily.
3. Turn off all accessories and both engines. Put both cars in Neutral or Park and set the handbrake.
4. Cover the cell caps with a rag—do not cover terminals.
5. If the terminals on the run-down battery are heavily corroded, clean them.
6. Identify the positive and negative posts on both batteries and connect the cables in the order shown.
7. Start the engine of the starting vehicle and run it at fast idle. Try to start the car with the dead battery. Crank it for no more than 10 seconds at a time and let it cool off for 20 seconds in between tries.
8. If it doesn't start in 3 tries, there is something else wrong.
9. Disconnect the cables in the reverse order.
10. Replace the cell covers and dispose of the rags.

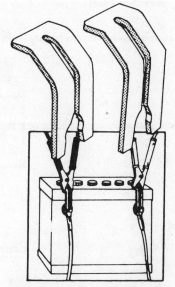

Side terminal batteries occasionally pose a problem when connecting jumper cables. There frequently isn't enough room to clamp the cables without touching sheet metal. Side terminal adaptors are available to alleviate this problem and should be removed after use.

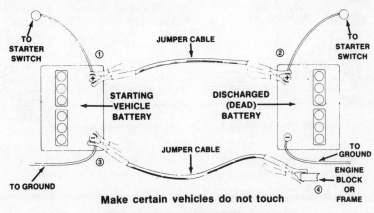

TO STARTER SWITCH

JUMPER CABLE

① ②

TO STARTER SWITCH

STARTING VEHICLE BATTERY

DISCHARGED (DEAD) BATTERY

TO GROUND

③

JUMPER CABLE

TO GROUND

④

ENGINE BLOCK OR FRAME

Make certain vehicles do not touch

This hook-up for negative ground cars only

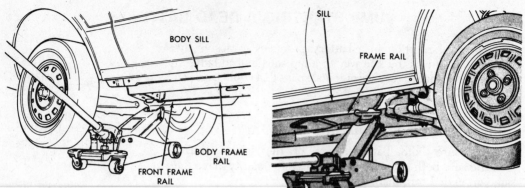

Frame rail jacking point—floor jack

Rear frame rail jacking point—floor jack

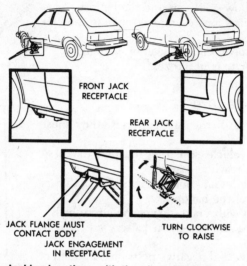

Jacking locations with tire changing jack

CONTROL ARM — CAUTION; DO NOT LIFT ON CONTROL ARMS

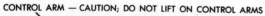

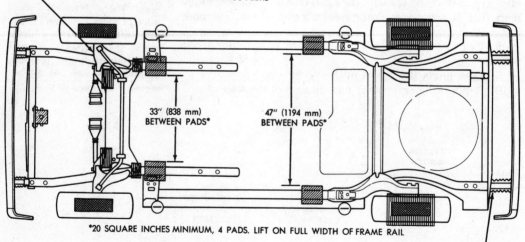

*20 SQUARE INCHES MINIMUM, 4 PADS. LIFT ON FULL WIDTH OF FRAME RAIL

TWIN POST LIFT POINTS
FRAME CONTACT OR FLOOR JACK
DRIVE ON HOIST
O SCISSORS JACK (EMERGENCY) LOCATIONS

Jacking and hoisting contact locations

rage—continual grinding on the starter will overheat the unit and make repair or replacement necessary.

JACKING

Floor jacks can be used to raise the car at the locations shown. In addition a front jacking point is located at the center of the front crossmember. Four door models only can be jacked at the extreme rear provided a 2″ x 4″ x 25″ (minimum dimensions) wood spacer is positioned as shown against the ledge of the rear bumper.

Jack receptacles are located at the front and rear of the body sill for use with jack supplied with a car. Do not use these lift points as bearing points for a floor jack.

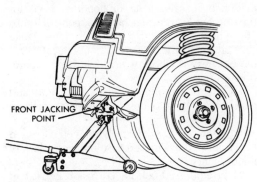

FRONT JACKING POINT

Front jacking point—floor jack

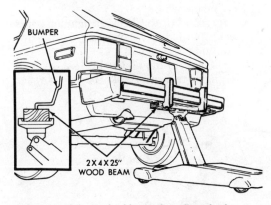

BUMPER

2 X 4 X 25″ WOOD BEAM

4-door model rear jacking point—floor jack

HOW TO BUY A USED CAR

Many people believe that a two or three year old used car is a better buy than a new car. This may be true; the new car suffers the heaviest depreciation in the first two years, but is not old enough to present a lot of costly repair problems. Whatever the age of the used car you might want to buy, this section and a little

patience will help you select one that should be safe and dependable.

Tips

1. First decide what model you want, and how much you want to spend.
2. Check the used car lots and your local newspaper ads. Privately owned cars are usually less expensive, however you will not get a warranty that, in most cases, comes with a used car purchased from a lot.
3. Never shop at night. The glare of the lights make it easy to miss faults on the body caused by accident or rust repair.
4. Try to get the name and phone number of the previous owner. Contact him/her and ask about the car. If the owner of the lot refuses this information, look for a car somewhere else.

A private seller can tell you about the car and maintenance. Remember, however, there's no law requiring honesty from private citizens selling used cars. There is a law that forbids the tampering with or turning back the odometer mileage. This includes both the private citizen and the lot owner. The law also requires that the seller or anyone transferring ownership of the car must provide the buyer with a signed statement indicating the mileage on the odometer at the time of transfer.

5. Write down the year, model and serial number before you buy any used car. Then dial 1-800-424-9393, the toll free number of the National Highway Traffic Safety Administration, and ask if the car has ever been included on any manufacturer's recall list. If so, make sure the needed repairs were made.
6. Use the "Used Car Checklist" in this section and check all the items on the used car you are considering. Some items are more important than others. You know how much money you can afford for repairs, and, depending on the price of the car, may consider doing any needed work yourself. Beware, however, of trouble in areas that will affect operation, safety or emission. Problems in the "Used Car Checklist" break down as follows:

  1–8: Two or more problems in these areas indicate a lack of maintenance. You should beware.
  9–13: Indicates a lack of proper care, however, these can usually be corrected with a tune-up or relatively simple parts replacement.
  14–17: Problems in the engine or transmission can be very expensive. Walk away from any car with problems in both of these areas.

7. If you are satisfied with the apparent condition of the car, take it to an independent di-

agnostic center or mechanic for a complete check. If you have a state inspection program, have it inspected immediately before purchase, or specify on the bill of sale that the sale is conditional on passing state inspection.

8. Road test the car—refer to the "Road Test Checklist" in this section. If your original evaluation and the road test agree—the rest is up to you.

Used Car Checklist

NOTE: *The numbers on the illustrations refer to the numbers on this checklist.*

1. *Mileage:* Average mileage is about 12,000 miles per year. More than average mileage may indicate hard usage. 1975 and later catalytic converter equipped models may need converter service at 50,000 miles.

2. *Paint:* Check around the tailpipe, molding and windows for overspray indicating that the car has been repainted.

3. *Rust:* Check fenders, doors, rocker panels, window moldings, wheelwells, floorboards, under floormats, and in the trunk for signs of rust. Any rust at all will be a problem. There is no way to check the spread of rust, except to replace the part or panel.

4. *Body appearance:* Check the moldings, bumpers, grille, vinyl roof, glass, doors, trunk lid and body panels for general overall condition. Check for misalignment, loose holdown clips, ripples, scratches in glass, rips or patches in the top. Mismatched paint, welding in the trunk, severe misalignment of body panels or ripples may indicate crash work.

5. *Leaks:* Get down and look under the car. There are no normal "leaks", other than water from the air conditioning condenser.

6. *Tires:* Check the tire air pressure. A common trick is to pump the tire pressure up to make the car roll easier. Check the tread wear, open the trunk and check the spare too. Uneven wear is a clue that the front end needs alignment. See the troubleshooting chapter for clues to the causes of tire wear.

7. *Shock absorbers:* Check the shock absorbers by forcing downward sharply on each corner of the car. Good shocks will not allow the car to bounce more than twice after you let go.

8. *Interior:* Check the entire interior. You're looking for an interior condition that agrees with the overall condition of the car. Reasonable wear is expected, but be suspicious of new seatcovers on sagging seats, new pedal pads, and worn armrests. These indicate an attempt to cover up hard use. Pull back the carpets and look for evidence of water leaks or flooding. Look for missing hardware, door handles, control knobs etc. Check lights and signal operations. Make sure all accessories (air conditioner, heater, radio etc.) work. Check windshield wiper operation.

9. *Belts and Hoses:* Open the hood and check all belts and hoses for wear, cracks or weak spots.

10. *Battery:* Low electrolyte level, corroded terminals and/or cracked case indicate a lack of maintenance.

11. *Radiator:* Look for corrosion or rust in the coolant indicating a lack of maintenance.

12. *Air filter:* A dirty air filter usually means a lack of maintenance.

13. *Ignition Wires:* Check the ignition wires for cracks, burned spots, or wear. Worn wires will have to be replaced.

14. *Oil level:* If the oil level is low, chances are the engine uses oil or leaks. Beware of water

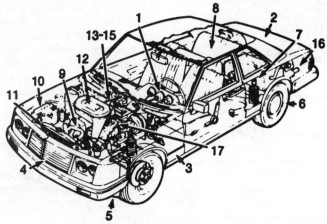

Check these areas when buying a used car. The "Used Car Checklist" gives an explanation of the numbered items

in the oil (cracked block), excessively thick oil (used to quiet a noisy engine), or thin, dirty oil with a distinct gasoline smell (internal engine problems).

15. *Automatic Transmission:* Pull the transmission dipstick out when the engine is running. The level should read "Full", and the fluid should be clear or bright red. Dark brown or black fluid that has distinct burnt odor signals a transmission in need of repair or over-haul.

16. *Exhaust:* Check the color of the exhaust smoke. Blue smoke indicates, among other problems, worn rings; black smoke can indicate burnt valves or carburetor problems. Check the exhaust system for leaks; it can be expensive to replace.

17. *Spark Plugs:* Remove one of the spark plugs (the most accessible will do). An engine in good condition will show plugs with a light tan or gray deposit on the firing tip. See the color Tune-Up tips section for spark plug conditions.

Road Test Check List

1. *Engine Performance:* The car should be peppy whether cold or warm, with adequate power and good pickup. It should respond smoothly through the gears.

2. *Brakes:* They should provide quick, firm stops with no noise, pulling or brake fade.

3. *Steering:* Sure control with no binding, harshness, or looseness and no shimmy in the wheel should be expected. Noise or vibration from the steering wheel when turning the car means trouble.

4. *Clutch (Manual Transmission):* Clutch action should give quick, smooth response with easy shifting. The clutch pedal should have about 1–1½ inches of free-play before it disengages the clutch. Start the engine, set the parking brake, put the transmission in first gear and slowly release the clutch pedal. The engine should begin to stall when the pedal is one-half to three-quarters of the way up.

5. *Automatic Transmission:* The transmission should shift rapidly and smoothly, with no noise, hesitation or slipping.

6. *Differential:* No noise or thumps should be present. Differentials have no "normal" leaks.

7. *Driveshaft, Universal Joints:* Vibration and noise could mean driveshaft problems. Clicking at low speed or coast conditions could mean worn U-joints.

8. *Suspension:* Try hitting bumps at different speeds. A car that bounces has weak shock absorbers. Clunks mean worn bushings or ball joints.

9. *Frame:* Wet the tires and drive in a straight line. Tracks should show two straight lines, not four. Four tire tracks indicate a frame bent by collision damage. If the tires can't be wet for this purpose, have a friend drive along behind you and see if the car appears to be traveling in a straight line.

Tune-Up and Performance Maintenance

2

TUNE-UP PROCEDURES

The procedures listed here are intended as specific procedures. More General procedures are given in Chapter 10, Troubleshooting.

Neither tune-up nor troubleshooting can be considered independently, since each has a direct bearing on the other.

An engine tune-up is a service designed to restore the maximum capability of power, performance, economy and reliability in an engine, and, at the same time, assure the owner of a complete check and more lasting results in efficiency and trouble-free performance. Engine tune-up becomes increasingly important each year, to ensure that pollutant levels are in compliance with federal emissions standards.

It is advisable to follow a definite and thorough tune-up procedure. Tune-up consists of three separate steps: Analysis, the process of determining whether normal wear is responsible for performance loss, and whether parts require replacement or service; Parts Replacement or Service; and Adjustment, where engine adjustments are returned to the original factory specifications.

The extent of an engine tune-up is usually determined by the length of time since the previous service, although the type of driving and the general mechanical condition of the engine must be considered. Specific maintenance should also be performed at regular intervals, depending on operating conditions.

Troubleshooting is a logical sequence of procedures designed to lead the owner or service man to the particular cause of trouble. The troubleshooting chapter of this manual is general in nature, yet specific enough to locate the problem. Service usually comprises two areas; diagnosis and repair. While the apparent cause of trouble, in many cases, is worn or damaged parts, performance problems are less obvious. The first job is to locate the problem and cause.

Once the problem has been isolated, refer to the appropriate section for repair, removal or adjustment procedures.

It is advisable to read the entire chapter before beginning a tune-up, although those who are more familiar with tune-up procedures may wish to go directly to the instructions.

Spark Plugs

A typical spark plug consists of a metal shell surrounding a ceramic insulator. A metal electrode extends downward through the center of the insulator and protrudes a small distance. Located at the end of the plug and attached to the side of the outer metal shell is the side electrode. The side electrode bends in at a 90° angle so that its tip is even with, and parallel to, the tip of the center electrode. The distance between these two electrodes (measured in thousandths of an inch) is called the spark plug gap. The spark plug in no way produces a spark but merely provides a gap across which the current can arc. The coil produces anywhere from 20,000 to 40,000 volts which travels to the distributor where it is distributed through the spark plug wires to the spark plugs. The current passes along the center electrode and jumps the gap to the side electrode, and, in so doing, ignited the air/fuel mixture in the combustion chamber.

SPARK PLUG HEAT RANGE

Spark plug heat range is the ability of the plug to dissipate heat. The longer the insulator (or the farther it extends into the engine), the hotter the plug will operate; the shorter the insulator the cooler it will operate. A plug that absorbs little heat and remains too cool will quickly accumulate deposits of oil and carbon since it is not hot enough to burn them off. This leads to plug fouling and consequently to misfiring. A plug that absorbs too much heat will have no

Tune-Up Specifications

Part numbers listed in this reference are not recommendations by Chilton for any product by brand name. They are references that can be used with interchange manuals and after market supplier catalogs to locate each brand supplier's discrete part number.
NOTE: When analyzing compression test results, look for uniformity among cylinders rather than specific pressures. The lowest reading cylinder should be withing 20% of the highest.

Year	Displ	Spark Plugs		Ignition Timing (deg) ▲		Intake Valve Opens (deg) ■	Fuel Pump Pressure (psi)	Idle Speed (rpm) ▲		Valve Lash (in.) ▲	
		Orig Type	Gap (in.)	Man Trans	Auto Trans			Man Trans	Auto Trans	Intake	Exhaust
'78	1.7L	RN-12Y	.035	15B	15B	23	4.5–6	900	900	.008–.012H	.016–.020H
'79	1.7L	RN-12Y	.035	15B	15B	14	4.4–5.8	900	900	.008–.012H	.016–.020H
'80	1.7L	RN-12Y	.035	12B ⑤	12B ⑤	14	4.4–5.8	900	900	.008–.012H	.016–.020H
'81	1.7L	P65–PR4 ①	.048 ②	12B ③	10B ④	14	4.4–5.8	900	900	.008–.012H	.016–.020H
	2.2L	P65–PR	.035	10B	10B	12	4.5–6.0	900	900	Hyd.	Hyd.
'82	1.7L	P65–PR	.035	20B	12B	14	4.4–5.8	900	900	.008–.012H	.016–.020H
	2.2L	P65–PR	.035	12B	12B	12	4.5–6.0	900	900	Hyd.	Hyd.
'83	1.7L	RN-12YC ⑥	.035	20°	12°	14	4.4–5.8	900	900	.008–.012H	.016–.020H
	2.2L	RN-12YC ⑥	.035	12° ⑦	12° ⑦	12	4.5–6.0	850	900	Hyd.	Hyd.
'84–'86	1.6L	RN-12YC ⑥	.035	12°	12°	16	4.5–6.0	850	1000	.012C	.014C
	2.2L	RN-12YC ⑥	.035	10° ⑧	10° ⑧	12	4.5–6.0	900 ⑧	900 ⑧	Hyd.	Hyd.

NOTE: *The underhood specifications sticker often reflects tune-up specification changes made in production. Sticker figures must be used if they disagree with those in this chart.*

▲ See text for procedure
■ Before Top Dead Center
① Canada: P65-PR
② Canada: .035
③ Canada: 5B
④ Canada: 10B
⑤ California: 10B
⑥ Replacement plug: RN-12Y
⑦ High-altitude: 6B
⑧ High-performance engine: 15°B @ 850 RPM—refer to VECI label under hood.

deposits, but, due to the excessive heat, the electrodes will burn away quickly and in some instances, preignition may result. Preignition takes place when plug tips get so hot that they glow sufficiently to ignite the fuel/air mixture before the actual spark occurs. This early ignition will usually cause a pinging during low speeds and heavy loads.

The general rule of thumb for choosing the correct heat range when picking a spark plug is: if most of your driving is long distance, high speed travel, use a colder plug; if most of your driving is stop and go, use a hotter plug. Original equipment plugs are compromise plugs, but most people never have occasion to change their plugs from the factory-recommended heat range.

REPLACING SPARK PLUGS

A set of spark plugs usually requires replacement after about 10,000 miles on cars with conventional ignition systems and after about 20,000 to 30,000 miles on cars with electronic ignition, depending on your style of driving. In normal operation, plug gap increases about 0.001 in. for every 1,000–2,500 miles. As the gap increases, the plug's voltage requirement also increases. It requires a greater voltage to jump the wider gap and about two to three times as much voltage to fire a plug at high speeds than at idle.

When you're removing spark plugs, you should work on one at a time. Don't start by removing the plug wires all at once, because unless you number them, they may become mixed up. Take a minute before you begin and number the wires with tape. The best location for numbering is near where the wires come out of the cap.

1. Twist the spark plug boot and remove the boot and wire from the plug. Do not pull on the wire itself as this will ruin the wire.

2. If possible, use a brush or rag to clean the area around the spark plug. Make sure that all the dirt is removed so that none will enter the cylinder after the plug is removed.

3. Remove the spark plug using the proper size socket. Turn the socket counterclockwise to remove the plug. Be sure to hold the socket straight on the plug to avoid breaking the plug, or rounding off the hex on the plug.

4. Once the plug is out, check it against the plugs shown in the color section to determine engine condition. This is crucial since plug readings are vital signs of engine condition.

5. Use a round wire feeler gauge to check the plug gap. The correct size gauge should pass through the electrode gap with a slight drag. If you're in doubt, try one size smaller and one larger. The smaller gauge should go through

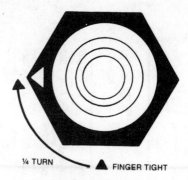

GASKET TYPE PLUGS

¼ TURN   ▲ FINGER TIGHT

TAPERED SEAT PLUGS (NO GASKET)

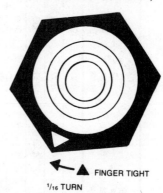

◀ ▲ FINGER TIGHT

¹⁄₁₆ TURN

Tighten the plugs as shown in the absence of a specified torque

easily while the larger one shouldn't go through at all. If the gap is incorrect, use the electrode bending tool on the end of the gauge to adjust the gap. When adjusting the gap, always bend the side electrode. The center electrode is nonadjustable.

6. Squirt a drop of penetrating oil on the threads of the new plug and install it. Don't oil the threads too heavily. Turn the plug in clockwise by hand until it is snug.

7. When the plug is finger tight, tighten it with a wrench. If you don't have a torque wrench, tighten the plug as shown.

8. Install the plug boot firmly over the plug. Proceed to the next plug.

CHECKING AND REPLACING SPARK PLUG CABLES

NOTE: *On 1980 and later models, to maintain proper sealing between the towers and the nipples, the cable and nipple assemblies should not be removed from the distributor cap or coil towers unless the nipple are damaged or the cables require replacement. Plug wires on 1980 and later models DO NOT pull from the distributer cap, they must be released from inside the cap.*

Visually inspect the spark plug cables for

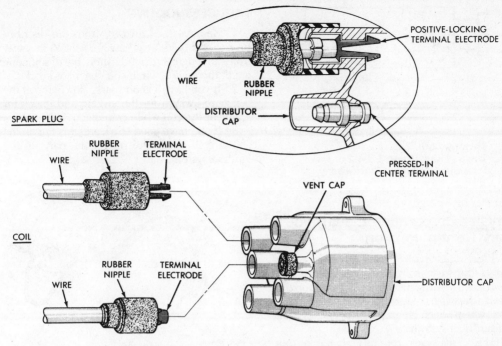

SPARK PLUG

COIL

Coil and spark plug wires—1980 and later models

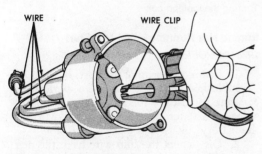

DISTRIBUTOR CAP

Removing the spark plug wires from the cap on 1980 and later models.

burns, cuts, or breaks in the insulation. Check the spark plug boots and the nipples on the distributor cap and coil. Replace any damaged wiring. If no physical damage is obvious, the wires can be checked with an ohmmeter for excessive resistance. (See the tune-up and troubleshooting section).

When installing a new set of spark plug cables, replace the cables one at a time so there will be no mixup. Start by replacing the longest cable first. Install the boot firmly over the spark plug. Route the wire exactly the same as the original. Insert the nipple firmly into the tower on the distributor cap. Repeat the process for each cable.

FIRING ORDER

To avoid confusion, replace spark plug wires or spark plugs one at a time.

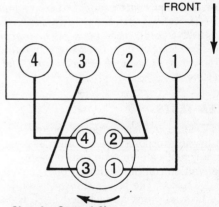

Chrysler Corp: 1.6L
Engine Firing Order: 1-3-4-2
Distributor Rotation: Clockwise

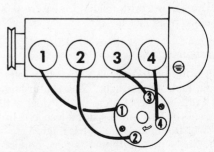

Chrysler Corp. 1.7L
Engine Firing Order: 1-3-4-2
Distributor Rotation: Clockwise

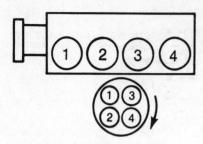

Chrysler Corp. 2.2L
Engine Firing Order: 1-3-4-2
Distributor Rotation: Clockwise

Chrysler Corporation Electronic Spark Control Ignition

The Electronic Spark Control System is the heart of the Lean Burn emission control system used by Chrysler. Omni and Horizon models use what is known as a Hall Effect ignition system which is controlled by signals from the lean Burn system.

NOTE: *This book contains simple testing procedures for your electronic ignition. More comprehensive testing on this system and other electronic control systems can be found in CHILTON'S GUIDE TO ELECTRONIC ENGINE CONTROLS, book part number 7535, available at most book sores and auto parts stores, or available directly from Chilton Co.*

SYSTEM TESTS

The electronic ignition system is controlled by the "Chrysler Corporation Lean Burn System," which is actually an emission control system.

The ignition coil can be tested on a conventional coil tester. The ballast resistor, mounted on the firewall, must be included in all tests. Primary resistance at 70°F should be 1.60–1.79 ohms for the Chrysler Prestolite coil, and 1.41–1.62 ohms for the Chrysler Essex coil. Secondary resistance should be 9400–11,700 ohms for the Prestolite, 8000–11,200 ohms for the Essex. The ballast resistor should measure 0.50–0.60 ohms resistance at 70°F.

EQUIPMENT

Some of the procedures in this section refer to an adjustable timing light. This is also known as a spark advance tester, i.e., a device that will measure how much spark advance is present going from one point, a base figure, to another. Since precise timing is very important to the Lean Burn System, do not attempt to perform any of the tests calling for an adjustable timing light without one.

TROUBLESHOOTING

1. Remove the coil wire from the distributor cap and hold it cautiously about ¼ in. away from an engine ground, then have someone crank the engine while you check for spark.

2. If you have a good spark, slowly move the coil wire away from the engine and check for arcing at the coil while cranking.

3. If you have good spark and it is not arcing at the coil, check the rest of the parts of the ignition system.

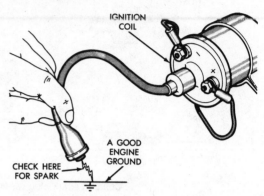

Testing the ignition coil

Engine Not Running—Will Not Start

1978–80 MODELS

1. Before performing this test, be sure the "Troubleshooting" test has been performed. Measure the battery specific gravity: it must be at least 1.220, temperature corrected. Measure the battery voltage and make a note of it.

2. Disconnect the thin wire from the negative coil terminal.

3. Remove the coil high tension lead at the distributor cap.

4. Turn the ignition On. While holding the coil high tension lead ¼ in. from a ground, connect a jumper wire from the negative coil terminal to a ground. A spark should be obtained from the high tension lead.

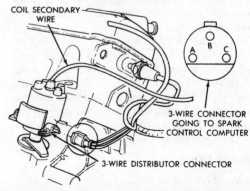

Distributor pick-up coil connector—1978–80

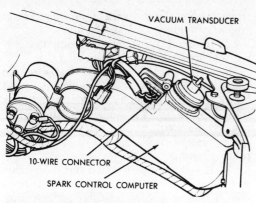

VACUUM TRANSDUCER

10-WIRE CONNECTOR

SPARK CONTROL COMPUTER

Spark control computer location

5. If there is no spark, use a voltmeter to test for at least 9 volts at the positive coil terminal (ignition On). If so, the coil must be replaced. If less than 9 volts is obtained, check the ballast resistor, wiring, and connections. If the car still won't start, proceed to Step 6.

6. If there was a spark in Step 4, turn the ignition Off, reconnect the wire to the negative coil terminal, and disconnect the distributor pick-up coil connector.

7. Turn the ignition On, and measure voltage between pin B of the pick-up coil connector on the spark control computer side, and a good engine ground. Voltage should be the same as the battery voltage measured in Step 1. If so, go to Step 11. If not, go to the next step.

NOTE: *Malfunction of the distributor pickup coil can be the result of the rotor not properly grounded to the distributor shaft. Remove the rotor and check the metal grounding tab to be sure it is not covered with plastic. If so, replace the rotor with a new one. Clean the top of the distributor shaft and install the rotor, pushing it onto the shaft so the metal tab contacts the shaft. Check for continuity between the interrupter vane and distributor housing. Do not try to start the engine with no continuity.*

8. Turn the ignition Off and disconnect the 10 terminal connector at the spark control computer.

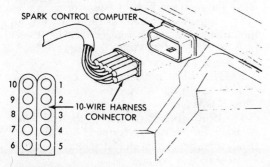

SPARK CONTROL COMPUTER

10 1
9   2
8   3   10-WIRE HARNESS
7   4   CONNECTOR
6   5

10-terminal wire harness

NOTE: *Do not remove grease from the 10-wire harness connector.*

9. Check for continuity between pin B of the pick-up coil connector on the computer side, and terminal 3 of the computer connector. If there is no continuity, the wire must be replaced. If continuity exists, go to the next step.

10. With the ignition On, connect a voltmeter between terminals 2 and 10 of the computer connector. Voltage should be the same as measured in Step 1. If so, the computer is defective and must be replaced.

11. Reconnect the 10 wire computer connector. Turn the ignition On. Hold the coil high tension lead (disconnected at the distributor cap) about ¼ in. from a ground. Connect a jumper wire between pins A and C of the distributor pick-up coil connector. If a spark is obtained, the distributor pick-up is defective and must be replaced. If not, go to the next step.

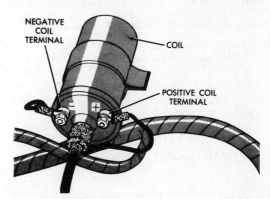

NEGATIVE COIL TERMINAL

COIL

POSITIVE COIL TERMINAL

Coil terminal location

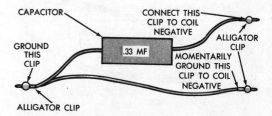

CAPACITOR

CONNECT THIS CLIP TO COIL NEGATIVE

ALLIGATOR CLIP

GROUND THIS CLIP

.33 MF

MOMENTARILY GROUND THIS CLIP TO COIL NEGATIVE

ALLIGATOR CLIP

Construct this special jumper wire to perform the no-start test on 1981 and later models

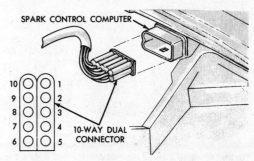

SPARK CONTROL COMPUTER

10 1
9   2
8   3
7   4   10-WAY DUAL
6   5   CONNECTOR

Removing the 10-way connector from the computer

12. Turn the ignition Off. Disconnect the 10 wire computer connector.

13. Check for continuity between pin C of the distributor connector and terminal 9 of the computer connector. Also check for continuity between pin A of the distributor connector and terminal 5 of the computer connector. If continuity exists, the computer is defective and must be replaced. If not, the wires are damaged. Repair them and recheck, starting at Step 11.

1981—AND LATER MODELS

1. Perform the "Troubleshooting" test before proceeding with the following. Make sure the battery is fully charged, then measure and record the battery voltage.

2. Remove the coil secondary wire from the distributor cap.

3. With the key on, use the special jumper wire and momentarily connect the negative terminal of the ignition coil to ground while holding the coil secondary wire (using insulated pliers and heavy gloves) about ¼ in. from a good ground. A spark should fire.

4. If spark was obtained, go to Step 9.

5. If no spark was obtained, turn off the ignition and disconnect the 10-wire harness going into the Spark Control Computer. **Do not remove the grease from the connector.**

6. With the ignition key on, use the special jumper wire and momentarily connect the negative terminal of the ignition coil to ground

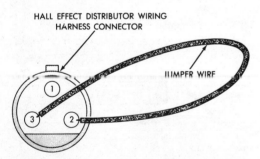

Jumping cavities 2 and 3 of the distributor harness connector

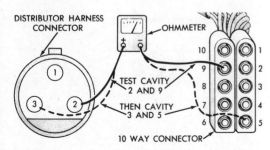

Testing cavities 2 and 9 then cavities 3 and 5 for continuity

while holding the coil wire ¼ in. from a good engine ground. A spark should fire.

7. If a spark is present, the computer output is shorted: replace the computer.

8. If no spark is obtained, measure the voltage at the coil positive terminal. It should be within 1 volt of battery voltage. If voltage is present but no spark is available when shorting negative terminal, replace the coil. If no voltage is present, replace the coil or check the primary wiring.

9. If voltage was obtained but the engine will not start, hold the carburetor switch open with a thin cardboard insulator and measure the voltage at the switch. It should be at least 5 volts. If voltage is present, go to Step 16.

10. If no voltage is present, turn the ignition switch off and disconnect the 10 wire harness going into the computer.

11. Turn the ignition switch on and measure the voltage at terminal 2 of the harness. It should be within 1 volt of battery voltage.

12. If no battery voltage is present, check for continuity between the battery and terminal 2 of the harness. If no continuity, repair fault and repeat Step 11.

13. If voltage is present turn ignition switch off and check for continuity between the carburetor switch and terminal 7 on connector. If no continuity is present, check for open wire between terminal 7 and the carburetor switch.

14. If continuity is present, check continuity between terminal 10 and ground. If continuity is present here, replace the computer. Repeat Step 9.

15. If no continuity is present, check for an open wire. If wiring is OK but the engine still won't start, go to next step.

16. Plug the 10 terminal dual connector back into the computer and turn the ignition switch on, hold the secondary coil wire near a good ground and disconnect the distributor harness connector. Using a regular jumper wire (not the special one mentioned earlier), jump terminal 2 to terminal 3 of the connector: a spark should fire at the coil wire. Make and break the connection at terminal 2 or 3 several times and check for good spark at the coil wire.

17. If spark is present at the coil wire but the engine won't start, replace the Hall Effect pick-up and check the rotor for cracks or burning. Replace as necessary.

NOTE: *When replacing a pick-up, always make sure rotor blades are grounded using an ohmmeter.*

18. If no spark is present at the coil wire, measure the voltage at terminal 1 of the distributor harness connector: it should be within 1 volt of battery voltage.

19. If correct, disconnect the 10 terminal dual

connector from the computer and check for continuity between terminal 2 of distributor harness and terminal 9 of the dual connector. Repeat test on terminal 3 of distributor harness and terminal 5 of dual connector. If no continuity, repair the harness. If continuity is present, replace the computer and repeat Step 16.

20. If no battery voltage is present in Step 18, turn off the ignition switch, disconnect the 10 terminal dual connector from the computer and check for continuity between terminal 1 of distributor harness and terminal 3 of dual connector. If no continuity, repair wire and repeat Step 16.

21. If continuity is present, turn the ignition switch on and check for battery voltage between terminal 2 and terminal 10 of the dual connector. If voltage is present, replace the computer and repeat Step 16. If no battery voltage is present, the computer is not grounded. Check and repair the ground wire and repeat Step 16.

POOR ENGINE PERFORMANCE

Before proceeding with these tests, be sure the ignition timing and idle speed are as specified.

Carburetor Switch Test

1. With the key OFF, disconnect the 10-wire harness from the Spark Control Computer.

2. With the throttle completely closed, check for continuity between pin 7 of the harness connector and a good ground. If there is no continuity, check the carburetor switch and wire. Recheck the timing.

3. With the throttle open, check for continuity between pin 7 of the harness connector and a good ground. There should be no continuity.

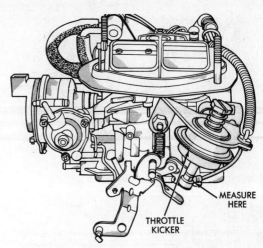

Carburetor switch continuity test—2.2L engine shown, 1.6L and 1.7L similar

Coolant Switch Test

1. With the key OFF, disconnect the wire from the coolant switch.

2. Connect one lead of an ohmmeter to a good ground, on the engine.

3. Connect the other lead to the terminal of the coolant switch. On a cold engine, (below 150°F) continuity should be present at the coolant switch. If not, replace the switch. On a warm engine (above 150°F) or on an engine at operating temperature (thermostat open), the ohmmeter should show no continuity. If it does, replace the coolant switch.

Start-up Advance Test—1978–79 Models

1. Connect an adjustable timing light to the engine so that the total timing advance can be checked.

2. Connect a jumper wire from the carburetor switch to a ground.

3. Start the engine and immediately adjust the timing light so that the basic timing light is seen on the timing plate of the engine. The meter (on the timing light) should show an 8° advance. Continue to observe the mark for 90 seconds, adjusting the light as necessary. The

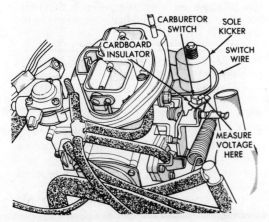

Carburetor switch insulator positioning—1.7L shown, 1.6L and 2.2L similar

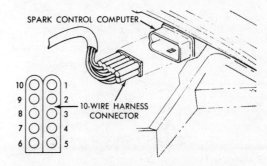

Carburetor switch continuity check

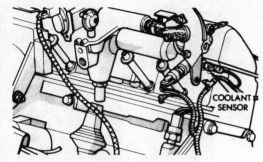

Coolant sensor location—1.6L engine

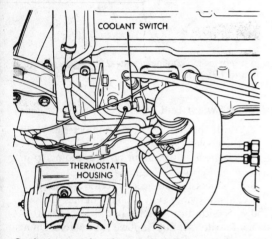

Coolant sensor location—1.7L engine

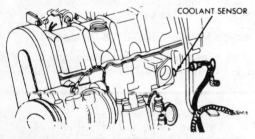

Coolant sensor location—2.2L engine

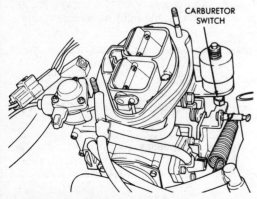

Location of carburetor switch

additional advance will slowly decrease to the basic timing signal over a period of about one minute. If not, replace the Spark Control Computer and recheck. If it is ok, go on to the next test. Do not remove the timing light or jumper wire. They will be used for the next test.

Speed Advance Test—1978–80 Models

1. Start and run the engine for 2 minutes.
2. Adjust the timing light so that the basic timing is shown at the timing indicator. Additional advance shown on the timing light meter should be:
   - 0–3° @ 1100 rpm
   - 8–12° @ 2000 rpm.

If not, replace the spark control computer and repeat the test. If as specified, go to the next test.

Spark Advance Test—1981–and Later Models

1. Check basic ignition timing and adjust if necessary.
2. Run the engine to obtain normal operating temperature. Check the operation of the coolant temperature sensor, refer to "coolant switch test" in this section.
3. Remove and plug the vacuum hose at the vacuum transducer.
4. Contrast an auxiliary vacuum pump to the vacuum transducer and apply 16 inches Hg. of vacuum.
5. Increase the engine speed to 2000 RPM, wait one minute and check for an increase in spark advance of about 12–20 degrees.
   NOTE: *The increase in advance is in addition to the basic advance.*
6. If the computer fails to obtain a reasonable amount of advance increase, replace the Spark Control Computer.

Vacuum Advance Test—1979–80 Models

The program for each computer is different. Specifications for individual computer numbers are:
   - 18–22° @ 2000 rpm (all part numbers)
   - 23–27° @ 3000 rpm (numbers 5206721, 5206784 and 5206793)
   - 28–32° @ 3000 rpm (numbers 5206785 and 5206790)

While performing these tests, use a metal exhaust tube. Use of rubber tube may cause a fire due to extremely high temperatures and a long test period.

If the spark control computer fails to meet these tests, it should be replaced.

1. Connect an adjustable timing light and tachometer.
2. Start the engine and warm it to normal operating temperature. Wait at least 1 minute

for start up advance to return to basic timing. Place the transmission in Neutral and apply the parking brake.

3. Check, and, if necessary, adjust the basic timing.

4. Remove the vacuum line from the vacuum transducer and plug the line.

5. Ground the carburetor switch.

6. Increase the engine speed to 1100 rpm.

7. Check the speed advance timing.

8. Increase speed to 2000 rpm. Remove the carburetor switch ground and connect the vacuum line to the vacuum transducer.

9. Check the Zero Time Offset. Timing should be:
   • 6–10°—computer number 5206721
   • 2–6°—computer number 5206784
   • 3–7°—computer number 5206785
   • 0–3°—computer number 5206790, 5206793

10. Allow the accumulator in the computer to "clock-up" for 8 minutes.

11. With the accumulator "clocked -up" and the speed at 1100 rpm, check the vacuum advance. It should be 0–3° at 1100 rpm.

12. Disconnect and plug the vacuum line from the transducer and increase the engine speed to 3000 rpm. Note the speed advance timing.

13. Reconnect the vacuum line to the transducer and recheck the vacuum advance.

14. Return the engine to curb idle. Connect the wire to the carburetor switch if applicable.

REMOVAL AND OVERHAUL

None of the components of the Lean Burn System (except the carburetor) may be taken apart and repaired. When a part is known to be bad, it should be replaced.

The Spark Control Computer is held on by mounting screws. First remove the battery, then disconnect the 10 terminal connectors and the air duct from the computer. Next remove the vacuum line from the transducer. Remove the

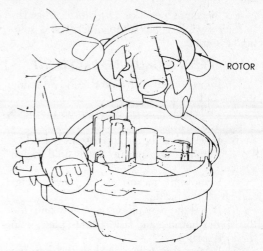

Removing or installing the Hall-effect distributor rotor

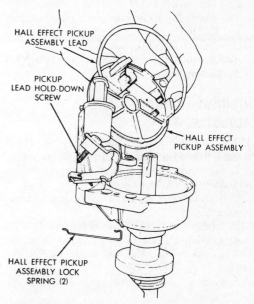

Removing or installing the Hall-effect pick-up assembly

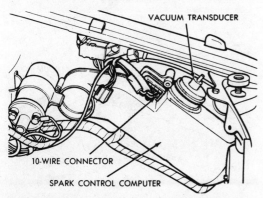

Spark control computer removal and installation

vacuum three screws securing the computer to the left front fender, and remove the computer.

To remove the vacuum transducer, replace the spark control computer.

NOTE: *When disconnecting the Spark Control Computer, check the following:*

1. *Discard any foam gasket found inside the connector cavity.*

2. *Be sure there is at least 1/4 in. silicone grease in the cavity connector.*

3. *Computers built after 1/78 have a piece of Butyl tape. If neither is present, clean the connector and cover the slotted latch with 3/4 in. wide electrical tape.*

If it becomes necessary to replace the carburetor switch, replace the bracket and solenoid assembly.

HALL EFFECT PICKUP REPLACEMENT

1. Loosen the distributor cap retaining screws and remove the cap.

2. Pull straight up on the rotor and remove it from the shaft.

3. Disconnect the pickup assembly lead.

4. Remove the pickup lead hold down screw.

5. Remove the pickup assembly lock springs and lift off the pickup.

6. Install the new pickup assembly onto the distributor housing and fasten it into place with the lock springs.

7. Fasten the pickup lead to the housing with the hold down screw.

8. Reconnect the lead to the harness.

9. Press the rotor back into place on the shaft. Do not wipe off the silicone grease on the metal portion of the rotor.

10. Replace the distributor cap and tighten the retaining screws.

Ignition Timing

ADJUSTMENT

The engine is timed on No. 1 cylinder, which is the left-hand side of the car, facing the car.

1. Connect a timing light according to the manufacturer's instructions.

2. Run the engine to normal operating temperature.

3. Make sure the idle speed is correct.

4. Loosen the distributor holddown screw just enough so that the distributor can be rotated.

5. Ground the carburetor switch on models so equipped.

6. Disconnect and plug the vacuum line at the Spark Control Computer (if so equipped).

7. Remove the timing hole access cover and aim the timing light at the hole in the clutch housing. Carefully rotate the distributor until

the mark is aligned with the pointer on the flywheel housing.

8. Tighten the distributor and recheck the timing.

9. Check, and if necessary adjust, the idle speed.

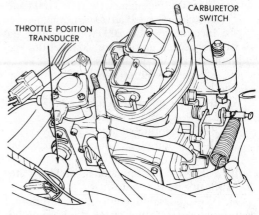

Carburetor switch location—1.7L engine

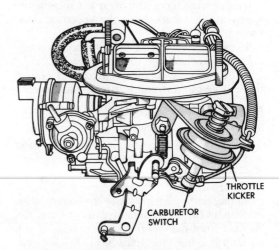

Carburetor switch location—2.2L engine

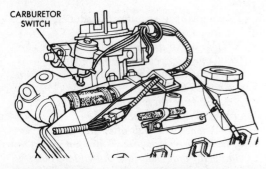

Carburetor switch location—1.6L engine

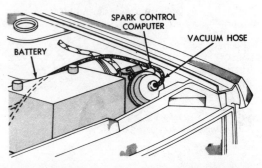

Spark control computer vacuum hose connection

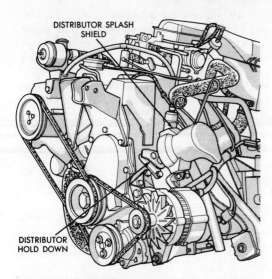

Loosen the distributor hold-down bolt to adjust the timing—1.6L engine shown

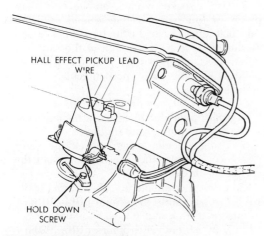

Distributor hold-down bolt—1.7L engine

Distributor hold-down bolt 2.2L engine

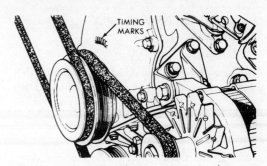

Timing marks—1.6L engine

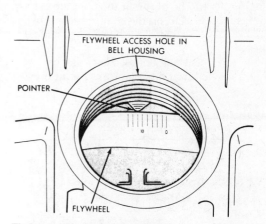

Timing marks—A-412 transaxle

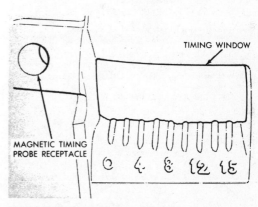

Timing marks—all models except A-412 transaxle and 1.6L engine

Valve Adjustment

Valve adjustment is not required as a matter of routine maintenance on the 1.6L and 1.7L engines. It is, however, necessary to check the valve clearance periodically. The 1.6L engine is an overhead valve design with adjustable rocker arms. The 1.7L engine clearance is adjusted by substituting discs located at the top of the cam followers. The discs are available in .05mm increments from 3.00 to 4.25mm. One disc is located in each cam follower. A special tool is required for the disc removal and installation. The 2.2L engine uses hydraulic valve lifters and does not require valve adjustment.

CHECKING/ADJUSTING VALVE CLEARANCE

1.6L Engine

The valve clearance should be checked with the engine cold and the piston at TDC (top dead center) on the compression stroke. The valves should be checked in the firing order 1-3-4-2.

1. Remove the valve cover.

2. Turn the crankshaft and watch the movement of the exhaust valves. When one is closing (moving upward) continue turning slowly until the inlet valve on the same cylinder just begins to open. This is called the "valve rocking" position. The piston in the opposite cylinder is then at TDC on the compression stroke, and its valve clearance can be checked and adjusted.

3. After checking both valve clearances, rotate the crankshaft one half turn, the next cylinder in the firing order should have its valves "rocking" and the pared cylinder can be adjusted.

4. To make an adjustment, loosen the locknut and turn the adjusting screw until the correct size feeler gauge is a sliding fit between the valve stem and the rocker arm. The cold clearance should be 0.25mm (.010in.) intake and 0.35mm (.012in.) exhaust.

5. When the correct clearance has been obtained, tighten the locknut securely while holding the adjusting screw.

6. Reinstall the valve cover.

1.7L Engine

The valve should be checked with the engine warm and be checked in the firing order 1-3-4-2.

1. Run the engine to normal operating temperature.

2. Remove the valve cover.

3. Use a socket wrench on the crankshaft pulley or bump the engine around until the camshaft lobes of No. 1 cylinder are positioned as shown. Due to the design of the camshaft lobes, it is not necessary that the lobes be pointing directly away (perpendicular) to the adjusting disc.

CAUTION: *Do not turn the engine using the camshaft pulley, and only turn the engine in the direction of normal rotation.*

4. Using a feeler gauge, check the valve clearance between the camshaft lobe and the valve adjusting disc.

Cold clearance should be .15–.25mm (.006–.010in.) intake and .35–.45mm (.014–.018in.) exhaust; warm clearance is .20–.30mm (.008–.012in.) intake and .40–.50mm (.016–.020in.) exhaust.

5. If the measure clearance is not as specified, the valve adjusting disc can be removed and replaced with another of the proper size to give the correct valve clearance.

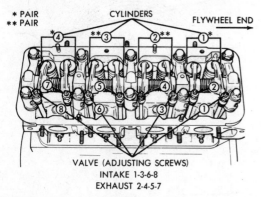

Valve adjustment locations—1.6L engine

VALVES 'ROCKING' ON CYLINDER NUMBER	ADJUST VALVES ON CYLINDER NUMBER
4	1
2	3
1	4
3	2

Making valve adjustment—1.6L engine

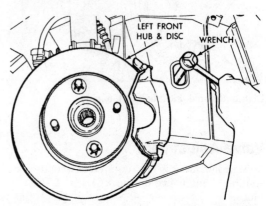

Rotate the 1.7L engine by inserting a wrench through the access hole

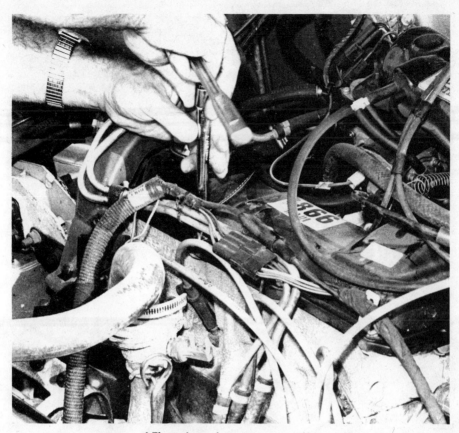

1.7L engine valve cover removal

The valves of cylinders 1, 3, 4, can be adjusted when No. 1 is positioned as shown on the 1.7L engine

Checking valve clearance with a feeler gauge on the 1.7L engine

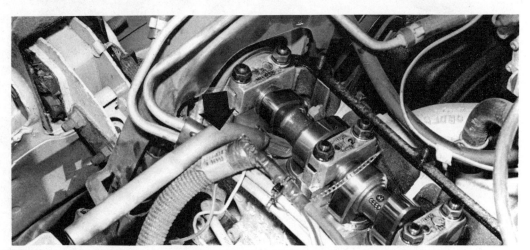

On the 1.7L engine, depress the cam followers with the special tool shown

On the 1.7L engine; remove the valve adjusting disc special tools shown.

Typical valve adjustment disc assortment for the 1.7L engine

Valve Adjusting Discs, 1.7

Thickness (mm)	Part Number	Thickness (mm)	Part Number
3.00	5240946	3.65	5240580
3.05	5240945	3.70	5240581
3.10	5240944	3.75	5240582
3.15	5240943	3.80	5240583
3.20	5240942	3.85	5240584
3.25	5240941	3.90	5240585
3.30	5240573	3.95	5240586
3.35	5240574	4.00	5240587
3.40	5240575	4.05	5240588
3.45	5240576	4.10	5240589
3.50	5240577	4.15	5240590
3.55	5240578	4.20	5240591
3.60	5240579	4.25	5240592

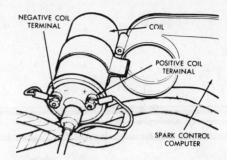

Tachometer connections

6. To remove the disc:

a. Depress the cam follower with Tool L-4417. This tool is necessary to remove the disc without damaging the camshaft or cylinder head.

b. Remove the valve adjusting disc with special removal pliers as shown in the illustration.

c. Calculate the thickness of a new disc and install one of the proper size. Be sure the number indicating the thickness of the disc (mm) faces down when installed.

d. Recheck the valve clearance.

7. Recheck or adjust all other valves in the same manner.

NOTE: *When the camshaft is in position to check the valves of No. 1 cylinder, cylinders No. 3 and 4 can also be checked or adjusted. It is only necessary to turn the engine one time to position the camshaft to check No. 2 cylinder.*

8. Reinstall the camshaft cover.

2.2L Engine

This engine has hydraulic valve lifter and no adjustment is required.

Idle Speed

TACHOMETER HOOKUP

1. Connect the red lead of the test tachometer to the negative primary terminal of the coil and the black lead to a good ground.

2. Turn the selector switch to the appro-

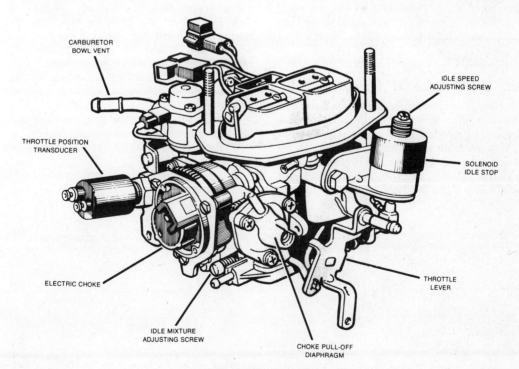

Holley 5220 carburetor

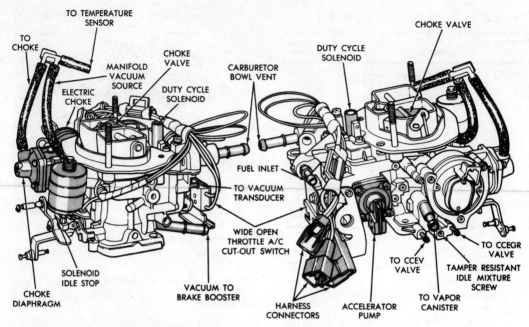

Holley 6520 carburetor, with air conditioning

priate cylinder position and read the idle on the 1000 rpm scale, if so equipped.

3. With the engine at normal operating temperature momentarily open the throttle to check for binding in the linkage. Make sure that the idle screw is against its stop.

4. Adjust the idle speed to specifications. If the engine is equipped with an idle solenoid, the solenoid must be energized and the adjusting screw must be resting on the solenoid plunger.

IDLE SPEED AND MIXTURE ADJUSTMENT

Chrysler recommends the use of a propane enrichment procedure to adjust the mixture. The equipment needed for this procedure is not readily available to the general public. An alternate method recommended by Chrysler is with the use of an exhaust gas analyzer. If this equipment is not available, and a mixture adjustment must be performed, follow this procedure:

1. Run engine to normal operating temperature.

2. Place the transmission in Neutral (MT) or Drive (AT), turn off the lights and air conditioning and make certain that the electric cooling fan is operating.

3. Disconnect the EGR vacuum line, disconnect the distributor electrical advance connector, and ground the carburetor idle stop switch (if equipped) with a jumper wire.

4. Connect tachometer according to the manufacturer's specifications. (See previous procedure).

5. Adjust the idle screw to achieve the curb idle figure listed on the underhood sticker.

6. Back out the mixture screw to achieve the fastest possible idle.

7. Adjust the idle screw to the specified curb idle speed.

ENGINE ELECTRICAL

Distributor

CAUTION: *1980 and later models have a different distributor cap. Never pull the wire from the cap. The wires are retained in the cap by means of internal clips in the wire towers. To remove a wire, first remove the distributor cap, then squeeze the clips ends together while gently removing the wire from the cap. Failure to follow this procedure will damage the core of the wire.*

Chrysler recommends that the wires not be removed from the cap for any reason other than replacement of a damaged wire or a wire that shows too much resistance.

REMOVAL AND INSTALLATION

1. Disconnect the distributor pickup lead wire at the harness connector and remove the splash shield (if so equipped).

2. Remove the distributor cap.

3. Rotate the engine crankshaft until the rotor is pointing toward the cylinder block. Make a mark on the block at this point for installation reference.

4. Remove the distributor holddown screw.

5. Carefully lift the distributor from the engine. The shaft will rotate slightly as the distributor is removed.

To install the distributor:

1. If the engine has been cranked over while the distributor was removed, rotate the crankshaft until the number one piston is at TDC on the compression stroke. This will be indicated by the O mark on the flywheel aligning with the pointer on the clutch housing. Position the rotor just ahead of the #1 terminal of the cap and lower the distributor into the engine. With the distributor fully seated, the rotor should be directly under the #1 terminal.

2. If the engine was not disturbed while the distributor was out, lower the distributor into the engine, engaging the gears and making sure

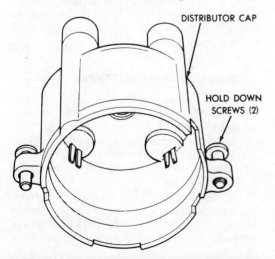

1980 and later distributor cap showing plug wire retaining clips. These clips double as rotor contacts.

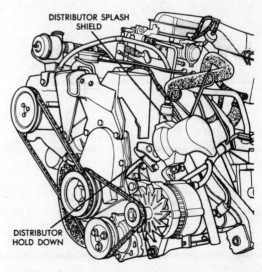

Distributor hold down bolt—1.6L engine

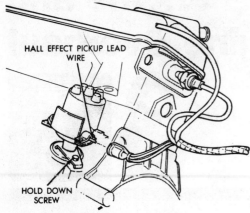

Distributor hold-down bolt—1.7L engine

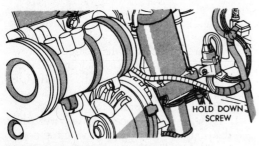

Distributor hold down bolt—2.2L engine

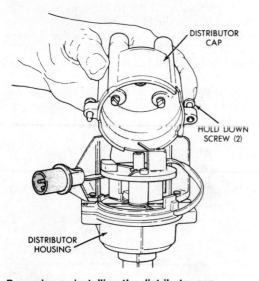

Removing or installing the distributor cap

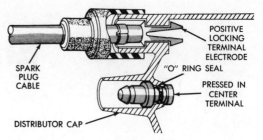

Coil and spark plug terminals—1980 and later models

Alternator

A conventional alternator is used. It has six built-in rectifiers which convert AC current to DC current. Current at the output terminal is DC. The main components of the alternator are: the rotor, stator, rectifiers, end shields and the drive pulley.

The electronic voltage regulator is a device which regulates the vehicle electrical system voltage by limiting the output voltage that is generated by the alternator. This is accomplished by controlling the amount of current that is allowed to pass through the alternator field windings. The regulator has no moving parts and requires no adjustment.

Ammeter fluctuation may be caused by an intermittent loss of alternator ground, which is easily corrected.

1. Do not remove the alternator from the car.

2. Remove the forward (black) through-bolt from the alternator and discard.

3. Assemble the ground strap (Part No. 5211756) under the head of the cadmium plated (silver) replacement through-bolt (Part No. 5206804).

4. Route the ground strap as shown.

5. Remove the bolt from the thermostat housing and assemble the other end of the ground strap under the bolt.

6. Tighten the bolt.

ALTERNATOR PRECAUTIONS

To prevent damage to the alternator and regulator, the following precautions should be taken when working with the electrical system.

1. Never reverse the battery connections.

2. Booster batteries for starting must be connected properly—positive-to-positive and negative-to-negative.

3. Disconnect the battery cables before using a fast charger; the charger has a tendency to force current through the diodes in the opposite direction for which they were designed. This burns out the diodes.

4. Never use a fast charger as a booster for starting the vehicle.

that the gasket is properly seated in the block. The rotor should line up with the mark made before removal.

3. Tighten the holddown screw and connect the wires. Install the distributor splash shield on models so equipped.

4. Check and adjust the ignition timing.

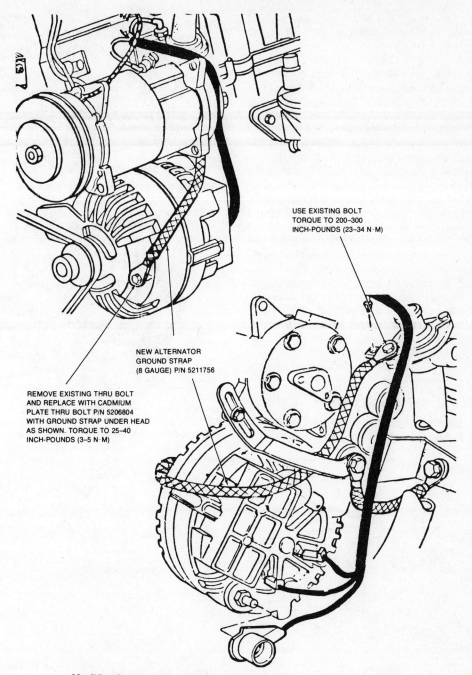

USE EXISTING BOLT
TORQUE TO 200–300
INCH-POUNDS (23–34 N·M)

NEW ALTERNATOR
GROUND STRAP
(8 GAUGE) P/N 5211756

REMOVE EXISTING THRU BOLT
AND REPLACE WITH CADMIUM
PLATE THRU BOLT P/N 5206804
WITH GROUND STRAP UNDER HEAD
AS SHOWN. TORQUE TO 25–40
INCH-POUNDS (3–5 N·M)

Modifications to improve alternator grounding on the 1.7L engine

5. Never disconnect the voltage regulator while the engine is running.

6. Avoid long soldering times when replacing diodes or transistors. Prolonged heat is damaging to AC generators.

7. Do not use test lamps of more than 12 volts (V) for checking diode continuity.

8. Do not short across or ground any of the terminals on the AC generator.

9. The polarity of the battery, generator, and regulator must be matched and considered before making any electrical connections within the system.

10. Never operate the alternator on an open circuit. Make sure that all connections within the circuit are clean and tight.

11. Disconnect the battery terminals when performing any service on the electrical system. This will eliminate the possibility of accidental reversal of polarity.

12. Disconnect the battery ground cable if arc welding is to be done on any part of the car.

Some 1978–79 Omni and Horizons may exhibit a tendency to inadequately charge the battery. This condition is probably due to a loose connection at the field terminals on the alternator.

A loose connection can be tested by disconnecting the 4-way connector between the alternator and engine harness. Test for continuity between the dark blue wire terminal in the connector and the male terminal brush assembly to which the dark blue wire is connected. Wiggle the alternator connection. More than 1 ohm resistance or an erratic reading indicates a loose connection. Repeat the test using the dark green wire instead of the dark blue wire.

Loose connections can be repaired.

1. Disconnect the loose female connections.
2. Replace the male terminal brush assembly on the alternator with part no. 4057928.
3. Remove the defective female terminal by peeling back the insulation and cutting the wire directly behind the terminal.
4. Crimp on a new female terminal and replace the connections.

REMOVAL AND INSTALLATION

1. Disconnect the battery ground cable.
2. Remove the wires from the alternator.

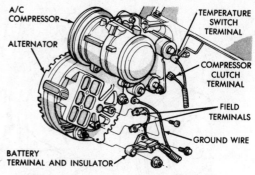

Alternator connections—Chrysler alternator

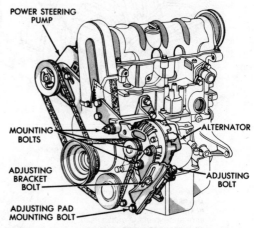

Alternator mounting details—Chrysler alternator

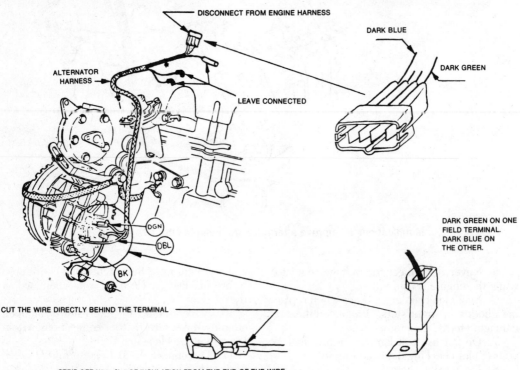

Modifications to alternator terminals

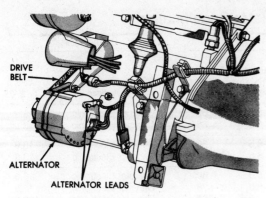

Alternator connections—Bosch alternator w/external regulator

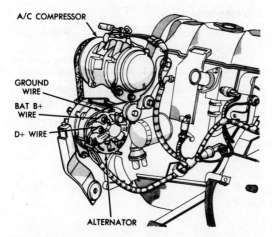

Alternator connections—bosch alternator w/internal regulator

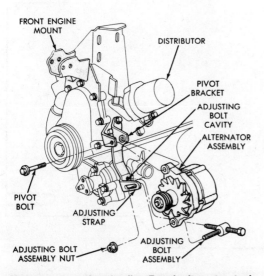

Alternator mounting details—Bosch alternator, typical

3. Support the alternator, remove the mounting bolts and lift out the unit.

4. Reverse the procedure for installation.

Regulator

NOTE: *Turbo models may be equipped with an in-line regulator. This type can only be serviced by replacing the power/logic module.*

REMOVAL AND INSTALLATION

1. Disconnect the battery ground cable.

2. Remove the wires from the regulator.

3. Remove the two sheet metal screws securing the regulator to the right side fender skirt.

4. Installation is the reverse of removal.

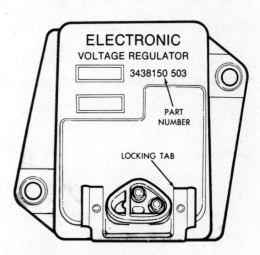

Electronic voltage regulator

Starter

The starter is an overrunning clutch drive type with a solenoid mounted on the starter motor. Six different type starters are used on Omni/Horizon models. Two each are built by Nippondenso, Bosch and Mitsubishi for manual and automatic transmission applications. Removal and installation procedures are the same for all units.

Some early production models may experience starter motor damage due to improper fit of the upper and lower steering column shrouds. Irregularities in the mating surface of the key cylinder area may cause the ignition key to bind, causing the starter to be continuously engaged. The condition can be corrected by loosening the shroud cover screws about 1½ turns.

If loosening the screws does not solve the problem, the covers will have to be replaced with new parts, which are available only in black and must be painted to match interior trim.

Alternator and Regulator Specifications

Year	Alternator		Field Current @ 12v (amp)	Output (amps)	Regulator	Volts @ 75°F
	Manufacturer	Identification			Manufacturer	
'79–'81	Chrysler	Yellow Tag	4.5–6.5	60	Chrysler Electronic	13.9
	Chrysler	Brown Tag	4.5–6.5	65	Chrysler Electronic	13.9
'82–'83	Chrysler	Yellow Tag	4.5–6.5	60	Chrysler Electronic	13.9
	Chrysler	Brown Tag	4.5–6.5	78	Chrysler Electronic	13.9
'84–'86	Chrysler	Yellow Tag	2.5–5.0	60	Chrysler Electronic	13.9
	Chrysler	Brown Tag	2.5–5.0	78	Chrysler Electronic	13.9
	Bosch	K1	2.5–5.0	65	Chrysler Electronic	13.9
	Bosch	N1	—	90	Bosch Integral	14.1

REMOVAL AND INSTALLATION

1. Disconnect the battery ground cable.
2. Remove the wires from the starter and solenoid.
3. Support the starter, remove the bolts and lift the unit out from the flywheel housing.
4. Installation is the reverse of removal.

OVERHAUL

Service procedures are similar for the Bosch, Mitsubishi and Nippondenso starters. The starter drive is an over-running clutch type with a solenoid mounted externally on the motor.

Disassembly

1. Disconnect the field coil wire from the solenoid terminal.
2. Remove the solenoid mounting screws and work the solenoid off the shift fork.
3. On Nippondenso units, remove the bearing cover, armature shaft lock, washer, spring, and seal.
4. On Bosch units, remove the bearing cover, armature shaft lock, and shim.
5. Remove the two through-bolts and the commutator end frame cover.
6. Remove the two brushes and the brush holder.

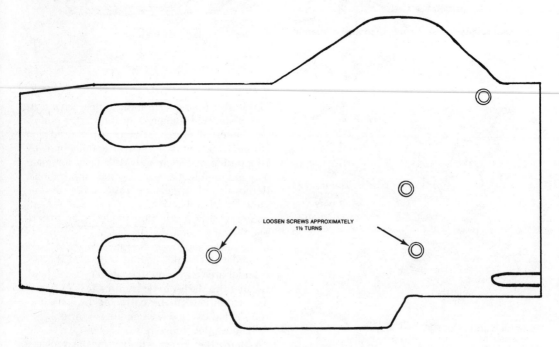

LOOSEN SCREWS APPROXIMATELY 1½ TURNS

BOTTOM VIEW OF LOWER SHROUD

Bottom view of lower shroud—loosen screws shown

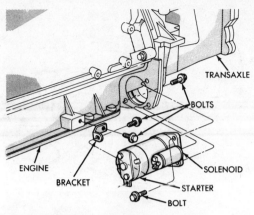

1.6L engine starter mounting

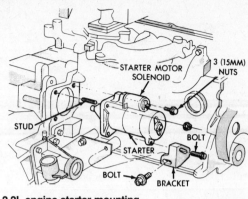

2.2L engine starter mounting

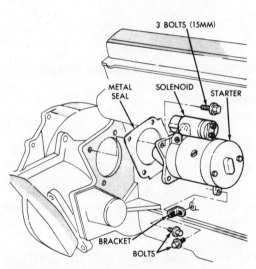

1.7L engine except w/A-412 manual transaxle—starter mounting

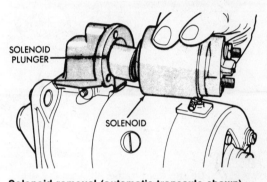

Solenoid removal (automatic transaxle shown)

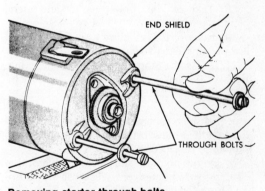

Removing starter through bolts

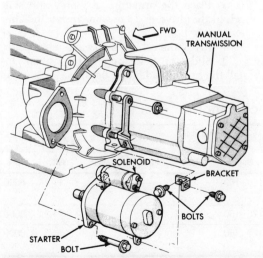

1.7L engine w/A-412 manual transaxle—starter mounting

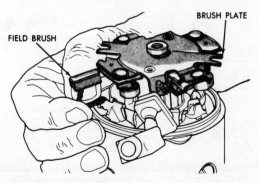

Brush assembly

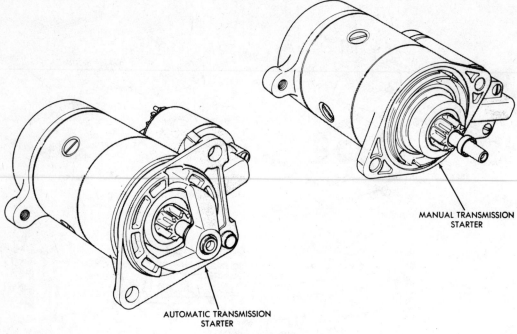

MANUAL TRANSMISSION
STARTER

AUTOMATIC TRANSMISSION
STARTER

Bosch Starters

7. Slide the field frame off over the armature.

8. Take out the shift lever pivot bolt.

9. Take off the rubber gasket and metal plate.

10. Remove the armature assembly and shift lever from the drive end housing.

11. Press the stop collar off the snap ring. Remove the snap-ring, stop collar, and clutch.

Inspection

1. Brushes that are worn more than one-half the length of new brushes, or are oil-soaked, should be replaced.

2. Do not immerse the starter clutch unit in cleaning solvent. Solvent will wash the lubricant from the clutch.

3. Place the drive unit on the armature shaft and, while holding the armature, rotate the pinion. The drive pinion should rotate smoothly in one direction only. The pinion may not rotate easily. If the clutch unit does not function properly, or if the pinion is worn, chipped, or burred, replace the unit.

Assembly

1. Lubricate the armature shaft and splines with SAE 10W–30 oil.

2. Install the clutch, stop collar, and lock ring on the armature.

3. Place the armature assembly and shift fork in the drive end housing. Install the shift lever pivot bolt.

4. Install the rubber gasket and metal plate.

5. Slide the field frame into position. Install the brush holder and brushes.

Starter Specifications

Year	Engine	Trans.	Manufacturer	Load Test*				No-Load Test		
				Amps	Volts	Torque (ft. lb.)	Amps	Volts	RPM
'78–'83	All	All	Bosch or Nippondenso	120–160	12	—	47	11	6600
'84–'86	1.6	All	Mitsubishi	120–160	12	—	47	11	6600
	2.2	All	Bosch or Nippondenso	120–160	12	—	47	11	6600

*To perform the load test, the engine should be up to operating temperature. Extremely heavy oil or tight engine will increase starter amperage draw.

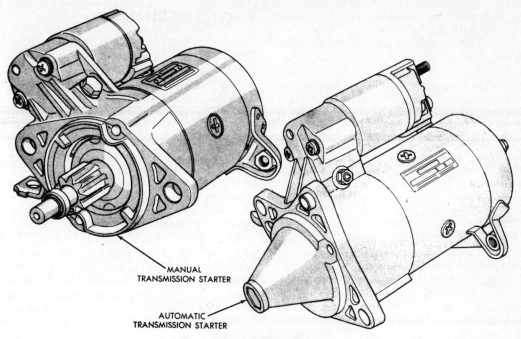

MANUAL
TRANSMISSION STARTER

AUTOMATIC
TRANSMISSION STARTER

Nippondenso Starters
Starter identification

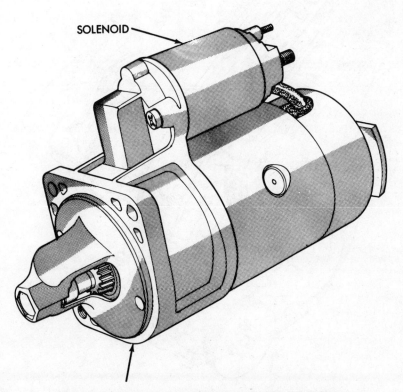

SOLENOID

Manual and Automatic transmission starter Mitsubishi Starter

6. Position the commutator end frame cover and install the through bolts.

7. On Nippondenso units, install the seal, spring, washer, armature shaft lock, and bearing cover.

8. On Bosch units, install the shim and armature shaft lock. Check that end play is 0.05–0.3 mm (0.002–0.012 in.). Install the bearing cover.

9. Assemble the solenoid to the shift fork and install the mounting screws.

10. Connect the field coil wire to the solenoid.

Battery

The battery is located conventionally, under the hood. It can be easily removed by disconnecting the battery cables and removing the hold-down bolts from the battery tray. Coat the terminals with a small amount of petroleum jelly after installation.

ENGINE MECHANICAL

There are three different engines used in the Omni/Horizon body styles. The 1.7 liter, basically a Volkswagen design, is used during the 1978 thru 1983 model years. The 2.2 liter engine, a Chrysler refined version of the 1.71 engine was introduced during the 1981 model year. In 1984 the 1.6 liter engine was introduced to replace the 1.7 liter engine. Below is a description of each of these engines.

The 1.6 Liter displacement engine is a four cylinder overhead valve engine with a cast iron block and an aluminum cylinder head. Five main bearings support the forged steel crankshaft with number three being the thrust bearing. The cast iron dual timing chain sprocket on the crankshaft, not only provides power for the timing chains, but it also acts as a vibration damper. The cast-iron camshaft is mounted on three babbitt bearings and a thrust plate lo-

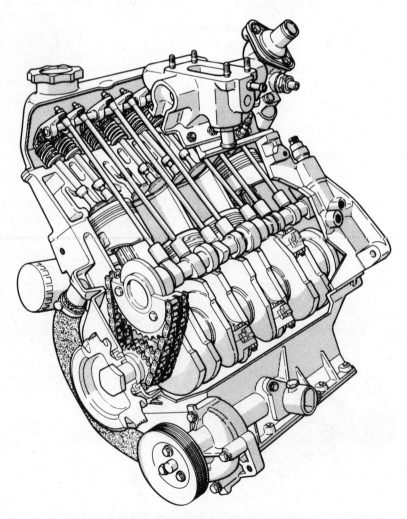

1.6L four cylinder engine—cut-away view

cated at the front bearing controls the camshaft end play. The camshaft itself is positioned left of the crankshaft, or toward the front of the car. The camshaft is driven by dual timing chains. These chains are enclosed by a cast aluminum timing cover which has the strobe ignition timing marks embossed on it. The cylinder head material is an aluminum alloy. The head is a "crossflow" design with in-line valves. The valve train design incorporates the use of mechanical tappets, push rods, and adjustable rocker arms. The spark plugs are located on the left side of the engine opposite the valves. The intake manifold is made of a cast aluminum alloy, cored with coolant passages for carburetor warm up. This manifold is located on the left side of the head. Embossed on the intake manifold is the cylinder number identification, firing order, and the direction of the distributor rotation. The exhaust manifold is made of nodular iron and is attached to the right side of the head (towards the rear of the car) and is held on by eight bolts.

The 1.7 Liter displacement engine is a four cylinder, overhead camshaft engine. The block is cast iron and the head is aluminum. A five main bearing forged steel crankshaft using no

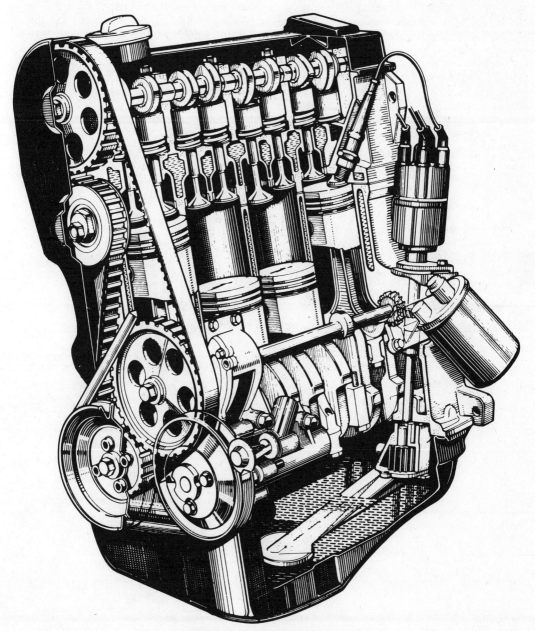

1.7L four cylinder engine—cut-away view

vibration damper is employed, rotated by cast aluminum pistons. A sintered iron timing belt sprocket is mounted on the end of the crankshaft. The intake manifold and oil filter base are aluminum. A steel reinforced belt drives the intermediate shaft and camshaft. The intermediate shaft drives the oil pump, distributor, and fuel pump. The cylinder head is lightweight aluminum alloy. The intake and exhaust manifolds are mounted on the same side of the cylinder head. The valves are opened and closed by the camshaft lobes operating on cupped cam followers which fit over the valves and springs. This design results in lighter valve train weight and fewer moving parts.

The 2.2 Liter displacement engine is a four cylinder, overhead camshaft design powerplant with a cast iron block and an aluminum cylinder head. The cast iron crankshaft is supported by five main bearings. No vibration dampener is used. The iron camshaft also has five bearing journals and there are flanges at the rear journal to control the camshaft end play. Sintered iron timing sprockets are mounted on both the camshaft and the crankshaft which are driven by the timing belt. The timing belt also drives an accessory shaft, housed in the forward-facing side of the block. The accessory shaft, in turn drives the fuel pump, oil pump and the distributor. The engine oil filter is attached to the base located at the left front of the block, toward the front of the car. The intake manifolds are cast aluminum and the exhaust manifolds are iron, both of which face the

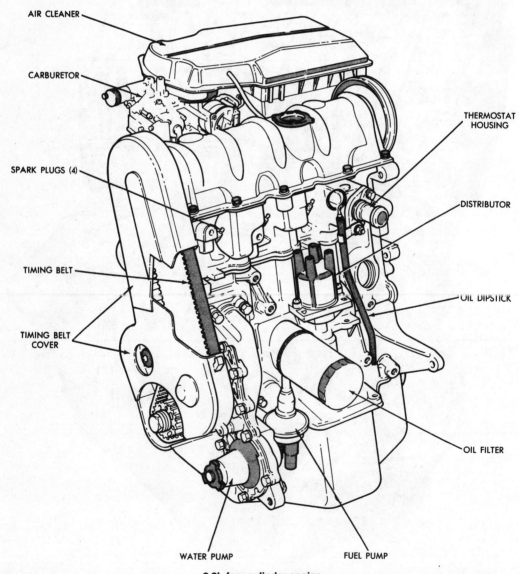

2.2L four cylinder engine

rear of the vehicle. The distributor, spark plugs, and oil filter are all located on the forward-facing side of the engine.

Engine Removal and Installation

Manual Transmission

NOTE: *The engine and transmission must be removed together, or the transmission should be completely removed from the car first. The following is for engine/transmission assembly removal.*

1. Disconnect the battery.
2. Mark the hood hinge outline and remove the hood.
3. Drain the cooling system.
4. Remove the radiator hoses and remove the radiator and shroud assembly.
5. Remove the air cleaner and hoses.
6. The air conditioning compressor does not have to be disconnected. Remove it from its bracket and position it out of the way. Securing it with wire is the best method.

NOTE: *On A/C cars do not disconnect any hoses from the A/C system. Disconnect compressor with hoses attached.*

7. Disconnect all wiring from the engine, alternator and carburetor.
8. Disconnect the fuel line, heater hoses and accelerator linkage.
9. Disconnect the air pump lines.
10. Remove the alternator.
11. Disconnect the clutch and speedometer cables.
12. Raise the vehicle and support it on jackstands.
13. Disconnect the driveshafts from the transmission and support them with wires.
14. Disconnect the exhaust pipe.
15. Remove the air pump.
16. Disconnect the transmission linkage.

Fuel, heater and accelerator connections

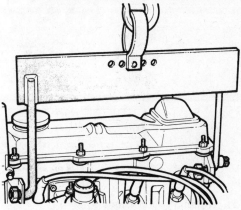

Attach a lifting sling to the engine

17. Lower the vehicle.
18. Attach a lifting fixture and a shop crane to the engine. Raise the engine slightly to take up the weight and disconnect the engine mounts in this order: front, right, left. Lift the engine from the car.

CAUTION: *On models with the A-460 transaxle, the left front engine mount is attached with two different types of mounting bolts. Two of the three bolts are of the pilot type with extended tips. These bolts must be installed in the positions shown in the accompanying illustration. Damage to the shift cover or difficult shifting may occur if the bolts are incorrectly installed.*

19. Lower the engine into place and loosely install all mounting bolts. When all mounts have been hand tightened, torque each to 40 ft. lbs.
20. Remove the lifting fixture and raise the vehicle, supporting it on jackstands.
21. Connect the driveshafts. Torque the bolts to 35 ft. lbs.
22. Connect the transmission linkage, install the air pump, connect the exhaust pipe and lower the vehicle.
23. Connect the clutch and speedometer cables.

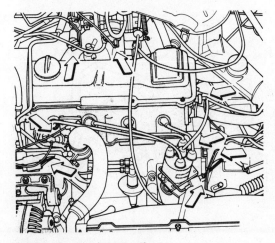

Engine electrical connections

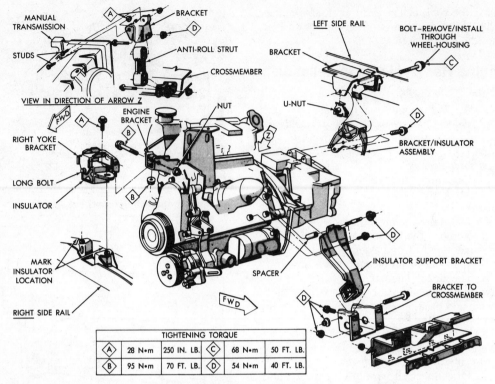

TIGHTENING TORQUE				
Ⓐ	28 N•m	250 IN. LB.	Ⓒ	68 N•m	50 FT. LB.
Ⓑ	95 N•m	70 FT. LB.	Ⓓ	54 N•m	40 FT. LB.

1.6L engine mounting brackets

24. Install the alternator.
25. Install the air pump lines.
26. Connect the fuel line, heater hoses and accelerator linkage.
27. Connect all wiring.
28. Mount the air conditioning compressor.
29. Install the air cleaner.
30. Install the radiator and hoses.
31. Fill the cooling system.
32. Install the hood.
33. Connect the battery.

34. Start the engine and run it to normal operating temperature.
35. Check the timing and adjust if necessary. Adjust the carburetor idle speed and mixture, and the transmission linkage.

Automatic Transmission

The engine is removed without the transmission.

1. Disconnect the battery.

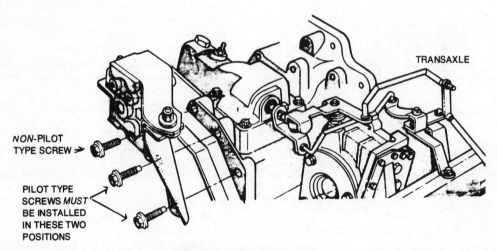

Left front engine mount—1.7L

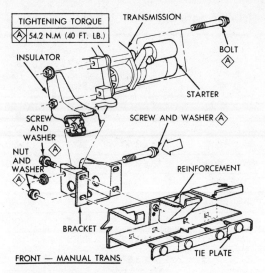

A	54.2 N.M (40 FT. LB.)

FRONT — MANUAL TRANS.

1.7L front engine mount

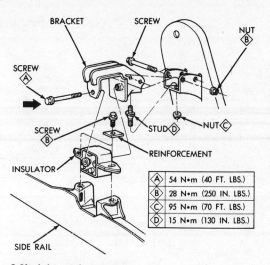

A	54 N•m	(40 FT. LBS.)
B	28 N•m	(250 IN. LBS.)
C	95 N•m	(70 FT. LBS.)
D	15 N•m	(130 IN. LBS.)

2.2L right engine mount

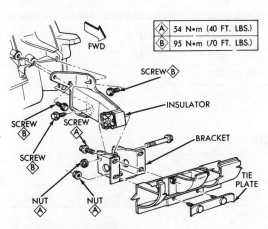

A	54 N•m	(40 FT. LBS.)
B	95 N•m	(70 FT. LBS.)

2.2L front engine mount

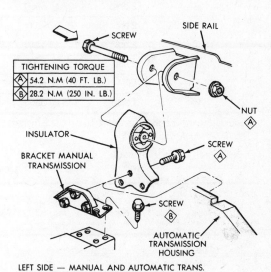

TIGHTENING TORQUE		
A	54.2 N.M	(40 FT. LB.)
B	28.2 N.M	(250 IN. LB.)

LEFT SIDE — MANUAL AND AUTOMATIC TRANS.

1.7L left engine mount

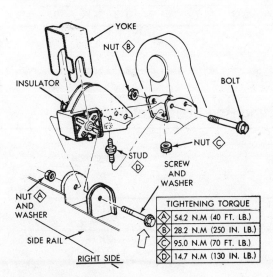

TIGHTENING TORQUE		
A	54.2 N.M	(40 FT. LB.)
B	28.2 N.M	(250 IN. LB.)
C	95.0 N.M	(70 FT. LB.)
D	14.7 N.M	(130 IN. LB.)

1.7L right engine mount

2. Scribe the outline of the hood hinges and remove the hood.

3. Drain the cooling system.

4. Disconnect the hoses from the radiator and engine.

5. Remove the air cleaner and hoses.

6. Disconnect the air conditioning compressor and set it aside, with refrigerant lines attached.

CAUTION: *Do not disconnect any of the refrigerant lines.*

7. Disconnect and tag all electrical connections from the engine.

8. Disconnect the fuel line, accelerator cable and heater hoses. Plug the lines to prevent leakage.

9. Remove the diverter valve and lines from the air pump.

General Engine Specifications

Engine	Year	Carb. Type	Horsepower @ rpm	Torque ft. lb. @ rpm	Bore x Stroke	Comp. Ratio	Oil. Press. (psi.) @ 2000 rpm
1.6L	'84	2 bbl.	64 @ 4800	87 @ 2800	3.17 x 3.07	8.8:1	58–87
1.7L	'78	2 bbl.	75 @ 5600	90 @ 3200	3.13 x 3.40	8.2:1	60–90
	'79	2 bbl.	70 @ 5200	85 @ 2800	3.13 x 3.40	8.2:1	60–90
	'80	2 bbl.	65 @ 5200	85 @ 2400	3.13 x 3.40	8.2:1	60–90
	'81–'82	2 bbl.	63 @ 5200	83 @ 2400	3.13 x 3.40	8.2:1	60–90
	'83	2 bbl.	63 @ 4800	83 @ 2400	3.13 x 3.40	8.2:1	60–90
2.2L	'81–'82	2 bbl.	84 @ 4800	111 @ 2800	3.44 x 3.62	8.5:1	50
	'83	2 bbl.	94 @ 5200	117 @ 3200	3.44 x 3.62	9.0:1	50
	①	2 bbl.	100 @ 5200	122 @ 3200	3.44 x 3.62	9.0:1	50
	②	2 bbl.	107 @ 5600	126 @ 3600	3.44 x 3.62	9.6:1	50
	'84–'86	2 bbl.	96 @ 5200	119 @ 3200	3.44 x 3.62	9.0:1	50
	①	2 bbl.	101 @ 5200	124 @ 3200	3.44 x 3.62	9.0:1	50
	②	2 bbl.	110 @ 5600	129 @ 3600	3.44 x 3.62	9.6:1	50
	③	EFI	110 @ 5600	129 @ 3600	3.44 x 3.62	—	50
	④	Turbo	146 @ 5200	170 @ 3600	3.44 x 3.62	—	50

① Standard engine in the Charger & Turismo 2.2 models
② High output engine used in the Shelby Charger
③ High output GLH
④ Turbo GLH

Valve Specifications

Engine	Seat Angle (deg)	Face Angle (deg)	Spring Test Pressure (lbs. @ in.)	Spring Installed Height (in.)	Stem to Guide Clearance (in.) Intake	Stem to Guide Clearance (in.) Exhaust	Stem Diameter (in.) Intake	Stem Diameter (in.) Exhaust
1.6L	46	45	—	—	.0015–.0027	.0022–.0035	.3137–.3143	.3129–.3136
1.7L	45	①	②	③	.020 ④ max	.027 ④ max	.3140	.3140
2.2L	45	45.5	⑤	1.65	.001–.003	.002–.004	.312–.313	.311–.312

① Intake: 45° 33' Exhaust: 43° 33'
② Outer: 101 @ .878 Inner: 49 @ .720
③ Outer: 1.28 Inner: 1.13
④ Measurement is made with the valve in the cylinder head positioned .400 in. above the cylinder head gasket surface.
⑤ Standard: 150 lbs. @ 122. Turbo: 175 @ 1.22

Crankshaft and Connecting Rod Specifications

Engine	Crankshaft Main Bearing Journal Dia.	Crankshaft Main Bearing Oil Clearance	Crankshaft Shaft End Play	Crankshaft Thrust on No.	Connecting Rod Journal Dia.	Connecting Rod Oil Clearance	Connecting Rod Side Clearance
1.6L	2.046–2.047	.0009–.0031	.003–.011	3	1.612–1.613	.0010–.0025	.006–.009
1.7L	2.124–2.128	.0008–.0030	.003–.007	3	1.809–1.813	.0011–.0034	.015
2.2L	2.362–2.363	.0003–.0031	.002–.007	3	1.968–1.969	.0008–.0034	.005–.013

Piston and Ring Specifications

Engine	Year	Ring Gap			Ring Side Clearance			Piston Clearance
		Top Compr.	Bottom Compr.	Oil Control	Top Compr.	Bottom Compr.	Oil Control	
1.6L	'84	.012–.018	.012–.018	.010–.016	.0018–.0028	.0018–.0028	.008 max	.0016–.0020
1.7L	'78–'79	.012–.018	.012–.018	.010–.016	.0008–.0020	.0008–.0020	.0008–.0020	.0011–.0270
	'80	.012–.018	.012–.018	.016–.045	.0016–.0028	.0008–.0020	.0008–.0020	.0004–.0015
	'81–'83	.012–.018	.012–.018	.016–.055	.0016–.0028	.0008–.0020	.008 max	.0004–.0015
2.2L	'81–'86	.011–.021	.011–.021	.015–.055	.0015–.0031	.0015–.0037	.008 max	.0005–.0015

Torque Specifications
(ft. lbs.)

Engine	Cyl. Head	Conn. Rod	Main Bearing	Crankshaft Bolt	Flywheel	Camshaft Cap Bolts	Camshaft Sprocket Bolts
1.6L	52	28	48	110	—	—	—
1.7L	60 ①	35 ③	47	58	55 ②	14	58
2.2L	45 ①	40 ①	30 ①	50	65	14	65

① Tighten to specified torque, then a ¼ turn more
② 50 ft. lbs. with auto. trans.
③ 1978 33 ft. lbs.

10. Remove the alternator.
11. Remove the upper bell housing bolts.
12. Raise and support the vehicle.
13. Remove the wheels and right and left splash shields.
14. Remove the power steering pump and set it aside. Do not disconnect the lines.
15. Remove the water pump and crankshaft pulleys.
16. Remove the front engine mounting bolt.
17. Remove the inspection cover from the transmission and remove the bolts from the flex plate.
18. Remove the starter.
19. Remove the remaining lower bell housing bolts.
20. Lower the vehicle and support the transmission with a jack.
21. Remove the oil filter and drain the oil.
22. Attach a lifting fixture to the engine and remove the engine.
23. Installation is the reverse of removal. Be sure to connect all lines, hoses and wires. Fill the engine with oil and coolant and test for leaks.

Rocker Arm/Camshaft Cover
REMOVAL AND INSTALLATION
1.6L Engine

1. Separate the crankcase ventilator hose from the valve cover.
2. Disconnect the diverter hose from the bracket.
3. Remove the six screws that retain the cover to the cylinder head and remove the cover.
4. To install, clean the cylinder head cover thoroughly, ensure that the cover rails are straight and then, install a new gasket.
5. Replace the six screws and tighten to 44 inch-pounds.
6. Connect the diverter hose to the bracket and the crankcase ventilator hose to the valve cover.

1.7L Engine

1. Separate the crankcase ventilator hose from the valve cover.
2. Remove the eight screws that retain the

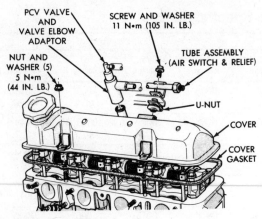

1.6L engine valve cover

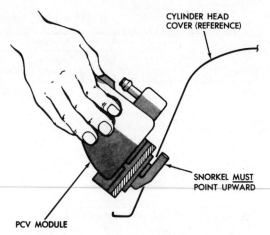

PCV module removal and installation—2.2L engine

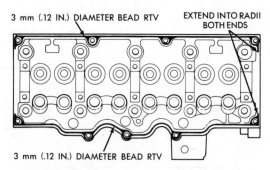

RTV gasket material application for camshaft cover—2.2L engine

cover to the cylinder head and remove the cover.

3. To install, clean the cylinder head cover thoroughly, ensure that the cover rails are straight, and then, install a new gasket.

4. Replace the eight screws and tighten to 48 inch-pounds.

5. Connect the crankcase ventilator hose to the valve cover.

2.2L Engine

1. Separate the crankcase ventilator hose from the PCV module.

2. Depress the retaining clip on the PCV module, turn the module counterclockwise and remove it from the cylinder head cover taking care not to damage the module of the cylinder head cover during the removal.

3. Remove the ten screws that retain the cover to the cylinder head and remove the cover.

4. To install, clean the cylinder head cover and its mating surface on the cylinder head thoroughly.

5. Depress the retaining clip on the PCV module, turn the module clockwise and install the PCV module into the cylinder head cover,

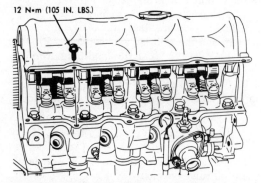

Camshaft cover—2.2L engine

check to see that the snorkle is positioned so that the open end is facing up. The snorkle should not be free to rotate.

6. Apply RTV gasket sealer in a continuous bead approximately ⅛ in. in diameter as shown in the illustration.

7. Install the ten screws that retain the cover to the cylinder head and tighten to 105 in.lbs.

8. Connect the crankcase ventilator hose to the PCV module.

Rocker Arm Shaft
REMOVAL AND INSTALLATION

1.6L Engine

NOTE: *Allow the cylinder head to cool before performing this procedure.*

1. Remove the cylinder head cover as previously described in "Rocker Arm/Camshaft Cover" in this chapter.

2. Loosen the cylinder head bolts evenly, beginning at the ends and working towards the center.

3. Tie the rocker arm assembly together with safety wire or equivalent.

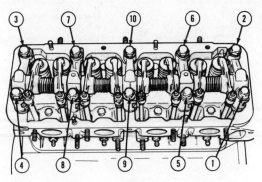

Remove the Rocker Arm/Cylinder Head bolts in numerical order.

Tie the rocker arm brackets together and then remove the entire assembly

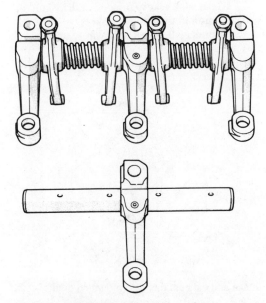

Rocker arm shaft assembly—1.6L engine

4. Remove the bolts and lift the rocker arm assembly off the cylinder head.

NOTE: *Before disassembly of the rocker arm assemblies, mark the component positions so they be installed in their original order.*

5. To disassemble, remove the retaining wire from the assembly. Slide the rocker shaft

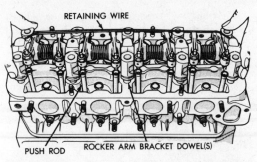

Install the push rods on the rocker arms and position the assembly in place.

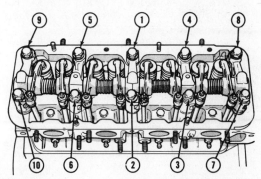

Head/Rocker Arm Assembly bolt tightening sequence

end brackets, rockers, and springs from the rocker shafts.

6. Check the fit of the rockers on the shafts, also check to see that the oil holes in the shafts are clear. Replace any worn components. If replacing the rocker shafts, the roll pin that secures it to the center bracket (no.2 or no.4) must be driven out.

7. To assemble, position the closed end of each rocker shaft so that they are at the outer ends of the assembly. Insert the rocker shaft into its center bracket (no.2 or no.4) with the flat on the shaft aligned with the hole in the bracket, and the plugged end right or left as required. Drive the roll pins back into the brackets.

8. Lubricate the components and assemblies with engine oil.

9. Tie the end brackets with wire to retain them as one assembly.

10. Position each rocker arm assembly on its dowel.

11. Lubricate the head bolt threads with engine oil and install through the rocker shaft brackets. Screw the bolts down finger tight while checking to see that each rocker adjusting screw engages its push rod. Remove the retaining wire.

12. Tighten the head bolts in progressive steps as shown in the illustration to 52 ft. lbs.

13. Start and run the engine to normal operating temperature, allow to cool down and retighten as described in step 12. Check valve clearance and adjust as necessary.

14. Replace the cylinder head cover as previously described in "Rocker Arm/Camshaft Cover" in this chapter.

Intake Manifold
REMOVAL AND INSTALLATION
1.6L Engine

1. Disconnect the battery.
2. Remove the air cleaner and disconnect all vacuum lines, electrical connections and fuel line from the carburetor.
3. Drain the cooling system. Disconnect the inlet hose from the water box to the heated intake manifold and the outlet hose to the heater.
4. Disconnect the EGR tube at the manifold.
5. Remove the eight mounting nuts and washers from the manifold and remove it from the engine.
6. Remove the carburetor from the manifold.
7. To install, clean all gasket surfaces, install new gaskets and torque the mounting nuts to 15 ft. lbs. The remaining procedures are reverse the removal.

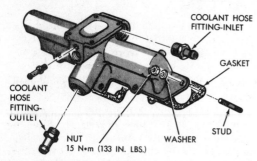

COOLANT HOSE FITTING-INLET

GASKET

COOLANT HOSE FITTING-OUTLET

NUT
15 N•m (133 IN. LBS.)

WASHER

STUD

Intake manifold—1.6L engine

1.7 L Engine

1. Remove the air cleaner and hoses.
2. Remove all wiring and any hoses connected to the carburetor and manifold.
3. Disconnect the accelerator linkage.
4. Remove the intake-to-exhaust manifold bolts.
5. Remove the manifold-to-head bolts and lift out the intake manifold.
6. Clean all gasket surfaces and, using new gaskets, install the manifold.
7. Connect all hoses and wires, and install the air cleaner.
8. Connect the accelerator linkage.

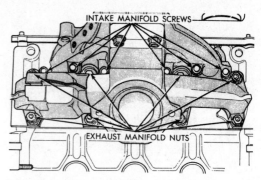

INTAKE MANIFOLD SCREWS

EXHAUST MANIFOLD NUTS

Intake and exhaust manifold mounting points—1.7L engine

2.2L Engine

NOTE: *Refer to turbocharger procedures which follows for turbo removal if equipped.*

1. Drain the cooling system.
2. Remove the air cleaner and hoses.
3. Remove all wiring and any hoses connected to the carburetor and manifold.
4. Disconnect the accelerator linkage and shift linkage (if equipped).
5. Remove the intake-to-exhaust manifold bolts.
6. Remove the manifold-to-head bolts and lift out the intake manifold.
7. Clean all gasket surfaces and install the intake manifold using new gaskets.
8. Connect all hoses and wires, and install the air cleaner.
9. Connect the accelerator linkage and shift linkage (if equipped).

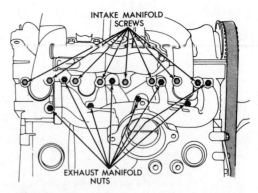

INTAKE MANIFOLD SCREWS

EXHAUST MANIFOLD NUTS

Intake and exhaust manifold mounting points—2.2L engine

Exhaust Manifold
REMOVAL AND INSTALLATION
1.6L Engine

1. Disconnect the battery.
2. Separate the carburetor air heater tube from the manifold stove.

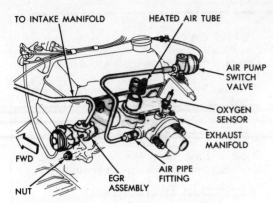

Exhaust manifold components—1.6L engine

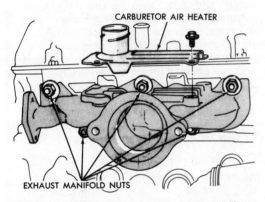

Exhaust manifold and carburetor heater—1.6L engine

3. Remove the oxygen sensor from the manifold.

4. Disconnect the air injection pipe from the manifold and separate the EGR assembly.

5. Raise the vehicle and support on jackstands, remove the exhaust pipe from the manifold.

6. Remove the exhaust manifold retaining nuts and remove the assembly.

7. Remove the carburetor air heater from the manifold.

8. To install, clean all gasket surfaces, install new gaskets and torque the mounting nuts to 15 ft. lbs. The remaining procedures are reverse the removal.

1.7L Engine

1. Follow the intake manifold removal procedures above.

2. Disconnect the exhaust pipe.

3. Unbolt and remove the exhaust manifold.

4. Clean the gasket surfaces, and using a new gasket, install the manifold.

2.2L Engine

NOTE: *Refer to turbocharger procedures which follows for turbo removal if equipped.*

1. Follow the intake manifold removal procedure above.

2. Disconnect the exhaust pipe.

3. Unbolt and remove the exhaust manifold.

4. Clean the gasket surfaces, and use a new gasket.

5. Installation is the reverse of removal.

Turbocharger

REMOVAL AND INSTALLATION

1. Disconnect the negative battery cable and drain the cooling system.

2. Disconnect the exhaust pipe from the turbocharger and the oxygen sensor electrical connector.

3. Remove the turbocharger-to-engine support bracket.

4. Loosen the oil drain back hose clamps and slide the hose down on the engine nipple.

5. Disconnect the turbocharger coolant tube nut at the engine outlet (below the power steering pump bracket) and the support bracket.

6. Remove the air cleaner assembly, the throttle body adaptor, the hose and the air cleaner box and bracket.

7. Disconnect the accelerator linkage, the throttle body electrical connector and the vacuum hoses.

8. Loosen the throttle body-to-turbocharger inlet hose clamps.

9. Remove the 3 throttle body-to-intake manifold screws and the throttle body.

10. Loosen the turbocharger discharge hose end clamp ONLY (the center band retains the deswirler).

11. At the fuel rail, remove the hose retainer bracket screw, the 4 intake bracket screws from the intake manifold and the 2 bracket-to-heat shield bracket clips. Lift the fuel rail (with the injectors, wiring harness and fuel lines intact) up and secure out of the way.

12. Disconnect the oil feed line from the turbocharger bearing housing.

13. Remove the 3 heat shield-to-intake manifold screws and the heat shield.

14. Disconnect the coolant return tube and hose assembly from the turbocharger and the water box. Remove the tube support bracket from the cylinder head and remove the assembly.

15. Remove the 4 turbocharger-to-exhaust manifold nuts. Lift the turbocharger off the studs, push down towards the passenger side, lift up and out of the engine compartment.

ENGINE OVERHAUL

Most engine overhaul procedures are fairly standard. In addition to specific parts replacement procedures and complete specifications for your individual engine, this chapter also is a guide to accepted rebuilding procedures. Examples of standard rebuilding practice are shown and should be used along with specific details concerning your particular engine.

Competent and accurate machine shop services will ensure maximum performance, reliability and engine life. Procedures marked with the symbol shown above should be performed by a competent machine shop, and are provided so that you will be familiar with the procedures necessary to a successful overhaul.

In most instances it is more profitable for the do-it-yourself mechanic to remove, clean and inspect the component, buy the necessary parts and deliver these to a shop for actual machine work.

On the other hand, much of the rebuilding work (crankshaft, block, bearings, pistons, rods, and other components) is well within the scope of the do-it-yourself mechanic.

Tools

The tools required for an engine overhaul or parts replacement will depend on the depth of your involvement. With a few exceptions, they will be the tools found in a mechanic's tool kit (see Chapter 1). More in-depth work will require any or all of the following:

• a dial indicator (reading in thousandths) mounted on a universal base
• micrometers and telescope gauges
• jaw and screw-type pullers
• scraper
• valve spring compressor
• ring groove cleaner
• piston ring expander and compressor
• ridge reamer
• cylinder hone or glaze breaker

• Plastigage®
• engine stand

Use of most of these tools is illustrated in this chapter. Many can be rented for a one-time use from a local parts jobber or tool supply house specializing in automotive work.

Occasionally, the use of special tools is called for. See the information on Special Tools and the Safety Notice in the front of this book before substituting another tool.

Inspection Techniques

Procedures and specifications are given in this chapter for inspecting, cleaning and assessing the wear limits of most major components. Other procedures such as Magnaflux and Zyglo can be used to locate material flaws and stress cracks. Magnaflux is a magnetic process applicable only to ferrous materials. The Zyglo process coats the material with a flourescent dye penetrant and can be used on any material. Check for suspected surface cracks can be more readily made using spot check dye. The dye is sprayed onto the suspected area, wiped off and the area sprayed with a developer. Cracks will show up brightly.

Overhaul Tips

Aluminum has become extremely popular for use in engines, due to its low weight. Observe the following precautions when handling aluminum parts:

• Never hot tank aluminum parts (the caustic hot-tank solution will eat the aluminum)

• Remove all aluminum parts (identification tag, etc.) from engine parts prior to hot-tanking.

• Always coat threads lightly with engine oil or anti-seize compounds before installation, to prevent seizure.

• Never over-torque bolts or spark plugs, especially in aluminum threads.

Stripped threads in any component can be repaired using any of several commercial repair kits (Heli-Coil, Microdot, Keen-serts, etc.)

When assembling the engine, any parts that will be in frictional contact must be pre-lubed to provide lubrication at initial start-up. Any product specifically formulated for this purpose can be used, but engine oil is not recommended as a pre-lube.

When semi-permanent (locked, but removable) installation of bolts or nuts is desired, threads should be cleaned and coated with Loctite® or other similar, commercial non-hardening sealant.

Repairing Damaged Threads

Several methods of repairing damaged threads are available. Heli-Coil® (shown here), Keenserts® and Microdot® are among the most widely used. All involve basically the same principle—drilling out stripped threads, tapping the hole and installing a pre-wound insert—making welding, plugging and oversize fasteners unnecessary.

Two types of thread repair inserts are usually supplied—a standard type for most Inch Coarse, Inch Fine, Metric Coarse and Metric Fine thread sizes and a spark plug type to fit most spark plug port sizes. Consult the individual manufacturer's catalog to determine exact applications. Typical thread repair kits will contain a selection of pre-wound threaded inserts, a tap (corresponding to the outside diameter threads of the insert) and an installation tool. Spark plug inserts usually differ because they require a tap equipped with pilot threads and a combined reamer/tap section. Most manufacturers also supply blister-packed thread repair inserts separately in addition to a master kit containing a variety of taps and inserts plus installation tools.

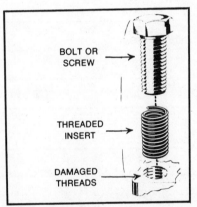
Damaged bolt holes can be repaired with thread repair inserts

BOLT OR SCREW
THREADED INSERT
DAMAGED THREADS

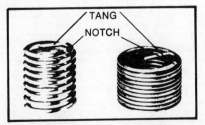
Standard thread repair insert (left) and spark plug thread insert (right)

TANG
NOTCH

Before effecting a repair to a threaded hole, remove any snapped, broken or damaged bolts or studs. Penetrating oil can be used to free frozen threads; the offending item can be removed with locking pliers or with a screw or stud extractor. After the hole is clear, the thread can be repaired, as follows:

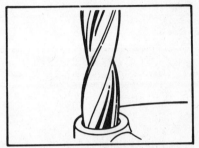
Drill out the damaged threads with specified drill. Drill completely through the hole or to the bottom of a blind hole

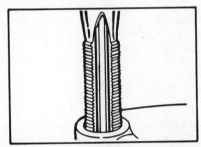
With the tap supplied, tap the hole to receive the thread insert. Keep the tap well oiled and back it out frequently to avoid clogging the threads

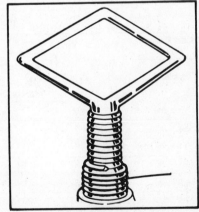
Screw the threaded insert onto the installation tool until the tang engages the slot. Screw the insert into the tapped hole until it is 1/4–1/2 turn below the top surface. After installation break off the tang with a hammer and punch

Standard Torque Specifications and Fastener Markings

In the absence of specific torques, the following chart can be used as a guide to the maximum safe torque of a particular size/grade of fastener.

- There is no torque difference for fine or coarse threads.
- Torque values are based on clean, dry threads. Reduce the value by 10% if threads are oiled prior to assembly.
- The torque required for aluminum components or fasteners is considerably less.

U.S. Bolts

SAE Grade Number	1 or 2			5			6 or 7		
Number of lines always 2 less than the grade number.									
Bolt Size (Inches)—(Thread)	Maximum Torque			Maximum Torque			Maximum Torque		
	Ft./Lbs.	Kgm	Nm	Ft./Lbs.	Kgm	Nm	Ft./Lbs.	Kgm	Nm
¼—20	5	0.7	6.8	8	1.1	10.8	10	1.4	13.5
—28	6	0.8	8.1	10	1.4	13.6			
5/16—18	11	1.5	14.9	17	2.3	23.0	19	2.6	25.8
—24	13	1.8	17.6	19	2.6	25.7			
⅜—16	18	2.5	24.4	31	4.3	42.0	34	4.7	46.0
—24	20	2.75	27.1	35	4.8	47.5			
7/16—14	28	3.8	37.0	49	6.8	66.4	55	7.6	74.5
—20	30	4.2	40.7	55	7.6	74.5			
½—13	39	5.4	52.8	75	10.4	101.7	85	11.75	115.2
—20	41	5.7	55.6	85	11.7	115.2			
9/16—12	51	7.0	69.2	110	15.2	149.1	120	16.6	162.7
—18	55	7.6	74.5	120	16.6	162.7			
⅝—11	83	11.5	112.5	150	20.7	203.3	167	23.0	226.5
—18	95	13.1	128.8	170	23.5	230.5			
¾—10	105	14.5	142.3	270	37.3	366.0	280	38.7	379.6
—16	115	15.9	155.9	295	40.8	400.0			
⅞— 9	160	22.1	216.9	395	54.6	535.5	440	60.9	596.5
—14	175	24.2	237.2	435	60.1	589.7			
1— 8	236	32.5	318.6	590	81.6	799.9	660	91.3	894.8
—14	250	34.6	338.9	660	91.3	849.8			

Metric Bolts

Relative Strength Marking	4.6, 4.8			8.8		
Bolt Markings						
Bolt Size Thread Size x Pitch (mm)	Maximum Torque			Maximum Torque		
	Ft./Lbs.	Kgm	Nm	Ft./Lbs.	Kgm	Nm
6 x 1.0	2–3	.2–.4	3–4	3–6	.4–.8	5–8
8 x 1.25	6–8	.8–1	8–12	9–14	1.2–1.9	13–19
10 x 1.25	12–17	1.5–2.3	16–23	20–29	2.7–4.0	27–39
12 x 1.25	21–32	2.9–4.4	29–43	35–53	4.8–7.3	47–72
14 x 1.5	35–52	4.8–7.1	48–70	57–85	7.8–11.7	77–110
16 x 1.5	51–77	7.0–10.6	67–100	90–120	12.4–16.5	130–160
18 x 1.5	74–110	10.2–15.1	100–150	130–170	17.9–23.4	180–230
20 x 1.5	110–140	15.1–19.3	150–190	190–240	26.2–46.9	160–320
22 x 1.5	150–190	22.0–26.2	200–260	250–320	34.5–44.1	340–430
24 x 1.5	190–240	26.2–46.9	260–320	310–410	42.7–56.5	420–550

CHECKING ENGINE COMPRESSION

A noticeable lack of engine power, excessive oil consumption and/or poor fuel mileage measured over an extended period are all indicators of internal engine wear. Worn piston rings, scored or worn cylinder bores, blown head gaskets, sticking or burnt valves and worn valve seats are all possible culprits here. A check of each cylinder's compression will help you locate the problems.

As mentioned in the "Tools and Equipment" section of Chapter 1, a screw-in type compression gauge is more accurate than the type you simply hold against the spark plug hole, although it takes slightly longer to use. It's worth it to obtain a more accurate reading. Follow the procedures below for gasoline and diesel-engined cars.

Gasoline Engines

1. Warm up the engine to normal operating temperature.
2. Remove all spark plugs.

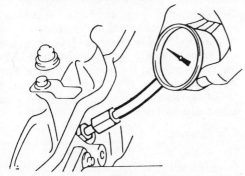

The screw-in type compression gauge is more accurate

3. Disconnect the high-tension lead from the ignition coil.
4. On carbureted cars, fully open the throttle either by operating the carburetor throttle linkage by hand or by having an assistant "floor" the accelerator pedal. On fuel-injected cars, disconnect the cold start valve and all injector connections.
5. Screw the compression gauge into the No. 1 spark plug hole until the fitting is snug.
   NOTE: *Be careful not to crossthread the plug hole. On aluminum cylinder heads use extra care, as the threads in these heads are easily ruined.*
6. Ask an assistant to depress the accelerator pedal fully on both carbureted and fuel-injected cars. Then, while you read the compression gauge, ask the assistant to crank the engine two or three times in short bursts using the ignition switch.

7. Read the compression gauge at the end of each series of cranks, and record the highest of these readings. Repeat this procedure for each of the engine's cylinders. Compare the highest reading of each cylinder to the compression pressure specifications in the "Tune-Up Specifications" chart in Chapter 2. The specs in this chart are maximum values.

A cylinder's compression pressure is usually acceptable if it is not less than 80% of maximum. The difference between each cylinder should be no more than 12–14 pounds.

8. If a cylinder is unusually low, pour a tablespoon of clean engine oil into the cylinder through the spark plug hole and repeat the compression test. If the compression comes up after adding the oil, it appears that that cylinder's piston rings or bore are damaged or worn. If the pressure remains low, the valves may not be seating properly (a valve job is needed), or the head gasket may be blown near that cylinder. If compression in any two adjacent cylinders is low, and if the addition of oil doesn't help the compression, there is leakage past the head gasket. Oil and coolant water in the combustion chamber can result from this problem. There may be evidence of water droplets on the engine dipstick when a head gasket has blown.

Diesel Engines

Checking cylinder compression on diesel engines is basically the same procedure as on gasoline engines except for the following:
1. A special compression gauge adaptor suitable for diesel engines (because these engines have much greater compression pressures) must be used.
2. Remove the injector tubes and remove the injectors from each cylinder.
   NOTE: *Don't forget to remove the washer underneath each injector; otherwise, it may get lost when the engine is cranked.*

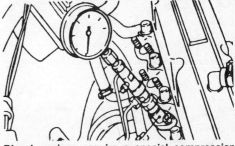

Diesel engines require a special compression gauge adaptor

3. When fitting the compression gauge adaptor to the cylinder head, make sure the bleeder of the gauge (if equipped) is closed.
4. When reinstalling the injector assemblies, install new washers underneath each injector.

Cylinder Head

REMOVAL AND INSTALLATION

1.6L Engine

NOTE: *The cylinder head must be cool before removing to avoid distortion.*

1. Disconnect the battery.
2. Drain the cooling system.
3. Remove the air cleaner assembly.
4. Disconnect all lines, hoses and wires from the head, manifold and carburetor.
5. Disconnect the accelerator linkage.
6. Remove the intake and exhaust manifolds.
7. If equipped with air conditioning, remove the compressor from the mounting brackets and support it out of the way. DO NOT remove the hoses from the compressor.
8. Remove the cylinder head cover as previously described in "Rocker Arm/Camshaft Cover" in this chapter.
9. Loosen the cylinder head bolts evenly, beginning at the ends and working towards the center.
10. Tie the rocker arm assembly together with safety wire or equivalent.
11. Remove the bolts and lift the rocker arm assembly off the cylinder head.
12. Label all the push rods so they be reinstalled in their original locations and remove them from the cylinder head.

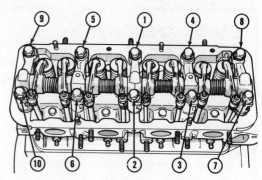

Cylinder head bolt tightening sequence—1.6L engine

13. Lift off the cylinder head and discard the gasket.
14. Installation is the reverse of removal. Make certain the gasket surfaces are thoroughly cleaned and are free of nicks or scratches. Always use a new head gasket and make certain the word "Dessus or Top" faces up when the gasket is laid on the engine block. Lubricate the head bolt threads with engine oil and install through the rocker shaft brackets. Screw the bolts down finger tight while checking to see that each rocker adjusting screw engages its push rod. Tighten the head bolts in progressive steps as shown in the illustration to 52 ft. lbs. Start and run the engine to normal operating temperature, allow to cool down and retorque as described above. Check valve clearance and adjust as necessary.

1.7L Engines

The engine should be cold before the cylinder head is removed. The head is retained by 10 socket head bolts.

1. Disconnect the battery.
2. Drain the cooling system.
3. Remove the air cleaner assembly.

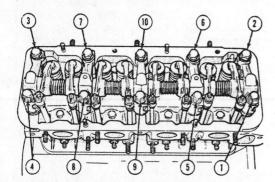

Cylinder head bolt removal sequence—1.6L engine

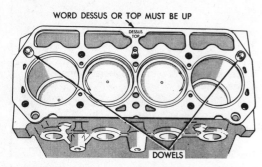

Cylinder head gasket mounting—1.6L engines

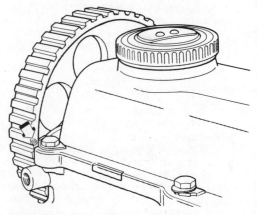

Aligning the 1.7L engine camshaft timing dot with the edge of the cylinder head

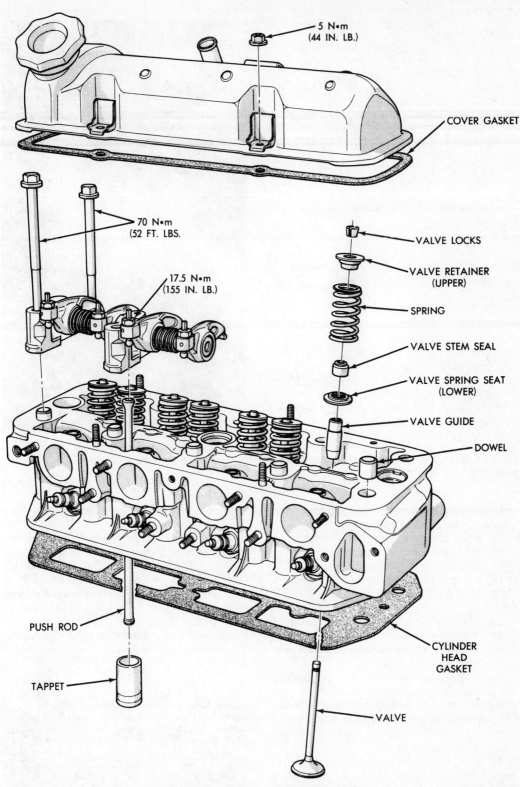

5 N•m
(44 IN. LB.)

COVER GASKET

70 N•m
(52 FT. LBS.)

17.5 N•m
(155 IN. LB.)

VALVE LOCKS

VALVE RETAINER
(UPPER)

SPRING

VALVE STEM SEAL

VALVE SPRING SEAT
(LOWER)

VALVE GUIDE

DOWEL

PUSH ROD

CYLINDER
HEAD
GASKET

TAPPET

VALVE

Cylinder head and valve assembly—1.6L engine

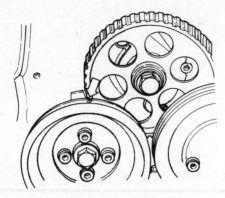

1.7L engine crankshaft-to-intermediate shaft timing mark alignment

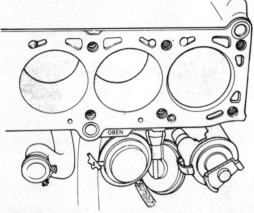

On the 1.7L engine, the head gasket is installed with the word OBEN facing up

1.7L engine timing belt installation

4. Disconnect all lines, hoses and wires from the head manifold and carburetor.

5. Disconnect the accelerator linkage.

6. Remove the distributor cap.

7. Disconnect the exhaust pipe.

8. Remove the carburetor.

9. Remove the intake and exhaust manifolds.

10. Remove the upper portion of the front cover.

11. Turn the engine by hand until all gear timing marks are aligned.

12. Loosen the drive belt tensioner and slip the belt off the camshaft gear.

NOTE: *The camshaft timing mark is on the back of the gear and is properly positioned when it is in line with the left corner of the camshaft cover at the head.*

13. If equipped with air conditioning, remove the compressor from the mounting brackets and support it out of the way with wires. Remove the mounting brackets from the head.

14. Remove the valve cover, gaskets and seals.

15. Remove head bolts in reverse order of the tightening sequence.

16. Lift off the head and discard the gasket.

17. Installation is the revers of removal. Make certain all gasket surfaces are thoroughly cleaned and are free of deep nicks or scratches. Always use new gaskets and seals. The word "OBEN" (Top) faces up. Never reuse a gasket or seal, even if it looks good. When positioning the head on the block, insert bolts 8 and 10 (see illustration) to align the head. Tighten bolts in the order shown in the illustration. Bolts should be

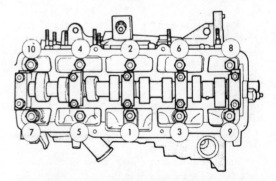

1.7L engine cylinder head torque sequence

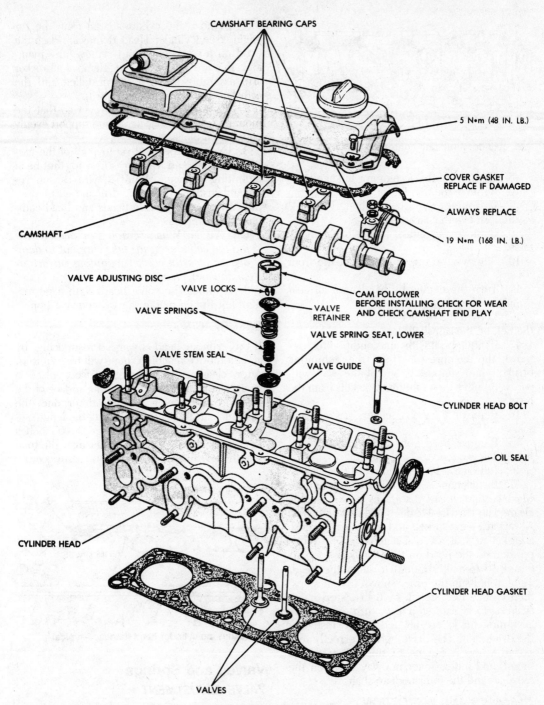

CAMSHAFT BEARING CAPS

5 N•m (48 IN. LB.)

COVER GASKET
REPLACE IF DAMAGED

ALWAYS REPLACE

19 N•m (168 IN. LB.)

CAMSHAFT

VALVE ADJUSTING DISC

VALVE LOCKS

VALVE SPRINGS

VALVE
RETAINER

CAM FOLLOWER
BEFORE INSTALLING CHECK FOR WEAR
AND CHECK CAMSHAFT END PLAY

VALVE SPRING SEAT, LOWER

VALVE STEM SEAL

VALVE GUIDE

CYLINDER HEAD BOLT

OIL SEAL

CYLINDER HEAD

CYLINDER HEAD GASKET

VALVES

1.7L cylinder head

tightened to 30 ft. lbs. in rotation, then tightened to 60 ft. lbs. When all bolts are at 60 ft. lbs., tighten each ¼ turn more in sequence. Make sure all timing marks are aligned before installing the drive belt. The drive belt is correctly tensioned when it can be twisted 90° with the thumb and index finger midway between the camshaft and intermediate shaft.

2.2L Engine

1. Disconnect the negative battery terminal.

2. Drain the cooling system.

3. Remove the air cleaner assembly.

4. Disconnect all lines, hoses and wires from the head, manifold and carburetor.

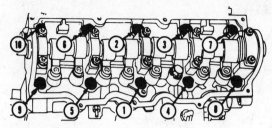

2.2L cylinder head bolt tightening sequence

5. Disconnect the accelerator linkage.

6. Remove the distributor cap.

7. Disconnect the exhaust pipe.

8. Remove the carburetor.

9. Remove the intake and exhaust manifolds.

10. Remove the upper portion of the front cover.

11. Turn the engine by hand until all gear timing marks are aligned.

12. Loosen the drive belt tensioner and slip the belt off the camshaft gear.

13. If equipped with air conditioning, remove the compressor from the mounting brackets and support it out of the way with wires. Remove the mounting brackets from the head.

14. Remove the valve cover, gaskets and seals.

15. Remove head bolts in reverse order of tightening sequence.

16. Lift off the head and discard the gasket.

17. Installation is the reverse of removal. Make certain all gasket surfaces are thoroughly cleaned and are free of deep nicks or scratches. Always use new gaskets and seals. Never reuse a gasket or seal, even if it looks good. When positioning the head on the block, insert bolts 8 and 10 (see illustration) to align the head. Tighten bolts in the order shown in four steps. Step 1: 30 ft. lbs., step 2: 45 ft. lbs., step 3: one again to 45 ft. lbs., step 4: ½ turn. Make sure all timing marks are aligned before installing the drive belt. The drive belt is correctly tensioned when it can be twisted 90° with the thumb and index finger midway between the camshaft and the intermediate shaft.

CLEANING AND INSPECTION

NOTE: *With the cylinder head removed from the engine, the rocker arm assemblies and camshaft removed, the valves, valve springs and valve stem oil seals can now be serviced.*

Since the machining of valve seats and valves, and the insertion of new valve guides or valve seats may tax the experience and equipment resources of the car owner, it is suggested that the cylinder head be taken to an automotive machine shop for rebuilding.

1. Remove the cylinder head from the car engine (see Cylinder Head Removal). Place the head on a workbench and remove any manifolds that are still connected. Remove all rocker arm assembly parts, if still installed and the camshaft (see Camshaft Removal).

2. Turn the cylinder head over so that the mounting surface is facing up and support evenly on wooden blocks.

3. Use a scraper and remove all of the gasket material and carbon stuck to the head mounting surface. Mount a wire carbon removal brush in an electric drill and clean away the carbon on the valve heads and head combustion chambers.

CAUTION: *When scraping or decarbonizing the cylinder head, take care not to damage or nick the gasket mounting surface or combustion chamber.*

4. Number the valve heads with a permanent felt-tipped marker for cylinder location.

RESURFACING

If the cylinder head is warped resurfacing, by an automotive machine shop, will be required. After cleaning the gasket surface, place a straight-edge across the mounting surface of the head. Using feeler gauges, determine the clearance at the center and along the lengths of both diagonals. If warpage exceeds .003 inches in a six inch span, or .006 inches over the total length the cylinder head must be resurfaced.

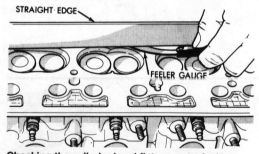

Checking the cylinder head flatness—typical

Valves and Springs
VALVE ADJUSTMENT

NOTE: *For all valve adjustment procedures please refer to Chapter 2 under "Valve Adjustment."*

REMOVAL AND INSTALLATION
1.6L Engine
CYLINDER HEAD REMOVED

1. Follow the procedures under "Cylinder head removal" in this chapter and remove the head.

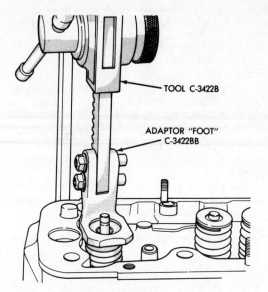

Removing the valve spring—1.6L engine

2. With the head removed from the engine block, compress the valve with a spring compressor tool.

3. Remove the valve retaining locks, spring retainer, spring, valve seals, and the spring seat.

4. Before removing the valves, remove any burrs from the valve stem lock grooves to prevent damage to the valve guides. Mark all the valves so they may be installed in their original position.

5. To install, coat the valve stems with oil and insert in the cylinder head. Install the spring seat on each guide.

6. Place a protective cap over the end of the valve, or wrap the lock grooves with tape to prevent the edges of the valve from damaging the oil seals.

7. Install the new valve stem seals on all of the valves. The seals should be pushed firmly and squarely over the valve guide and down until it bottoms out.

8. Install the valve springs and retainers. Compress the valve spring only enough to install the locks, being careful not to misalign the direction of compression.

9. The remaining procedures are reverse the removal.

1.7L Engine

CYLINDER HEAD NOT REMOVED

1. Remove the rocker arm cover.

2. Remove the camshaft as described later in this chapter.

3. Remove the spark plugs.

4. Turn the crankshaft until the piston of the cylinder being serviced is in the BDC, bottom dead center position.

5. With an airline adapter and an air hose installed into the spark plug hole, apply 90–122 psi of air pressure.

6. Compress the valve spring with tool L-4419 or equivalent.

7. Remove the adjusting disc, valve keeper, spring retainer and valve spring.

8. Remove the seal by pulling side-to-side with a pair of long nose pliers or the C-4745 Seal Remover tool may be used.

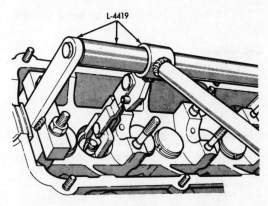

Compressing the valve spring—1.7L engine

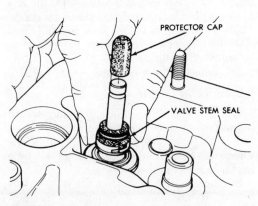

Installing valve stem seals—1.6L engine

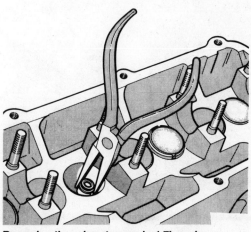

Removing the valve stem seal—1.7L engine

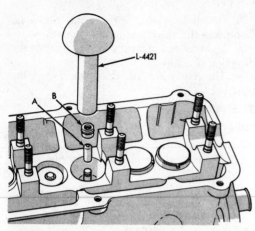

Installing valve stem seals—1.7L engine

9. Place a protective cap over the end of the valve, or wrap the lock grooves with tape to prevent the edges of the valve from damaging the oil seals.

10. Install the new valve stem seals on all of the valves. The seals should be pushed firmly and squarely over the valve guide with tool L-4421 or equivalent and down until it bottoms out.

11. To install, reverse the removal procedures.

2.2L Engine

CYLINDER HEAD NOT REMOVED

1. Remove the rocker arm cover.

2. For each rocker arm, rotate the cam until the base circle is in contact with the rocker arm.

3. Depress the valve spring using tool 4682 or equivalent and slide the rocker arm out. Label all rocker arms so that they may be reassembled in their original order.

4. Remove the hydraulic lash adjusters.

5. Rotate the crankshaft so that the cylin-

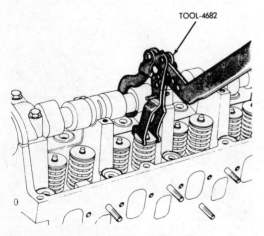

Removing the valve springs—2.2L engine

der is at TDC with the intake and exhaust valves closed.

6. With an airline adapter and an air hose installed into the spark plug hole, apply 90–120 psi of air pressure.

7. Using tool 4682 or equivalent compress the valve spring and remove the valve locks.

8. Remove the valve spring.

9. Remove the seal by pulling side-to-side with a pair of long nose pliers.

10. To install, install the spring seat on each guide.

11. Place a protective cap over the end of the valve, or wrap the lock grooves with tape to prevent the edges of the valve from damaging the oil seals.

12. Install the new valve stem seals on all of the valves. The seals should be pushed firmly and squarely over the valve guide and down until it bottoms out.

NOTE: *When using tool 4682 the valve locks can become dislocated. Check to be certain that both locks are in position after removing the tool.*

13. Install the valve springs and retainers. Compress the valve spring with tool 4682 or equivalent, only enough to install the locks, being careful not to misalign the direction of compression.

14. Check the installed spring height of the springs. This measurement should be made from the lower edge of the spring to its upper edge, not including the spring seat.

15. Install the rocker arms and adjusters in their original locations. Check the clearance between the projecting ears of the rocker arm and the valve spring retainers. At least .020 in. clearance must be present, if necessary, the rocker arm ears may have to be ground to obtain this clearance.

16. Check the dry lash. Dry lash is the amount of clearance that exists between the base circle of the installed camshaft and the rocker arm pad when the adjuster is completely collapsed. Dry lash should be .024–.060 in. The adjusters must be drained to perform this check. Refill the adjusters before final assembly and allow 10 minutes for the adjusters to bleed down before rotating the cam.

17. Reinstall the rocker arm cover.

VALVE INSPECTION

1. Clean the valves thoroughly and discard burned, warped, or cracked valves.

2. If the valve face is only lightly pitted, the valve may be refaced to an angle of 45° by a qualified machine shop.

3. Measure the valve stem for wear at various points and check it against the specifications shown in the "Valve Specifications" chart.

FOR DIMENSIONS,
REFER TO
SPECIFICATIONS

CHECK FOR
BENT STEM

DIAMETER

VALVE FACE ANGLE

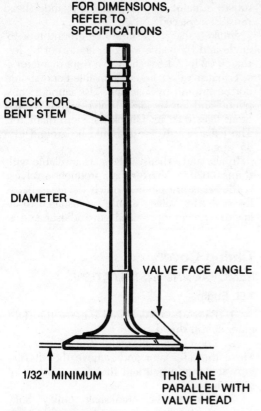

1/32″ MINIMUM

THIS LINE
PARALLEL WITH
VALVE HEAD

Critical valve dimensions

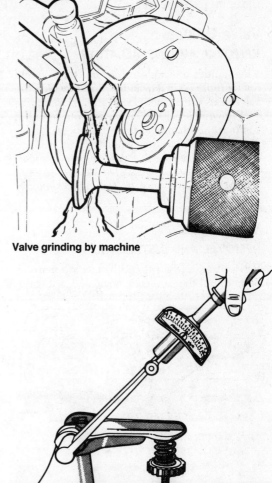

Valve grinding by machine

VALVE REFACING

Using a valve grinder, resurface the valves according to the specifications given in the "Valve Specifications" chart.

>   NOTE: *The valve face angle is not always identical to the valve seat angle.*

A minimum margin of ⅟₃₂ in. should remain after grinding the valve. The valve stem top should also be squared and resurfaced, by placing the stem in the V-block of the grinder, and turning it while pressing lightly against the grinding wheel.

CHECK SPRINGS

Whenever the valves have been removed for inspection, reconditioning or replacement, the valve springs should be tested. To test the spring tension you will need special tool C-647 or equivalent. Place the spring over the stud on the table and lift the compressing lever to set the tone device. Pull on the torque wrench until a ping is heard. Take a reading on the torque wrench at this instant. Multiply this reading by two. The resulting specification is the spring load at the test length. Refer to the "Valve Specifications" chart for specifications. Inspect each valve spring for squareness with a steel square and a surface plate, test the spring from

Testing the valve spring pressure with special tool C-647

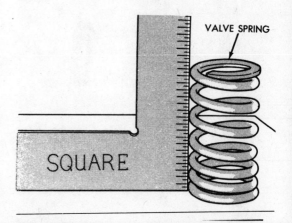

VALVE SPRING

SQUARE

Checking the valve spring free height and squareness

both ends. If the spring is more than ¹⁄₁₆ out of square, replace the spring.

Valve Guides

REMOVAL AND INSTALLATION

Valve guides are replaceable, but they should not be replaced in a cylinder head in which the valve seats cannot be refaced.

Worn guides should be pressed out from the combustion chamber side and new guides pressed in as far as they will go.

NOTE: *Service valve guides have a shoulder. Once the guide is seated, do not use more than 1 ton pressure or the guide shoulder could break.*

Valve Seats

REMOVAL AND INSTALLATION

Valve seats can be refaced if they are worn or burned, but the correction angle and seat width

must be maintained. If not, the cylinder head must be replaced.

Intake valve seats should be ground to a 45° angle and the valve margin should not be less than 0.02 in. Check the valve stem diameter.

Exhaust valves are sodium filled and should not be ground by machine. Use lapping compound and lap by hand. Valve margin should be at least 0.02 in. Check the stem diameter. The exhaust valve seat should be ground to a 45° angle.

Intake and exhaust valves are available with stems 0.020 in. shorter than production valves. If the seats are cut too much during repairs, these shorter valves should be installed to allow the use of proper sized valve adjusting discs.

Timing Cover

REMOVAL AND INSTALLATION

1.6L Engine

1. Raise the vehicle and remove the right inner splash shield.

2. Loosen the alternator adjusting screw. Move the alternator and remove the alternator/water pump belt and the air pump belt (if so equipped).

3. Remove the crankshaft pulley bolt, washer, and pulley.

4. Drain the cooling system through the water pump drain plug and remove the water pump to timing cover hose.

5. Raise the timing cover end of the engine and carefully support.

6. Remove the bolts supporting the engine mount bracket to the timing cover and block.

NOTE: *Two of the cover to block screws pass through the tubular locating dowels. Make*

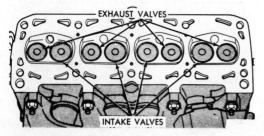

Valve identification

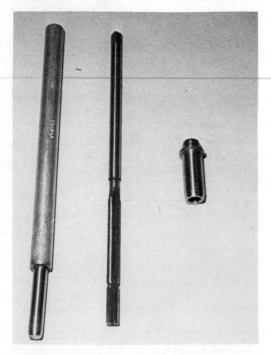

Valve guide tools

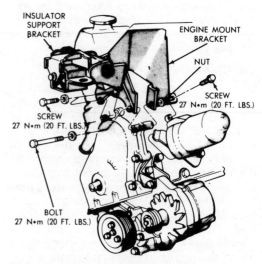

Engine mounting bracket—1.6L engine

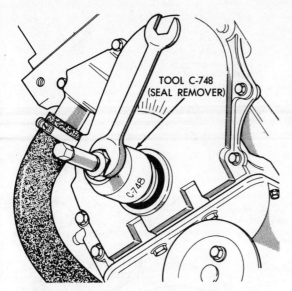

Removing the timing cover oil seal—1.6L engine

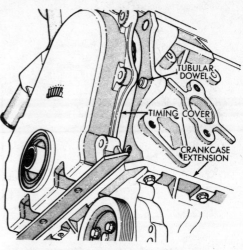

Installing the timing cover—1.6L engine

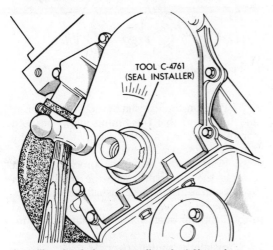

Installing the timing cover oil seal—1.6L engine

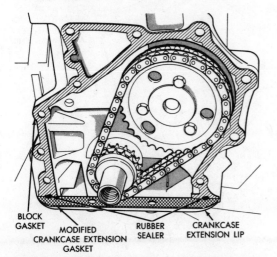

Timing cover gasket mounting—1.6L engine

sure the dowels DO NOT fall into the crank-case extension during the cover removal.

7. Remove the crankcase extension to cover and the cover to block screws and remove the cover.

8. To remove the oil seal, install the seal removal tool C-748 or equivalent over the crankshaft nose and turn tightly into the seal. Tap the side of the thrust to loosen and remove the seal.

9. To install the oil seal, position tool C-4761 or equivalent on the seal and drive the seal into the timing cover until the tool stops against the cover.

10. To install the timing cover, reverse the removal procedures.

1.7L Engines

1. Loosen the alternator mounting bolts, pivot the alternator and remove the drive belt.

2. Do the same thing with the air conditioning compressor.

3. Remove the cover retaining nuts, washers and spacers.

4. Remove the cover.

5. Installation is the reverse of removal.

2.2L Engines

1. Loosen the alternator mounting bolts, pivot the alternator and remove the drive belt.

2. Do the same thing with the air conditioning compressor.

3. Remove the cover retaining nuts, washers and spacers.

4. Remove the cover.

5. Installation is the reverse of removal.

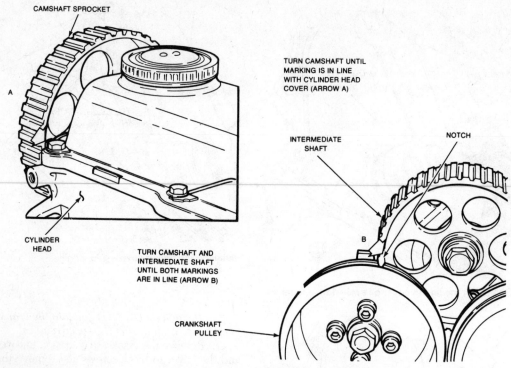

CAMSHAFT SPROCKET

TURN CAMSHAFT UNTIL MARKING IS IN LINE WITH CYLINDER HEAD COVER (ARROW A)

INTERMEDIATE SHAFT

NOTCH

A

CYLINDER HEAD

TURN CAMSHAFT AND INTERMEDIATE SHAFT UNTIL BOTH MARKINGS ARE IN LINE (ARROW B)

B

CRANKSHAFT PULLEY

1.7L engine valve train timing marks

Timing Chain and Gears
REMOVAL AND INSTALLATION
1.6L Engine

1. Remove the timing cover as outlined earlier.

2. Remove the camshaft sprocket bolts and remove the sprocket and chain.

3. Remove the crankshaft gear with a pilot adapter tool C-4760 and gear puller C-3894-A or equivalent.

4. To install, align the crankshaft sprocket with the key and drive it onto the shaft.

5. Position the camshaft sprocket into place and turn it so that the timing marks on both sprockets are on a line passing through the sprocket centers as shown in the illustration.

6. Remove the camshaft sprocket without turning the camshaft, place the timing chain over it and reinstall the camshaft sprocket.

7. Recheck the timing marks. Install and torque the camshaft sprocket bolts to 113 in. lbs.

8. Install the timing cover.

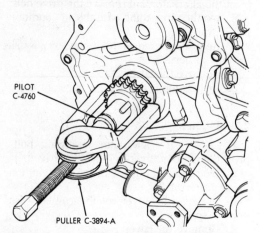

PILOT C-4760

PULLER C-3894-A

Removing the crankshaft sprocket—1.6L engine

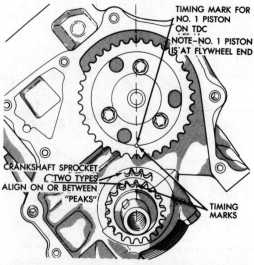

TIMING MARK FOR NO. 1 PISTON ON TDC NOTE–NO. 1 PISTON IS AT FLYWHEEL END

CRANKSHAFT SPROCKET TWO TYPES ALIGN ON OR BETWEEN "PEAKS"

TIMING MARKS

Alignment of the camshaft and crankshaft sprockets

Timing Belt

REMOVAL AND INSTALLATION

1.7L Engines

The timing belt is designed to last a long time without requiring tension adjustments. If the belt is removed or replaced, basic valve timing must be checked and the belt retensioned.

1. Remove the timing belt cover.
2. While holding the large hex on the tension pulley, loosen the pulley nut.
3. Remove the belt from the tensioner.
4. Slide the belt off the three toothed pulleys.
5. Using the larger bolt on the crankshaft pulley, turn the engine until the #1 cylinder is at TDC of the compression stroke. At this point the valves for the #1 cylinder will be closed and the timing mark will be aligned with the pointer on the flywheel housing. Make sure that the timing mark on the rear face of the camshaft pulley is aligned with the lower left corner of the valve cover.
6. Check that the V-notch in the crankshaft pulley aligns with the dot mark on the intermediate shaft.

CAUTION: *If the timing marks are not per-*

On the 1.7L engine the belt tension is correct when the belt can be twisted 90° at the mid-point of its longest run

fectly aligned, poor engine performance and probable engine damage will result!

7. Install the belt on the pulleys.
8. Adjust the tension by turning the large tensioner hex to the right. Tension is correct when the belt can be twisted 90° with the thumb and forefinger, midway between the camshaft and intermediate pulleys.
9. Tighten the tensioner locknut to 32 ft. lb.
10. Install the timing belt cover and check the ignition timing.

2.2L Engines

1. Remove the timing belt cover.
2. While holding the large hex on the tension pulley, loosen the pulley nut.
3. Remove the belt from the tensioner.
4. Slide the belt off the three toothed pulleys.
5. Using the larger bolt on the crankshaft pulley, turn the engine until the #1 cylinder is at TDC of the compression stroke. At this point the valves for the #1 cylinder will be closed and the timing mark will be aligned with the pointer on the flywheel housing. Make sure that the dots on the cam sprocket and cylinder head are aligned.
6. Check that the V-notch in the crankshaft pulley aligns with the dot mark on the intermediate shaft.

CAUTION: *If the timing marks are not perfectly aligned, poor engine performance and probable engine damage will result!*

7. Install the belt on the pulleys.
8. Adjust the tensioner by turning the large tensioner hex to the right. Tension is correct when the belt can be twisted 90° with the thumb and forefinger, midway between the camshaft and intermediate pulleys.
9. Tighten the tensioner locknut to 32 ft. lb.
10. Install the timing belt cover and check the ignition timing.

Camshaft

REMOVAL AND INSTALLATION

1.6L Engine

NOTE: *The camshaft has an integral oil pump/distributor helical drive gear and an eccentric which drives the fuel pump. These items must be removed to enable camshaft removal.*

1. Remove the valve cover, rocker arms, push rods and tappets. Label these items so they may be installed in their original locations.
2. Remove the timing cover.

Timing Belt Wear

DESCRIPTION	FLAW CONDITIONS

1. Hardened back surface rubber

Back surface glossy. Non-elastic and so hard that even if a finger nail is forced into it, no mark is produced.

2. Cracked back surface rubber

3. Cracked or exfoliated canvas

4. Badly worn teeth (initial stage)

Canvas on load side tooth flank worn (Fluffy canvas fibers, rubber gone and color changed to white, and unclear canvas texture)

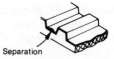

5. Badly worn teeth (last stage)

Canvas on load side tooth flank worn down and rubber exposed (tooth width reduced)

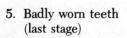

6. Cracked tooth bottom

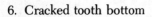

7. Missing tooth

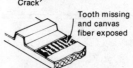

8. Side of belt badly worn

NOTE: *Normal belt should have clear-cut sides as if cut by a sharp knife.*

9. Side of belt cracked

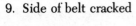

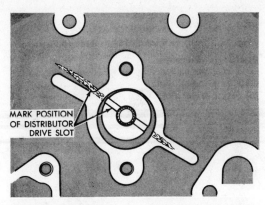

Marking the position of the distributor driveshaft—
1.6L engine

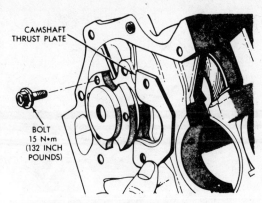

Camshaft thrust plate—1.6L engine

3. Remove the timing chain and sprockets.

4. Remove the oil pump and fuel pump.

5. Remove the distributor and drive housing, mark the crankcase in relation to the distributor drive slot.

6. With a magnet, remove the distributor drive from the driveshaft spindle.

7. Remove the oil pump shaft drive gear circlip.

NOTE: *Place a clean rag in the cavity around the gear to prevent the circlip from falling into the crankcase.*

8. Tap the driveshaft toward the oil pump side of the crankcase until the gear and thrust washer are free from the spline, and remove the gear and washer.

9. Pull the driveshaft out from the oil pump side of the crankcase.

10. Remove the camshaft thrust plate and carefully remove the camshaft.

11. Installation is the reverse of the removal. Lubricate the camshaft, bearings, tappets, rockers and push rods. Lubricate the thrust plate and install with the open end up towards the cylinder head.

NOTE: *If a new camshaft or tappets have been installed, one pint of Chrysler oil conditioner 3419130 or an equivalent break in lubricant should be added to the crankcase.*

1.7L Engine

1. Remove the timing belt cover.
2. Remove the timing belt.
3. Remove the air cleaner assembly.
4. Remove the valve cover.
5. Remove the Nos. 1, 3, and 5 camshaft bearing caps.

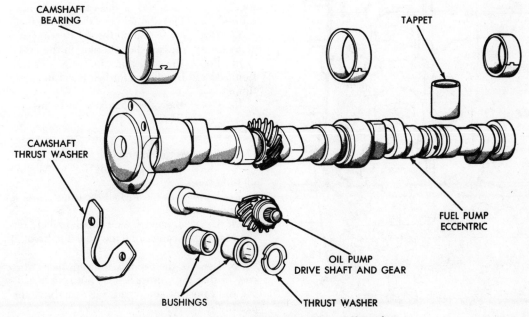

Camshaft and oil pump/distributor drive—1.6L engine

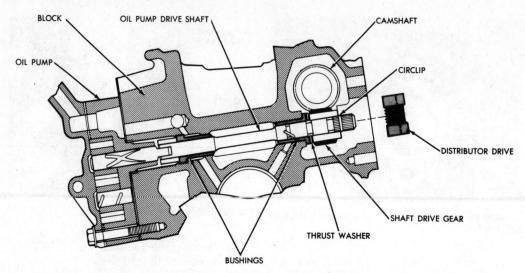

Oil pump/distributor driveshaft—1.6L engine

6. Loosen caps 2 and 4 diagonally and in increments.

7. Lift the camshaft out.

8. Lubricate the camshaft journals and lobes

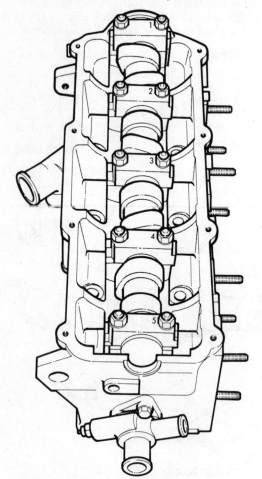

1.7L engine bearing cap installation

with engine assembly lubricant and position it in the head.

9. Install a new oil seal.

10. Install the Nos. 1, 3, 5 bearing caps and torque the nuts to 14 ft. lbs.

NOTE: *All bearing caps are slightly offset. They should be installed so that the numbers on the cap read right side up from the driver's seat.*

11. Install the Nos. 2 and 4 caps and diagonally torque the nuts to 14 ft. lbs.

NOTE: *All bearing caps are slightly offset. They should be installed so that the numbers on the cap read right side up from the driver's seat.*

12. Position a dial indicator so that the feeler touches the front end of the camshaft. Check for end play. Play should not exceed .006 in.

13. Place a new seal on the #1 bearing cap. If necessary, replace the end plug in the head.

14. Follow the procedures under Timing Belt Removal and Installation for belt installation and timing.

15. Check the valve clearance and ignition.

2.2L Engine

1. Remove the timing belt.

2. Mark the rocker arms for installation identification.

3. Loosen the camshaft bearing capnuts several turns each.

4. Using a wooden or rubber mallet, rap the rear of the camshaft a few times to break it loose.

5. Remove the capnuts and caps being very careful that the camshaft does not cock. Cocking the camshaft could cause irreparable damage to the bearings.

6. Check all oil holes for blockage.

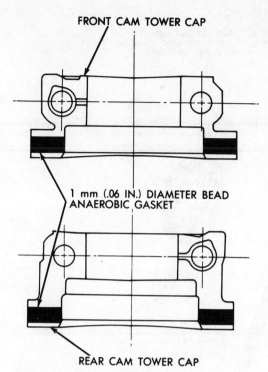

FRONT CAM TOWER CAP

1 mm (.06 IN.) DIAMETER BEAD ANAEROBIC GASKET

REAR CAM TOWER CAP

2.2L engine camshaft tower cap showing sealer location

7. Install the bearing caps with #1 at the timing belt end and #5 at the transmission end. Caps are numbered and have arrows facing forward. Cap nut torque is 14 ft. lb.

8. Apply RTV silicone gasket material as per the accompanying picture.

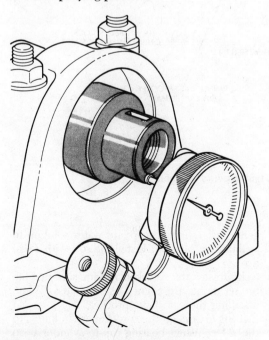

Measuring camshaft end-play—typical

9. Install the bearing caps before the seals are installed.

10. The rest of the procedure is the reverse of disassembly.

CAMSHAFT ENDPLAY CHECK

1. Move the camshaft as far forward as possible.

2. Install a dial indicator as per the accompanying picture.

3. Zero the indicator, push the camshaft backward, then forward as far as possible and record the play. Maximum play should be .006 in.

Timing Sprockets and Oil Seal
REMOVAL AND INSTALLATION
1.7L Engine

The camshaft, intermediate shaft, and crankshaft pulleys are located by keys on their respective shafts and each is retained by a bolt. To remove any or all of the pulleys, first remove the timing belt cover and belt and then use the following procedure.

NOTE: *When removing the crankshaft pulley, don't remove the four socket head bolts which retain the outer belt pulley to the timing belt pulley.*

1. Remove the center bolt.

2. Gently pry the pulley off the shaft.

3. If the pulley is stubborn in coming off, use a gear puller. Don't hammer on the pulley.

4. Remove the pulley and key. The oil seal may now be carefully pried out. Special tools are available for this purpose, but a screwdriver can be used.

5. Install the pulley in the reverse order of removal.

6. Install a new seal using a seal installation tool.

7. Tighten the center bolt to 58 ft. lbs.

8. Install the timing belt, check valve timing, tension belt, and install the cover.

2.2L

1. Raise and support the car on jackstands.

2. Remove the right inner splash shield.

3. Remove the crankshaft pulley.

4. Unbolt and remove both halves of the timing belt cover.

5. Take up the weight of the engine with a jack.

6. Remove the right engine mount bolt and raise the engine slightly.

7. Remove the timing belt tensioner and remove the belt.

8. Remove the crankshaft sprocket bolt, and with a puller, remove the sprocket.

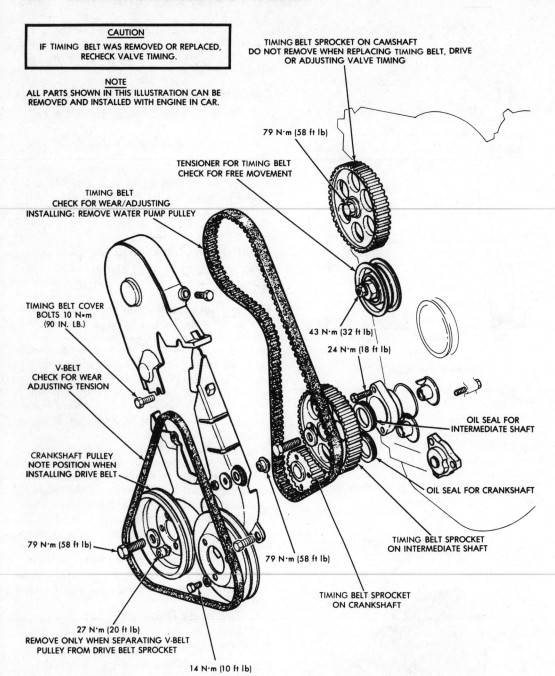

CAUTION
IF TIMING BELT WAS REMOVED OR REPLACED,
RECHECK VALVE TIMING.

NOTE
ALL PARTS SHOWN IN THIS ILLUSTRATION CAN BE
REMOVED AND INSTALLED WITH ENGINE IN CAR.

TIMING BELT SPROCKET ON CAMSHAFT
DO NOT REMOVE WHEN REPLACING TIMING BELT, DRIVE
OR ADJUSTING VALVE TIMING

79 N·m (58 ft lb)

TENSIONER FOR TIMING BELT
CHECK FOR FREE MOVEMENT

TIMING BELT
CHECK FOR WEAR/ADJUSTING
INSTALLING: REMOVE WATER PUMP PULLEY

TIMING BELT COVER
BOLTS 10 N·m
(90 IN. LB.)

43 N·m (32 ft lb)

24 N·m (18 ft lb)

V-BELT
CHECK FOR WEAR
ADJUSTING TENSION

OIL SEAL FOR
INTERMEDIATE SHAFT

CRANKSHAFT PULLEY
NOTE POSITION WHEN
INSTALLING DRIVE BELT

OIL SEAL FOR CRANKSHAFT

79 N·m (58 ft lb)

79 N·m (58 ft lb)

TIMING BELT SPROCKET
ON INTERMEDIATE SHAFT

TIMING BELT SPROCKET
ON CRANKSHAFT

27 N·m (20 ft lb)
REMOVE ONLY WHEN SEPARATING V-BELT
PULLEY FROM DRIVE BELT SPROCKET

14 N·m (10 ft lb)

1.7L engine front cover, timing gears and belt

9. Using special Tool C-4679 or its equiv-alent, remove the crankshaft seal.

10. Unbolt and remove the camshaft and intermediate shaft sprockets.

11. To install the crankshaft seal, first polish the shaft with 400 grit emery paper. If the seal has a steel case, lightly coat the OD of the seal with Loctite Stud N' Bearing Mount® or its equivalent. If the seal case is rubber coated, generously apply a soap and water solution to facilitate installation. Install the seal with a seal driver.

12. Install the sprockets making sure that the timing marks are aligned as illustrated. When installing the camshaft sprocket, make certain that the arrows on the sprocket are in line with the #1 camshaft bearing cap-to-cylinder head line.

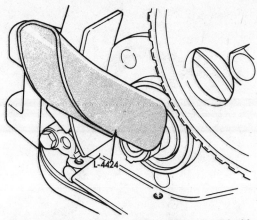

Removing 1.7L engine crankshaft front oil seal with tool L-4424

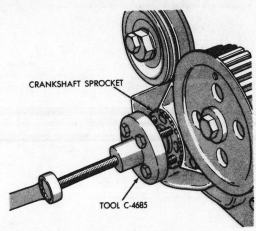

2.2L engine crankshaft sprocket removal

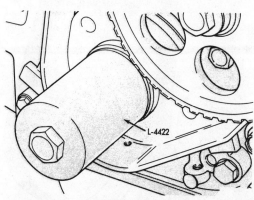

Installing 1.7L engine crankshaft front oil seal with tool L-4422

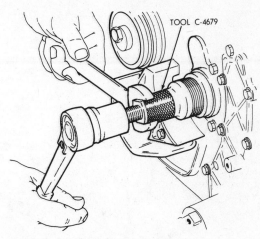

2.2L engine oil seal remover tool

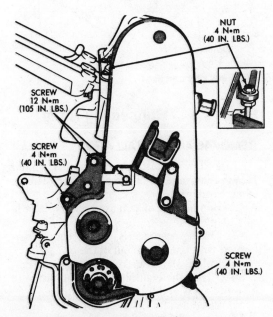

2.2L engine front cover installation

13. The small hole in the camshaft sprocket must be at the top and in line with the vertical center line of the engine.

14. Rotate the engine two full revolutions and recheck timing mark positioning.

15. Install the belt.

16. Rotate the engine to the #1 piston TDC position.

17. Install the belt tensioner and place tool C-4703 on the large hex nut.

18. Reset the belt tension so that the axis of the tool is about 15° off of horizontal.

19. Turn the engine clockwise two full revolutions to #1 TDC.

20. Tighten the tensioner locknut using a weighted wrench to the following torques:
  • Timing belt cover bolts, 105 in. lb.
  • Camshaft sprocket bolt, 65 ft. lb.
  • Crankshaft sprocket bolt, 50 ft. lb.
  • Intermediate shaft sprocket bolt, 65 ft. lb.

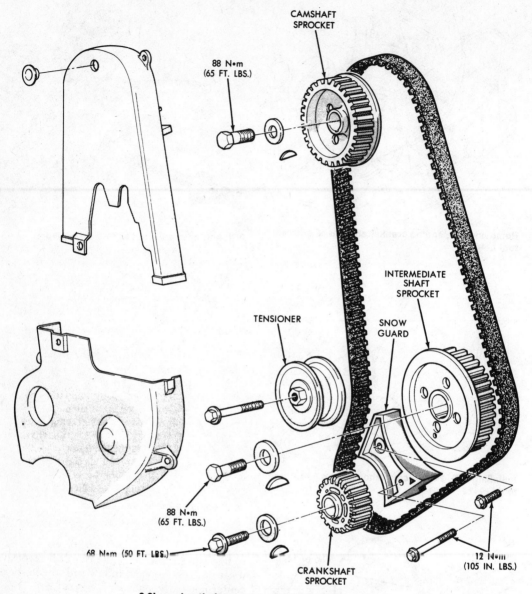

CAMSHAFT
SPROCKET

88 N•m
(65 FT. LBS.)

INTERMEDIATE
SHAFT
SPROCKET

TENSIONER

SNOW
GUARD

88 N•m
(65 FT. LBS.)

68 N•m (50 FT. LBS.)

12 N•m
(105 IN. LBS.)

CRANKSHAFT
SPROCKET

2.2L engine timing cover, sprockets, belt and seal

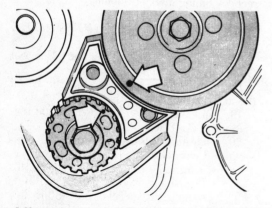

2.2L engine crankshaft and intermediate shaft timing mark alignment

Pistons and Connecting Rods

REMOVAL AND INSTALLATION

1. Follow the instructions under "Cylinder Head" removal and "Timing Belt" or "Timing Chain" removal.

2. Remove the oil pan as described later in this chapter.

3. This procedure is much easier performed with the engine out of the car.

4. Pistons should be removed in the order: 1-3-4-2. Turn the crankshaft until the piston to be removed is at the bottom of its stroke.

5. Place a cloth on the head of the piston to be removed and, using a ridge reamer, re-

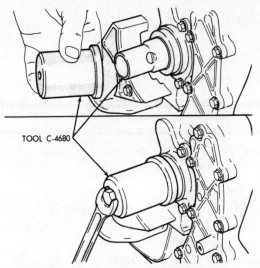

Installing the shaft seal on any of the 2.2L engine shafts

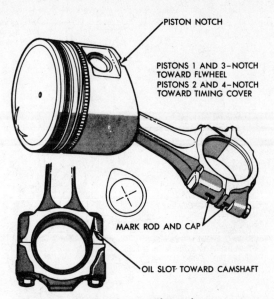

PISTON NOTCH

PISTONS 1 AND 3-NOTCH TOWARD FLWHEEL
PISTONS 2 AND 4-NOTCH TOWARD TIMING COVER

MARK ROD AND CAP

OIL SLOT TOWARD CAMSHAFT

1.6L engine piston and connecting rod

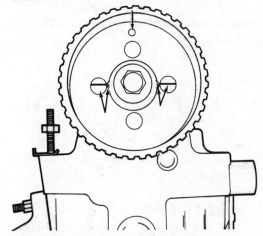

2.2L camshaft timing mark alignment

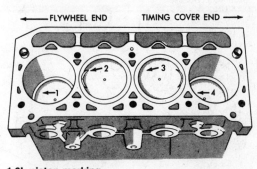

←FLYWHEEL END   TIMING COVER END →

1.6L piston marking

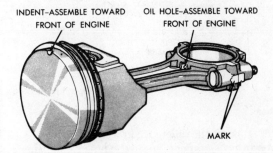

INDENT-ASSEMBLE TOWARD FRONT OF ENGINE   OIL HOLE-ASSEMBLE TOWARD FRONT OF ENGINE

MARK

2.2L engine piston and connecting rod

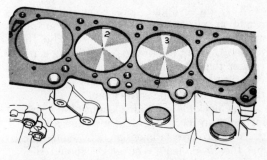

2.2L piston marking

move the deposits from the upper end of the cylinder bore.

NOTE: *Never remove more than 1/32 in. from the ring travel area when removing the ridges.*

6. Mark all connecting rod bearing caps so that they may be returned to their original locations in the engine. The connecting rod caps are marked with rectangular forge marks which must be mated during assembly and be installed on the intermediate shaft side of the engine. Mark all pistons so they can be returned to their original cylinders.

CAUTION: *Don't score the cylinder walls or the crankshaft journal.*

7. Using an internal micrometer, measure the bores across the thrust faces of the cylinder and parallel to the axis of the crankshaft at a minimum of four equally spaced locations. The bore must not be out-of-round by more than 0.005 in. and it must not taper more than 0.010

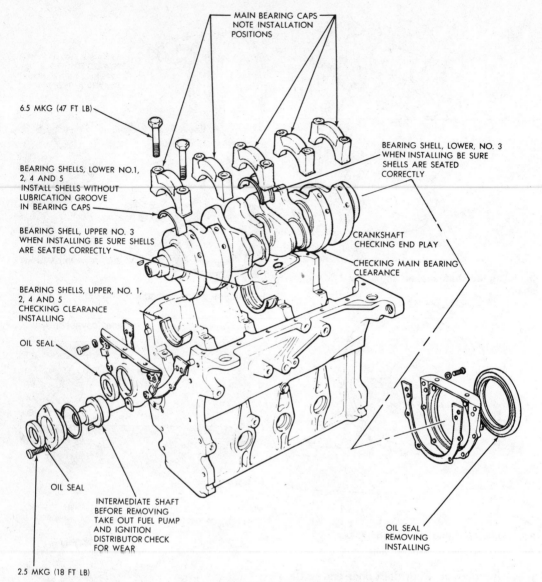

MAIN BEARING CAPS
NOTE INSTALLATION
POSITIONS

6.5 MKG (47 FT LB)

BEARING SHELLS, LOWER NO.1,
2, 4 AND 5
INSTALL SHELLS WITHOUT
LUBRICATION GROOVE
IN BEARING CAPS

BEARING SHELL, UPPER NO. 3
WHEN INSTALLING BE SURE SHELLS
ARE SEATED CORRECTLY

BEARING SHELLS, UPPER, NO. 1,
2, 4 AND 5
CHECKING CLEARANCE
INSTALLING

OIL SEAL

BEARING SHELL, LOWER, NO. 3
WHEN INSTALLING BE SURE
SHELLS ARE SEATED
CORRECTLY

CRANKSHAFT
CHECKING END PLAY

CHECKING MAIN BEARING
CLEARANCE

OIL SEAL

INTERMEDIATE SHAFT
BEFORE REMOVING
TAKE OUT FUEL PUMP
AND IGNITION
DISTRIBUTOR CHECK
FOR WEAR

OIL SEAL
REMOVING
INSTALLING

2.5 MKG (18 FT LB)

1.7L cylinder block and crankshaft

in. Taper is the difference in wear between two bore measurements in any cylinder. See the "Engine Rebuilding" section for complete details.

8. If the cylinder bore is in satisfactory condition, place each ring in the bore in turn and square it in the bore with the head of the piston. Measure the ring gap. If the ring gap is greater than the limit, get a new ring. If the ring gap is less than the limit, file the end of the ring to obtain the correct gap.

9. Check the ring side clearance by installing rings on the piston, and inserting a feeler gauge of the correct dimension between the ring and the lower land. The gauge should slide freely around the ring circumference without binding. Any wear will form a step on the lower land. Remove any pistons having high steps. Before checking the ring side clearance, be sure that the ring grooves are clean and free of carbon, sludge, or grit.

10. Piston rings should be installed so that their ends are at three equal spacings. Avoid installing the rings with their ends in line with the piston pin bosses and the thrust direction.

11. Install the pistons in their original bores, if you are reusing the same pistons. Install short lengths of rubber hose over the connecting rod bolts to prevent damage to the cylinder walls or rod journal.

12. Install a ring compressor over the rings on the piston. Lower the piston and rod assem-

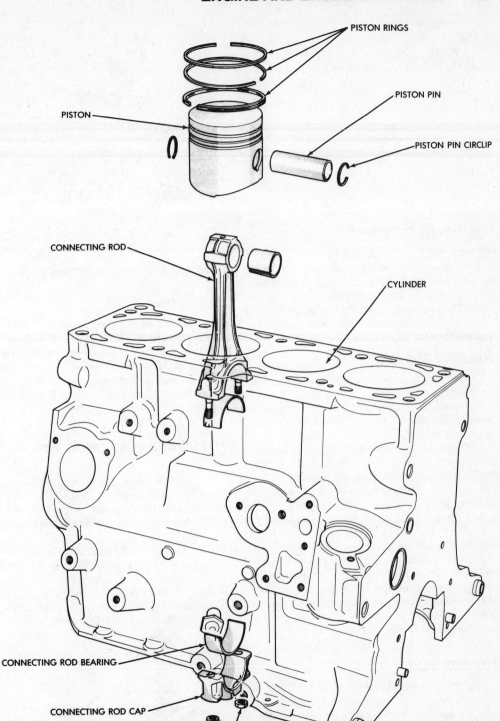

PISTON RINGS

PISTON

PISTON PIN

PISTON PIN CIRCLIP

CONNECTING ROD

CYLINDER

CONNECTING ROD BEARING

CONNECTING ROD CAP

4.5 mkg (33 ft lb)
OIL CONTACTING SURFACE

Piston and rings—all engines similar

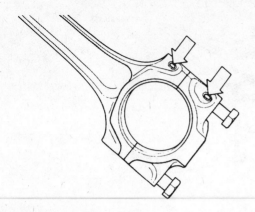

Connecting rod match marks

bly into the bore until the ring compressor contacts the block. Using a wooden hammer handle, push the piston into the bore while guiding the rod onto the journal.

NOTE: *On the 1.7 and 2.2L engines the arrow on the piston should face toward the front (drive belt) of the engine.*

CLEANING AND INSPECTION

1. Use a piston ring expander and remove the rings from the piston.

2. Clean the ring grooves using an appropriate cleaning tool, exercise care to avoid cutting too deeply.

3. Clean all varnish and carbon from the piston with a safe solvent. Do not use a wire brush or caustic solution on the pistons.

4. Inspect the pistons for scuffing, scoring, cracks, pitting or excessive ring groove wear. If wear is evident, the piston must be replaced.

5. Have the piston and connecting rod assembly checked by a machine shop for correct alignment, piston pin wear and piston diameter. If the piston has "collapsed" it will have to be replaced or knurled to restore original diameter. Connecting rod bushing replacement, piston pin fitting and piston changing can be handled by the machine shop.

CYLINDER BORE

Check the cylinder bore for wearing using a telescope gauge and a micrometer, measure the cylinder bore diameter perpendicular to the piston pin at a point 2½ inches below the top of the engine block. Measure the piston skirt perpendicular to the piston pin. The difference between the two measurements is the piston clearance. If the clearance is within specifications, finish honing or glaze breaking is all that is required. If clearance is excessive a slightly oversize piston may be required. If greatly oversize, the engine will have to be bored and .010 inch or larger oversized pistons installed.

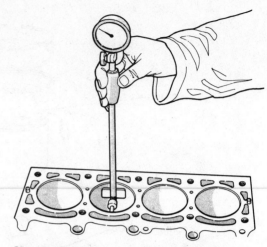

Checking the cylinder bore with bore gauge

PISTON PINS

The pin connecting the piston and connecting rod is press fitted. If too much free play develops take the piston assemblies to the machine shop and have oversize pins installed. Installing new rods or pistons requires the use of a press—have the machine shop handle the job for you.

FITTING AND POSITIONING PISTON RINGS

1. Take the new piston rings and compress them, one at a time into the cylinder that they will be used in. Press the ring about one inch below the top of the cylinder block using an inverted piston.

2. Use a feeler gauge and measure the distance between the ends of the ring, this is called, measuring the ring end-gap. Compare the reading to the one called for in the specifications table. File the ends of the ring with a fine file to obtain necessary clearance.

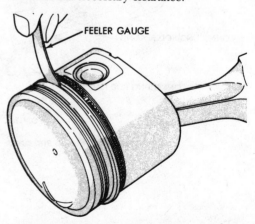

FEELER GAUGE

Checking piston ring side clearance

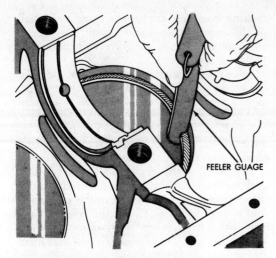

Checking piston ring end gap

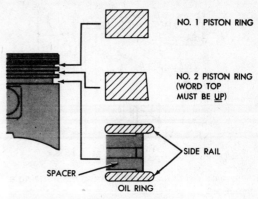

Piston ring installation—1.6L engine

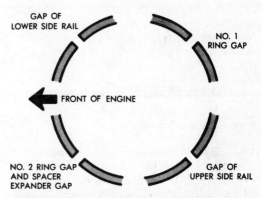

Piston ring end gap positioning—2.2L engine

NOTE: *If inadequate ring end-gap is utilized ring breakage will result.*

3. Inspect the ring grooves on the piston for excessive wear or taper. If necessary have the grooves recut for use with a standard ring and spacer. The machine shop can handle the job for you.

4. Check the ring groove by rolling the new piston ring around the groove to check for burrs or carbon deposits. If any are found, remove with a fine file. Hold the ring in the groove and measure side clearance with a feeler gauge. If clearance is excessive, spacer(s) will have to be added.

NOTE: *Always add spacers above the piston ring.*

5. Install the rings on the piston, lower ring first using a ring installing tool. Consult the instruction sheet that comes with the rings to be sure they are installed with the correct side up. A mark on the ring usually faces upward.

6. When installing oil rings; first, install the ring in the groove. Hold the ends of the ring butted together (they must not overlap) and install the bottom rail (scraper) with the end about one inch away from the butted end of the control ring. Install the top rail about an inch away from the butted end of the control but on the opposite side from the lower rail.

7. Install the two compression rings.

8. Consult the illustration with piston ring set instruction sheet for ring positioning, arrange the rings as shown, install a ring compressor and insert the piston and rod assembly into the engine.

Crankshaft and Bearings

1. Rod bearings can be installed when the pistons have been removed for servicing (rings etc) or, in most cases, while the engine is still in the car. Rearing replacement, however, is far easier with the engine out of the car and disassembled.

2. For in car service, remove the oil pan, spark plugs and front cover if necessary. Turn the engine until the connecting rod to be ser-

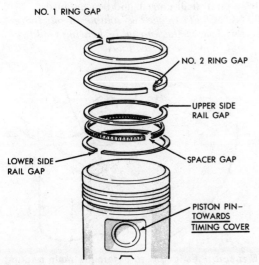

Piston ring positioning—1.6L engine

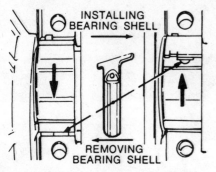

Remove or install the upper bearing insert using a roll-out pin

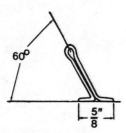

Home-made bearing roll-out pin

viced is at the bottom of it's travel. Remove the bearing cap, place two pieces of rubber hose over the rod cap bolts and push the piston and rod assembly up the cylinder bore until enough room is gained for bearing insert removal. Take care not to push the rod assembly up too far or the top ring will engage the cylinder ridge or come out of the cylinder and require head removal for reinstallation.

3. Clean the rod journal, the connecting rod end and the bearing cap after removing the old bearing inserts. Install the new inserts in the rod and bearing cap, lubricate them with oil. Position the rod over the crankshaft journal and install the rod caps. Make sure the cap and rod numbers match, torque the rod nuts to specifications.

4. Main bearings may be replaced while the engine is still in the car by "rolling" them out and in.

5. Special roll-out pins are available from automotive parts houses or can be fabricated from a cotter pin. The roll out pin fits in the oil hole of the main bearing journal. When the crankshaft is rotated opposite the direction of the bearing lock tab, the pin engages the end of the bearing and "rolls" out the insert.

6. Remove main bearing cap and roll out upper bearing insert. Remove insert from main bearing cap. Clean the inside of the bearing cap and crankshaft journal.

7. Lubricate and roll upper insert into position, make sure the lock tab is anchored and the insert is not "cocked." Install the lower

bearing insert into the cap; lubricate and install on the engine. Make sure the main bearing cap is installed facing in the correct direction and torque to specifications.

8. With the engine out of the car. Remove the intake manifold, cylinder head, front cover, timing gears and/or chain, oil pan, oil pump and flywheel.

9. Remove the piston and rod assemblies. Remove the main bearing caps after marking them for position and direction.

10. Remove the crankshaft bearing inserts and rear main oil seal. Clean the engine block and cap bearing saddles. Clean the crankshaft and inspect for wear. Check the bearing journals with a micrometer for out-of-round condition and to determine what size rod and main bearing inserts to install.

11. Install the main bearing upper inserts and rear main oil seal half into the engine block.

12. Lubricate the bearing inserts and the crankshaft journals. Slowly and carefully lower the crankshaft into position.

13. Install the bearing inserts and rear main seal into the bearing caps, install the caps working from the middle out. Torque cap bolts to specifications in stages, rotate the crankshaft after each torque stage.

14. Remove bearing caps, one at a time and check the oil clearance with Plastigage.® Reinstall if clearance is within specifications. Check the crankshaft end-play, if within specifications install connecting rod and piston assemblies with new rod bearing inserts. Check connecting rod bearing oil clearance and rod side play, if correct and assemble the rest of the engine.

BEARING OIL CLEARANCE

Remove cap from the bearing to be checked. Using a clean, dry rag, thoroughly clean all oil from crankshaft journal and bearing insert.

NOTE: *Plastigage® is soluble in oil; therefore, oil on the journal or bearing could result in erroneous readings.*

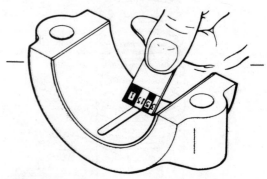

Measure Plastigage® to determine main bearing clearance

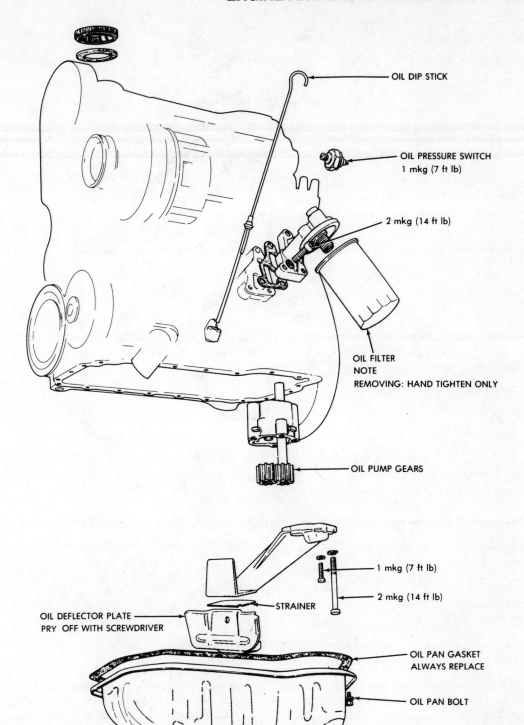

OIL DIP STICK

OIL PRESSURE SWITCH
1 mkg (7 ft lb)

2 mkg (14 ft lb)

OIL FILTER
NOTE
REMOVING: HAND TIGHTEN ONLY

OIL PUMP GEARS

1 mkg (7 ft lb)

2 mkg (14 ft lb)

STRAINER

OIL DEFLECTOR PLATE
PRY OFF WITH SCREWDRIVER

OIL PAN GASKET
ALWAYS REPLACE

OIL PAN BOLT

3 mkg (22 ft lb)

1.7L engine lubricating system components

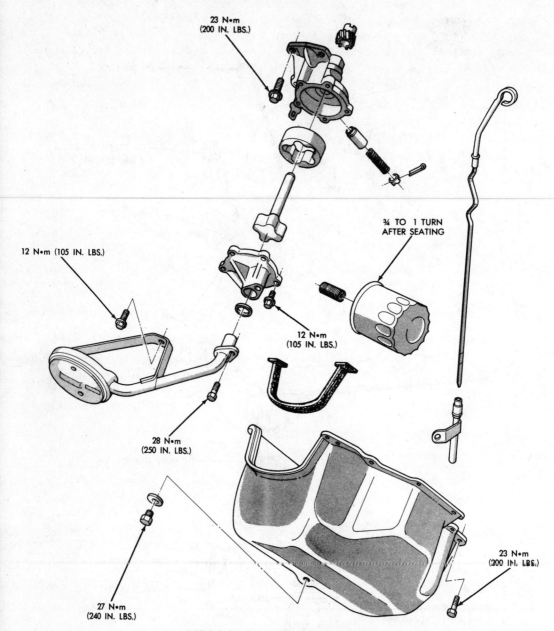

23 N•m
(200 IN. LBS.)

12 N•m (105 IN. LBS.)

¾ TO 1 TURN
AFTER SEATING

12 N•m
(105 IN. LBS.)

28 N•m
(250 IN. LBS.)

23 N•m
(200 IN. LBS.)

27 N•m
(240 IN. LBS.)

2.2L lubricating system components

Place a piece of Plastigage® along the full width of the insert, reinstall cap, and torque to specifications.

NOTE: *Specifications are given in the engine specifications earlier in this chapter.*

Remove bearing cap, and determine clearance by comparing width of Plastigage® to the scale on Plastigage envelope. Journal taper is determined by comparing width of the Plastigage® strip near its ends. Rotate crankshaft 90° and retest, to determine journal eccentricity.

NOTE: *Do not rotate crankshaft with Plastigage® installed. If bearing insert and journal appear intact, and are within tolerances, no further main bearing service is required. If bearing or journal appear defective, cause of failure should be determined before replacement.*

CRANKSHAFT END-PLAY/CONNECTING ROD SIDE PLAY

Place a pry bar between a main bearing cap and crankshaft casting taking care not to damage any journals. Pry backward and forward measure the distance between the thrust bearing (center main 3) and crankshaft with a feeler gauge. Compare reading with specifications. If too great a clearance is determined, a larger thrust bearing or crank machining may be required. Check with an automotive machine shop for their advice.

Connecting rod clearance between the rod and crankthrow casting can be checked with a feeler gauge. Pry the rod carefully to one side as far as possible and measure the distance on the other side of the rod.

CRANKSHAFT REPAIRS

If a journal is damaged on the crankshaft, repair is possible by having the crankshaft machined, after removal from engine to a standard undersize. Consult the machine shop for their advice.

Oil Pan

REMOVAL AND INSTALLATION

1. Drain the oil pan.
2. Support the pan and remove the attaching bolts.
3. Lower the pan and discard the gaskets.
4. Clean all gasket surfaces thoroughly and install the pan using gasket sealer and a new gasket.
5. Torque the pan bolts to 7 ft. lbs. on the 1.6L, 1.7L and 17 ft. lb. on the 2.2L.
6. Refill the pan, start the engine, and check for leaks.

Oil Pump

REMOVAL AND INSTALLATION

1.6L Engine

1. Drain the crankcase oil and remove the oil filter.
2. While holding the cover and housing together, remove the seven mounting bolts and pull the assembly from the engine block.
3. To install, seal all the oil pump attaching bolt threads with an oil resistant sealer.
4. Install new gaskets on the pump, housing to block and housing to cover.
5. Place the cover on the housing and insert two bolts to maintain alignment.
6. Install the housing into the block and rotate the assembly until the driving gear shaft engages the slot in the driveshaft.
7. Align the bolt pattern to the block, install the remaining five bolts and tighten to 9 ft. lbs.
8. Install the oil filter and refill the crankcase.

1.7L and 2.2L Engines

1. Remove the oil pan.
2. Remove the two pump mounting bolts.

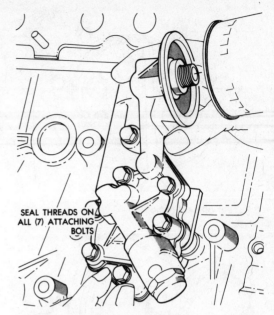

SEAL THREADS ON ALL (7) ATTACHING BOLTS

Oil pump assembly—1.6L engine

3. Pull the oil pump down and out of the engine.
4. Installation is the reverse of removal. Torque pump mounting bolts to 14 ft. lbs. on the 1.7L and 9 ft. lb on the 2.2L.

Rear Main Seal

REMOVAL AND INSTALLATION

The rear main seal is located in a housing on the rear of the block. To replace the seal it is necessary to remove the engine.

1. Remove the transmission and flywheel.
CAUTION: *Before removing the transmission, align the dimple on the flywheel with the pointer on the flywheel housing. The transmission will not mate with the engine during installation unless this alignment is observed.*

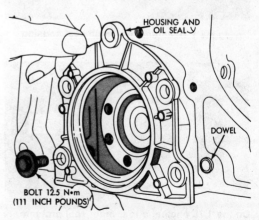

HOUSING AND OIL SEAL

DOWEL

BOLT 12.5 N•m (111 INCH POUNDS)

Rear main oil seal housing—1.6L engine

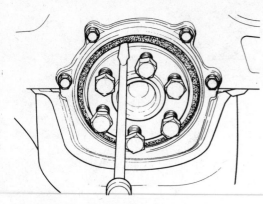

2.2L rear oil seal removal

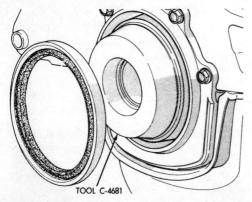

TOOL C-4681

2.2L rear main oil seal installation

Prying the 1.7L engine rear main seal housing

On the 1.7L engine, a rear main seal protector is needed when installing the new seal

2. Very carefully, pry the old seal out of the support ring with a suitable tool.

3. Coat the new seal with clean engine oil and press it into place with a flat piece of metal. Take great care not to scratch the seal or crankshaft.

4. Install the flywheel and transmission.

ENGINE COOLING

The cooling system consists of a radiator, overflow tank, water pump, thermostat, coolant temperature switch, electric fan and radiator fan switch. The use of an electric fan is necessitated by the transversely mounted engine. A radiator bypass system is used for faster warmup.

Radiator
REMOVAL AND INSTALLATION

1. Move the temperature selector to full on.
2. Open the radiator drain cock.
3. When the coolant reserve tank is empty, remove the radiator cap.
4. Remove the hoses.
5. Remove the upper and lower mounting brackets.
6. Remove the shroud.
7. Remove the fan motor attaching bolts.
8. Remove the top radiator attaching bolts.
9. Remove the bottom radiator attaching bolts.
10. Lift radiator from engine compartment.
11. Installation is the reverse of removal.

Water Pump
REMOVAL AND INSTALLATION

1.6L Engine

1. Remove the radiator cap and drain the cooling system.
2. Remove the drive belts.
3. Disconnect the water pump to block coolant hose at the pump.
4. Remove the water pump pulley.
5. Remove the four water pump to crankcase extension bolts and remove the water pump assembly.
6. Installation is the reverse of removal. Be sure to use a new gasket.

1.7L Engine

1. Drain the cooling system.
2. Remove the drive belts.
3. Remove the water pump pulley.
4. Unbolt the compressor and/or air pump brackets from the water pump and secure them out of the way.

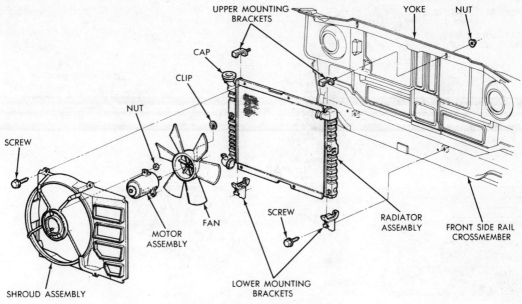

Radiator, fan and shroud—typical

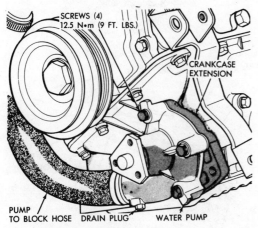

1.6L engine water pump

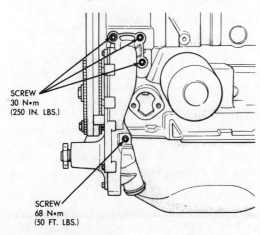

2.2L engine water pump

5. Position the bypass hose lower clamp in the center of the hose and disconnect the heater hose.

6. Unbolt and remove the water pump. Discard the gasket and clean the gasket surfaces.

7. Installation is the reverse of removal. Torque the water pump bolts to 25 ft. lbs., the alternator adjusting bolt to 30–50 ft. lbs.; the pulley bolts to 85–125 in. lbs.

2.2L Engine

1. Drain the cooling system.
2. Remove the upper radiator hose.
3. Without disconnecting any hoses, remove the air conditioning compressor from its brackets and set it out of the way.
4. Remove the alternator.
5. Disconnect the lower hose, the bypass hose and then, unbolt and remove the water pump.
6. Installation is the reverse of removal. Torque the three upper bolts to 20 ft. lb.; the lower bolt to 50 ft. lb.

Thermostat

REMOVAL AND INSTALLATION

1. Drain the cooling system to a level below the thermostat.
2. Remove the hose(s) from the thermostat housing.
3. Remove the thermostat housing.
4. Remove the thermostat and discard the gasket. Clean the gasket surfaces thoroughly.
5. Using a new gasket, position the ther-

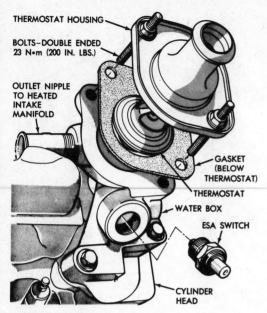

1.6L engine thermostat and water box

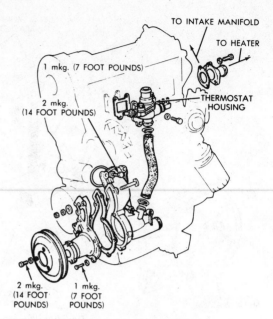

1.7L engine water pump and thermostat

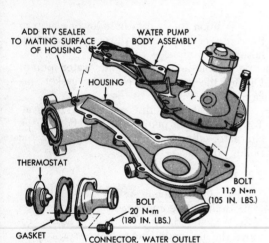

2.2L engine thermostat and water pump

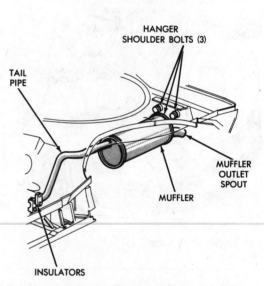

Tail pipe with muffler, typical

mostat and install the housing and bolts. Make sure that the thermostat is seated properly.

6. Refill the cooling system.

EXHAUST SYSTEM

Exhaust Pipes, Mufflers and Tailpipes

REMOVAL

1. Raise and support the car on jackstands.
2. Apply penetrating oil such as Liquid Wrench®, WD-40®, CRC®, or equivalent to all nuts, clamps and components being removed. Let stand while the penetrants act.

3. If the tail pipe is integral with the muffler, (most original pipes), cut the tail pipe close to the muffler with a hacksaw or pipe cutter.

4. Remove all clamps and supports from the exhaust system to aid in proper alignment of components when installing aftermarket parts.

5. When removing the tail pipe, raise and support the rear of the car to take the weight off of the springs and to provide clearance for parts removal.

6. Thoroughly clean the mating ends of all parts with a wire brush, making sure that they are free of rust, dirt and scale. Discard all worn, rusted or broken clamps and insulators

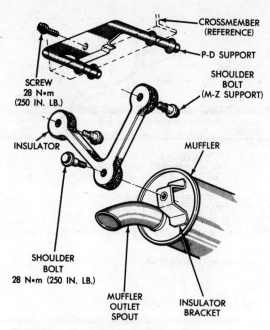

Tail pipe and muffler support insulator

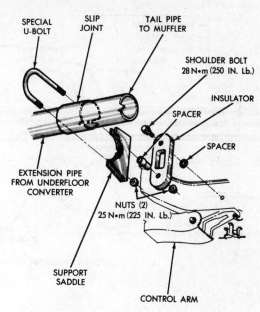

Exhaust pipe extension assembly-to-tail pipe

INSTALLATION

1. Assemble all parts, clamps, supports and insulators loosely, to provide for proper alignment.

2. Beginning at the front of the system, align and clamp each part maintaining proper clearance between parts and body members.

3. Tighten all clamps and supports.

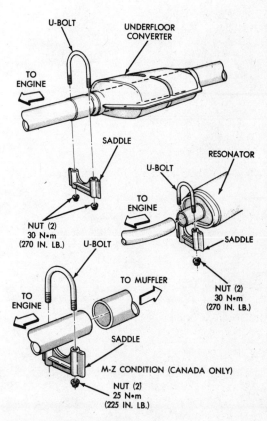

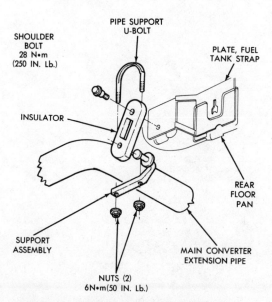

Underfloor converter extension pipe support

Mid-connection slip joint

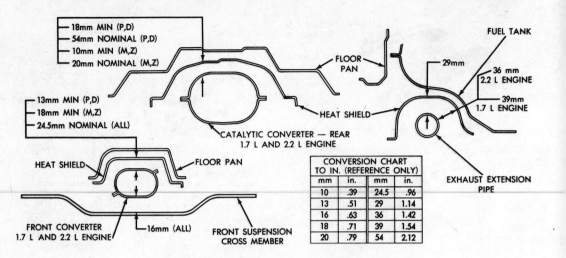

- 18mm MIN (P,D)
- 54mm NOMINAL (P,D)
- 10mm MIN (M,Z)
- 20mm NOMINAL (M,Z)

FLOOR PAN

FUEL TANK

29mm

36 mm 2.2 L ENGINE

39mm 1.7 L ENGINE

- 13mm MIN (P,D)
- 18mm MIN (M,Z)
- 24.5mm NOMINAL (ALL)

HEAT SHIELD

CATALYTIC CONVERTER — REAR 1.7 L AND 2.2 L ENGINE

HEAT SHIELD

FLOOR PAN

EXHAUST EXTENSION PIPE

FRONT CONVERTER 1.7 L AND 2.2 L ENGINE

16mm (ALL)

FRONT SUSPENSION CROSS MEMBER

CONVERSION CHART TO IN. (REFERENCE ONLY)			
mm	in.	mm	in.
10	.39	24.5	.96
13	.51	29	1.14
16	.63	36	1.42
18	.71	39	1.54
20	.79	54	2.12

Proper exhaust system component clearances

Emission Controls and Fuel Systems

4

EMISSION CONTROLS

Several different systems are used on each car. Most require no service and those which may require service also require sophisticated equipment for testing purposes. Following is a brief description of each system.

Catalytic Converter

Two catalysts are used in a small one located just after the exhaust manifold and a larger one located under the car body. Catalysts promote complete oxidation of exhaust gases through the effect of a platinum coated mass in the catalyst shell. Two things act to destroy the catalyst, functionally: excessive heat and leaded gas. Ex-

cessive heat during misfiring and prolonged testing with the ignition system in any way altered is the most common occurrence. Test procedures should be accomplished as quickly as possible, and the car should not be driven when misfiring is noted.

CAUTION: *Operation of any type including idling should be avoided if engine misfiring occurs. Alteration or deterioration of the ignition system or fuel system must be avoided to prevent overheating the catalytic converter.*

All converter equipped cars are equipped with a special fuel filler neck that prevents the use of any filler nozzle except those designed for unleaded fuel. As a reminder to the operator, a decal "UNLEADED GASOLINE" is located near the fuller neck, and on the dash.

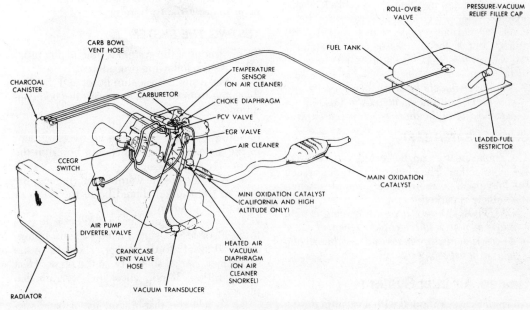

Emission control system

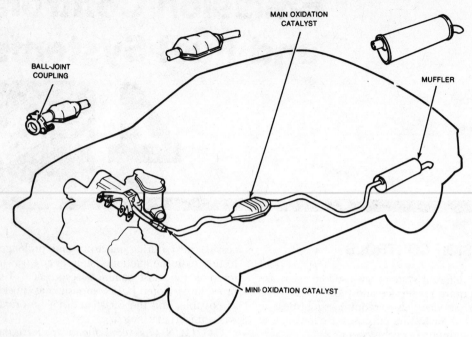

Exhaust system with catalytic converter

Electric Choke System

An electric heater and switch are sealed within the choke system, with electricity supplied from the oil pressure sending unit. A minimum of 4 psi oil pressure is required to close the contacts and send current to the choke control switch.

The electric choke unit is located on the side of the carburetor. The initial setting is made by the manufacturer, but it is adjustable. The thermostat housing mark is positioned opposite a specified reference line on the black plastic adapter, after which, the 3 screws are tightened. No normal service of this system is required, but it, for any reason, the 3 retaining screws are loosened, the adjustment must be made again.

NOTE: *If the choke is removed, be careful you don't lose the small plastic bushing located between the thermostat loop and pin.*

CHOKE HEATER TEST

The choke heater can be tested with a direct B+ connection. The choke valve should reach the fully open position within 5 minutes, when the vehicle is parked.

CAUTION: *Do not operate the engine with a loss of power to the choke. This will cause a very rich mixture and result in abnormally high exhaust temperatures.*

Heated Air Inlet System

All engines are equipped with a vacuum device located in the carburetor air cleaner intake. A small door is operated by a vacuum diaphragm and a thermostatic spring. When the air temperature outside is 40°F or lower, the door will block off air entering from outside and allow air channelled from the exhaust manifold area to enter the intake. This air is heated by the hot manifold. At 65°F or above, the door fully blocks off the heated air. At temperatures in between, the door is operated in intermediate positions. During acceleration the door is controlled by engine vacuum to allow the maximum amount of air to enter the carburetor.

TESTING THE SYSTEM

To determine if the system is functioning properly, use the following procedures.

1. Make sure all vacuum hoses and the flexible pipe from the heat stove are in good condition.

2. On a cold engine and the outside air temperature less than 50°F, the heat control door in the air cleaner snorkel should be up in the up or "Heat On" position.

3. With the engine warmed and running, the door in the snorkel should be in the down or "Heat Off" position.

4. Remove the air cleaner. Allow it to cool to 50°F, or less. Using a hand vacuum pump, apply 20 in./Hg to the sensor. The door in the air cleaner snorkel should be in the up or "Heat On" position. If not, check the vacuum diaphragm.

5. To test the diaphragm, use a hand vacuum pump to apply about 20 in./Hg to the dia-

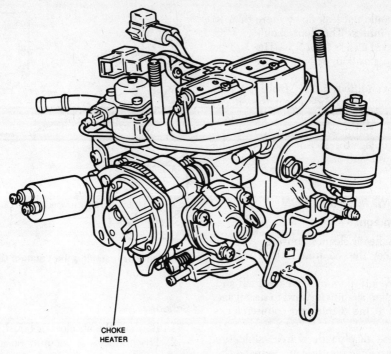

CHOKE
HEATER

Choke heater on carburetor

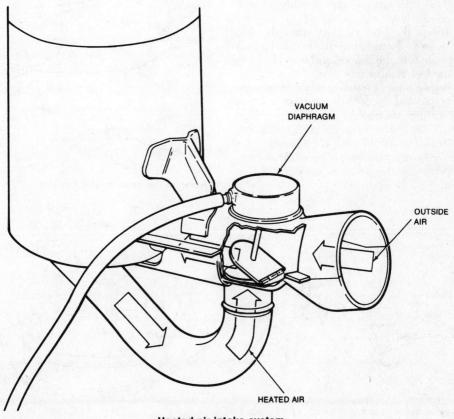

VACUUM
DIAPHRAGM

OUTSIDE
AIR

HEATED AIR

Heated air intake system

phragm. It should not leak down more than 10 in./Hg in 3 minutes. The door should not lift from the snorkel at less than 2 in./Hg, and be in the full up position with no more than 4 in./Hg.

6. If these conditions in Step 6 are not met, replace the diaphragm and repeat the checks in Steps 2 and 3. If the vacuum diaphragm performs properly, but proper temperature is not maintained, replace the sensor and repeat the checks in Steps 2 and 3.

REMOVAL AND INSTALLATION

Vacuum Diaphragm

1. Remove the air cleaner housing.
2. Disconnect the vacuum hose from the diaphragm.
3. Drill through the metal (welded) tab and tip the diaphragm slightly forward to disengage the lock. Rotate the diaphragm counterclockwise.
4. When the diaphragm is free, slide the complete assembly to one side and remove the operating rod from the heat control door.
5. With the diaphragm removed, check the door for freedom of operation. When the door is raised, it should fall freely when released. If not, check the snorkel walls for interference, or check the hinge pin.
6. Insert the operating rod into the heat control door. Position the diaphragm tangs in the openings in the snorkel and turn clockwise until the lock is engaged.
7. Apply 9 in. of vacuum to the diaphragm hose nipple and check to be sure the heat control door operates freely.

CAUTION: *Manually operating the heat control door could cock the operating rod and restrict proper operation of the system.*

8. Assemble the air cleaner and install it on the car. Test the operation.

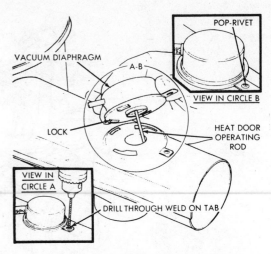

Removing or installing the vacuum diagraphm

Sensor

1. Remove the air cleaner housing.
2. Disconnect the vacuum hoses from the sensor and remove the retainer clips. Discard

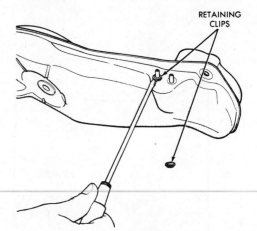

Remove the sensor retaining clip

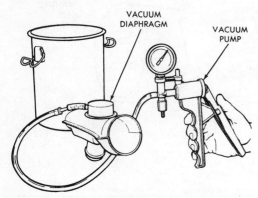

Testing vacuum diaphragm with hand vacuum pump

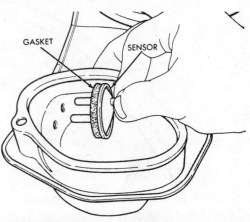

Install the gasket and sensor

the old clips; new ones are supplied with a new sensor.

3. Remove the sensor and gasket.

4. Install a new gasket and sensor. Hold the sensor in place and install new retainer clips. Be sure the gasket forms a tight air seal. Do not attempt to adjust the sensor.

Exhaust Gas Recirculation System

This system reduces the amount of oxides of nitrogen in the exhaust by allowing a predetermined amount of hot exhaust gases to recirculate and dilute the incoming fuel/air mixture. The principal components of the system are the EGR valve and the Coolant Control Exhaust Gas Recirculation Valve (CCEGR). The former is located in the intake manifold and directly regulates the flow of exhaust gases into the intake. The latter is located in the thermostat housing and overrides the EGR valve when coolant temperature is below 125°F.

Ported vacuum uses a slot in the carburetor throttle body which is exposed to an increasing percentage of manifold vacuum as the throttle opens. The throttle bore port is connected to the EGR valve. The flow rate of recirculation is dependent on manifold vacuum, throttle position and exhaust gas back pressure. Recycling at wide open throttle is eliminated, by calibrating the valve opening point above the manifold vacuum available at wide open throttle, which provides maximum performance.

3. Allow the engine to idle in Neutral for 70 seconds, with the throttle closed. Abruptly accelerate the engine to about 2000 rpm, but not more than 3000 rpm.

4. Visible movement of the EGR valve stem should occur during this operation. Movement can be seen by the position of the groove on the EGR valve stem. You may have to repeat the operation several times to definitely ascertain movement.

Inspect the EGR valve for deposits, particularly around the poppet and seat area. If deposits amount to more than a thin film, the valve should be cleaned. Apply a liberal amount of manifold heat control valve solvent to the poppet and seat area and allow the deposits to soften. Open the valve with an external vacuum source and remove the deposits, with a suitable sharp tool.

CAUTION: *During the cleaning operation, do not spill solvent on the valve diaphragm or it will cause failure of the diaphragm. Do not push on the diaphragm to operate the valve; use an external vacuum source.*

An alternate procedure to this messy operation is to simply replace the valve if it is extremely clogged.

NOTE: *A new EGR valve was used on models built after February 20, 1978. Vehicles built prior to the change can increase fuel economy slightly by using the new EGR valve (part no. 4131219) and gasket (part no. 3671425).*

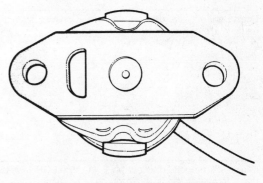

Bottom view (poppet seat area) of EGR valve

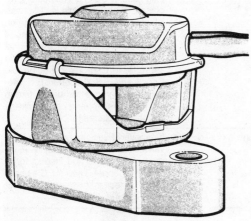

EGR valve

TESTING THE SYSTEM

EGR Valve

1. Inspect all hose connections between the carburetor, intake manifold and EGR valve.

2. Check the valve with the engine warmed and running.

CCEGR Valve

This valve is mounted in the thermostat housing and is color coded yellow for its calibrated temperature of 120–130°F. During warm-up, when engine coolant temperature exceeds 125°F, the valve opens, allowing vacuum to reach the EGR valve, causing recirculation of exhaust gasses.

1. Remove the valve from the housing.

2. Place it an ice bath below 40°F. so that the threaded portion of the valve is covered.

EGR Diagnosis

NOTE: *All tests must be made with fully warm engine running continuously for at least two minutes*

Condition	Possible Cause	Correction
EGR valve stem does not move on system test.	(a) Check, leaking, disconnected or plugged hoses.	(a) Verify correct hose connections and leak check and confirm that all hoses are open. If defective hoses are found, replace hose harness.
	(b) Defective EGR valve.	(b) Disconnect hose harness from EGR valve. Connect external vacuum source, 10 in./Hg or greater, to valve diaphragm while checking valve movement. If no valve movement occurs, replace valve. If valve opens, approx. ⅛" travel, clamp off supply hose to check for diaphragm leakage. Valve should remain open 30 seconds or longer. If leakage occurs, replace valve. If valve is satisfactory, evaluate control system.
EGR valve stem does not move on system test, operates normally on external vacuum source.	(a) Defective thermal control valve.	(a) Disconnect CCEGR valve and bypass the valve with a short length of ³⁄₁₆" tubing. If normal movement of the EGR valve is restored, replace the thermal valve.
	(b) Defective control system—Plugged passages.	(b) Ported Vacuum Control System: Remove carburetor and inspect port (slot type) in throttle bore and associated vacuum passages in carburetor throttle body including limiting orifice at hose end of passages. Use suitable solvent to remove deposits and check for flow with light air pressure. Normal operation should be restored to ported vacuum control EGR system.
Engine will not idle, dies out on return to idle or idle is very rough or slow. EGR valve open at idle.	(a) Control system defective.	(a) Disconnect hose from EGR valve and plug hose. If idle is unsatisfactory, replace EGR valve. If idle is still unsatisfactory, install a vacuum guage on ported signal tap and observe gauge for vacuum reading. If vacuum signal is greater than 1 inch/Hg, check idle set (refer to Carburetor, Engine Idle Check and Set Procedure). If vacuum is ok, remove carburetor, Group 14, Fuel System, and check linkage and throttle blades for binding.
Engine will not idle, dies out on return to idle or idle is rough or slow. EGR valve closed at idle.	(a) High EGR valve leakage in closed position.	(a) If removal of vacuum hose from EGR valve does not correct rough idle, remove EGR valve and inspect to insure that poppet is seated. Clean deposits if necessary or replace EGR valve if found defective.

3. Connect a hand vacuum pump to the valve nipple corresponding to the yellow stripe hose. Apply 10 in. vacuum. There should be no more than 1 in. drop in vacuum in one (1) minute. If the vacuum reading falls off, the valve should be replaced.

Air Injection System

This systems job is to reduce carbon monoxide and hydrocarbons to required levels. The system adds a controlled amount of air to exhaust gases, via an air pump and induction tubes,

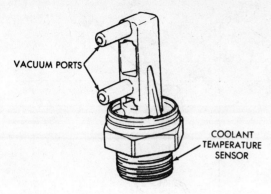

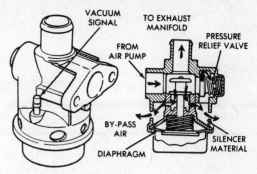

AIR pump diverter valve

CCEGR valve

causing oxidation of the gases. The California and other American cars, introduces air through the head at the exhaust port. The system is composed of an air pump, a combination diverter/pressure-relief valve, hoses, a check valve to protect the hoses from exhaust gas, and an injection tube.

NOTE: *The system is not noiseless. A certain squeal is present in pump operation.*

SERVICING THE SYSTEM

For proper operation of the system, the drive belt should be in good condition and properly tensioned. The air pump is not a serviceable item; if necessary, it should be replaced.

NOTE: *Do not attempt to disassemble the pump or clamp it in a vise.*

Complaints of road load surge at about 40–60 mph on 1978 Federal models equipped with manual transmission and AIR pump can be corrected, in most cases, by installing a kit (Part No. 4131207).

The kit consists of a vacuum bleed, an idle air bleed, a carburetor ID tag, main metering jet, air horn gasket and hose routing label.

1. Remove the carburetor air horn.
2. Replace the primary main metering jet with the one supplied in the kit.

3. Install the new carburetor air horn gasket.
4. Install the air horn.
5. Install the idle air bleed in the opening next to the primary choke housing. It should be installed flush with the surface. Use a driver (brass drift) larger than the diameter of the bleed fitting.
6. Install the vacuum bleed between the EGR ported vacuum nipple of the carburetor and install the CCEGR valve hose in place of the existing plastic reducer. The large end of the vacuum bleed should be toward the carburetor.
7. Install the new hose routing label over the old one.
8. Install the new carburetor ID tag under the air horn screw in place of the old one.

REMOVAL AND INSTALLATION

Air Pump

1. Disconnect and tag the hoses from the pump.
2. Loosen the air pump idler pivot and adjusting bolts. Remove the drive belt.
3. Remove the air pump pulley and attaching bolts.
4. Remove the air pump.
5. Installation is the reverse of removal. Tension the drive belt (see Chapter 1).

Diverter Valve

Servicing the diverter valve is limited to replacement. If the valve fails it will become extremely noisy. If air escapes from the silencer at idle speed, either the diverter valve or the relief valve has failed and the entire valve assembly should be replaced.

1. Remove the air and vacuum hoses.
2. Remove the 2 screws holding the diverter valve to the mounting flange and remove the valve.
3. Remove the old gasket.

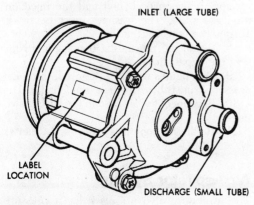

AIR pump

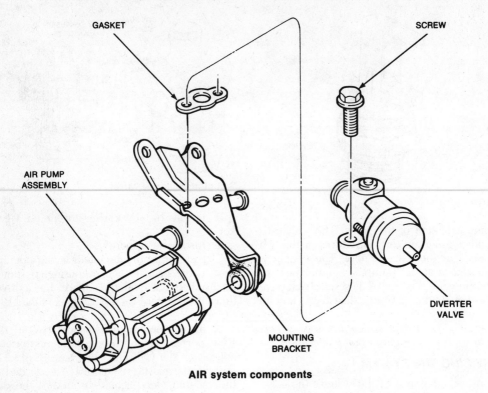

AIR system components

4. Installation is the reverse of removal. Use a new gasket and connect the hoses properly.

Check Valve

The check valve is not repairable; if necessary to service it, replace it with a new one. The valve can be tested by removing the hose from the valve inlet tube. If exhaust gasses escape from the inlet tube the valve has failed. On California cars, if the tube nut joint is leaking, retorque the nut to 25–35 ft. lbs. If the adapter to the exhaust manifold joint is leaking, retorque the connection to a maximum of 40 ft. lbs. On Canadian cars, if the air injection tube to the head joint is leaking, retorque the hollow bolts to 20 ft. lbs.

CALIFORNIA CARS

1. Release the clamp and disconnect the air hose from the check valve.
2. Remove the tube nut holding the injection tube to the exhaust manifold.
3. Remove the injection tube from the engine.
4. Installation is the reverse of removal.

CANADIAN CARS

1. Release the clamp and remove the air hose from the check valve inlet.
2. On A/C cars, remove the air conditioning compressor from the mount.

CAUTION: *Do not disconnect any A/C system hoses.*

Remove the 4 isolated rubber compressor mounting bracket bolts and the compressor-to-cylinder head bolt. Set the compressor aside and keep it upright.

3. Drain the cooling system to a level below the thermostat housing.
4. Remove the housing from the bypass hose.
5. Remove the 4 hollow bolts holding the injection tube assembly to the cylinder head.
6. Install the injection tube assembly on the cylinder head. The 4 copper washers must be used between the tube assembly and the cylinder head.
7. Install the 4 hollow bolts with copper washers between each bolt and the injection tube assembly. The washers must be used. Torque the bolts to 20 ft. lbs.
8. Install the thermostat housing and connect the bypass hose.
9. On engines with A/C, reinstall the compressor. Adjust the drive belt (see Chapter 1).
10. Reconnect the air hose to the check valve inlet.
11. Refill the cooling system (see Chapter 1).

Air Aspirator System

The aspirator valve utilizes exhaust pressure pulsation to draw clean air from the inside of

CHILTON'S
FUEL ECONOMY
& TUNE-UP TIPS

Tune-up • Spark Plug Diagnosis • Emission Controls

Fuel System • Cooling System • Tires and Wheels

General Maintenance

CHILTON'S FUEL ECONOMY & TUNE-UP TIPS

Fuel economy is important to everyone, no matter what kind of vehicle you drive. The maintenance-minded motorist can save both money and fuel using these tips and the periodic maintenance and tune-up procedures in this Repair and Tune-Up Guide.

There are more than 130,000,000 cars and trucks registered for private use in the United States. Each travels an average of 10-12,000 miles per year, and, and in total they consume close to 70 billion gallons of fuel each year. This represents nearly ⅔ of the oil imported by the United States each year. The Federal government's goal is to reduce consumption 10% by 1985. A variety of methods are either already in use or under serious consideration, and they all affect you driving and the cars you will drive. In addition to "down-sizing", the auto industry is using or investigating the use of electronic fuel delivery, electronic engine controls and alternative engines for use in smaller and lighter vehicles, among other alternatives to meet the federally mandated Corporate Average Fuel Economy (CAFE) of 27.5 mpg by 1985. The government, for its part, is considering rationing, mandatory driving curtailments and tax increases on motor vehicle fuel in an effort to reduce consumption. The government's goal of a 10% reduction could be realized — and further government regulation avoided — if every private vehicle could use just 1 less gallon of fuel per week.

How Much Can You Save?

Tests have proven that almost anyone can make at least a 10% reduction in fuel consumption through regular maintenance and tune-ups. When a major manufacturer of spark plugs sur-

TUNE-UP

1. Check the cylinder compression to be sure the engine will really benefit from a tune-up and that it is capable of producing good fuel economy. A tune-up will be wasted on an engine in poor mechanical condition.

2. Replace spark plugs regularly. New spark plugs alone can increase fuel economy 3%.

3. Be sure the spark plugs are the correct type (heat range) for your vehicle. See the Tune-Up Specifications.

Heat range refers to the spark plug's ability to conduct heat away from the firing end. It must conduct the heat away in an even pattern to avoid becoming a source of pre-ignition, yet it must also operate hot enough to burn off conductive deposits that could cause misfiring.

The heat range is usually indicated by a number on the spark plug, part of the manufacturer's designation for each individual spark plug. The numbers in bold-face indicate the heat range in each manufacturer's identification system.

Manufacturer	Typical Designation
AC	R **45** TS
Bosch (old)	WA **145** T30
Bosch (new)	HR **8** Y
Champion	RBL **15** Y
Fram/Autolite	4**15**
Mopar	P-**62** PR
Motorcraft	BRF-**42**
NGK	BP **5** ES-15
Nippondenso	W **16** EP
Prestolite	14GR **5** 2A

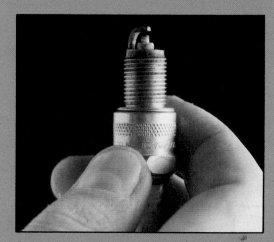

Periodically, check the spark plugs to be sure they are firing efficiently. They are excellent indicators of the internal condition of your engine.

On AC, Bosch (new), Champion, Fram/Autolite, Mopar, Motorcraft and Prestolite, a higher number indicates a hotter plug. On Bosch (old), NGK and Nippondenso, a higher number indicates a colder plug.

4. Make sure the spark plugs are properly gapped. See the Tune-Up Specifications in this book.

5. Be sure the spark plugs are firing efficiently. The illustrations on the next 2 pages show you how to "read" the firing end of the spark plug.

6. Check the ignition timing and set it to specifications. Tests show that almost all cars have incorrect ignition timing by more than 2°.

veyed over 6,000 cars nationwide, they found that a tune-up, on cars that needed one, increased fuel economy over 11%. Replacing worn plugs alone, accounted for a 3% increase. The same test also revealed that 8 out of every 10 vehicles will have some maintenance deficiency that will directly affect fuel economy, emissions or performance. Most of this mileage-robbing neglect could be prevented with regular maintenance.

Modern engines require that all of the functioning systems operate properly for maximum efficiency. A malfunction anywhere wastes fuel. You can keep your vehicle running as efficiently and economically as possible, by being aware of your vehicle's operating and performance characteristics. If your vehicle suddenly develops performance or fuel economy problems it could be due to one or more of the following:

PROBLEM	POSSIBLE CAUSE
Engine Idles Rough	Ignition timing, idle mixture, vacuum leak or something amiss in the emission control system.
Hesitates on Acceleration	Dirty carburetor or fuel filter, improper accelerator pump setting, ignition timing or fouled spark plugs.
Starts Hard or Fails to Start	Worn spark plugs, improperly set automatic choke, ice (or water) in fuel system.
Stalls Frequently	Automatic choke improperly adjusted and possible dirty air filter or fuel filter.
Performs Sluggishly	Worn spark plugs, dirty fuel or air filter, ignition timing or automatic choke out of adjustment.

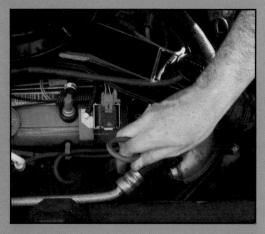

Check spark plug wires on conventional point type ignition for cracks by bending them in a loop around your finger.

Be sure that spark plug wires leading to adjacent cylinders do not run too close together. (Photo courtesy Champion Spark Plug Co.)

7. If your vehicle does not have electronic ignition, check the points, rotor and cap as specified.

8. Check the spark plug wires (used with conventional point-type ignitions) for cracks and burned or broken insulation by bending them in a loop around your finger. Cracked wires decrease fuel efficiency by failing to deliver full voltage to the spark plugs. One misfiring spark plug can cost you as much as 2 mpg.

9. Check the routing of the plug wires. Misfiring can be the result of spark plug leads to adjacent cylinders running parallel to each other and too close together. One wire tends to pick up voltage from the other causing it to fire "out of time".

10. Check all electrical and ignition circuits for voltage drop and resistance.

11. Check the distributor mechanical and/or vacuum advance mechanisms for proper functioning. The vacuum advance can be checked by twisting the distributor plate in the opposite direction of rotation. It should spring back when released.

12. Check and adjust the valve clearance on engines with mechanical lifters. The clearance should be slightly loose rather than too tight.

SPARK PLUG DIAGNOSIS

Normal

APPEARANCE: This plug is typical of one operating normally. The insulator nose varies from a light tan to grayish color with slight electrode wear. The presence of slight deposits is normal on used plugs and will have no adverse effect on engine performance. The spark plug heat range is correct for the engine and the engine is running normally.

CAUSE: Properly running engine.

RECOMMENDATION: Before reinstalling this plug, the electrodes should be cleaned and filed square. Set the gap to specifications. If the plug has been in service for more than 10-12,000 miles, the entire set should probably be replaced with a fresh set of the same heat range.

Oil Deposits

APPEARANCE: The firing end of the plug is covered with a wet, oily coating.

CAUSE: The problem is poor oil control. On high mileage engines, oil is leaking past the rings or valve guides into the combustion chamber. A common cause is also a plugged PCV valve, and a ruptured fuel pump diaphragm can also cause this condition. Oil fouled plugs such as these are often found in new or recently overhauled engines, before normal oil control is achieved, and can be cleaned and reinstalled.

RECOMMENDATION: A hotter spark plug may temporarily relieve the problem, but the engine is probably in need of work.

Incorrect Heat Range

APPEARANCE: The effects of high temperature on a spark plug are indicated by clean white, often blistered insulator. This can also be accompanied by excessive wear of the electrode, and the absence of deposits.

CAUSE: Check for the correct spark plug heat range. A plug which is too hot for the engine can result in overheating. A car operated mostly at high speeds can require a colder plug. Also check ignition timing, cooling system level, fuel mixture and leaking intake manifold.

RECOMMENDATION: If all ignition and engine adjustments are known to be correct, and no other malfunction exists, install spark plugs one heat range colder.

Photos Courtesy Fram Corporation

Carbon Deposits

APPEARANCE: Carbon fouling is easily identified by the presence of dry, soft, black, sooty deposits.

CAUSE: Changing the heat range can often lead to carbon fouling, as can prolonged slow, stop-and-start driving. If the heat range is correct, carbon fouling can be attributed to a rich fuel mixture, sticking choke, clogged air cleaner, worn breaker points, retarded timing or low compression. If only one or two plugs are carbon fouled, check for corroded or cracked wires on the affected plugs. Also look for cracks in the distributor cap between the towers of affected cylinders.

RECOMMENDATION: After the problem is corrected, these plugs can be cleaned and reinstalled if not worn severely.

MMT Fouled

APPEARANCE: Spark plugs fouled by MMT (Methycyclopentadienyl Maganese Tricarbonyl) have reddish, rusty appearance on the insulator and side electrode.

CAUSE: MMT is an anti-knock additive in gasoline used to replace lead. During the combustion process, the MMT leaves a reddish deposit on the insulator and side electrode.

RECOMMENDATION: No engine malfunction is indicated and the deposits will not affect plug performance any more than lead deposits (see Ash Deposits). MMT fouled plugs can be cleaned, regapped and reinstalled.

High Speed Glazing

APPEARANCE: Glazing appears as shiny coating on the plug, either yellow or tan in color.

CAUSE: During hard, fast acceleration, plug temperatures rise suddenly. Deposits from normal combustion have no chance to fluff-off; instead, they melt on the insulator forming an electrically conductive coating which causes misfiring.

RECOMMENDATION: Glazed plugs are not easily cleaned. They should be replaced with a fresh set of plugs of the correct heat range. If the condition recurs, using plugs with a heat range one step colder may cure the problem.

Ash (Lead) Deposits

APPEARANCE: Ash deposits are characterized by light brown or white colored deposits crusted on the side or center electrodes. In some cases it may give the plug a rusty appearance.

CAUSE: Ash deposits are normally derived from oil or fuel additives burned during normal combustion. Normally they are harmless, though excessive amounts can cause misfiring. If deposits are excessive in short mileage, the valve guides may be worn.

RECOMMENDATION: Ash-fouled plugs can be cleaned, gapped and reinstalled.

Detonation

APPEARANCE: Detonation is usually characterized by a broken plug insulator.

CAUSE: A portion of the fuel charge will begin to burn spontaneously, from the increased heat following ignition. The explosion that results applies extreme pressure to engine components, frequently damaging spark plugs and pistons.

Detonation can result by over-advanced ignition timing, inferior gasoline (low octane) lean air/fuel mixture, poor carburetion, engine lugging or an increase in compression ratio due to combustion chamber deposits or engine modification.

RECOMMENDATION: Replace the plugs after correcting the problem.

Photos Courtesy Champion Spark Plug Co.

EMISSION CONTROLS

13. Be aware of the general condition of the emission control system. It contributes to reduced pollution and should be serviced regularly to maintain efficient engine operation.

14. Check all vacuum lines for dried, cracked or brittle conditions. Something as simple as a leaking vacuum hose can cause poor performance and loss of economy.

15. Avoid tampering with the emission control system. Attempting to improve fuel econ-

FUEL SYSTEM

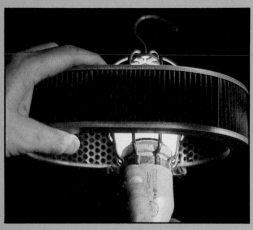

Check the air filter with a light behind it. If you can see light through the filter it can be reused.

Extremely clogged filters should be discarded and replaced with a new one.

18. Replace the air filter regularly. A dirty air filter richens the air/fuel mixture and can increase fuel consumption as much as 10%. Tests show that ⅓ of all vehicles have air filters in need of replacement.

19. Replace the fuel filter at least as often as recommended.

20. Set the idle speed and carburetor mixture to specifications.

21. Check the automatic choke. A sticking or malfunctioning choke wastes gas.

22. During the summer months, adjust the automatic choke for a leaner mixture which will produce faster engine warm-ups.

COOLING SYSTEM

29. Be sure all accessory drive belts are in good condition. Check for cracks or wear.

30. Adjust all accessory drive belts to proper tension.

31. Check all hoses for swollen areas, worn spots, or loose clamps.

32. Check coolant level in the radiator or expansion tank.

33. Be sure the thermostat is operating properly. A stuck thermostat delays engine warm-up and a cold engine uses nearly twice as much fuel as a warm engine.

34. Drain and replace the engine coolant at least as often as recommended. Rust and scale

TIRES & WHEELS

38. Check the tire pressure often with a pencil type gauge. Tests by a major tire manufacturer show that 90% of all vehicles have at least 1 tire improperly inflated. Better mileage can be achieved by over-inflating tires, but never exceed the maximum inflation pressure on the side of the tire.

39. If possible, install radial tires. Radial tires deliver as much as ½ mpg more than bias belted tires.

40. Avoid installing super-wide tires. They only create extra rolling resistance and decrease fuel mileage. Stick to the manufacturer's recommendations.

41. Have the wheels properly balanced.

omy by tampering with emission controls is more likely to worsen fuel economy than improve it. Emission control changes on modern engines are not readily reversible.

16. Clean (or replace) the EGR valve and lines as recommended.

17. Be sure that all vacuum lines and hoses are reconnected properly after working under the hood. An unconnected or misrouted vacuum line can wreak havoc with engine performance.

---

23. Check for fuel leaks at the carburetor, fuel pump, fuel lines and fuel tank. Be sure all lines and connections are tight.

24. Periodically check the tightness of the carburetor and intake manifold attaching nuts and bolts. These are a common place for vacuum leaks to occur.

25. Clean the carburetor periodically and lubricate the linkage.

26. The condition of the tailpipe can be an excellent indicator of proper engine combustion. After a long drive at highway speeds, the inside of the tailpipe should be a light grey in color. Black or soot on the insides indicates an overly rich mixture.

27. Check the fuel pump pressure. The fuel pump may be supplying more fuel than the engine needs.

28. Use the proper grade of gasoline for your engine. Don't try to compensate for knocking or "pinging" by advancing the ignition timing. This practice will only increase plug temperature and the chances of detonation or pre-ignition with relatively little performance gain.

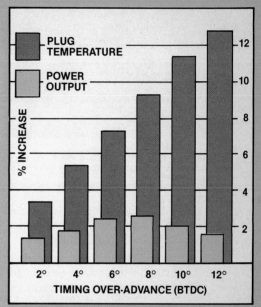

Increasing ignition timing past the specified setting results in a drastic increase in spark plug temperature with increased chance of detonation or preignition. Performance increase is considerably less. (Photo courtesy Champion Spark Plug Co.)

---

that form in the engine should be flushed out to allow the engine to operate at peak efficiency.

35. Clean the radiator of debris that can decrease cooling efficiency.

36. Install a flex-type or electric cooling fan, if you don't have a clutch type fan. Flex fans use curved plastic blades to push more air at low speeds when more cooling is needed; at high speeds the blades flatten out for less resistance. Electric fans only run when the engine temperature reaches a predetermined level.

37. Check the radiator cap for a worn or cracked gasket. If the cap does not seal properly, the cooling system will not function properly.

---

42. Be sure the front end is correctly aligned. A misaligned front end actually has wheels going in differed directions. The increased drag can reduce fuel economy by .3 mpg.

43. Correctly adjust the wheel bearings. Wheel bearings that are adjusted too tight increase rolling resistance.

Check tire pressures regularly with a reliable pocket type gauge. Be sure to check the pressure on a cold tire.

GENERAL MAINTENANCE

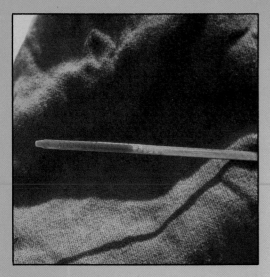

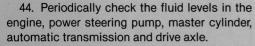

Check the fluid levels (particularly engine oil) on a regular basis. Be sure to check the oil for grit, water or other contamination.

A vacuum gauge is another excellent indicator of internal engine condition and can also be installed in the dash as a mileage indicator.

44. Periodically check the fluid levels in the engine, power steering pump, master cylinder, automatic transmission and drive axle.

45. Change the oil at the recommended interval and change the filter at every oil change. Dirty oil is thick and causes extra friction between moving parts, cutting efficiency and increasing wear. A worn engine requires more frequent tune-ups and gets progressively worse fuel economy. In general, use the lightest viscosity oil for the driving conditions you will encounter.

46. Use the recommended viscosity fluids in the transmission and axle.

47. Be sure the battery is fully charged for fast starts. A slow starting engine wastes fuel.

48. Be sure battery terminals are clean and tight.

49. Check the battery electrolyte level and add distilled water if necessary.

50. Check the exhaust system for crushed pipes, blockages and leaks.

51. Adjust the brakes. Dragging brakes or brakes that are not releasing create increased drag on the engine.

52. Install a vacuum gauge or miles-per-gallon gauge. These gauges visually indicate engine vacuum in the intake manifold. High vacuum = good mileage and low vacuum = poorer mileage. The gauge can also be an excellent indicator of internal engine conditions.

53. Be sure the clutch is properly adjusted. A slipping clutch wastes fuel.

54. Check and periodically lubricate the heat control valve in the exhaust manifold. A sticking or inoperative valve prevents engine warm-up and wastes gas.

55. Keep accurate records to check fuel economy over a period of time. A sudden drop in fuel economy may signal a need for tune-up or other maintenance.

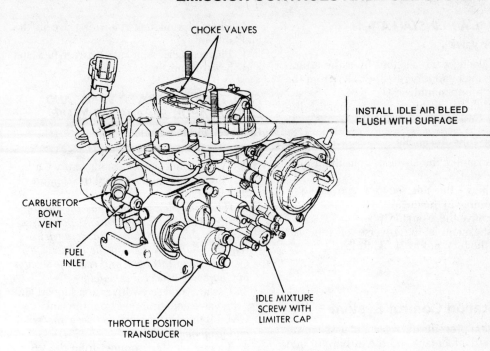

CHOKE VALVES

INSTALL IDLE AIR BLEED
FLUSH WITH SURFACE

CARBURETOR
BOWL
VENT

FUEL
INLET

IDLE MIXTURE
SCREW WITH
LIMITER CAP

THROTTLE POSITION
TRANSDUCER

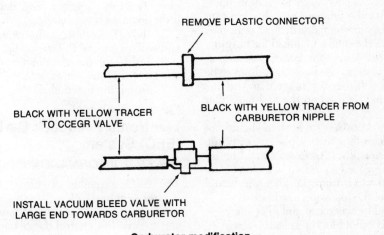

REMOVE PLASTIC CONNECTOR

BLACK WITH YELLOW TRACER
TO CCEGR VALVE

BLACK WITH YELLOW TRACER FROM
CARBURETOR NIPPLE

INSTALL VACUUM BLEED VALVE WITH
LARGE END TOWARDS CARBURETOR

Carburetor modification

the air cleaner into the exhaust system. The function is to reduce HC (hydrocarbon) emissions. It is located in a tube between the exhaust manifold and the air cleaner.

TESTING THE SYSTEM

To determine if the air aspirator valve has failed, disconnect the hose from the aspirator inlet. With the engine idling in Neutral, vacuum exhaust pulses can be felt at the aspirator inlet. If hot exhaust gas is escaping from the aspirator inlet, the valve has failed and should be replaced.

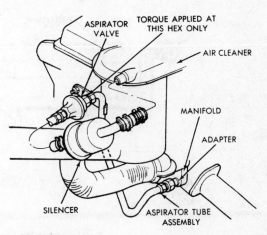

ASPIRATOR
VALVE

TORQUE APPLIED AT
THIS HEX ONLY

AIR CLEANER

MANIFOLD

ADAPTER

SILENCER

ASPIRATOR TUBE
ASSEMBLY

AIR aspirator system

REMOVAL AND INSTALLATION
Aspirator Valve

1. Disconnect the air hose from the aspirator valve inlet and unscrew the valve from the aspirator tube assembly.
2. Installation is the reverse of removal. Replace the hose if it has hardened.

Aspirator Tube Assembly

1. Disconnect the air hose from the aspirator valve inlet.
2. Remove the nut securing the aspirator tube assembly to the engine.
3. Remove the aspirator tube.
4. Installation is the reverse of removal. Tighten the tube nut to 25–35 ft. lbs.

Evaporation Control System

This system prevents the release of gasoline vapors from the fuel tank and the carburetor into the atmosphere. The system is vacuum operated and draws the fumes into a charcoal canister where they are temporarily held until they are drawn into the intake manifold for burning. For proper operation of the system and to prevent gas tank failure, the lines should never be plugged, and no other cap other than the one specified should be used on the fuel tank filler neck.

The Evaporation Control System should not require service other than replacement of the charcoal canister filter. All hoses should be inspected and replaced if cracked or leaking. Any loss of fuel or vapor from the filler cap would indicate one of the following conditions:

1. Poor seal between cap and filler neck,
2. Malfunction of fuel cap release valve,
3. Plugged vent line roll-over valve in the fuel tank, or
4. Plugged vapor vent lines between fuel tank and charcoal canister.

FUEL TANK ROLL-OVER VALVE AND LIQUID VAPOR SEPARATOR VALVE
Removal and Installation

1. Remove the fuel tank.
2. Wedge the blade of a suitable pry bar between the rubber grommet and the support rib on the fuel tank.

NOTE: *Chrysler recommends the use of 2 screwdrivers for this operation. Before performing this operation with screwdrivers, read the Safety Notice on the acknowledgements page of this book and read the section in Chapter 1 concerning Safety.*

3. Use a second screwdriver as a support and pry the valve and grommet from the tank.

CAUTION: *Do not pry between the valve and grommet.*

4. To remove the grommet from the valve, place the valve upright on a flat surface and push down on the grommet.
5. Install the rubber grommet in the fuel tank and work it around the curled lip.
6. Lubricate the grommet with engine oil and twist the valve down into the grommet.
7. Install the fuel tank.

Electronic Feedback Carburetor (EFC) System
GENERAL INFORMATION

The EFC system is essentially an emissions control system which utilizes an electronic signal, generated by an exhaust gas oxygen sensor, to precisely control the air-fuel mixture ra-

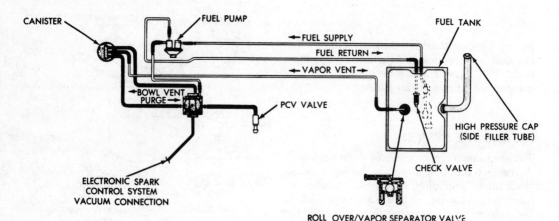

Fuel evaporation control system schematic

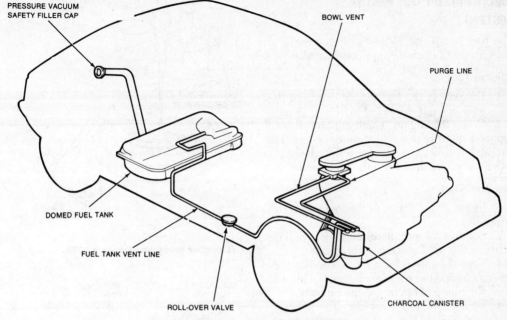

Components of Fuel Evaporation system

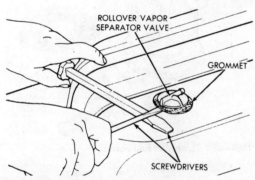

Removing rollover/vapor separation valve from fuel tank

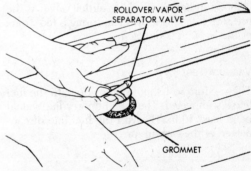

Installing the rollover/vapor separator valve

tio in the carburetor. This allows the engine to produce exhaust gases of the proper composition to permit the use of a three-way catalyst. The three-way catalyst is designed to convert the three pollutants (1) Hydrocarbons (HC), (2) Carbon Monoxide (CO), and (3) Oxides of Nitrogen (NOx) into harmless substances.

There are two operating modes in the EFC system:

(1) Open Loop—Air fuel ratio is controlled by information programmed into the computer at manufacture.

(2) Closed Loop—Air fuel ratio is varied by the computer based on information supplied by the oxygen sensor.

When the engine is cold, the system will be operating in the open loop mode. During that time, the air fuel ratio will be fixed at a richer level. This will allow proper engine warm-up.

Also during this period, air injection (from the air injection pump) will be injected upstream in the exhaust manifold.

TESTING

Testing requires sophisticated equipment not available to the general public, and/or, prohibitively expensive. Therefore, no testing procedures are given here.

FUEL SYSTEM

The fuel system consists of the fuel tank, fuel pump, fuel filter, carburetor, fuel lines and vacuum lines.

Mechanical Fuel Pump

TESTING

The fuel pump can be tested in a variety of ways, depending on the equipment available.

Volume Test

1. Disconnect the fuel supply line from the carburetor (leave it connected to the fuel pump).
2. Crank the engine. The fuel pump should supply 1 quart of fuel in 1 minute or less. Do not catch the fuel in a styrofoam container.
3. Reconnect the line to the carburetor.

Pressure Test

1. Insert a "tee" fitting in the fuel line at the carburetor.
2. Connect a 6 inch (maximum) piece of hose between the "tee" and a pressure gauge.
3. Vent the pump for a few seconds to relieve air trapped in the fuel chamber. This will allow the pump to operate at full capacity.
4. Operate the engine at idle. The pressure should be 4–6 psi and remain constant or return slowly to zero when the engine is stopped. An instant drop to zero when the engine is stopped indicates a leaking outlet valve. If the pressure is too high, the main spring is too strong or the air vent is plugged.

Vacuum Test

The vacuum test should be made with the fuel line disconnected. The minimum reading should be at least 10 in./Hg with the fuel line disconnected at the carburetor.

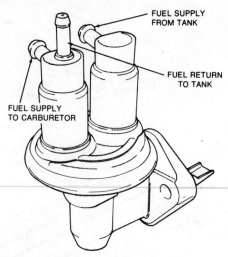

1.7L engine fuel pump through 1980

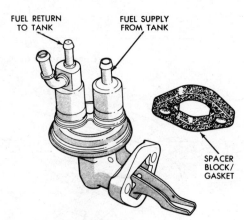

1981–83 1.7L engine fuel pump

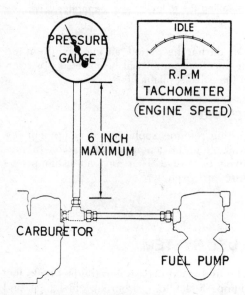

Testing fuel pump pressure

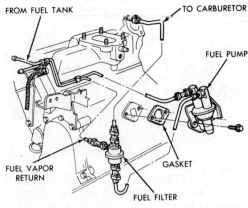

1.6L fuel line routing

Inlet Valve Test

A vacuum gauge is needed to test the inlet valve.

1. Disconnect the fuel inlet line at the fuel pump.

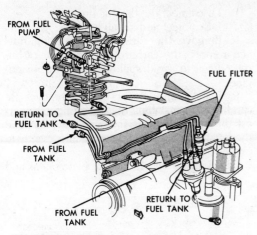

FROM FUEL PUMP

FUEL FILTER

RETURN TO FUEL TANK

FROM FUEL TANK

RETURN TO FUEL TANK

FROM FUEL TANK

1.7L fuel line routing

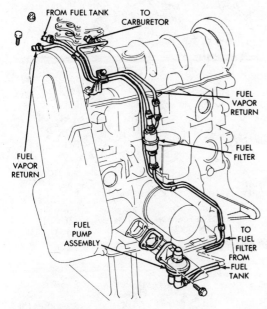

FROM FUEL TANK

TO CARBURETOR

FUEL VAPOR RETURN

FUEL VAPOR RETURN

FUEL FILTER

FUEL PUMP ASSEMBLY

TO FUEL FILTER

FROM FUEL TANK

2.2L fuel line routing

2. Connect a vacuum gauge to the inlet fitting of the fuel pump.

3. Crank the engine.

4. There should a noticeable vacuum present, not alternated by blowback.

5. If blowback is present, the inlet valve is not seating properly and the pump should be replaced.

6. Remove the vacuum gauge and reconnect the fuel line.

REMOVAL AND INSTALLATION

A mechanical fuel pump is located on the left side of the engine. To remove the pump, disconnect the fuel and vapor lines and remove the attaching bolts. Installation is the reverse of removal. Always use a new gasket when in-

stalling the pump and make certain the gasket surfaces are clean.

Electric Fuel Pump (Turbocharged Models)

1. Raise and support the rear of the vehicle. Release the pressure in the fuel system.

2. Disconnect the negative battery terminal.

3. Remove the fuel tank cap and the fuel tube-to-quarter panel screws.

4. Remove the draft tube cap from the sending unit, connect a siphon hose to the draft tube and siphon the fuel from the tank.

5. Disconnect the fuel pump wiring connector from the lock ring cap. Wrap a cloth around the fuel hose and remove the fuel hose from the lock ring cap.

6. Disconnect and lower the fuel tank from the vehicle.

7. Using a non-metallic drift and a hammer, remove the lock ring by driving it counterclockwise.

8. Remove the fuel pump and O-ring seal from the tank. Check the in-tank filter and replace it, if necessary.

9. To install, use a new O-ring seal and reverse the removal procedures. Start the vehicle and check for leaks.

Carburetor

Holley models 5220 and 6520 are used. Each unit is a staged 2-barrel unit.

REMOVAL AND INSTALLATION

Do not attempt to remove the carburetor from a hot engine that has just been run. Allow the engine to cool sufficiently. When removing the

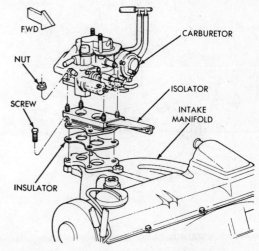

FWD

CARBURETOR

NUT

ISOLATOR

SCREW

INTAKE MANIFOLD

INSULATOR

Carburetor removal and installation—typical

carburetor, it should not be necessary to disturb the intake manifold isolator mounting screws, unless you have determined that a leak exists in the isolator.

1. Disconnect the negative battery cable.

2. Remove the air cleaner.

3. Remove the fuel filler cap to relieve pressure.

4. Disconnect the fuel inlet fitting and catch any excess fuel that may flow out.

5. Disconnect all electrical connections. Tag these for installation.

6. Disconnect the throttle linkage.

7. Disconnect and tag all hoses.

8. Remove the carburetor mounting nuts and remove the carburetor. Hold the carburetor level to avoid spilling fuel on a hot engine.

9. Installation is the reverse of removal. Be careful when installing the mounting nut nearest the fast idle lever. It is very easy to bend the lever. Tighten the mounting nuts evenly to prevent vacuum leaks.

Check to be sure the choke plate opens and

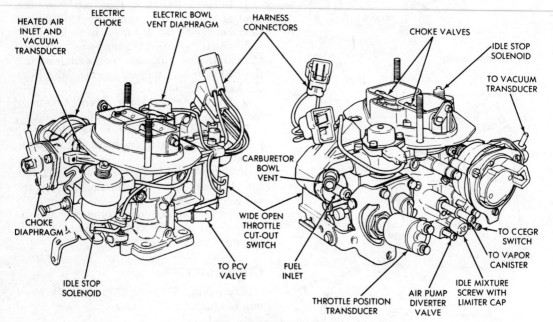

1978 Holley 5220 Carburetor (with A/C)

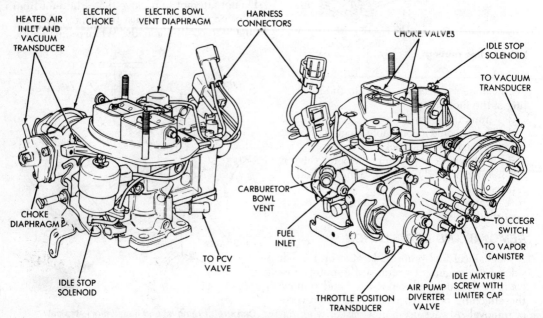

1978 Holley 5220 Carburetor (w/o A/C)

closes fully and that full throttle travel is obtained.

ADJUSTMENTS

NOTE: *Before attempting any adjustments, complaints of fuel loading on a cold engine on all 1978 models (except those with Federal emission package and aspirator and manual transmission) can be cured by removing the secondary choke blade and choke blade attaching screws and discarding. This* *change has been incorporated in production as of May 15, 1978.*

Float Setting and Float Drop

1. Remove and invert the air horn.
2. Insert a .480 inch gauge between the air horn and float.
3. If necessary, bend the tang on the float arm to adjust.
4. Turn the air horn right side up and allow the float to hang freely. Measure the float drop

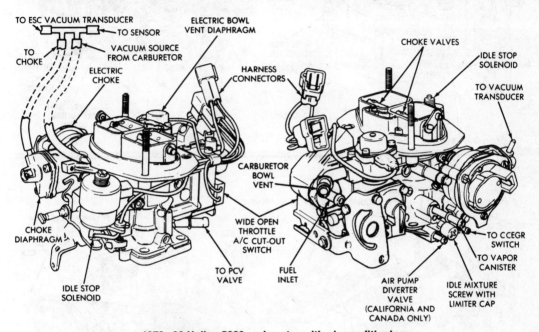

1979–80 Holley 5220 carburetor with air conditioning

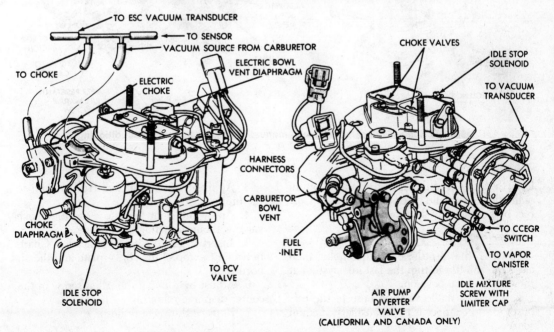

1979–80 Holley 5220 carburetor without air conditioning

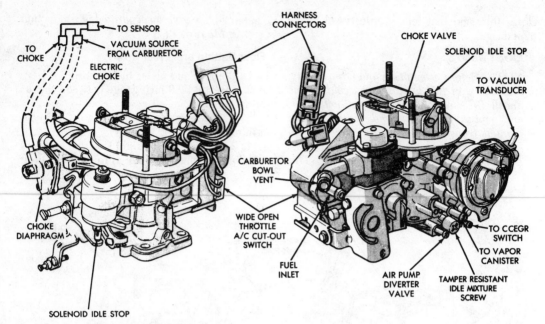

1981–82 Holley 5220 carburetor with manual transaxle and air conditioning

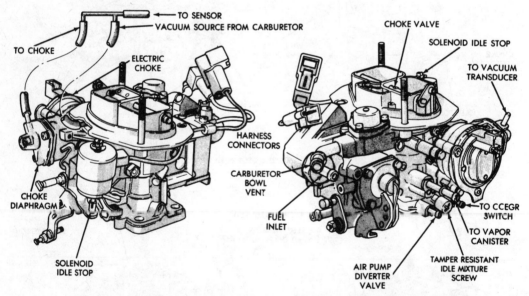

1981–82 Holley 5220 carburetor with manual transaxle, without air conditioning

from the bottom of the air horn to the bottom of the float. It should be exactly ⅞ inches. Correct by bending the float tang.

Vacuum Kick

1. Open the throttle, close the choke, then close the throttle to trap the fast idle system at the closed choke position.

2. Disconnect the vacuum hose to the carburetor and connect it to an auxiliary vacuum source.

3. Apply at least 15 inches Hg. vacuum to the unit.

4. Apply sufficient force to close the choke valve without distorting the linkage.

5. Insert a gauge (see Specification Chart) between the top of the choke plate and the air horn wall.

6. Adjust by rotating the Allen screw in the center diaphragm housing.

7. Replace the vacuum hose.

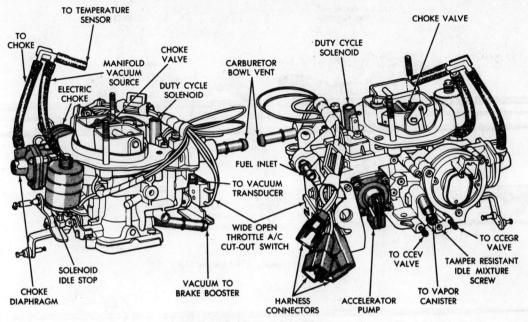

1981–82 Holley 6520 carburetor

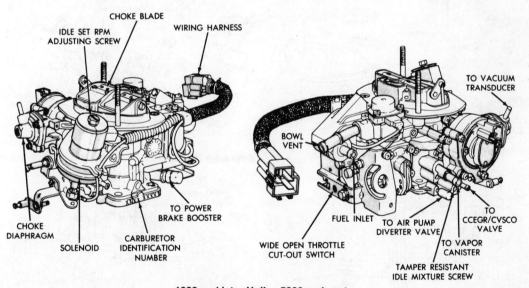

1983 and later Holley 5220 carburetor

Throttle Position Transducer

1978 ONLY

1. Disconnect the wire from the transducer.
2. Loosen the locknut.
3. Place an $\frac{11}{16}$ inch gauge between the outer portion of the transducer and the mounting bracket.
4. To adjust the gap, turn the transducer.
5. Tighten the locknut.

Fast Idle

1. Remove the top of the air cleaner.
2. Disconnect and plug the EGR vacuum line. On 2.2L engines, disconnect the two-way electrical connector at the carburetor (red and tan wires).
3. Plug any open vacuum lines, which were connected to the air cleaner.
4. Do not disconnect the vacuum line to the spark control computer. Instead, use a jumper wire to ground the idle stop switch. The air conditioning should be off.
5. Disconnect the engine cooling fan at the radiator and complete the circuit at the plug with a jumper wire to energize the fan.
6. Set the brake, place the transmission in

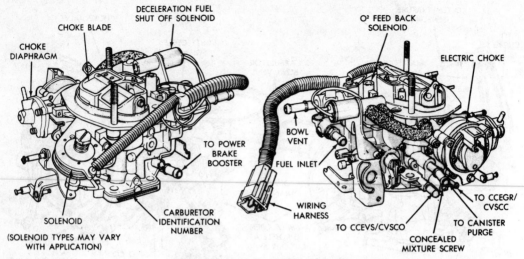

1983 and later Holley 6520 carburetor

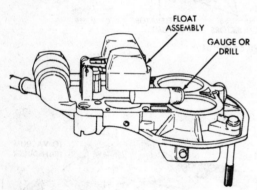

Checking float level

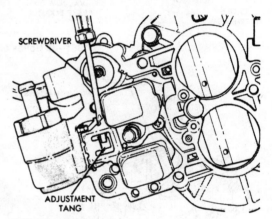

Adjusting float level

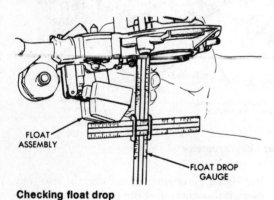

Checking float drop

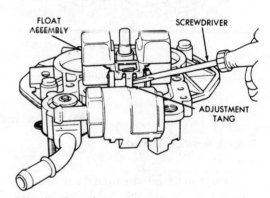

Adjusting float drop

Neutral and position the first step of the fast idle cam under the adjusting screw.

7. Connect a tachometer according to the manufacturer's specifications.

8. Start the engine and observe the idle speed. With the choke fully open, the speed should remain steady. If it gradually increases, the idle stop switch is not properly grounded.

9. Turn the adjusting screw to give the specified rpm. Do not adjust with the screw contacting the plastic cam.

10. Operate the throttle linkage a few times and return the screw to the first cam step to recheck rpm.

Throttle Stop Speed Adjustment (w/o Air Conditioning)

1. The engine should be fully warmed.
2. Put the transmission in Neutral and set the parking brake.
3. Turn the headlights off.
4. Using a jumper wire, ground the idle stop carburetor switch.
5. Disconnect the idle stop solenoid wire at the connector.
6. Adjust the throttle stop speed screw to 700 rpm.
7. Reconnect the idle stop solenoid wire.
8. Disconnect the jumper wire from the carburetor switch.

OVERHAUL

Efficient carburetion depends greatly on careful cleaning and inspection during overhaul, since dirt, gum, varnish, water in or on the carburetor parts are mainly responsible for poor performance.

Carburetor overhaul should be performed in a clean, dust-free area. Carefully disassemble the carburetor, keeping look-alike parts segregated. Note all jet sizes.

Once the carburetor is disassembled, wash all parts (except diaphragms, electric choke

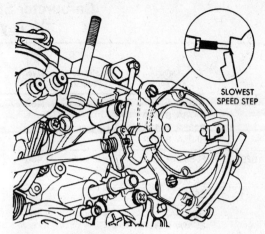

Adjusting fast idle speed

units, pump plunger and any other plastic, leather or fiber parts) in clean carburetor solvent. Do not leave the parts in solvent any longer than necessary to sufficiently loosen the deposits. Excessive cleaning may remove the special finish from the float bowl and choke valve bodies, leaving them unfit for service. Rinse all parts in clean solvent and blow dry with compressed air. Wipe all plastic, leather or fiber parts with a clean, lint-free cloth.

Blow out all passages and jets with compressed air and be sure there are no restrictions or blockages. Never use wire to clean jets, fuel passages or air bleeds.

Check all parts for wear or damage. If wear or damage is found, replace the complete assembly. Especially check the following.

1. Check the float and needle seat for wear. If any is found, replace the assembly.
2. Check the float 'hinge pin for wear and

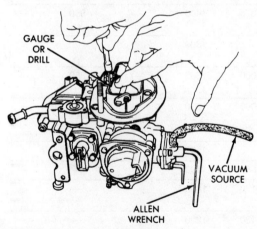

Adjusting choke vacuum kick

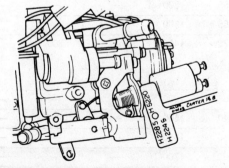

Adjusting throttle position transducer

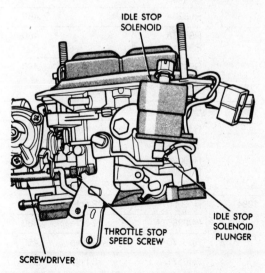

Adjusting throttle stop speed (w/o A/C)

Carburetor Specifications
Holley 5220

Year	Carb Part No.	Accelerator Pump	Dry Float Level (in.)	Vacuum Kick (in.)	Fast Idle RPM (w/fan)	Throttle Position Transducer (in.)	Throttle Stop Speed RPM	Choke
1978	R-8376A, 8378A, 8384A, 8439A, 8441A, 8505A, 8507A	#2 hole	.480	.070	1100	.547	700	2 Rich
1979	R-8524A, 8526A, 8532A, 8534A, 8528A, 8530A	#2 hole	.480	.040	1700	—	700	2 Rich
	R8525A, 8541A, 8531A, 8533A, 8527A, 8529A	#2 hole	.480	.070	1400	—	700	2 Rich
1980	R8838A R8839A R9110A R9111A	—	.480	.040	1700	—	700	—
	R8726A R8727A R9108A	—	.480	.070	1400	—	700	—
	R9109A	—	.480	.100	1400	—	700	—
1981	R9058A R9059A	—	.480	.040	1400	—	850	—
	R9056A R9057A	—	.480	.070	1400	—	850	—
	R9064A R9065A				1300			
	R9684A R9685A	—	.480	.060	1300	—	850	—
1982	R9582A R9583A R9584A	—	.480	.060	1200	—	—	—
	R9585A				1500			
	R9820A	—	.480	.080	1200	—	—	—
	R9513A R9514A	—	.480	.120	1400	—	—	—
	R9499A R9511A R9512A	—	.480	.130	1200	—	—	—
1983	R40020A	#3 hole	.480	.055	1300	—	—	—
	R40022A	#3 hole	.480	.055	1500	—	—	—
	R40023A R40024 R40025A R40026A	#2 hole	.480	.070	1400	—	700	—
1984	R400601A	#2 hole	.480	.055	1200	—	—	—
	R400851A	#2 hole	.480	.040	1500	—	—	—
	R40170A	#3 hole	.480	.060	1650	—	—	—
	R40171A	#3 hole	.480	.060	1700	—	—	—
	R400671A	#3 hole	.480	.070	1500	—	—	—
	R400681A	#3 hole	.480	.070	1700	—	—	—

Carburetor Specifications
Holley 6520

Year	Carb. Part No.	Dry Float Setting (in.)	Solenoid Idle Stop (rpm)	Fast Idle Speed (rpm)	Vacuum Kick (in.)
1981	R9060A R9061A	.480	850	1100	.030
	R9125A R9126A	.480	850	1200	.030
	R9052A R9053A	.480	850	1400	.070
	R9054A R9055A	.480	850	1400	.040
	R9602A R9603A	.480	850	1500	.065
	R9604A R9605A	.480	850	1600	.065
1982	R9824A	.480	900	1400	.065
	R9503A R9504A R9750A R9751A	.480	850	1300	.085
	R9822A R9823A	.480	850	1400	.080
	R9505A R9506A R9752A R9753A	.480	900	1600	.100
1983	R40080A R40081A	.480	850	1400	.045
	R40003A R40007A	.480	775	1400	.070
	R40010A R40004A	.480	900	1500	.080
	R40012A R4008A	.480	900	1600	.070
	R40014A R40006A	.480	850	1275	.080
1984	R400581A	.480	850	1400	.070
	R401071A	.480	1000	1600	.055
	R400641A R400811A	.480	800	1500	.080
	R400651A R400821A	.480	900	1600	.080
	R40071A R40122A	.480	850	1500	.080

the floats for distortion or dents. Replace the float if fuel has leaked into it.

3. Check the throttle and choke shaft bores for out-of-round. Damage or wear to the throttle arm, shaft or shaft bore will often require replacement of the throttle body. These parts require close tolerances and an air leak here can cause poor starting and idling.

4. Inspect the idle mixture adjusting needles for burrs or grooves. Burrs or grooves will usually require replacement of the needles since a satisfactory idle cannot be obtained.

Carburetor Specifications
Holley 5220/6520

Year/ Part No.	Dry Float Setting	Solenoid Idle Stop	Fast Idle Speed (rpm)	Vacuum Kick (in.)
1985				
R40058A	.480	①	①	.070
R40060A	.480	①	①	.055
R40116A	.480	①	①	.095
R40117A	.480	①	①	.095
R40134A	.480	①	①	.075
R40135A	.480	①	①	.075
R40138A	.480	①	①	.075
R40139A	.480	①	①	.075
1986				
R400581A	.480	①	①	.070
R400602A	.480	①	①	.055
R401341A	.480	①	①	.075
R401351A	.480	①	①	.075
R401381A	.480	①	①	.075
R401391A	.480	①	①	.075
R401161A	.480	①	①	.095
R401171A	.480	①	①	.095

① Refer to specification on VECI label under the hood.

5. Test the accelerator pump check valves. They should pass air one way only. Test for proper seating by blowing and sucking on the valve. If the valve is satisfactory, wash the valve again to remove breath moisture.

6. Check the bowl cover for warping with a straightedge.

7. Closely inspect the valves and seats for wear or damage, replacing as necessary.

8. After the carburetor is assembled, check the choke valve for freedom of operation.

Carburetor overhaul kits are recommended for each overhaul. These kits contain all gaskets and new parts to replace those that deteriorate most rapidly. Failure to replace all parts supplied with the kit (especially gaskets) can result in poor performance later.

Some carburetor manufacturers supply overhaul kits of three types—minor repair, major repair and gasket kits. They basically consist of:

Minor Repair Kits:
• All gaskets
• Float needle valve
• Volume control screw
• All diaphragms
• Pump diaphragm spring

Major Repair Kits:
• All jets and gaskets
• All diaphragms
• Float needle valve
• Volume control screw
• Pump ball valve
• Main jet carrier
• Float
• Complete intermediate rod
• Intermediate pump lever
• Complete injector tube
• Assorted screws and washers

Gasket Kits:
• All gaskets.

After cleaning and checking all components, reassemble the carburetor using new parts, using the exploded views in the car sections, if necessary. Make sure that all screws and jets are tight in their seats, but do not overtighten or the tips will be distorted. Do not tighten needle valves into their seats or uneven jetting will result. Always use new gaskets and adjust the float.

ELECTRONIC FUEL INJECTION

NOTE: *This book contains simple testing and service procedures for your fuel injection system. More comprehensive testing and diagnosis procedures may be found in CHILTON'S GUIDE TO FUEL INJECTION AND FEEDBACK CARBURETORS, book part number 7488, available at most book stores and auto parts stores, or available directly from Chilton Co.*

Multi-Point Fuel Injection

The turbocharged multi-point electronic fuel injection system combines an electronic fuel and spark advance control system with a turbocharged intake system.

A digital pre-programmed computer, known as a Logic Module, regulates ignition timing, air-fuel ratio, emission control devices, cooling fan, charging system, turbocharger wastegate, and idle speed. The Logic Module has the ability to update and revise its commands to meet all driving conditions.

Component Servicing

CAUTION: *RELEASE FUEL SYSTEM PRESSURE before removing any system components. Refer to the Fuel Filter section in Chapter 1 for instructions.*

Throttle Body

REMOVAL AND INSTALLATION

EFI

1. Release the pressure in the fuel system.
2. Disconnect the negative battery terminal.
3. Disconnect the fuel injector wiring connector and the 6-way connector from the throttle body.
4. Remove the ground wire from the 6-way connector and the air cleaner hose.
5. Remove the throttle cable, the speed control and the transmission kickdown cables, if equipped.
6. Remove the return spring and the vacuum hoses.
7. Loosen the fuel delivery and the return hose clamps, wrap a towel around each hose and twist the hose from the connection.
8. Remove the mounting screws and the throttle body from the vehicle.
9. To install, use a new gasket and reverse the removal procedures. Torque the throttle body mounting screws to 17 ft. lbs.

Multi-Point

1. Release the pressure in the fuel system.
2. Disconnect the negative battery cable.
3. Remove the air cleaner-to-throttle body screws and the air cleaner adaptor.
4. Remove the accelerator, the speed control, the transmission kickdown cables and the return spring.

5. Disconnect the 6-way electrical connector from the throttle body.
6. Remove the vacuum hoses from the throttle body.
7. Loosen the throttle body-to-turbocharger hose clamp.
8. Remove the throttle body-to-intake manifold screws and the throttle body from the vehicle.
9. To install, use a new gasket and reverse the removal procedures.

Fuel Injector

REMOVAL AND INSTALLATION

EFI

1. Release the pressure in the fuel system.
2. Disconnect the negative battery cable.
3. Remove the 4 screws securing the fuel inlet chamber-to-throttle body.
4. Remove the pressure regulator-to-throttle body vacuum tube.
5. Place a towel around the fuel inlet chamber and lift the chamber off of the throttle body.
6. Pull the injector from the throttle body.
7. Remove the upper/lower O-rings, the snap ring, the seal and the washer from the fuel injector.
8. To install, use new O-rings, seal and washer, then reverse the removal procedures. Torque the inlet chamber screws to 35 inch lbs.

Multi-point

1. Release the pressure in the fuel system.
2. Disconnect the negative battery cable.

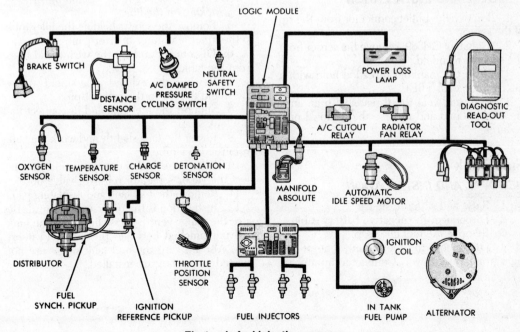

Electronic fuel injection sensors

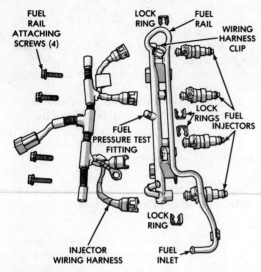

Fuel rail and injectors

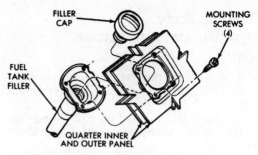

Fuel filter mounting—typical

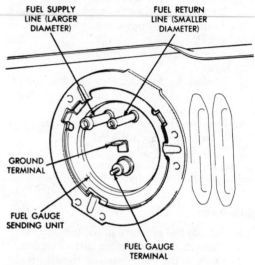

Fuel tank lines and wing

3. Remove the electrical wiring connectors from the injectors.

4. Disconnect the fuel rail from the delivery line and the pressure regulator.

5. Remove the hold down clamps and the fuel injectors/fuel rail as an assembly.

6. To remove a fuel injector from the fuel rail, remove the locking ring and separate the injector from the fuel rail.

7. To install, use new gaskets and seals and reverse the removal procedures.

Oxygen Sensor

REMOVAL AND INSTALLATION

1. Remove the bullet connector from the tip of the sensor.

2. Using tool C-4589, remove the sensor from the exhaust manifold.

3. Clean the manifold threaded hole with a tap (18 mm x 1.5 x 6E).

4. To install, coat the threads with an antisieze compound and reverse the removal procedures.

Fuel Tank

REMOVAL AND INSTALLATION

1. Raise and support the car.

2. Disconnect the negative battery cable.

3. Remove the fuel filler cap.

4. Disconnect the fuel supply line at the right front shock tower. Connect a drain or siphon line and empty the tank into another container.

NOTE: *Do not begin the siphoning process by sucking on the line.*

5. Remove the screws holding the filler tube to the inner and outer quarter panel.

6. Disconnect and tag the wiring and lines from the tank.

7. Remove the exhaust pipe shield. Allow the shield to rest on the exhaust pipe.

8. Support the fuel tank and disconnect the fuel tank straps.

9. Lower the tank slightly and work the tank from the filler tube.

10. Lower the tank some more and disconnect the vapor separator roll-over valve hose.

11. Remove the fuel tank and insulating pad.

12. Installation is the reverse of removal. Be sure the vapor vent hose is clipped to the tank and not pinched between the tank and floorpan. Also be sure the fuel tank straps are not twisted when they are installed.

Chassis Electrical

5

UNDERSTANDING AND TROUBLESHOOTING ELECTRICAL SYSTEMS

For any electrical system to operate, it must make a complete circuit. This simply means that the power flow from the battery must make a complete circle. When an electrical component is operating, power flows from the battery to the component, passes through the component causing it to perform its function (lighting a light bulb, for example) and then returns to the battery through the ground of the circuit. This ground is usually (but not always) the metal part of the vehicle on which the electrical component is mounted.

Perhaps the easiest way to visualize this is to think of connecting a light bulb with two wires attached to it to your vehicle battery. The battery in your vehicle has two posts (negative and positive). If one of the two wires attached to the light bulb was attached to the negative post of the battery and the other wire was attached to the positive post of the battery, you would have a complete circuit. Current from the battery would flow out one post, through the wire attached to it and then to the light bulb, causing it to light. It would then leave the light bulb, travel through the other wire, and return to the other post of the battery.

The normal automotive circuit differs from this simple example in two ways. First, instead of having a return wire from the bulb to the battery, the light bulb returns the current to the battery through the chassis of the vehicle. Since the negative battery cable is attached to the chassis and the chassis is made of electrically conductive metal, the chassis of the vehicle can serve as a ground wire to complete the circuit. Secondly, most automotive circuits contain switches to turn components on and off as required.

There are many types of switches, but the most common simply serves to prevent the passage of current when it is turned off. Since the switch is a part of the circle necessary for a complete circuit, it operates to leave an opening in the circuit, and thus an incomplete or open circuit, when it is turned off.

Some electrical components which require a large amount of current to operate also have a relay in their circuit. Since these circuits carry a large amount of current, the thickness of the wire (gauge size) in the circuit is also greater. If this large wire were connected from the component to the control switch on the instrument panel, and then back to the component, a voltage drop would occur in the circuit. To prevent this potential drop in voltage, an electromagnetic switch (relay) is used. The large wires in the circuit are connected from the vehicle battery to one side of the relay, and from the opposite side of the relay to the component. The relay is normally open, preventing current from passing through the circuit. An additional, smaller, wire is connected from the relay to the control switch for the circuit. When the control switch is turned on, it completes the circuit. This closes the relay and allows current to flow from the battery to the component. The horn, headlight, and starter circuits are three which use relays.

You have probably noticed how the vehicle's instrument panel lights get brighter the faster you rev the engine. This happens because your alternator (which supplies the battery) puts out more current at speeds above idle. This is normal. However, it is possible for larger surges of current to pass through the electrical system of your car. If this surge of current were to reach an electrical component, it could burn the component out. To prevent this from happening, fuses are connected into the current supply wires of most of the major electrical systems of your vehicle. The fuse serves to head off the surge at the pass. When an electrical current of excessive power passes through the component's fuse, the fuse blows out and breaks the circuit, saving it from destruction.

The fuse also protects the component from damage if the power supply wire to the component is grounded before the current reaches the component.

There is another important rule to the complete circle circuit. *Every complete circuit from a power source must include a component which is using the power from the power source.* If you were to disconnect the light bulb from the previous example of a light bulb being connected to the battery by two wires together (take our word for it—don't try it) the result would literally be shocking. A similar thing happens (on a smaller scale) when the power supply wire to a component or the electrical component itself becomes grounded before the normal ground connection for the circuit. To prevent damage to the system, the fuse for the circuit blows to interrupt the circuit—protecting the components from damage. Because grounding a wire from a power source makes a complete circuit—less the required component to use the power—this phenomenon is called a short circuit. The most common causes of short circuits are: the rubber insulation on a wire breaking or rubbing through to expose the current carrying core of the wire to a metal part of the vehicle, or a short) switch.

Some electrical systems on the vehicle are protected by a circuit breaker which is, basically, a self-repairing fuse. When either of the above-described events takes place in a system which is protected by a circuit breaker, the circuit breaker opens the circuit the same way a fuse does. However, when either the short is removed from the circuit or the surge subsides, the circuit breaker resets itself and does not have to be replaced as a fuse does.

The final protective device in the chassis electrical system is a fuse link. A fuse link is a wire that acts as a fuse. It is connected between the starter relay and the main wiring harness for the car. This connection is under the hood, very near a similar fuse link which protects all the chassis electrical components. It is the probable cause of trouble when none of the electrical components function, unless the battery is disconnected or dead.

Electrical problems generally fall into one of three areas:

1. The component that is not functioning is not receiving current.
2. The component itself is not functioning.
3. The component is not properly grounded.

Problems that fall into the first category are by far the most complicated. It is the current

supply system to the component which contains all the switches, relays, fuses, etc.

The electrical system can be checked with a test light and a jumper wire. A test light is a device that looks like a pointed screwdriver with a wire attached to it. It has a light bulb in its handle. A jumper wire is a piece of insulated wire with an alligator clip attached to each end.

If a light bulb is not working, you must follow a systematic plan to determine which of the three causes is the villain.

1. Turn on the switch that controls the inoperable bulb.
2. Disconnect the power supply wire from the bulb.
3. Attach the ground wire on the test light to a good metal ground.
4. Touch the probe end of the test light to the end of the power supply wire that was disconnected from the bulb. If the bulb is receiving current, the test light will go on.

NOTE: *If the bulb is one which works only when the ignition key is turned on (turn signal), make sure the key is turned on.*

If the test light does not go on, then the problem is in the circuit between the battery and the bulb. As mentioned before, this includes all the switches, fuses, and relays in the system. The problem is an open circuit between the battery and the bulb. If the fuse is blown and, when replaced, immediately blows again, there is a short circuit in the system which must be located and repaired. If there is a switch in the system, bypass it with a jumper wire. This is done by connecting one end of the jumper wire into the switch, and the other end of the jumper wire to the wire coming out of the switch. If the test light lights with the jumper wire installed, the switch or whatever was bypassed is defective.

NOTE: *Never substitute the jumper wire for the bulb, as the bulb is the component required to use the power from the power source.*

5. If the bulb in the test light goes on, then the current is getting to the bulb that is not working in the vehicle. This eliminates the first of the three possible causes. Connect the power supply wire and connect a jumper wire from the bulb to a good metal ground. Do this with the switch which controls the bulb turned on, and also the ignition switch turned on if it is required for the light to work. If the bulb works with the jumper wire installed, then it has a bad ground. This is usually caused by the metal area on which the bulb mounts to the car being coated with some type of foreign matter or rust.

6. If neither test located the source of the trouble, then the light bulb itself is defective.

The above test procedure can be applied to

any of the components of the chassis electrical system by substituting the component that is not working for the light bulb. *Remember that for any electrical system to work, all connections must be clean and tight.*

HEATER

Heater Assembly

REMOVAL AND INSTALLATION

Without Air Conditioning

1978–79

1. Disconnect the battery and drain the cooling system.

2. Remove the center outside air floor vent housing.

3. Remove the ash tray.

4. Remove the two defroster duct adapter screws. The left one is reached through the ash tray opening.

5. Remove the defrost duct adapter and push the flexible hose up out of the way.

6. Disconnect the temperature control cable.

7. Disconnect the blower motor wiring connector.

8. Disconnect the hoses from the heater core and plug the core openings.

9. Remove the two nuts retaining the heater unit to the firewall.

10. Remove the glove compartment and door.

11. Remove the screw attaching the heater brace bracket to the instrument panel.

12. Remove the heater assembly support

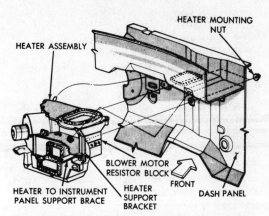

Removing or installing the heater

strap nut. Disconnect the strap from the plenum stud and lower the heater from the instrument panel.

13. Disconnect the control cable and remove the unit from the car.

14. Connect the control cable and raise the unit into position so that the core tubes and mounting studs fit through their holes in the firewall.

15. Install the support strap and hand tighten the nut.

16. Install and tighten the two heater-to-firewall nuts.

17. Unplug and connect the core tubes.

18. Install the defroster duct adaptor.

19. Install the ash tray.

20. Install the center outside air floor vent housing.

21. Install the glove compartment.

22. Refill the cooling system.

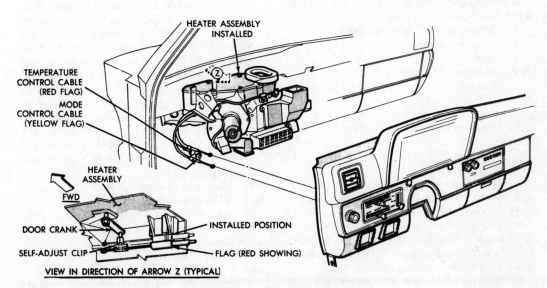

Heater control holders and attachment

1980 AND LATER

1. Disconnect the battery ground.
2. Drain the cooling system.
3. Disconnect the blower motor wiring connector.
4. Remove the ash tray.
5. Depress the retaining tab and pull the temperature control cable out of the receptacle on the heater.
6. Remove the glove compartment and door.
7. Disconnect the heater hoses at the core tubes, and cover the tube openings to prevent spillage.
8. Remove the two nuts holding the heater case to the firewall.
9. Remove the wire connector from the blower motor resistor block.
10. Remove the bolt holding the heater support brace to the instrument panel.
11. Remove the heater support bracket nut. Disconnect the strap from the plenum stud and lower the heater from the instrument panel.
12. Depress the tab on the retainer and pull the mode control door cable from the heater.
13. Move the heater to the right and remove it from the car.
14. Installation is the reverse of removal.

With Air Conditioning

1978–79

This procedure requires the discharge, evacuation, recharge and leak testing of the system. This is a relatively dangerous operation, since contact with refrigerant can cause injury.

During installation, a small can of refrigerant oil will be necessary.

1. Disconnect the battery ground.
2. Drain the coolant.
3. Disconnect the temperature door cable from the heater-evaporator unit.
4. Disconnect the temperature door cable from the retaining clips.
5. Remove the glovebox.
6. Disconnect the vacuum harness from the control head.
7. Disconnect the blower motor lead and anti-diesel relay wire.
8. Remove the seven screws fastening the right trim bezel to the instrument panel. Starting at the right side, swing the bezel clear and remove it.
9. Remove the three screws on the bottom of the center distribution duct cover and slide the cover rearward and remove it.
10. Remove the center distribution duct.
11. Remove the defroster duct adaptor.

12. Remove the H-type expansion valve, located on the right side of the firewall:
    a. remove the 5/16 in. bolt in the center of the plumbing sealing plate.
    b. carefully pull the refrigerant lines toward the front of the car, taking care to avoid scratching the valve sealing surfaces.
    c. remove the two 1/4–20 Allen head cap screws and remove the valve.
13. Cap the pipe openings at once. Wrap the valve in a plastic bag.
14. Disconnect the hoses from the core tubes.
15. Disconnect the vacuum lines at the intake manifold and water valve.
16. Remove the unit-to-firewall retaining nuts.
17. Remove the panel support bracket.
18. Remove the right cowl lower panel.
19. Remove the instrument panel pivot bracket screw from the right side.
20. Remove the screws securing the lower instrument panel at the steering column.
21. Pull back the carpet from under the unit as far as possible.
22. Remove the nut from the evaporator-heater unit-to-plenum mounting brace and blower motor ground cable. While supporting the unit, remove the brace from its stud.
23. Lift the unit, pulling it rearward to allow clearance. These operations may require two people.
24. Slowly lower the unit taking care to keep the studs from hanging-up on the insulation.
25. When the unit reaches the floor, slide it rearward until it is out from under the instrument panel.
26. Remove the unit from the car.

CAUTION: *When installing the unit in the car, care must be taken that the vacuum lines to the engine compartment do not hang-up on the accelerator or become trapped between the unit and the firewall. If this happens, kinked lines will result and the unit will have to be removed to free them. Proper routing of these lines will require two people. The portion of the vacuum harness which is routed through the steering column support MUST be positioned BEFORE the distribution housing is installed. The harness MUST be routed ABOVE the temperature control cable.*

27. Place the unit on the floor as far under the panel as possible.
28. Raise the unit carefully, at the same time pull the lower instrument panel rearward as far as possible.
29. Position the unit in place and attach the brace to the stud.
30. Install the lower ground cable and attach the nut.

31. Install and tighten the unit-to-firewall nuts.

32. Reposition the carpet and install, but do not tighten the right instrument panel pivot bracket screw.

33. Place a piece of sheet metal or thin cardboard against the evaporator-heater assembly to center the assembly duct seal.

34. Position the center distributor duct in place making sure that the upper left tab comes in through the left center A/C outlet opening and that each air take-off is properly inserted in its respective outlet.

NOTE: *Make sure that the radio wiring connector does not interfere with the duct*

35. Install and tighten the screw securing the upper left tab of the center air distribution duct to the instrument panel.

36. Remove the sheet metal or cardboard from between the unit and the duct.

NOTE: *Make sure that the unit seal is properly aligned with the duct opening.*

37. Install and tighten the two lower screws fastening the center distribution duct to the instrument panel.

38. Install and tighten the screws securing the lower instrument panel at the steering column.

39. Install and tighten the nut securing the instrument panel to the support bracket.

40. Make sure that the seal on the unit is properly aligned and seated against the distribution duct assembly.

41. Tighten the instrument panel pivot bracket screw and install the right cowl lower trim.

42. Slide the distributor duct cover assembly onto the center distribution duct so that the notches lock into the tabs and the tabs slide over the rear and side ledges of the center duct assembly.

43. Install the three screws securing the ducting.

44. Install the right trim bezel.

45. Connect the vacuum harness to the control head.

46. Connect the blower lead and the anti-diesel wire.

47. Install the glove box.

48. Connect the temperature door cable.

49. Install new O-rings on the evaporator plate and the plumbing plate. Coat the new O-rings with clean refrigerant oil.

50. Place the H-valve against the evaporator sealing plate surface and install the two ½–20NC throughbolts. Torque to 6–10 ft. lb.

51. Carefully hold the refrigerant line connector against the valve and install the 5⁄16–18-NC bolt. Torque to 14–20 ft. lb.

52. Install the heater hoses at the core tubes.

53. Connect the vacuum lines at the manifold and water valve.

54. Install the condensate drain tube.

55. Have the system evacuated, charged and leak tested by a trained technician.

1980 AND LATER

This procedure requires the discharge, evacuation, recharge and leak testing of the system. This is a relatively dangerous operation, since, contact with refrigerant can cause injury.

1. Discharge the system.

2. Drain the cooling system.

3. Disconnect the battery.

4. Disconnect the heater hoses at the core tubes. Cap the tube openings to prevent spillage.

5. Disconnect the vacuum lines at the intake manifold and the water valve. Tag the lines for installation.

6. Remove the "H" valve:

a. Disconnect the wire from the low pressure cut-off switch.

b. Remove the bolt in the center of the plumbing sealing plate.

c. Pull the refrigerant line assembly toward the front of the car. Take care to avoid scratching the valve sealing surfaces with the tube pilots.

d. Hold the H valve, remove the two allen head screws and lift out the valve.

7. Unclamp and remove the condensation drain.

8. Remove the nuts holding the heater/evaporator case to the firewall.

9. Depress the tab and unhook the cable retainer from the case.

10. Remove the glove compartment.

11. Disconnect the vacuum harness from the A/C control head.

12. Disconnect the blower feed wire and the anti-diesel solenoid wires.

13. Remove the seven screws retaining the right trim bezel to the instrument panel. Starting at the right side, swing the trim bezel clear of the panel and remove it.

14. Remove the three screws securing the center distribution duct to the instrument panel and remove it.

15. Remove the defroster duct adapter.

16. Remove the instrument panel support bracket.

17. Remove the instrument panel pivot bracket screw from the right side.

18. Remove the screws securing the instrument panel to the steering column.

19. Pull the carpet away from the case.

20. Remove the nut securing the case to the plenum and ground cable.

21. Support the case and remove the plenum bracket.

22. Lift the case and pull it rearward as far as possible to clear the panel. The lower panel may have to be pulled rearward to aid in case removal.

NOTE: *Two people will make this job a lot easier.*

23. When the case clears the panel, lower it slowly so that the studs don't hang up in the panel liner.

24. Lower the case to the floor and remove it from the car.

CAUTION: *When installing the unit, make sure that none of the vacuum lines is kinked. Kinked lines would require removal of the unit again.*

25. Place the case on the floor as far forward as possible.

26. Lift the unit being careful of the studs. Manipulate the panel to aid installation of the case.

27. Attach the brace to the stud. Install the ground wire and tighten the nut.

28. Install and tighten the case-to-firewall nuts.

29. Install the drain tube.

30. Install the heater hoses.

31. Install the vacuum lines.

32. Install the "H" valve.

33. Reposition the carpet.

34. Install, but don't tighten the right side instrument panel pivot bracket screw.

35. Install the defroster duct adapter, making certain that the opening is properly aligned.

36. Place a piece of thin cardboard against the evaporator/heater assembly-to-center distribution duct seal.

37. Position the center distribution duct in place. Make sure that the upper left tab comes out through the left center duct. Each end air outlet must be properly aligned with its respective spot cooler.

NOTE: *Be certain that the radio wiring connecter does not interfere with the center duct.*

38. Install and tighten the screw retaining the upper left tab of the center duct.

39. Remove the cardboard. Make sure that the evaporator/heater seal is properly aligned with the top of the center duct opening.

40. Install and tighten the two lower center duct-to-panel screws.

41. Installation of all remaining parts is the reverse of the removal sequence. Fill the cooling system; evacuate, charge and leak test the A/C system.

Blower Motor

REMOVAL AND INSTALLATION

Without Air Conditioning

The blower motor is located under the instrument panel on the left side of the heater assembly.

1. Disconnect the motor wiring.

2. Remove the left outlet duct.

3. Remove the motor retaining screws and remove the motor.

4. Installation is the reverse of removal.

Air Conditioned Cars

1. Disconnect the battery ground.

2. Remove the three screws securing the glovebox to the instrument panel.

3. Disconnect the wiring from the blower and case.

4. Remove the blower vent tube from the case.

5. Loosen the recirculating door from its bracket and remove the actuator from the housing. Leave the vacuum lines attached.

6. Remove the seven screws attaching the recirculating housing to the A/C unit and remove the housing.

7. Remove the three mounting flange nuts and washers.

8. Remove the blower motor from the unit.

9. Installation is the reverse of removal. Replace any damaged sealer.

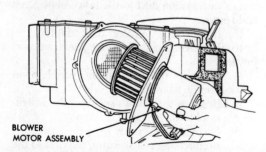

BLOWER
MOTOR ASSEMBLY

Removing or installing the blower motor

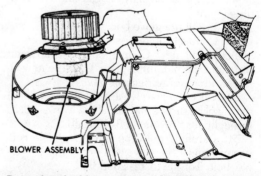

BLOWER ASSEMBLY

Removing the blower motor (with A/C)

Heater Core

REMOVAL AND INSTALLATION

Without Air Conditioning

1. Remove the heater assembly as described earlier.
2. Remove the left outlet duct.
3. Remove the blower motor.
4. Remove the defroster duct adapter.
5. Remove the outside air and defroster door cover.
6. Remove the defroster door.
7. Remove the defroster door control rod.
8. Remove the core cover.
9. Lift the core from the unit.
10. Installation is the reverse of removal.

With Air Conditioning

NOTE: *Core removal requires removal of the entire heater assembly.*

1. Remove the heater/evaporator assembly.
2. Place the unit on a workbench. On the inside-the-car-side, remove the ¼-20 nut from the mode door actuator on the top cover and the two retaining clips from the front edge of the cover. To remove the mode door actuator, remove the two screws securing it to the cover.
3. Remove the fifteen screws attaching the cover to the assembly and lift off the cover. Lift the mode door out of the unit.

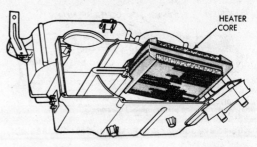

Removing the heater core

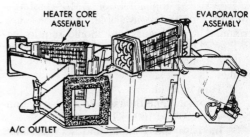

Removing the heater core and evaporator coil

4. Remove the screw from the core retaining bracket and lift out the core.
5. Place the core in the unit and install the bracket.
6. Install the actuator arm.

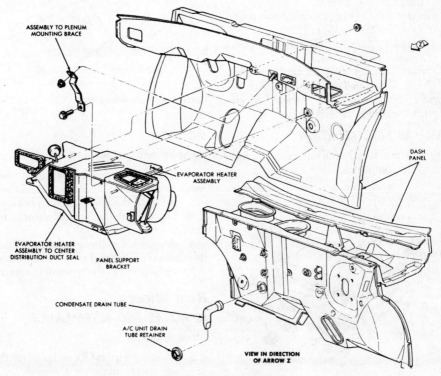

Heater/evaporator assembly

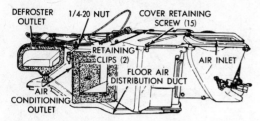

DEFROSTER OUTLET · 1/4-20 NUT · COVER RETAINING SCREW (15) · RETAINING CLIPS (2) · AIR INLET · FLOOR AIR DISTRIBUTION DUCT · AIR CONDITIONING OUTLET

Heater/evaporator unit positioned for disassembly

RADIO

AM, AM/FM monaural, or AM/FM stereo multiplex units are available. All radios are trimmed at the factory and should require no further adjustment. However, after a repair or if the antenna trim is to be verified, proceed as follows:

1. Turn radio on.
2. Manually tune the radio to a weak station between 1400 and 1600 KHz on AM.
3. Increase the volume and set the tone control to full treble (clockwise).
4. Viewing the radio from the front, the trimmer control is a slot-head located at the rear of the right side. Adjust it carefully by turning it back and forth with a screwdriver until maximum loudness is achieved.

NOTE: *Some 1978 and early production 1979 cars exhibit an ignition noise interfering with radio reception. This can be corrected by installing the following items:*

1. *Ground Strap (Engine-mount-to-frame) (Chrysler Part No. 5211212)*
2. *Ground Strap (Engine-to-Cowl) (Chrysler Part No. 5211211).*
3. *Ground Strap (A/C Evaporator-to-Cowl) (Chrysler Part No. 5211210)*

Ground straps can also be obtained in kit form from local radio or CB shops.

REMOVAL AND INSTALLATION

1. Remove the bezel attaching screws and open the glove compartment.

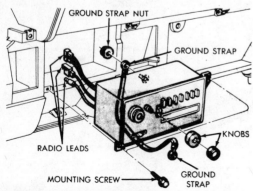

GROUND STRAP NUT · GROUND STRAP · KNOBS · RADIO LEADS · MOUNTING SCREW · GROUND STRAP

Radio removed or installation

2. Remove the bezel, guiding the right end around the glove compartment and away from the panel.
3. Disconnect the radio ground strap and remove the two radio mounting screws.
4. Pull the radio from the panel and disconnect the wiring and antenna lead.
5. Installation is the reverse of removal.

WINDSHIELD WIPERS

Front Wipers

WIPER REFILL

See Chapter 1 for wiper refill replacement.

WIPER BLADE REPLACEMENT

1. Lift the wiper arm away from the glass.
2. Depress the release lever on the bridge and remove the blade assembly from the arm.
3. Lift the tab and pinch the end bridge to release it from the center bridge.
4. Slide the end bridge from the blade element and the element from the opposite end bridge.
5. Assembly is the reverse of removal. Make sure that the element locking tabs are securely locked in position.

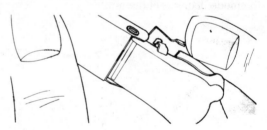

Removing front wiper arm

MOTOR

Removal and Installation

1. Disconnect the linkage from the motor carnk arm.
2. Remove the wiper motor plastic cover.
3. Disconnect the wiring harness from the motor.
4. Remove the three mounting bolts from the motor bracket and remove the motor.
5. Installation is the reverse of removal.

Rear Wipers

REMOVAL AND INSTALLATION

Blade and Arm

1. Turn the wipers ON and position the blade at a convenient place on the glass by turning the ignition OFF.

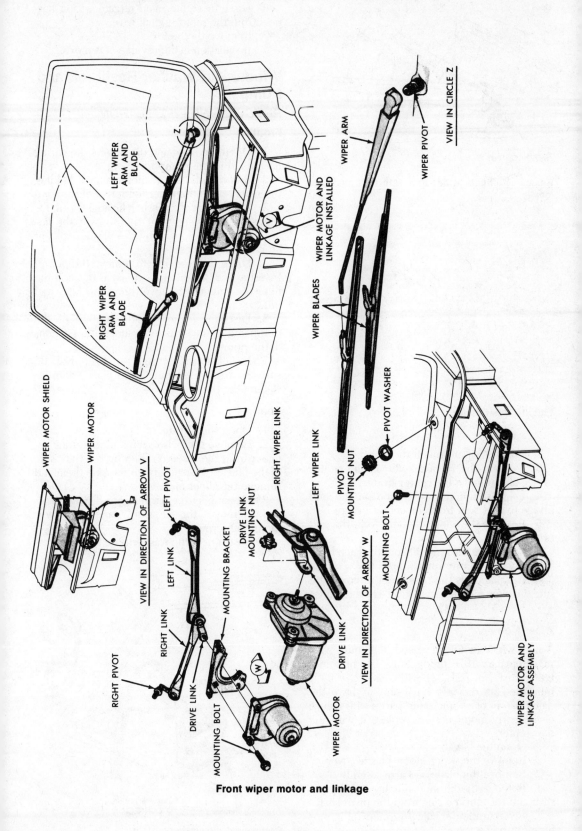

LEFT WIPER ARM AND BLADE

RIGHT WIPER ARM AND BLADE

WIPER MOTOR SHIELD

WIPER MOTOR

VIEW IN DIRECTION OF ARROW V

LEFT PIVOT

LEFT LINK

MOUNTING BRACKET

RIGHT LINK

RIGHT PIVOT

DRIVE LINK

MOUNTING BOLT

WIPER MOTOR

DRIVE LINK MOUNTING NUT

RIGHT WIPER LINK

LEFT WIPER LINK

DRIVE LINK

VIEW IN DIRECTION OF ARROW W

PIVOT MOUNTING NUT

MOUNTING BOLT

WIPER MOTOR AND LINKAGE ASSEMBLY

WIPER ARM

WIPER PIVOT

VIEW IN CIRCLE Z

WIPER MOTOR AND LINKAGE INSTALLED

WIPER BLADES

PIVOT WASHER

Front wiper motor and linkage

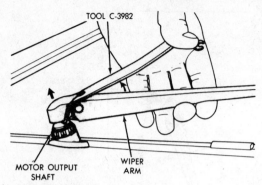

Removing liftgate wiper arm with tool available locally

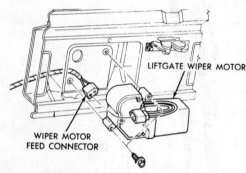

Liftgate wiper motor

2. Lift the wiper arm off the glass.

3. Depress the release lever on the center bridge and remove the center bridge.

4. Depress the release button on the end bridge to release it from the center bridge.

5. Remove the wiper element from the end bridge.

6. To remove the arm, pull out the latch knob and remove the arm from the pivot.

7. Installation is the reverse of removal. Be sure the element is engaged in all 4 bridge claws.

Wiper Motor

A new wiper motor was used beginning with mid-February 1978 production. The new motor is Part No. 5211024 with date code 0378 imprinted on red ink. Early motors have the date code in black ink (same part no.) If failure of the early motor occurs, replace it with the new motor.

1. Open the liftgate.

2. Remove the wiper motor plastic cover.

3. Remove the blade and arm assembly.

4. Remove the chrome nut from the pivot shaft and the chrome ring from the pivot shaft.

5. From inside the tailgate, remove the motor mounting screws.

6. Disconnect the main liftgate wiring harness from the motor pigtail wire.

7. Remove the motor.

8. Installation is the reverse of removal.

Windshield Washer Reservoir and Pump

REMOVAL AND INSTALLATION

Front

1. Open the hood and disconnect the wiring harness from the pump.

2. Remove the sheet metal screws holding the reservoir to the inner fender shield.

3. Disconnect the washer hose and remove the reservoir. Keep your thumb over the liquid outlet to avoid spilling the washer solvent on painted surfaces.

4. Drain the reservoir to remove the pump. Insert a $19/32''$ socket and extension through the filler opening and remove the pump filter and nut.

5. Disconnect the outside portion of the pump and remove the inner and outer portions of the pump.

6. Installation is the reverse of removal. Be sure the rubber grommet is in place when installing the pump.

Rear

1. Open the liftgate.

2. Remove the plastic cap and mounting retainer from the reservoir filler on the right side of the liftgate. Reach through the side drain and remove the sheet metal screws.

3. Disconnect the wiring from the pump.

4. Remove the 2 side panel reservoir mounting screws.

5. Disconnect the washer hose from the reservoir.

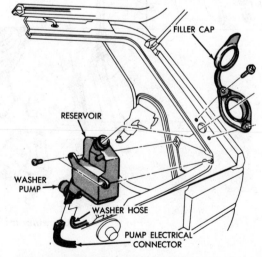

Rear windshield washer system

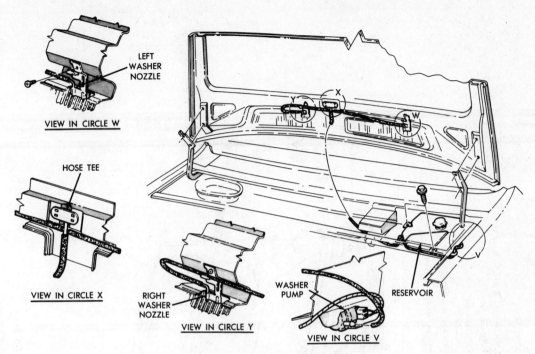

LEFT WASHER NOZZLE

VIEW IN CIRCLE W

HOSE TEE

VIEW IN CIRCLE X

RIGHT WASHER NOZZLE

VIEW IN CIRCLE Y

WASHER PUMP

RESERVOIR

VIEW IN CIRCLE V

Front windshield washer system

6. Remove the reservoir and pump from the side panel through the aperture panel access hole. Try not to spill windshield washer solvent on the paint.

7. Drain the reservoir to remove the pump. Insert a $^{19}/_{32}''$ socket and extension through the filler opening and remove the pump filter and nut.

8. Disconnect the outside portion of the pump and remove the inner and outer parts of the pump.

9. Installation is the reverse of removal. Be sure the rubber grommet is in place when installing the pump.

INSTRUMENT PANEL

The fuel, temperature and oil pressure gauges work on the constant voltage principle through a common voltage limiter which pulses to provide intermittent current to the gauge system.

Cluster Assembly
REMOVAL AND INSTALLATION
1978–83

1. Remove the two lens assembly lower attaching retaining springs by pulling rearward with a pliers.

2. Allow the lens assembly to drop as it is pulled rearward.

3. Remove the speedometer assembly (two screws).

4. Remove the two wiring harness connectors.

5. Remove the two (1978–79), or four (1980–83) cluster attaching screws.

6. (1978–79 only) Pull the two upper spring retainers away from the panel.

7. If equipped with a clock, reach behind the panel and disconnect the wires.

8. Remove the cluster assembly.

9. Installation is the reverse of removal.

Rattles in a 1978 or 1979 instrument cluster may be caused by loose or missing upper cluster mounting clips. To correct rattles, a screw (Chrysler Part No. 9414172) in the screw holes provided in the upper part of the cluster.

1984 AND LATER

1. Remove the two lower cluster bezel retaining screws.

2. Allow the bezel to drop slightly as it is moved rearward and remove the bezel.

3. Remove the four screws attaching the cluster to the base panel.

4. Pull the cluster rearward and disconnect the speedometer cable and the wiring connector.

5. Remove the cluster assembly from the instrument panel.

6. To install, reverse the removal procedure.

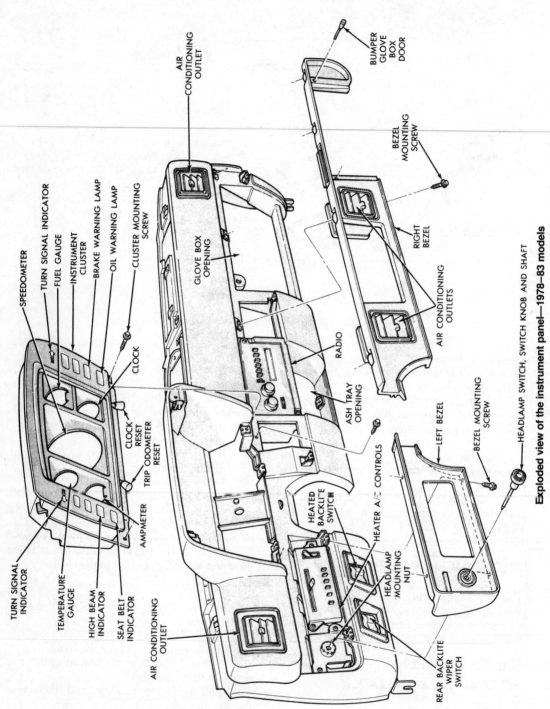

Exploded view of the instrument panel—1978–83 models

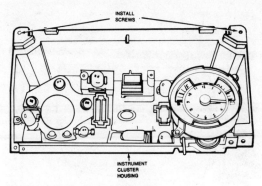

Instrument cluster modification

Speedometer Cable
REMOVAL AND INSTALLATION

1. Reach under the instrument panel and depress the spring clip retaining the cable to the speedometer head (on some models, cluster removal may be necessary). Pull the cable back and away from the head.

2. If the core is broken, raise and support the vehicle and remove the cable retaining screw from the cable bracket. Carefully slide the cable out of the transaxle.

3. Coat the new core sparingly with speedometer cable lubricant and insert it in the cable. Install the cable at the transaxle, lower the car and install the cable at the speedometer head.

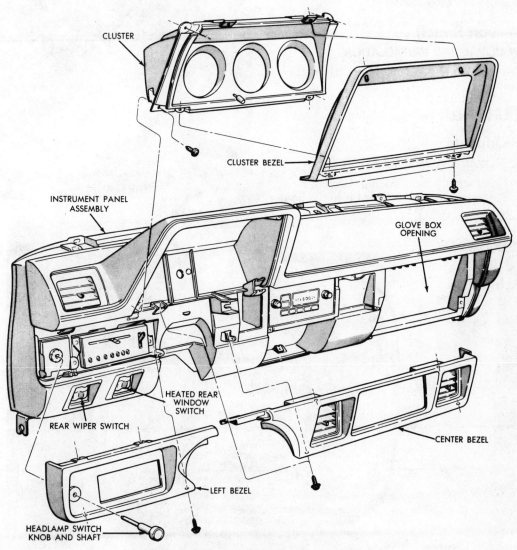

Typical instrument panel—1984 and later

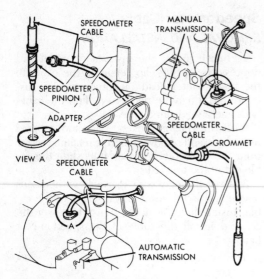

Speedometer cable mounting

Headlight bezel mounting screws—typical

Ignition Switch

REMOVAL AND INSTALLATION

See Chapter 7 for Ignition Switch replacement.

LIGHTING

Headlights

REMOVAL AND INSTALLATION

1. Be sure the light switch is OFF.
2. Remove the 4 screws that hold the headlight bezel in place.

Headlight socket

Headlight retaining ring screws

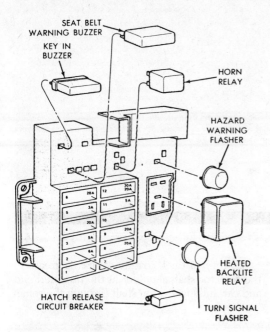

Fuse block—1978-79 models

3. Remove the headlight bezel. Pull the bezel away and disconnect the parking/turn signal light. Twist to remove the light and socket.

4. Set the bezel aside.

5. Remove the 4 screws securing the headlight retainer and remove the retainer.

6. Pull the headlight out and disconnect the socket.

7. Install a new headlight in the reverse order of removal. Check the operation of the lights before completing the assembly.

Headlight Switch

REMOVAL AND INSTALLATION

1. Disconnect the battery ground.
2. Pull the headlight knob from the switch.
3. Unscrew the collar from the instrument panel side of the switch.
4. Push the switch through the panel and let it drop; disconnect the wires.
5. Installation is the reverse of removal.

FUSES, FUSIBLE LINKS AND CIRCUIT BREAKERS

Fusible Links

Fusible links are used to prevent major wire harness damage in the event of a short circuit or an overload condition in electrical circuits. each fusible link is of a fixed value for a specific

electrical load. Should a link fail, the cause of the failure must be determined and repaired prior to installing a new link of the same value.

Circuit Breakers

Circuit breakers are used along with the fusible links to protect electrical system components such as headlamps, windshield wipers, electric windows, tailgate front and rear switches. The circuit breakers are located either in the switch or mounted on/near the lower lip of the instrument panel, to the right or left side of the steering column.

FUSE PANELS

The fuse panel is used to house the fuses that protect the individual or combined electrical circuits within the vehicle. The turn signal flasher, the hazard warning flasher and the seat belt warning buzzer/timer are located on the fuse panel for quick identification and replacement. The fuses are usually identified by abbreviated circuit names or number, with the number of the rated fuse needed to protect the circuit printed below the fuse holder.

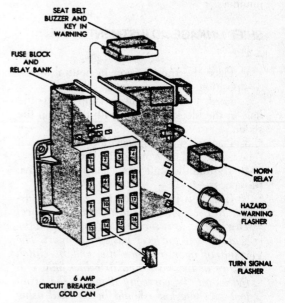

Fuse block—1980-84

WIRING DIAGRAMS

Wiring diagrams have been left out of this book. As cars have become more complex and available with longer and longer option lists, wiring diagrams have grown in size and complexity also. It has become virtually impossible to provide a readable reproduction in a reasonable number of pages.

Drive Train

+6

MANUAL TRANSAXLE

The Omni and Horizon models use four types of manual transaxles, the A412 VW design 4-spd., the Chrysler design A460 4-spd., the A465 5-spd., and the A525 close ratio 5-spd. used in the high performance models.

A pad, located on top of the clutch housing contains the transaxle and VIN identification numbers.

SHIFT LINKAGE ADJUSTMENT
A-412

1. Place the transmission in neutral at the 3–4 position.
2. Loosen the shift tube clamp. Align the hole in the blocker bracket with the tab in the slider.
3. Place a ⅝ inch spacer between the shift tube flange and the yoke at the shift base.
4. Tighten the shift tube clamp and remove the spacer.
NOTE: *It is possible for the manual transaxle to become locked in two gears at once. This will occur if the interlock blocker on the gearshift selector lever has spread apart. The result of operating like this will be clutch failure at the least, and driveline failure at the worst. To correctly diagnose the problem, the interlock should be checked using the following procedure:*
1. Disconnect the shift linkage operating lever from the transaxle selector shaft.
2. Remove the transaxle detent spring assembly and selector shaft boot.
3. Remove the aluminum selector shaft plug.
4. Place the transaxle in neutral and pull the selector shaft assembly out of the case.
5. Measure the interlock blocker gap "A," in the accompanying picture. If gap "A" exceeds .330 in. replace the gearshift selector shaft assembly.

6. Apply a thick coating of chassis grease to the selector shaft shoulder at the threaded end and carefully insert the shaft through the selec-

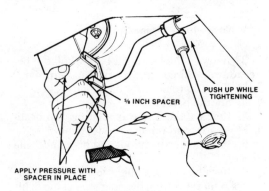

A-412 shift linkage adjustment

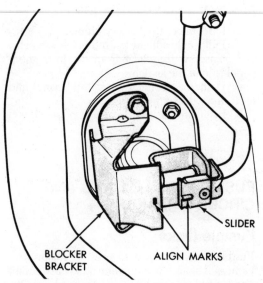

On the A-412, align the marks on the blocker and slides

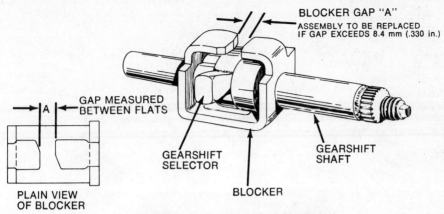

Checking the A-412 interlock blocker

tor shaft oil seal. Reverse steps 1–4 to install.

7. Adjust the shift linkage.

A-460

1. From the left side of the car, remove the lockpin from the transaxle selector shaft housing.

2. Reverse the lockpin and insert it in the same threaded hole while pushing the selector shaft into the selector housing. A hole in the selector shaft will align with the lockpin, allowing the lockpin to be screwed into the housing. This will lock the selector shaft in the 1-2 neutral position.

3. Raise and support the vehicle on jackstands.

4. Loosen the clamp bolt that secures the gearshift tube to the gearshift connector.

5. Make sure that the gearshift connector slides and turns freely in the gearshift tube.

6. Position the shifter mechanism connector assembly so that the isolator is contacting the standing flange and the rib on the isolator is aligned front and back with the hole in the

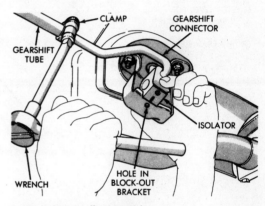

A-460 linkage adjustment

block-out bracket. Hold the connector in this position while tightening the clamp bolt on the gearshift tube to 14 ft. lb.

7. Lower the car.

8. Remove the lockpin from the selector shaft housing and install it the original way in the housing.

9. Tighten the lockpin to 105 in. lb.

10. Check shifter action.

A465 and A525

1. From the left side of the car, remove the lockpin from the transaxle selector shaft housing.

2. Reverse the lockpin and insert it in the same threaded hole while pushing the selector shaft into the selector housing. A hole in the selector shaft will align with the lockpin, allowing the lockpin to be screwed into the housing. This will lock the selector shaft in the 1-2 neutral position.

3. Remove the gearshift knob, the retaining nut and the pull-up ring.

4. Remove the console attaching screws and remove the console.

5. Make two cable adjusting pins as shown in the illustration.

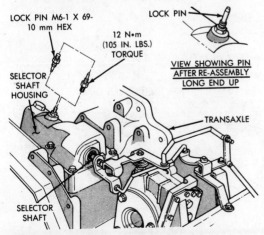

A-460, 465, and 525 transaxles pinned in the 1st to 2nd neutral position for linkage adjustment

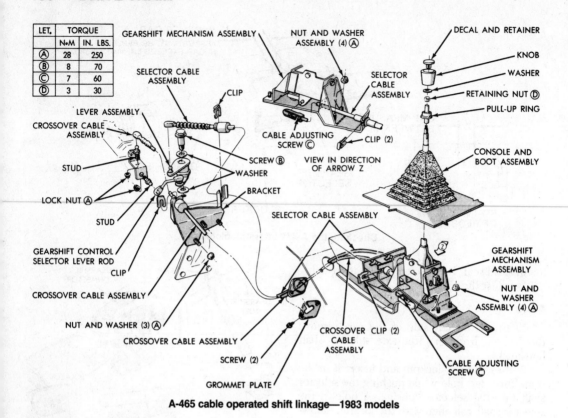

LET.	TORQUE	
	N•M	IN. LBS.
Ⓐ	28	250
Ⓑ	8	70
Ⓒ	7	60
Ⓓ	3	30

GEARSHIFT MECHANISM ASSEMBLY

NUT AND WASHER ASSEMBLY (4) Ⓐ

DECAL AND RETAINER

KNOB

WASHER

RETAINING NUT Ⓓ

PULL-UP RING

SELECTOR CABLE ASSEMBLY

SELECTOR CABLE ASSEMBLY

CLIP

CABLE ADJUSTING SCREW Ⓒ

CLIP (2)

VIEW IN DIRECTION OF ARROW Z

CONSOLE AND BOOT ASSEMBLY

LEVER ASSEMBLY

CROSSOVER CABLE ASSEMBLY

STUD

LOCK NUT Ⓐ

STUD

SCREW Ⓑ

WASHER

BRACKET

GEARSHIFT CONTROL SELECTOR LEVER ROD

CLIP

CROSSOVER CABLE ASSEMBLY

SELECTOR CABLE ASSEMBLY

GEARSHIFT MECHANISM ASSEMBLY

NUT AND WASHER ASSEMBLY (4) Ⓐ

NUT AND WASHER (3) Ⓐ

CROSSOVER CABLE ASSEMBLY

SCREW (2)

GROMMET PLATE

CROSSOVER CABLE ASSEMBLY

CLIP (2)

CABLE ADJUSTING SCREW Ⓒ

A-465 cable operated shift linkage—1983 models

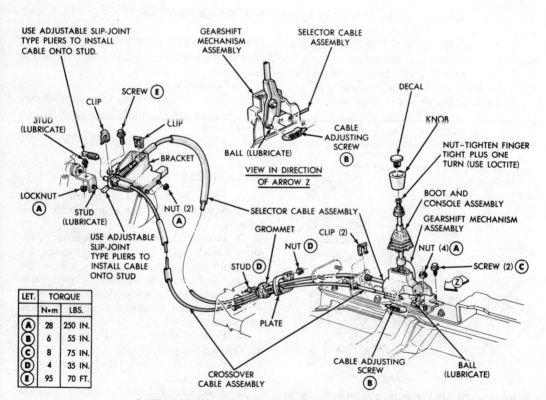

USE ADJUSTABLE SLIP-JOINT TYPE PLIERS TO INSTALL CABLE ONTO STUD.

GEARSHIFT MECHANISM ASSEMBLY

SELECTOR CABLE ASSEMBLY

DECAL

CLIP

SCREW Ⓔ

CLIP

KNOB

STUD (LUBRICATE)

BRACKET

CABLE ADJUSTING SCREW Ⓑ

NUT–TIGHTEN FINGER TIGHT PLUS ONE TURN (USE LOCTITE)

BALL (LUBRICATE)

VIEW IN DIRECTION OF ARROW Z

LOCKNUT Ⓐ

STUD (LUBRICATE)

NUT (2) Ⓐ

BOOT AND CONSOLE ASSEMBLY

GEARSHIFT MECHANISM ASSEMBLY

USE ADJUSTABLE SLIP-JOINT TYPE PLIERS TO INSTALL CABLE ONTO STUD

SELECTOR CABLE ASSEMBLY

GROMMET

NUT Ⓓ

CLIP (2)

NUT (4) Ⓐ

SCREW (2) Ⓒ

STUD Ⓓ

PLATE

LET.	TORQUE	
	N•m	LBS.
Ⓐ	28	250 IN.
Ⓑ	6	55 IN.
Ⓒ	8	75 IN.
Ⓓ	4	35 IN.
Ⓔ	95	70 FT.

CROSSOVER CABLE ASSEMBLY

CABLE ADJUSTING SCREW Ⓑ

BALL (LUBRICATE)

A-465 and A-525 cable operated shift linkage—1984 models

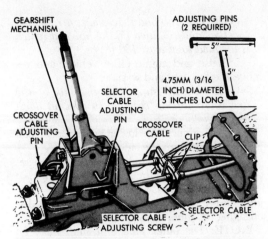

Make two cable adjusting pins—A-465, A-525 transaxles

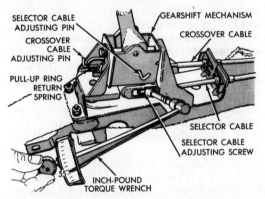

Adjusting the selector cable—A-465, A-525 transaxles

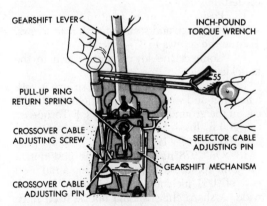

Adjusting the crossover cable—A-465, A-525 transaxles

6. Adjust the selector cable and torque the adjusting screw to 60 in. lbs. on 1983 models, or 55 in. lbs. on 1984 and later models.

NOTE: *Proper torque of the selector cable and the crossover cable adjusting screw is important for proper operation of the shift linkage.*

7. Adjust the crossover cable and torque the adjusting screw to 60 in. lbs. on 1983 models, or 55 in. lbs. on 1984 and later models.

8. Remove the lock pin from the selector shaft housing and reinstall the lock pin in the selector shaft housing so that the long end is pointing up. Torque the lock pin to 105 in. lbs.

9. Check for proper operation of the shift cables.

10. Reinstall the console, pull-up ring, retaining nut and the gearshift knob.

REMOVAL AND INSTALLATION

A-412

NOTE: *Anytime the differential cover is removed, a new gasket should be formed from RTV sealant. See Chapter 1.*

1. Remove the engine timing mark access plug.

2. Rotate the engine to align the drilled mark on the flywheel with the pointer on the engine.

3. Disconnect the battery ground.

4. Disconnect the shift linkage rods.

5. Disconnect the starter and ground wires.

6. Disconnect the backup light switch wire.

7. Remove the starter.

8. Disconnect the clutch cable.

9. Disconnect the speedometer cable.

10. Support the weight of the engine from

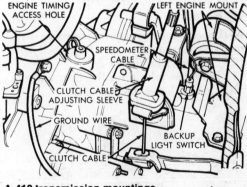

A-412 transmission mountings

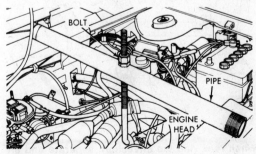

Fabricated engine support fixture

above, preferably with a shop hoist or the fabricated holding fixture.

11. Raise and support the vehicle.

12. Disconnect the drive shafts and support them out of the way.

13. Remove the left splash shield.

14. Drain the transaxle.

15. Unbolt the left engine mount.

16. Remove the transaxle-to-engine bolts.

17. Slide the transaxle to the left until the mainshaft clears, then, carefully lower it from the car.

18. Installation is the reverse of removal.

19. Adjust the clutch cable.

20. Adjust the shift linkage.

21. Fill the transaxle.

A-460, A-465 and A-525

1. Disconnect the battery.

2. Install an engine lifting fixture on the engine.

3. Disconnect the shift linkage.

4. Remove both front wheels.

5. Remove the left front splash shield.

6. Follow the procedures under "Halfshaft Removal and Installation."

7. The removal of the unit is the same as that for the automatic transaxle, except that no torque converter is used.

8. Installation is the reverse of removal.

Halfshaft

REMOVAL AND INSTALLATION

A-412 Models

NOTE: *Anytime the differential cover is removed, a new gasket should be formed from RTV sealant. See Chapter 1.*

1. With the vehicle on the floor and the brakes applied, loosen the hub nut.

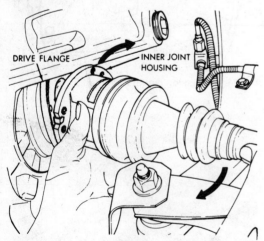

DRIVE FLANGE

INNER JOINT HOUSING

When removing the driveshaft, separate and tilt the joint housing to prevent leakage

NOTE: *The hub and driveshafts are splined together and retained by the hub nut which is torqued to at least 180 ft. lbs.*

2. Raise and support the vehicle and remove the hub nut and washer.

NOTE: *Always support both ends of the driveshaft during removal to prevent damage to the boots.*

3. Disconnect the lower control arm ball joint stud nut from the steering knuckle.

4. Remove the Allenhead screws which secure the CV joint to the transmission flange.

5. Holding the CV housing, push the outer joint and knuckle assembly outward while disengaging the inner housing from the flange face.

NOTE: *The outer joint and shaft must be supported during disengagement of the inner joint.*

Quickly turn the open end of the joint upward to retain as much lubricant as possible, then carefully pull the outer joint spline out of the hub. Cover the joint with a clean towel to prevent dirt contamination.

6. Before installation, make sure that any lost lubricant is replaced. The only lubricant specified is Chrysler part number 4131389. No other lubricant of any type is to be used, as premature failure of the joint will result.

7. Clean the joint body and mating flange face.

8. Install the outer joint splined shaft into the hub. Do not secure with the nut and washer.

9. Early production vehicles were built with a cover plate between the hub and flange face. This cover is not necessary and should be discarded.

10. Position the inner joint in the transmission drive flange and secure it with *new* screws. Torque the screws to 37–40 ft. lb.

11. Connect the lower control arm to the knuckle.

12. Install the outer joint and secure it with a *new* nut and washer. Torque the nut with the car on the ground and the brake set. Torque is:

• 200 ft. lbs.—1978

• 180 ft. lbs.—1979 and later

13. On 1978 models, stake the new nut to the joint spindle using a tool having a radiused end of .063 inch and approximately 7/16 inch wide. A sharp chisel should not be used since the collar will probably be split.

NOTE: *1979 and later models use a cotter pin and nut-lock to retain the nut. Staking is unnecessary.*

14. After attaching the driveshaft, if the inboard boot appears to be collapsed or deformed, vent the inner boot by inserting a round-tipped, small diameter rod between the boot and the shaft. As venting occurs, boot will return to its original shape.

A-460, A-465, A-525 and Automatic Transmission Models

The inboard CV joints are retained by circlips in the differential side gears. The circlip tangs are located on a machined surface on the inner end of the stub shaft.

1. With the car on the ground, loosen the hub nut, which has been torqued to 200 ft. lbs.

2. Drain the transaxle differential and remove the cover.

NOTE: *Anytime the transaxle differential cover is removed, a new gasket should be formed from RTV sealant. See Chapter 1.*

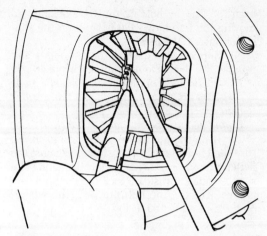

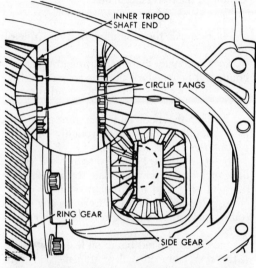

Rotate the driveshaft to expose the circlip retainer

Compress the circlip tongs and push the shaft toward the side gear

3. To remove the right-hand driveshaft, disconnect the speedometer cable and remove the cable and gear before removing the driveshaft.

4. Rotate the driveshaft to expose the circlip tangs.

5. Compress the circlip with needle nose pliers and push the shaft into the side gear cavity.

6. Remove the clamp bolt from the ball stud and steering knuckle.

7. Separate the ball joint stud from the steering knuckle, by prying against the knuckle leg and control arm.

8. Separate the outer CV joint splined shaft

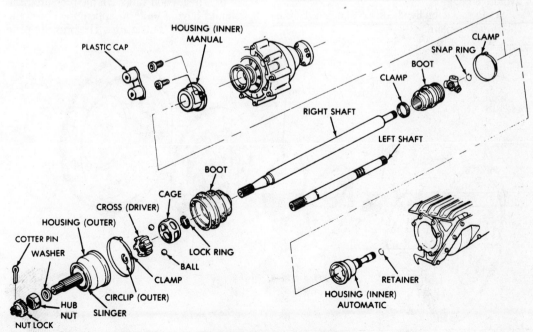

Exploded view of driveshafts

from the hub by holding the CV housing and moving the hub away. Do not pry on the slinger or outer CV joint.

9. Support the shaft at the CV joints and remove the shaft. Do not pull on the shaft.

NOTE: *Removal of the left shaft may be made easier by inserting the blade of a thin prybar between the differential pinion shaft and prying against the end face of the shaft.*

10. Installation is the reverse of removal. Be sure the circlip tangs are positioned against the flattened end of the shaft before installing the shaft. A quick thrust will lock the circlip in the groove. Tighten the hub nut with the wheels on the ground to 180 ft. lbs.

CLUTCH

The clutch is a single dry disc unit, with no adjustment for wear provided in the clutch itself. Adjustment is made through an adjustable sleeve in the pedal linkage.

Clutch Disc

REMOVAL AND INSTALLATION

1. Remove the transmission as described earlier.

NOTE: *Chrysler recommends the use of special tool L-4533 for disc alignment on the A-412 and tool C-4676 for the A-460, A-465 and A-525 transaxles.*

2. Loosen the flywheel-to-pressure plate bolts diagonally, one or two turns at a time to avoid warpage.

3. Remove the flywheel and clutch disc from the pressure plate.

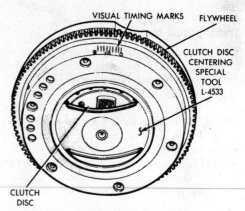

Centering the A-412 clutch disc

4. Remove the retaining ring and release plate.

5. Diagonally loosen the pressure plate-to-crankshaft bolts. Mark all parts for reassembly.

6. Remove the bolts, spacer and pressure plate.

7. The flywheel and pressure plate surfaces should be cleaned thoroughly with fine sandpaper.

8. It is a false economy to replace either the clutch disc or pressure plate separately, since this will only lead to premature failure of the other component. In order to reuse any of the components, the following conditions should be met:

a. There should be no oil leakage through the rear main oil seal or transmission front oil seal.

b. The friction surface of the pressure plate should have a uniform appearance over the entire surface contact area. The pressure plate

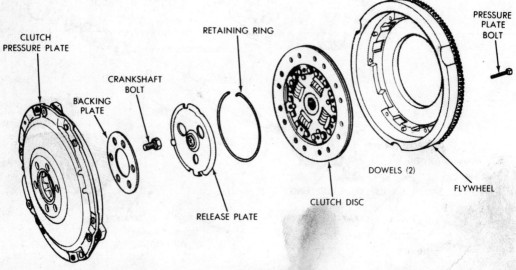

A-412 clutch

A-412 clutch dowel pin hole

A-412 clutch dowel pin

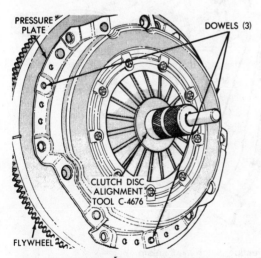

A-460, 465, and 525 clutch disc alignment

may be improperly mounted or sprung if a heavy wear pattern occurs directly opposite a light wear pattern.

c. The friction face of the flywheel should be free from discoloration, burned areas, cracks or grooves. Frequently the face of the flywheel must be machined smooth before installing a new clutch.

d. The disc should be free of oil or grease. If it is worn to within less than 0.015 in. of the rivet heads, replace the disc.

e. Check the pressure plate for flatness. It should be flat within 0.020 in. across the friction area, and be free from cracks, burns, grooves or ridges.

f. Inspect the cover outer mounting flange for flatness, burrs, nicks, or dents.

g. The 2 dowels in the flywheel should be tight and undamaged.

h. Inspect the center of the release plate for cracks or heavy wear. Wear up to 0.010 in. is acceptable.

If the clutch assembly does not meet these conditions, it should be replaced.

9. Align marks and install the pressure plate, spacer and bolts. Coat the bolts with thread compound and torque them to 55 ft. lbs.

10. Install the release plate and retaining ring.

11. Using special tool L-4533, C-4676 or their equivalent, install the clutch disc and flywheel on the pressure plate.

CAUTION: *Make certain that the drilled mark on the flywheel is at the top, so that the two dowels on the flywheel align with the proper holes in the pressure plate.*

12. Install the six flywheel bolts and tighten them to 14.5 ft. lb. on A-412 equipped models, and 21 ft. lb. on A-460, A-465, and A-525 equipped models.

13. Remove the aligning tool.

14. Install the transmission.

15. Adjust the freeplay.

CLUTCH FREEPLAY ADJUSTMENT

A-412

1. Pull up on the clutch plate.

2. While holding the cable up, rotate the adjusting sleeve downward until a snug contact is made against the grommet.

3. Rotate the sleeve slightly to allow the end of the sleeve to seat in the rectangular hole in the grommet.

A-460, A-465, and A-525

This unit has a self-adjusting clutch. No manual adjustment is possible.

AUTOMATIC TRANSAXLE

The automatic transaxle combines a torque converter, fully automatic 3-speed transmission, final drive gearing and differential into a compact front wheel drive system.

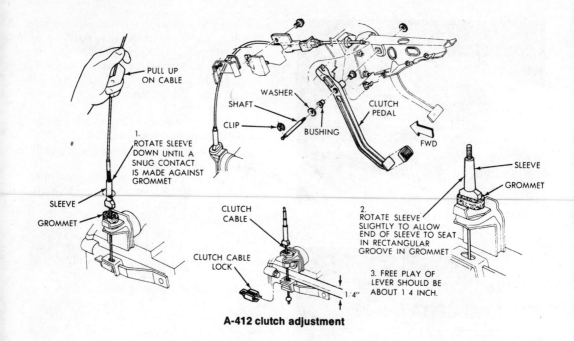

A-412 clutch adjustment

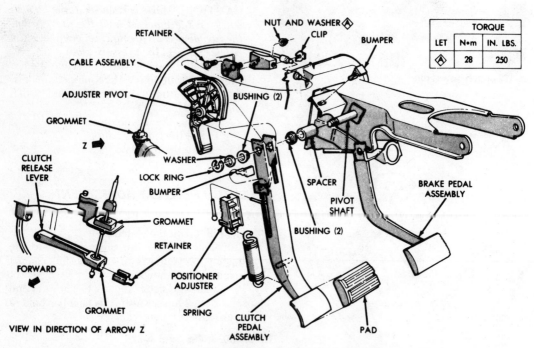

A-460, 465, and A-525 self adjusting clutch mechanism

SHIFT LINKAGE ADJUSTMENT

NOTE: *When it is necessary to disconnect the linkage cable from the lever, which uses plastic grommets as retainers, the grommets should be replaced.*

1. Make sure that the adjustable swivel block is free to slide on the shift cable.

2. Place the shift lever in Park.

3. With the linkage assembled, and the swivel lock bolt loose, move the shift arm on the transaxle into the "Park" position.

4. Hold the shift arm in position with a force

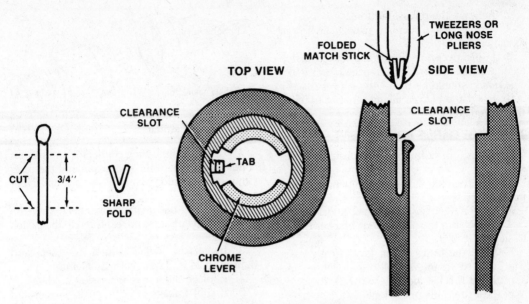

Automatic transmission shifter modification

of about 10 lbs. and tighten the adjuster swivel lock bolt to 8 ft. lb.

5. Check the linkage action.

NOTE: *The automatic transmission gear selector release button may pop up in the knob when shifting from PARK to DRIVE. This is caused by inadequate retention of the selector release knob retaining tab. The release button will always work but the loose button can be annoying. A sleeve (Chrysler Part No. 5211984) and washers (Chrysler Part No. 6500380) are available to cure this condition. If these are unavailable, do the following:*

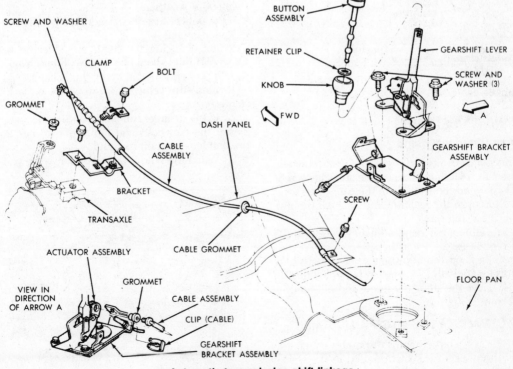

Automatic transmission shift linkage

1. Remove the release button.
2. Cut and fold a standard paper match stem as shown.
3. Using tweezers, insert the folded match as far as possible into the clearance slot as shown. The match should be below the knob surface.
4. Insert the button, taking care not to break the button stem.

THROTTLE CABLE ADJUSTMENT

1. Adjust the idle speed as previously described.
2. Run the engine to normal operating temperature.
3. Loosen the adjustment bracket lock screw.
4. Make sure the adjustment bracket is free to slide in its slot.
5. Hold the transmission lever firmly rearward against its internal stop and tighten the adjustment bracket lock screw to 9 ft. lb.
6. Test the cable operation.

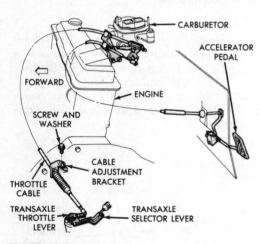

Throttle cable

BAND ADJUSTMENTS

Front (Kickdown) Band

Chrysler recommends that the band be adjusted at each fluid change. The adjusting screw is located on the left side of the case.

1. Loosen the lock nut and back off the nut above five full turns.
2. Tighten the band adjusting screw to 72 inch pounds.
3. Back off the adjusting screw exactly 2.5 turns except with 1.6L engine, back off 3 turns.
4. Hold the adjusting screw and tighten the locknut to 35 ft. lb.

NEUTRAL START SWITCH ADJUSTMENT

The neutral start circuit is the center contact of the three-terminal switch located in the transmission case.

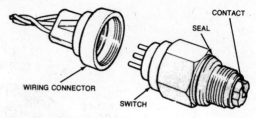

Neutral safety switch

1. Remove the wiring connector and test for continuity between the center pin and the case. Continuity should exist only in Park and Neutral.
2. Remove the switch and check that the operating lever fingers are centered in the switch opening.
3. Install the switch and a new seal and tighten to 24 ft. lb. Retest with a lamp.
4. Replace the lost transmission fluid.
5. If shift linkage adjustment is correct and the switch still malfunctions, replace the switch.

PAN REMOVAL AND INSTALLATION, FLUID AND FILTER CHANGE

NOTE: *RTV silicone sealer is used in place of a pan gasket.*

Chrysler recommends no fluid or filter changes during the normal service life of the car. Severe usage requires a fluid and filter change every 15,000 miles. Severe usage is defined as:

a. more than 50% heavy city traffic during 90°F weather.

b. police, taxi or commercial operation or trailer towing.

When changing the fluid, only Dexron or Dexron II fluid should be used. A filter change should be performed at every fluid change.

1. Raise the vehicle and support it on jack stands.
2. Place a large container under the pan, loosen the pan bolts and tap at one corner to break it loose. Drain the fluid.
3. When the fluid is drained remove the pan bolts.

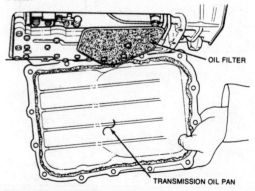

Removing transmission oil pan

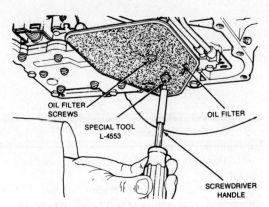

Automatic transmission oil filter attaching screws

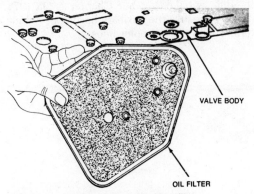

Removing automatic transmission filter

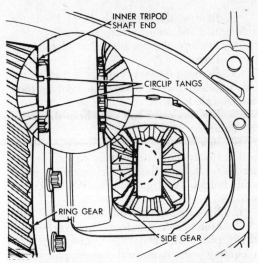

Rotate the driveshafts to expose the circlip ends

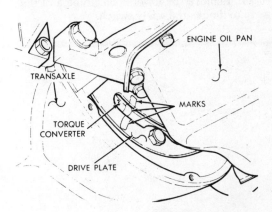

Matchmark the torque converter and drive plate

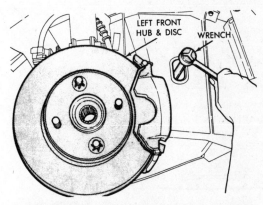

Access plug (in right splash shield) to rotate engine by hand

4. Remove the retaining screws and replace the filter. Tighten the screws to 35 inch pounds.

5. Clean the fluid pan, peel off the old RTV silicone sealer and install the pan, using a ⅛ inch bead of new RTV sealer. Always run the sealer bead inside the bolt holes. Tighten the pan bolts to 10–12 ft. lb.

6. Pour the specified amount of Dexron or Dexron II fluid through the filler tube.

7. Start the engine and idle it for at least 2 minutes. Set the parking brake and move the selector through each position, ending in Park.

8. Add sufficient fluid to bring the level to the FULL mark on the dipstick. The level should be checked in Park, with the engine idling at normal operating temperature.

REMOVAL AND INSTALLATION

The automatic transaxle can be removed with the engine installed in the car, but, the transaxle and torque converter must be removed as an assembly. Otherwise the drive plate, pump bushing or oil seal could be damaged. The drive plate will not support a load—no weight should be allowed to bear on the drive plate.

1. Disconnect the negative battery cable.

2. Disconnect the throttle and shift linkage from the transaxle.

3. Raise and support the car. Remove the front wheels. Refer to "Halfshaft Removal and Installation" to remove or install the halfshafts.

4. Remove the oil cooler hoses.

5. Remove the left splash shield. Drain the differential and remove the cover.

6. Remove the speedometer adaptor, cable and gear.

7. Remove the sway bar.

8. Remove both lower ball joint-to-steering knuckle bolts.

9. Pry the lower ball joint from the steering knuckle.

10. Remove the driveshaft from the hub.

11. Rotate both driveshafts to expose the circlip ends. Note the flat surface on the inner ends of both axle tripod shafts. Pry the circlip out.

12. Remove both driveshafts.

13. Matchmark the torque converter and drive plate. Remove the torque converter mounting bolts. Remove the access plug in the right splash shield to rotate the engine.

14. Remove the lower cooler tube and the wire to the neutral safety switch.

15. Install some means of supporting the engine.

16. Remove the upper bell-housing bolts.

17. Remove the engine mount bracket from the front crossmember.

18. Support the transmission.

19. Remove the front mount insulator through-bolts and the bell housing mount.

21. Remove the long through-bolt from the left-hand engine mount.

22. Raise the transaxle and pry it away from the engine.

23. Installation is the reverse of removal. Fill the differential with DEXRON® automatic transmission fluid before lowering the car. Form a new gasket from RTV sealant when installing the differential cover. See Chapter 1. On 1978 models, be sure the auxiliary horn does not interfere with the oil cooler lines.

FRONT SUSPENSION

A MacPherson type front suspension, with vertical shock absorbers attached to the upper fender reinforcement and the steering knuckle, is used. Lower control arms, attached inboard to a cross-member and outboard to the steering knuckle through a ball joint, provide lower steering knuckle position. During steering maneuvers, the upper strut and steering knuckle turn as an assembly.

Strut

REMOVAL AND INSTALLATION

NOTE: *A new bonded mount assembly is now used on late 1978 and later models, replacing the double nut, bearing retainer, isola-*

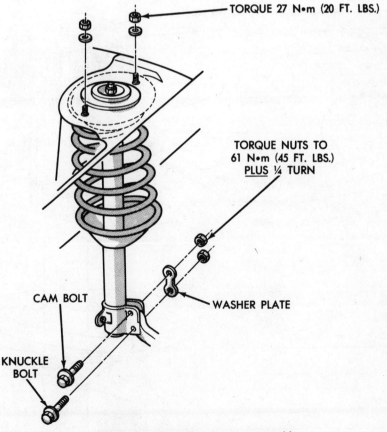

TORQUE 27 N•m (20 FT. LBS.)

TORQUE NUTS TO
61 N•m (45 FT. LBS.)
<u>PLUS</u> ¼ TURN

CAM BOLT

WASHER PLATE

KNUCKLE BOLT

Removing or installing the strut assembly

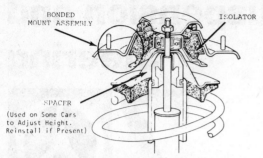

Modified version of strut damper mount

tor and strut retainer previously used. To remove the welded nut, grind the hex flats for proper wrench fit.

1. Raise and support the vehicle.
2. Remove the wheel.
3. NOTE: *If the original strut is to be assembled to the original knuckle, mark the cam adjusting bolt. Remove the cam adjusting bolt, through bolt and brake hose bracket retaining screw.*
4. Remove the strut mounting screws and remove the strut.
5. Installation is the reverse of removal. Po-

sition the knuckle leg in the strut and install the upper (cam) and lower through-bolts. Index the cam bolt with the match marks. Torque the strut mounting screws to 20 ft. lbs.; the brake hose bracket screw to 10 ft. lbs.; the cam bolt to 45 ft. lbs. plus ¼ turn, and the wheel nuts to 80 ft. lbs.

Spring

REMOVAL AND INSTALLATION

NOTE: *A spring compressor is required to remove the spring from the strut. A crow's foot adaptor and torque wrench are also required.*

1. Remove the struts.
2. Compress the spring, using a reliable coil spring compressor.
3. Hold the strut rod and remove the rod nut.
4. Remove the retainers and bushings.
5. Remove the spring.

NOTE: *Springs are not interchangeable from side to side.*

CAUTION: *When removing the spring from*

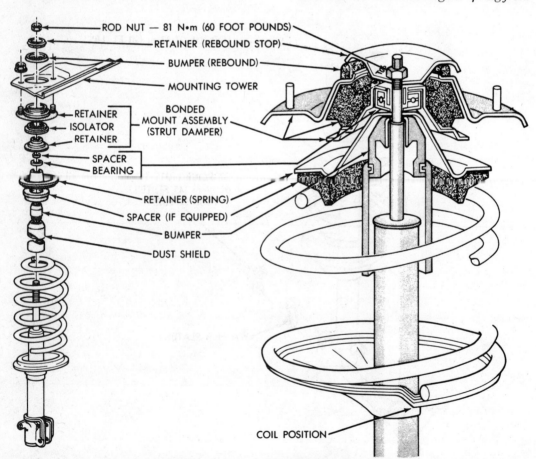

First version of strut damper mount

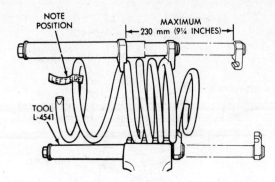

Remove or install the coil spring

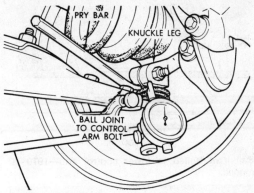

Checking ball joints

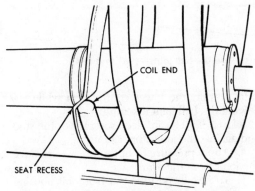

Be sure the lower coil end seats in the recess

the compressor, open the compressor evenly and not more than 9¼ inches.

6. Assembly is the reverse of disassembly in the following order:
- Bumper dust shield
- Spring seat
- Upper spring retainer
- Bearing and spacer
- Mount assembly
- Rebound bumper
- Retainer
- Rod nut

NOTE: *Torque rod nut to 55 ft. lbs. before removing the spring compressor. Use a crow's foot adaptor to tighten the nut while holding the rod with an open end wrench.*

Be sure the lower coil end of the spring is seated in the seat recess.

Ball Joints

INSPECTION

1. Raise and support the vehicle.
2. With the suspension fully extended (at full travel) clamp a dial indicator to the lower control arm with the plunger indexed against the steering knuckle leg.
3. Zero the dial indicator.

4. Use a stout bar to pry on the top of the ball joint housing-to-lower control arm bolt with the bar tip under the steering knuckle leg.
5. Measure the axial travel of the steering knuckle leg in relation to the control arm by raising and lowering the steering knuckle as in Step 4.
6. If the travel is more than 0.050 in., the ball joint should be replaced.

REPLACEMENT

1978 Models

The lower ball joints are permanently lubricated, operate with no free play, and are riveted in place. The rivets must be drilled out and replaced with special bolts.

NOTE: *To avoid damage to the control arm surface adjacent to the ball joint during drilling, the use of a center punch and a drill press are strongly recommended.*

1. Remove the lower control arm.
2. Position the assembly with the ball joint up.
3. Center punch the rivets on the ball joint housing side.
4. Using a drill press with a ¼ inch bit, drill out the center of the rivet.
5. Using a ½ inch bit, drill the center of the rivet until the bit makes contact with the ball joint housing.
6. Using a ⅜ inch bit, drill the center of the rivet. Remove the remainder of the rivet with a punch.
7. Position the new ball joint on the control arm and tighten the bolts to 60 ft. lbs.
8. Install the control arm and tighten the ball joint clamp bolt to 50 ft. lbs.; the pivot bolt to 105 ft. lbs. and the stub strut to 70 ft. lbs.

1979–80

The ball joint housing is bolted to the lower control arm with the joint stud retained in the steering knuckle by a clamp bolt.

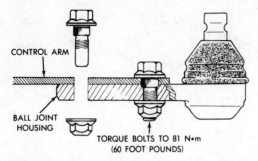

Ball joint bolted to lower control arm—1979–80 models

1. Raise and support the car.
2. Remove the steering knuckle-to-ball joint stud clamp bolt and separate the stud from the knuckle leg.
3. Remove the 2 bolts holding the ball joint housing to the lower control arm.
4. Remove the ball joint housing.
5. Install a new ball joint housing to the control arm. Torque the retaining bolts to 60 ft. lbs.
6. Install the ball joint stud in the steering knuckle. Tighten the clamp bolt to 50 ft. lbs.
7. Lower the car.

1981 and Later

NOTE: *This procedure requires special tools and machine shop services.*

The ball joint is pressed into the lower control arm on these models and is retained to the steering knuckle by a clamp bolt. The lower control arm must be removed from the vehicle and placed in a press to perform this operation.

1. Pry off the rubber grease seal.
2. Position the Receiving Cup tool C-4699-

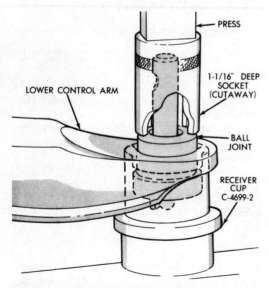

Removing the ball joint—1981 and later

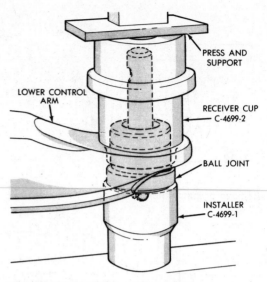

Installing the ball joint—1981 and later

2 to support the lower control arm while receiving the ball joint assembly.
3. Install a 1¹⁄₁₆ in. deep socket over the stud and against the joint upper housing.
4. Apply pressure from the press to remove the joint from the arm.
5. To install, position the ball joint housing into the control arm cavity.
6. Place the assembly in the press with the installer tool C-4699-1 supporting the lower control arm.
7. Align and press the assembly until the ball joint bottoms against the control arm cavity down flange.
8. With a 1½ in. socket, press the seal onto the ball joint housing so that it seats against the lower control arm.

Lower Control Arm

REMOVAL AND INSTALLATION

1. Raise and support the vehicle.
2. Remove the front inner pivot through bolt, the rear stub strut nut, retainer and bushing, and the ball joint-to-steering knuckle clamp bolt.
3. Separate the ball joint stud from the steering knuckle by prying between the ball stud retainer on the knuckle and the lower control arm.

CAUTION: *Pulling the steering knuckle out from the vehicle after releasing it from the ball joint can separate the inner C/V joint.*

4. Remove the sway bar-to-control arm nut and reinforcement and rotate the control arm over the sway bar. Remove the rear stub strut bushing, sleeve and retainer.

NOTE: *The substitution of fasteners other*

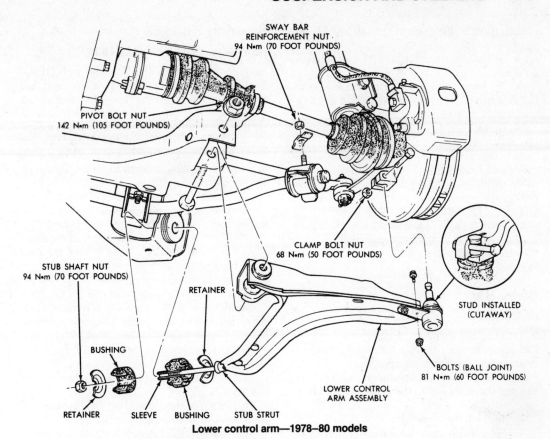

SWAY BAR
REINFORCEMENT NUT
94 N•m (70 FOOT POUNDS)

PIVOT BOLT NUT
142 N•m (105 FOOT POUNDS)

STUB SHAFT NUT
94 N•m (70 FOOT POUNDS)

RETAINER

CLAMP BOLT NUT
68 N•m (50 FOOT POUNDS)

STUD INSTALLED
(CUTAWAY)

BUSHING

RETAINER   SLEEVE   BUSHING   STUB STRUT

LOWER CONTROL
ARM ASSEMBLY

BOLTS (BALL JOINT)
81 N•m (60 FOOT POUNDS)

Lower control arm—1978–80 models

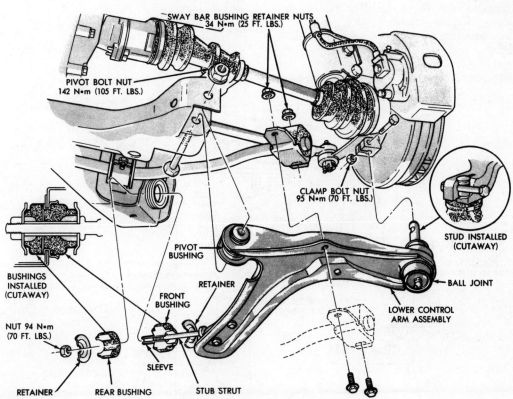

SWAY BAR BUSHING RETAINER NUTS
34 N•m (25 FT. LBS.)

PIVOT BOLT NUT
142 N•m (105 FT. LBS.)

BUSHINGS
INSTALLED
(CUTAWAY)

NUT 94 N•m
(70 FT. LBS.)

RETAINER   REAR BUSHING   STUB STRUT

PIVOT
BUSHING

RETAINER

FRONT
BUSHING

SLEEVE

CLAMP BOLT NUT
95 N•m (70 FT. LBS.)

STUD INSTALLED
(CUTAWAY)

BALL JOINT

LOWER CONTROL
ARM ASSEMBLY

Lower control arm—1981 and later

than those of the grade originally used is not recommended.

5. Install the retainer, bushing and sleeve on the stub strut.

6. Position the control arm over the sway bar and install the rear stub strut and front pivot into the crossmember.

7. Install the front pivot bolt and loosely install the nut.

8. Install the stub strut bushing and retainer and loosely assemble the nut.

9. Position the sway bar bracket and stud through the control arm and install the retainer and nut. Tighten the nut to 10 ft. lb.

10. Install the ball joint stud into the steering knuckle and install the clamp bolt. Torque the clamp bolt to 50 ft. lb.

Sway Bar
REMOVAL AND INSTALLATION

1. Raise and support the car.

2. Remove the nut from the control arm end bushing and reinforcement plates.

3. Remove the nut, retainers and insulator holding the sway bar to the crossmember linkage.

4. Remove the sway bar.

5. Inspect the sway bar for distortion or fatigue cracks in the metal. Replace any damaged or distorted bushings.

6. Installation is the reverse of removal.

Steering Knuckle
REMOVAL AND INSTALLATION

Service or repair to the bearing, hub, brake dust shield or the steering knuckle itself will require removal of the knuckle. Before attempting this operation, be aware that to reassemble the components it is necessary to torque the front hub nut to at least 180 ft. lbs. You will need a large torque wrench to read that high and a great deal of strength to attain that much torque on the nut.

1. Remove the cotter pin and nut-lock.

2. Loosen the hub nut while the car is resting on the wheels with the brakes applied.

NOTE: *The hub and driveshaft are splined together through the knuckle and retained by the hub nut.*

3. Raise and support the car.

4. Remove the wheel and tire.

5. Remove the hub nut. Be sure the splined driveshaft is free to separate from the spline in hub when the knuckle is removed.

6. Disconnect the tie rod end from the steering arm.

7. Disconnect the brake hose retainer from the strut.

8. Remove the clamp bolt holding the ball joint stud in the steering knuckle.

9. Remove the brake caliper adaptor screw and washers.

10. Support the caliper on a wire hook.

11. Remove the brake disc.

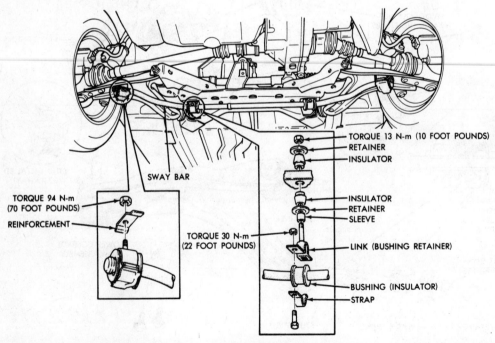

Sway bar

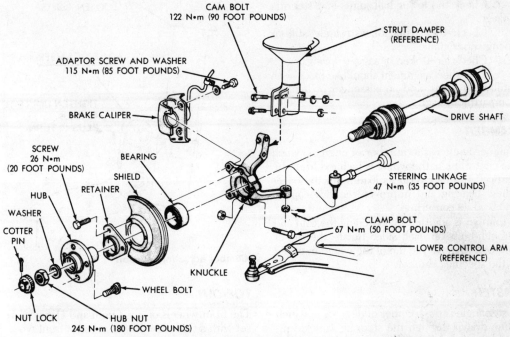

CAM BOLT
122 N•m (90 FOOT POUNDS)

STRUT DAMPER
(REFERENCE)

ADAPTOR SCREW AND WASHER
115 N•m (85 FOOT POUNDS)

BRAKE CALIPER

DRIVE SHAFT

SCREW
26 N•m
(20 FOOT POUNDS)

BEARING

SHIELD

STEERING LINKAGE
47 N•m (35 FOOT POUNDS)

HUB

RETAINER

WASHER

COTTER
PIN

CLAMP BOLT
67 N•m (50 FOOT POUNDS)

LOWER CONTROL ARM
(REFERENCE)

KNUCKLE

WHEEL BOLT

NUT LOCK

HUB NUT
245 N•m (180 FOOT POUNDS)

Exploded view of front suspension (steering knuckle)—typical

12. Matchmark the camber adjusting cams and loosen both bolts.

13. Support the steering knuckle and remove the cam adjusting and through-bolts. Remove the upper knuckle leg out of the strut bracket and lift the knuckle from the ball joint stud.

NOTE: *Do not allow the driveshaft to hang during this procedure.*

14. Service procedures requiring hub removal also require that a new bearing be installed.

15. Installation is the reverse of removal. A new hub nut is required. When the car is rest-

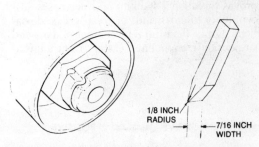

1/8 INCH
RADIUS

7/16 INCH
WIDTH

Staking the nut retainer in place in 1978 models

ing in the wheels, with the brakes applied, tighten the hub nut to:
- 200 ft. lbs.—1978 models
- 180 ft. lbs.—1979 and later models

On 1978 models, stake the hub nut in place. 1979 and later models use a coter pin and nutlock.

Wheel Alignment

Wheel alignment requires the use of fairly sophisticated equipment to accurately measure the geometry of the front end. The information is given here so that the owner will be aware of what is involved, not so that he can do the work himself.

Before the wheels are aligned, the following checks should be made, since these are factors that will influence the wheel alignment settings.

1. All tires should be of the same size and up to the recommended pressures.

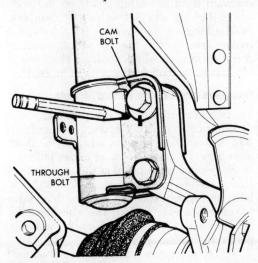

CAM
BOLT

THROUGH
BOLT

Matchmark the cam bolts

2. Check the lower ball joints and steering linkage.

3. Check the struts for extremely stiff or spongy operation.

4. Check for broken or sagged springs.

5. The wheel alignment should be made with a full tank of gas, and no passenger or luggage compartment load.

CAMBER

Camber angle is the number of degrees which the centerline of the wheel is inclined from the vertical. Camber reduces loading of the outer wheel bearing and improves the tire contact patch while cornering.

Camber is adjusted by loosening the cam and through-bolts on each side. Rotate the upper cam bolt to move the top of the wheel in or out to the specified camber.

CASTER

Caster angle is the number of degrees in which a line drawn through the steering knuckle pivots is inclined from the vertical, toward the front or rear of the car. Positive caster improves directional stability and decreases susceptibility to crosswinds or road surface deviations. Other than the replacement of damaged suspension components, caster is not adjustable.

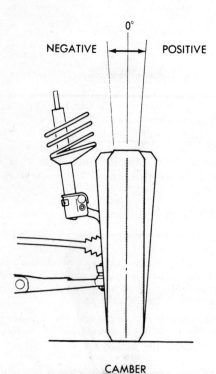

CAMBER

Front suspension camber

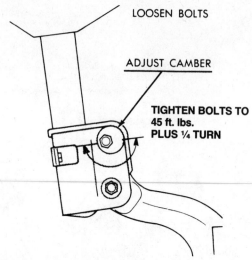

Camber adjusting location

TOE-OUT

The front wheels on the Omni and Horizon are set with a slight toe out, as on most front wheel drive cars, to counteract the tendency of the driving wheels to toe-in excessively. Toe out is the amount, measured in inches, that the wheels are closer together at the rear than at the front. Toe is checked with the wheels straight-ahead. The tie-rod linkage is adjustable. Loosen the nuts and clamps and adjust the length of the tie-rod for correct toe out.

REAR SUSPENSION

All Except Pickup Models

A trailing, independent arm assembly, with integral sway bar is used. The wheel spindles are attached to two trailing arms which extend rearward from mounting points on the body where they are attached with shock absorbing, oval bushings. A crossmember is welded to the trailing arms, just to the rear of the bushings. A coil spring over shock absorber strut assembly, similar to the front suspension, is used.

Rampage and Scamp Pickup Models

The rear suspension on the Rampage and Scamp pickup models uses leaf springs mounted to a tubular axle. The conventional type rear shock absorbers are mounted on an angle, outboard at the bottom and inboard at the top. This design is used to provide greater side-to-side stability and weight carrying capacity in addition to controlling ride motion. The wheel spindles are attached to the axle assembly and supported by the leaf springs.

NOTE: *It is important that aftermarket load leveling devices are NOT installed on this*

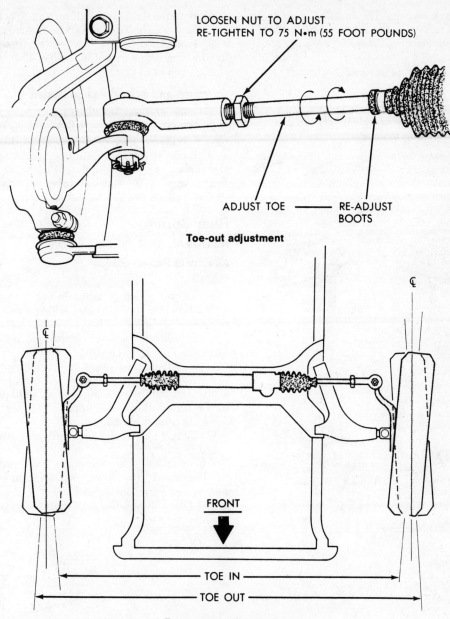

LOOSEN NUT TO ADJUST
RE-TIGHTEN TO 75 N•m (55 FOOT POUNDS)

ADJUST TOE ——— RE-ADJUST
BOOTS

Toe-out adjustment

FRONT

TOE IN

TOE OUT

Front suspension geometry

Wheel Alignment Specifications
(caster is not adjustable)

Year	Front Camber		Toe-Out (in.)		Rear Camber	
	Range (deg)	Preferred	Front	Rear	Range (deg)	Preferred
'78	¼N to ¾P	5⁄16P	⅛ out to 0	5⁄32 out to 1⁄32 in	1½N to ½N	1N
'79–'81	¼N to ¾P	5⁄16P	5⁄32 out to ⅛ in	5⁄32 out to 11⁄32 in	1½N to ½N	1N
'82–'86	¼N to ¾P	5⁄16P	7⁄32 in to ⅛ out	5⁄32 out to 11⁄32 in	1¼N to ¼N ①	½N

① Rampage/Scamp: 1⅛N to ⅛N

suspension system. The installation of these devices will cause the rear brake height sensing proportioning valve to sense a light load condition that is actually a loaded condition being created by these add-on devices.

Shock Absorber

REMOVAL AND INSTALLATION

All Except Pickup Models

1. Remove the protective cap from the upper mounting nut.
2. Remove the upper mounting nut, isolator retainer and isolator.
3. Raise and support the vehicle.

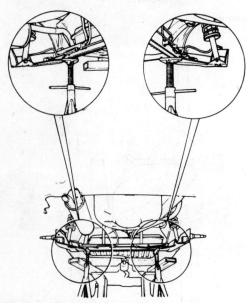

Supporting the rear axle

4. Remove the lower strut mounting bolt.
5. Remove the strut and spring assembly.
6. Installation is the reverse of removal. Torque the lower mounting bolt to 40 ft. lbs.; the upper nut to 20 ft. lbs.

Rampage and Scamp Pickup Models

1. Raise and support the truck.
2. Remove the nuts and bolts securing the upper and lower ends of the shock absorber.
3. Remove the shock absorber and inspect the rubber eye and bushings. If these are defective, replace the shock absorber assembly.
4. Installation is the reverse of the removal.

Rear Spring

REMOVAL AND INSTALLATION

All Except Pickup Models

The use of a coil spring compressor, such as Chrysler part #L-4514, is necessary.

1. Remove the strut and spring assembly as described earlier.
2. Install the spring compressor on the spring and place it in a vise.

CAUTION: *Always grip 4 or 5 coils and never extend the retractors beyond 9¼ inches.*

3. Tighten the retractors evenly until pressure is removed from the upper spring seat.
4. Loosen the retaining nut.

CAUTION: *Be very careful when loosening the retaining nut. If the spring is not properly compressed, serious injury could result.*

5. Remove the lower isolator, pushrod sleeve, and upper spring seat.
6. Carefully slip the strut from the spring.

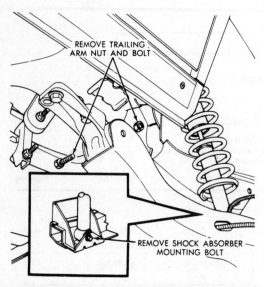

Trailing arm and shock absorber mounting bolts

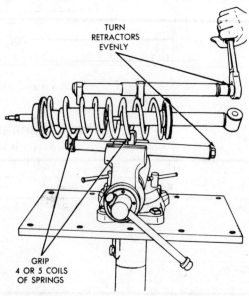

Removing coil spring from rear shock absorber

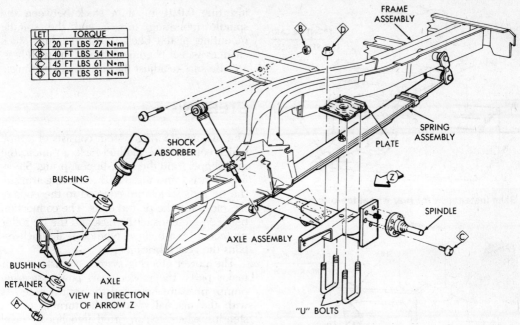

LET	TORQUE	
A	20 FT LBS	27 N•m
B	40 FT LBS	54 N•m
C	45 FT LBS	61 N•m
D	60 FT LBS	81 N•m

FRAME ASSEMBLY

SHOCK ABSORBER

BUSHING

SPRING ASSEMBLY

PLATE

SPINDLE

BUSHING

RETAINER

AXLE

VIEW IN DIRECTION OF ARROW Z

AXLE ASSEMBLY

"U" BOLTS

Rear shock absorber mounting—Rampage and Scamp models

7. Remove the rebound bumper and dust shield from the strut.

8. Remove the lower spring seat.

9. Carefully and evenly, remove the compressor from the spring.

10. Install the compressor on the spring, gripping four or five coils.

11. Compress the spring.

12. Install the lower spring seat, dust shield and rebound bumper on the strut.

13. Slip the unit inside the coil spring and install the upper spring seat.

14. Make sure that the level surfaces on the seats are in position with the spring.

15. Install the sleeve on the pushrod and install the retaining nut. Torque the nut to 20 ft. lbs.

16. Install the lower isolator.

17. Install the strut and spring assembly.

Rampage and Scamp Pickup Models

1. Raise the vehicle and support the frame on jackstands while relieving the weight on the rear springs.

2. Disconnect the rear brake proportioning valve spring. Disconnect the lower ends of the shock absorbers at the axle brackets.

3. Loosen and remove the "U" bolt nuts and remove the "U" bolts and spring plates.

4. Lower the rear axle assembly, allowing the springs to hang free.

5. Loosen and remove the front pivot bolt from the front spring hanger.

6. Loosen and remove the rear spring shackle nuts and remove the shackles from the spring.

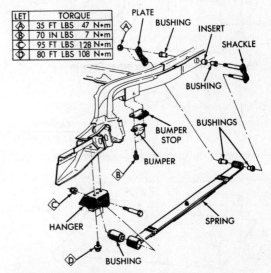

LET	TORQUE	
A	35 FT LBS	47 N•m
B	70 IN LBS	7 N•m
C	95 FT LBS	128 N•m
D	80 FT LBS	108 N•m

PLATE

BUSHING

INSERT

SHACKLE

BUSHING

BUSHINGS

BUMPER STOP

BUMPER

HANGER

SPRING

BUSHING

Rear leaf spring installation—Rampage and Scamp pickup models

7. Installation is the reverse of the removal procedure, taking note of the tightening specifications shown in the illustration.

Rear Wheel Bearings

See Chapter 1.

Rear Wheel Alignment

Due to the design of the rear suspension, it is possible to adjust both the camber and toe-in of the rear wheels. Alignment is controlled by

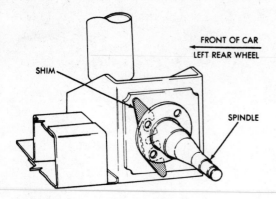

Shim installation for rear wheel toe-out

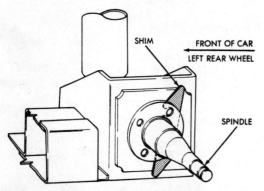

Shim installation for rear wheel toe-in

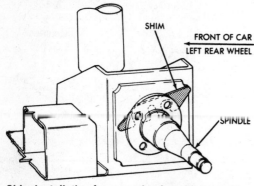

Shim installation for rear wheel positive camber

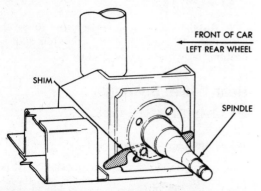

Shim installation for rear wheel negative camber

inserting 0.010 in. shim stock between the spindle mounting surface and the spindle mounting plate. Each 0.010 in. shim stock changes wheel alignment by approximately 0° 18′. Be sure to adjust the rear wheel bearings.

STEERING

The manual steering system consists of a tube which contains the toothed rack, a pinion, the rack slipper, and the rack slipper spring. Steering effort is transmitted to the steering arms by the tie rods which are coupled to the ends of the rack, and the tie rod ends. The connection between the ends of the rack and the tie rod is protected by a bellows type oil seal which retains the gear lubricant.

The power steering system consists of four major parts: the power gear, power steering pump, pressure hose and the return hose. As with the manual system, the turning of the steering wheel is converted into linear travel through the meshing of the helical pinion teeth with the rack teeth. Power assist is provided by an open center, rotary type, three-way control valve which directs fluid to either side of the rack control piston.

Steering Wheel
REMOVAL AND INSTALLATION

1. Remove the horn button and horn switch.
2. Remove the steering wheel nut.
3. Using a steering wheel puller, remove the steering wheel.
4. Align the master serration in the wheel hub with the missing tooth on the shaft. Torque the shaft nut to 60 ft. lbs.

CAUTION: *Do not torque the nut against the steering column lock or damage will occur.*

5. Replace the horn switch and button.

Turn Signal Switch
REMOVAL AND INSTALLATION

1. Disconnect the electrical connector at column.

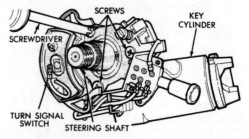

Turn signal switch

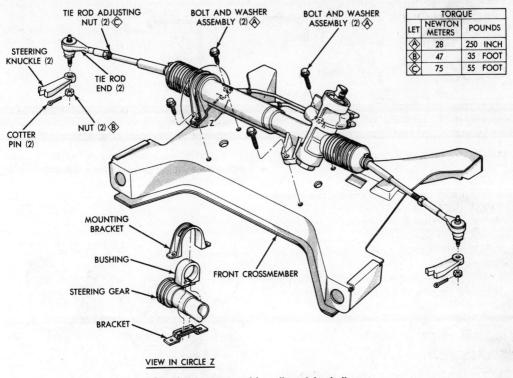

TORQUE		
LET	NEWTON METERS	POUNDS
Ⓐ	28	250 INCH
Ⓑ	47	35 FOOT
Ⓒ	75	55 FOOT

VIEW IN CIRCLE Z

Steering gear assembly—all models similar

2. Remove the steering wheel as described earlier.

3. Remove the lower column cover.

4. Remove the wash/wipe switch.

5. Remove the wiring clip and the three screws securing the turn signal switch.

6. Installation is the reverse of removal.

Ignition and Steering Lock
REMOVAL AND INSTALLATION

1. Remove the steering wheel.

2. Remove the upper and lower column covers.

3. Using a hacksaw blade, cut the upper ¼ inch from the key cylinder retainer pin boss.

4. Using a drift, drive the roll pin from the housing and remove the key cylinder.

5. Insert the new cylinder into the housing, making sure that it engages the lug on the ignition switch driver. Install the roll pin.

Ignition Switch
REMOVAL AND INSTALLATION

1. Remove the connector from the switch.

2. Place the key in the LOCK position.

3. Remove the key.

4. Remove the two mounting screws from the switch and pushrod to drop below the jacket.

5. Rotate the switch 90 degrees to permit removal of the switch from the pushrod.

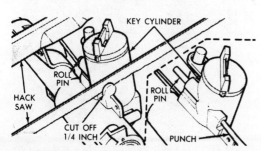

Remove the roll pin in key cylinder

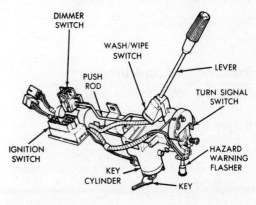

Steering column switch components

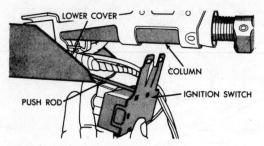

Ignition switch removal

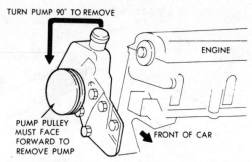

Power steering pump removal and installation—1.7L and 2.2L engines

6. To install the switch, position the switch in LOCK (second detent from the top).

7. Place the switch at right angles to the column and insert the pushrod.

8. Align the switch on the bracket and install the screws.

9. With a light rearward load on the switch, tighten the screws. Check for proper operation.

Tie Rod End

REPLACEMENT

1. Loosen the jam nut which connects the tie rod end to the knuckle. Mark the tie rod position on the threads.

2. Using a ball joint separator, remove the tie rod end from the knuckle.

3. Install a new tie rod end in reverse of removal. Torque the end nut to 50 ft. lbs.; the locknut to 65 ft. lbs.

4. Check alignment.

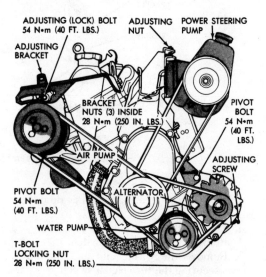

Power steering pump mounting—1.6L engine

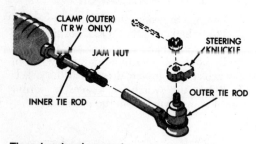

Tie rod end replacement

Power Steering Pump

REMOVAL AND INSTALLATION.

1. Disconnect the power steering hoses from the pump.

2. Remove the adjusting bolt and slip off the belt.

3. Support the pump, remove the mounting bolts and lift out the pump.

4. Installation is the reverse of removal. Adjust the belt to specifications. See Chapter 1.

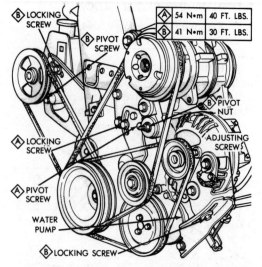

Power steering pump mounting—1.7L and 2.2L engines

Steering Gear

REMOVAL AND INSTALLATION

1. Raise and support the front of the vehicle. Remove front wheels.

2. Remove the cotter pins, the castle nuts and the tie rod ends (using a ball joint puller) from the steering knuckles.

3. If equipped, remove the antirotational link from the crossmember and the air diverter valve bracket, from the left-side of the crossmember.

NOTE: *The lower universal joint is removed with the steering gear.*

4. Drive out the lower roll pin attaching the pinion shaft to the lower universal joint. Use a back-up, to protect the universal joint, while driving the roll pin.

5. Support the front suspension crossmember with a hydraulic jack. Remove the 2 rear nuts attaching the crossmember to the frame. Loosen the 2 front bolts attaching the crossmember to the frame and lower the crossmember slightly for access to the boot seal shields.

6. Remove the splash and the boot seal shields.

7. If equipped, remove the oil tubes from the power steering pump.

8. Remove the steering gear bolts from the front suspension crossmember.

9. Remove the steering gear from the left side of the vehicle.

10. To install, reverse the removal procedures. The right rear crossmember bolt is a pilot bolt that correctly locates the crossmember, tighten it first. Torque the 4 crossmember bolts to 90 ft. lbs. and the steering gear attaching bolts to 21 ft. lbs.

Brakes

BRAKE SYSTEM

A conventional front disc/rear drum setup is used. The front discs are single piston caliper types; the rear drums are activated by a conventional top mounted wheel cylinder. Disc brakes require no adjustments, the drum brakes are self adjusting by means of the parking brake cable. The only variances in the system from those found on the majority of vehicles are that the system is diagonally balanced, that is, the front left and right rear are on one system and the front right and left rear on the other. No proportioning valve is used. Power brakes are optional.

Adjustment

All disc brakes are inherently self-adjusting. No adjustment is possible. Even though the drum brakes are self-adjusting in normal use, there are times when a manual adjustment is required, such as after installing new shoes or if it is required to back the shoes off the drum. A star wheel with screw type adjusters is provided for these occasions.

1. Remove the access slot plug from the backing plate.

2. Using a brake adjusting spoon pry downward (left side) or upward (right side) on the end of the tool (starwheel teeth moving up) to tighten the brakes. The opposite applies to loosen the brakes.

NOTE: *It will be necessary to use a small screwdriver to hold the adjusting lever away from the starwheel. Be careful not to bend the adjusting lever.*

3. When the brakes are tight almost to the point of being locked, back off on the starwheel 10 clicks. The starwheel on each set of brakes (front or rear) must be backed off the same number of turns to prevent brake pull from side to side.

Adjusting rear brakes

4. When all brakes are adjusted, check brake pedal travel and then make several stops, while backing the car up, to equalize all the wheels.

TESTING ADJUSTER

1. Raise the vehicle on a hoist, with a helper in the car, to apply the brakes.

2. Loosen the brakes by holding the adjuster lever away from the starwheel and backing off the starwheel approximately 30 notches.

3. Spin the wheel and brake drum in reverse and apply the brakes. The movement of the secondary shoe should pull the adjuster lever up, and when the brakes are released the lever should snap down and turn the starwheel.

4. If the automatic adjuster doesn't work, the drum must be removed and the adjuster components inspected carefully for breakage, wear, or improper installation.

Brake Specifications

All measurements given are (in.) unless noted

Model	Lug Nut Torque (ft./lb.)	Master Cylinder Bore	Brake Disc		Brake Drum			Minimum Lining Thickness	
			Minimum Thickness	Maximum Run-Out	Diameter	Max Machine O/S	Max Wear Limit	Front	Rear
1978–80	80–85	0.625	0.431 ②	①	7.87	7.927	7.927	③	5/16
1981–82	80–85	0.875	0.431 ②	0.004	7.87	7.927	7.927	③	5/16
1983–86	80–85 ④	0.827	0.431 ②	0.004	7.87	7.927	7.927	③	5/16

NOTE: *Minimum lining thickness is as recommended by the manufacturer. Because of variations in state inspection regulations, the minimum allowable thickness may be different than recommended by the manufacturer.*
① Maximum 0.005 in. total combined run-out of disc and hub.
  Run-out of disc (installed on hub)—0.005 in.
  Run-out of hub (disc removed)—0.002 in.
② Thickness of new disc—0.490–0.505 in.
③ 5/16 in.—minimum thickness of lining and backing plate at any point.
④ 1984 and later—95 ft. lbs.

Master Cylinder

REMOVAL AND INSTALLATION

With Power Brakes

1. Disconnect the primary and secondary brake lines from the master cylinder. Plug the openings.
2. Remove the nuts attaching the cylinder to the power brake booster.
3. Slide the master cylinder stright out, away from the booster.
4. Position the master cylinder over the studs on the booster, align the pushrod with the master cylinder piston and tighten the nuts to 16 ft. lbs.
5. Connect the brake lines.
6. Bleed the brakes.

With Non-Power Brakes

1. Disconnect the primary and secondary brake lines and install plugs in the master cylinder openings.
2. Disconnect the stoplight switch mounting bracket from under the instrument panel.
3. Pull the brake pedal backward to disengage the pushrod from the master cylinder piston.
NOTE: *This will destroy the grommet.*
4. Remove the master cylinder-to-firewall nuts.
5. Slide the master cylinder out and away from the firewall. Be sure to remove all pieces of the broken grommet.
6. Install the boot on the pushrod.
7. Install a new grommet on the pushrod.
8. Apply a soap and water solution to the grommet and slide it firmly into position in the primary piston socket. Move the pushrod from side to side to make sure it's seated.

9. From the engine side, press the pushrod through the master cylinder mounting plate and align the mounting studs with the holes in the cylinder.
10. Install the nuts and torque them to 16 ft. lbs.
11. From under the instrument panel, place the pushrod on the pin on the pedal and install a new retaining clip.
CAUTION: *Be sure to lubricate the pin.*
12. Install the brake lines on the master cylinder.
13. Bleed the system.

OVERHAUL

CAUTION: *Do not hone the master cylinder bore. Honing will remove the anodized finish.*
1. Clean the housing and reservoir.
2. Remove the reservoir caps and empty the fluid.
3. Clamp the master cylinder in a soft-jawed vise.
4. Pull the reservoir from the master cylinder housing.
5. Remove the reservoir grommets.
6. Use needle nosed pliers to remove the secondary piston pin from inside the housing.
7. Remove the snap-ring from the outer end of the housing.
8. Slide the primary piston out of the master cylinder bore.
9. Tap the open end of the cylinder on the bench to remove the secondary piston. If it sticks in the bore, it can be removed with light air pressure.
NOTE: *If air pressure is used to remove the piston, new cups must be installed.*
10. Note the position of the rubber cups and remove all except the primary cup.

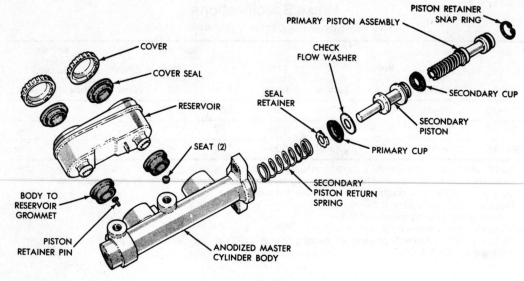

Master cylinder exploded view

NOTE: *Do not remove the primary cup from the primary piston. If the cup is worn, the entire primary piston assembly should be replaced.*

11. If the brass tube seats are not reusable, replace them using a suitable tool.

12. Wash the entire housing in clean brake fluid and inspect for pitting or scratches. If any are found, replace the housing. If the pistons are corroded, they should be replaced. Discard all used rubber parts and replace piston caps and seals.

13. Before assembly, dip all parts in clean brake fluid.

14. Install the check flow washer.

15. Install the secondary piston into the master cylinder bore. Be sure the cup lips enter the bore evenly. Keep well lubricated with brake fluid.

16. Center the primary piston spring retainer on the secondary piston and push the piston assemblies into the bore up to the primary piston cup.

17. Work the cup into the bore and push the piston in up to the secondary seal. Work the cup into the bore and push on the piston until fully seated.

18. Depress the piston and install the snapring.

19. Tap the secondary piston retainer pin into the housing.

20. Install new tube seats.

21. Install the reservoir grommets in the housing. Lubricate the area with clean brake fluid and install the reservoir. All the lettering should be properly read from the left side of the reservoir when it is properly installed. Make

sure the bottom of the reservoir touches the top of the grommet.

Pressure Differential Valve and Warning Light Switch

The brake system is split diagonally. That means that the right rear and left front brakes are connected to the same reservoir. Both systems are routed through, but separated by, the pressure differential valve, which also contains the warning switch. The function of the valve is to activate the switch in the event of brake system malfunction. The warning light switch is the latching type. It will automatically recenter itself after the repair is made and brake pedal depressed.

The bulb can be checked each time the ignition switch is turned to the ON position or each time the parking brake is set.

Height Sensing Proportioning Valve

The Rampage and Scamp pickup models use a height sensing dual proportioning valve in addition to the regular differential warning switch. This valve is located under the bed just forward of the rear axle. It automatically provides optimum brake balance front-to-rear regardless of the vehicle load condition. The valve modulates the pressure to the rear brakes sensing the vehicle load condition through relative movement between the rear axle and the load floor.

NOTE: *It is important that aftermarket load leveling devices are NOT installed on this*

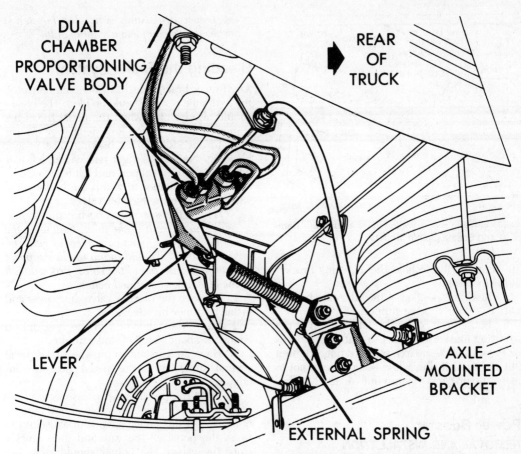

DUAL
CHAMBER
PROPORTIONING
VALVE BODY

REAR
OF
TRUCK

LEVER

AXLE
MOUNTED
BRACKET

EXTERNAL SPRING

Rear brake height sensing proportioning valve—Rampage and Scamp pickup models

brake/suspension system. The installation of these devices will cause the rear brake height sensing proportioning valve to sense a light load condition that is actually a loaded condition being created by these add-on devices.

TESTING

When a premature rear wheel slide is obtained on brake application, it could be an indication that the fluid pressure to the rear brakes is above the reduction ratio for the rear line pressure and that the proportioning valve is malfunctioning. To test the valve use the following procedures.

NOTE: *During the testing, leave the front brake lines connected to the valve.*

1. Disconnect the external spring at the valve end.

2. Install one gauge and "T" of tool set C-4007-A in the line from either master cylinder port and brake valve assembly.

3. Install the second gauge from tool set C-4007-A to either rear brake line. Bleed the rear brake system.

4. Have a second person exert pressure on

the brake pedal (holding pressure) to get a reading on the valve inlet gauge and check the reading on the outlet gauge. The inlet pressure should read 1000 psi and the outlet pressure should read between 530 and 770 psi. If either is not as specified, replace the valve.

INSTALLATION AND ADJUSTMENT

NOTE: *After installing a new height sensing proportioning valve, both rear brakes should be bled.*

1. Raise the vehicle and support on jackstands so that the rear suspension is hanging free and the shock absorbers are fully extended. Leave the wheels and tires on the truck to help keep the suspension in the full rebound position.

2. Loosen the spring adjusting bracket nuts "A" and "B" as shown in the illustration.

3. Push the valve lever "C" rearward until it bottoms and hold it there.

4. Rotate the spring adjusting bracket "D" rearward until all the free play has been removed from the spring. (Be careful not to stretch the spring). While holding the adjusting bracket in position, release the valve lever. Tighten nut

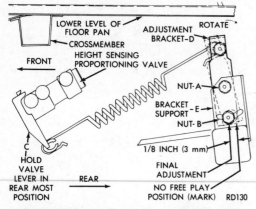

Height sensing proportioning valve adjusting—Rampage and Scamp pickup models

"B" temporarily, to hold the adjusting bracket in this position.

5. Mark the position of the adjusting bracket nut "B" on the bracket support "E."

6. Loosen nut "B" and rotate the top of the adjusting bracket rearward so that nut "B" is ⅛ in. forward of the no free play position. Tighten nut "B" to 21 ft. lbs. while being careful not to move the bracket. Tighten nut "A" to 21 ft. lbs.

Power Booster

REMOVAL AND INSTALLATION

1. Remove the master cylinder; it can be pulled far enough out of the way to allow booster removal without disconnecting the brake lines.

2. Disconnect the vacuum hose from the booster.

3. Under the instrument panel, pry the retainer clip center tang over the end of the brake pedal pin and pull the retainer clip from the pin. Discard the clip.

4. Remove the four booster attaching nuts.

5. Remove the booster from the vehicle.

6. Position the booster on the firewall.

7. Torque the nuts to 20 ft. lbs.

8. Carefully position the master cylinder on the booster.

9. Install the mounting nuts and torque them to 18 ft. lbs.

10. Connect the vacuum hose to the booster.

11. Coat the bearing surface of the pedal pin with chassis lube.

12. Connect the pushrod to the pedal pin and install a new clip.

13. Check the stoplight operation. With vacuum applied to the power brake unit and pressure applied to the pedal, the master cylinder should vent (force a jet of fluid through the front chamber vent port).

CAUTION: *Do not attempt to disassemble*

the power brake unit, since the booster is serviced as a complete assembly only.

Bleeding the Brake System

Anytime a brake line has been disconnected the hydraulic system should be bled. The brakes should also be bled when the pedal travel becomes unusually long ("soft pedal") or the car pulls to one side during braking. The proper bleeding sequence is: right rear wheel, left rear wheel, right front caliper, and left front caliper. You'll need a helper to pump the brake pedal while you open the bleeder valves.

NOTE: *If the system has been drained, first refill it with fresh brake fluid. Following the above sequence, open each bleeder valve by ½ to ¾ of a turn and pump the brake pedal until fluid runs out of the valve. Proceed with the bleeding as outlined below.*

1. Remove the bleeder valve dust cover and install a rubber bleeder hose.

2. Insert the other end of the hose into a container about ⅓ full of brake fluid.

3. Have an assistant pump the brake pedal several times until the pedal pressure increases.

4. Hold the pedal under pressure and then start to open the bleeder valve about ½ to ¾ of a turn. At this point, have your assistant depress the pedal all the way and then quickly close the valve. The helper should allow the pedal to return slowly.

NOTE: *Keep a close check on the brake fluid in the reservoir and top it up as necessary throughout the bleeding process.*

5. Keep repeating this procedure until no more air bubbles can be seen coming from the hose in the brake fluid.

6. Remove the bleeder hose and install the dust cover.

7. Continue the bleeding at each wheel in sequence.

NOTE: *Don't splash any brake fluid on the paintwork. Brake fluid is very corrosive and will eat paint away. Any fluid accidentally spilled on the body should be immediately flushed off with water.*

FRONT DISC BRAKES

Omnis and Horizon models use a floating caliper front disc brake.

Disc Brake Pads

INSPECTION

Disc pads (lining and shoe assemblies) should be replaced in axle sets (both wheels) when the thickness of the shoe and lining is less than $5/16$ inch.

NOTE: *State inspection specifications take precedence over these general recommendations.*

Note that disc pads in floating caliper type brakes may wear at an agle, and measurement should be made at the narrow end of the taper. Tapered linings should be replaced if the taper exceeds $1/8$ in. from end to end (the difference between the thickest and thinnest points).

Always replace both sets on each wheel whenever one pad needs replacing.

NOTE: *Brake squeal is inherent in disc brakes. If the squeal is objectionable and constant it can be reduced by installing new brake pads (Chrysler Part No. 4176767). After 1000 miles of city driving these new compound pads should reduce noise, although a very low level of noise may be present under certain conditions.*

REMOVAL AND INSTALLATION

Kelsey Hayes Type

1. Raise and support the car.
2. Remove the wheels.
3. Remove the caliper guide pins and anti-rattle springs.
4. Remove the caliper by slowly sliding the caliper off the brake disc. Hang the caliper by a piece of stiff wire. Do not allow it to hang by the brake line.
5. Remove the outboard brake pad from the adaptor.
6. Slide the inboard pad out of the adaptor.

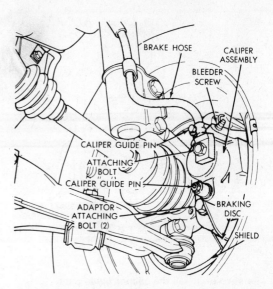

Front caliper attaching points

7. To install the pads, place new pads in the adaptor.
8. Loosen the rear cap of the master cylinder reservoir and slowly push the caliper pistons back into the housing.

CAUTION: *Be sure the reservoir does not overflow, especially onto painted surfaces.*

9. Hold the outboard lining in position and carefully slide the caliper into position on the adaptor.
10. Install the guide pins (lightly lubricated with silicone grease) and anti-rattle springs. The anti-rattle spring clips are installed with the closed loop toward the center of the car.
11. Bleed the brakes.
12. Install the wheels.

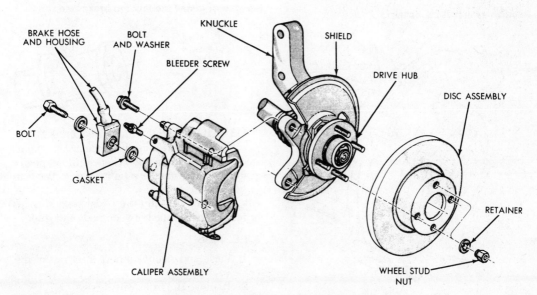

Exploded view of disc brake components

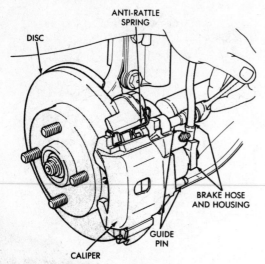

Remove or install the caliper guide pins

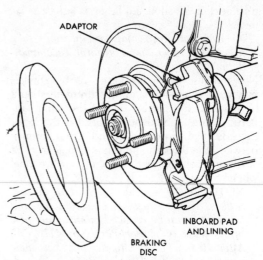

Remove or install the brake disc

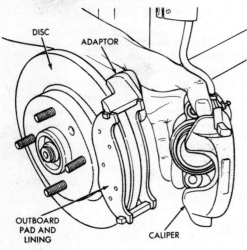

Remove or install the caliper

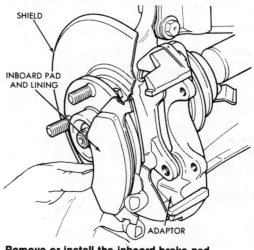

Remove or install the inboard brake pad

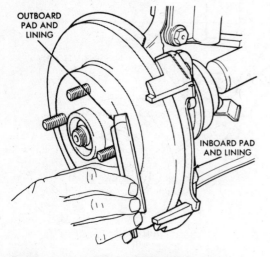

Remove or install the outboard brake pad

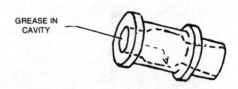

CAUTION: *Tighten the wheels in an every-other-nut rotation until all wheels are tightened to ½ specification. Repeat the sequence until all lug nuts are tight to full specification.*

After assembly, pump the pedal several times to remove clearance between pads and rotors.

A.T.E. Type

1. Raise and safely support the front of the vehicle.

2. Remove the front wheels.

3. Remove the hold-down spring from the

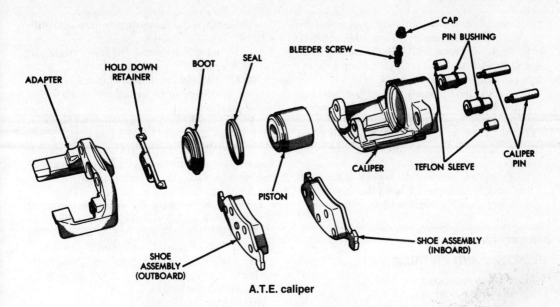

ADAPTER · HOLD DOWN RETAINER · BOOT · SEAL · BLEEDER SCREW · CAP · PIN BUSHING · PISTON · CALIPER · TEFLON SLEEVE · CALIPER PIN · SHOE ASSEMBLY (OUTBOARD) · SHOE ASSEMBLY (INBOARD)

A.T.E. caliper

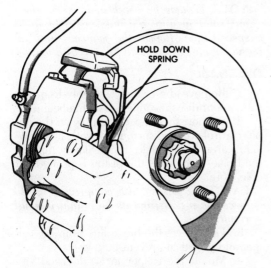

HOLD DOWN SPRING

Hold-down spring removal—A.T.E.

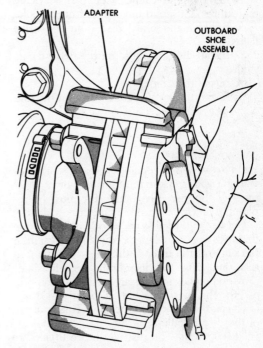

ADAPTER · OUTBOARD SHOE ASSEMBLY

Outboard pad—A.T.E.

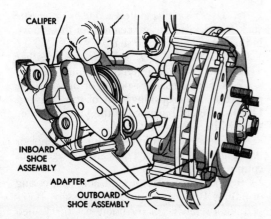

CALIPER · INBOARD SHOE ASSEMBLY · ADAPTER · OUTBOARD SHOE ASSEMBLY

Caliper and inboard pad—A.T.E.

caliper by pushing in at the middle of the spring and pushing it outwards.

3. Loosen, but do not remove the caliper guide pins until the caliper is free from the mount. Removal of the guide pins is necessary only if the bushings or sleeves require replacement.

4. Lift the caliper out and away from the disc rotor. The inboard pad will remain in the caliper.

5. Support the caliper so that no strain is on

the hose. Remove the inboard pad from the caliper. Lift the outboard pad from the adapter.

6. Push the piston back into the caliper bore. Install the inboard pad with the clamp locating it in the caliper piston.

7. Install the outboard pad in the adapter. Position the caliper over the rotor and secure with the guide pins. Carefully tighten the guide pins to 18–22 ft. lbs. Install the hold-down spring. Mount the front wheels and lower the vehicle.

8. Pump the brake pedal several times until a firm pedal is obtained. Check the master cylinder level. Road test the vehicle.

Brake Disc
REMOVAL AND INSTALLATION

1. Raise and support the car.
2. Remove the wheels.
3. Remove the caliper (see pad servicing procedures). Suspend the caliper from a hook.
4. Remove the brake disc from the drive flange studs.
5. Install the brake disc on the drive flange studs.
6. Install the caliper.
7. Install the wheels. See NOTE at the end of the previous procedure.

INSPECTION

Light scoring is acceptable. Heavy scoring or warping will necessitate refinishing or replacement of the disc. The brake disc must be replaced if cracks or burned marks are evident.

Check the thickness of the disc. Measure the thickness at 12 equally spaced points 1 inch from the edge of the disc. If thickness varies more than 0.0005 in. the disc should be refinished, provided equal amounts are out from each side and the thickness does not fall below 0.431 in.

Check the run-out of the disc. Total run-out of the disc installed on the car should not exceed 0.0005 in. The disc can be resurfaced to correct minor variations as long as equal amounts are cut from each side and the thickness is at least 0.431 in. after resurfacing.

Check the run-out of the hub (disc removed). It should not be more than 0.002 in. If so, the hub should be replaced.

Caliper
REMOVAL AND INSTALLATION

NOTE: *Refer to A.T.E. pad servicing if A.T.E. Caliper.*
1. Raise and support the car.
2. Remove the wheels.

3. Remove the caliper guide pins and anti-rattle springs.
4. Remove the caliper by slowly sliding it off the adaptor.

NOTE: *If the old pads are being reused, mark them so they can be installed in their original position.*

5. If the caliper is being removed for overhaul, disconnect and plug the brake line.
6. Installation is the reverse of removal. Loosen the rear master cylinder reservoir cap and slowly push the caliper pistons back into the housing.

CAUTION: *Be sure the reservoir does not overflow, especially onto painted surfaces.*

7. Hold the outboard pad in position and slide the caliper onto the adaptor.
8. Install the guide pins and anti-rattle springs.
9. Bleed the brakes.
10. Install the wheels.

NOTE: *Tighten the wheels in an every-other-nut rotation until the nuts are tight to ½ specification. Repeat the sequence until all the lug nuts are tight to full specification.*

OVERHAUL

1. Remove the caliper assembly from the car *without* disconnecting the hydraulic line.
2. Support the caliper assembly on the upper control arm and surround it with shop towels to absorb any brake fluid. Slowly depress the brake pedal until the piston is pushed out of its bore.

CAUTION: *Do not use compressed air to force the piston from its bore; injury could result.*

3. Disconnect the brake line from the caliper and plug it to prevent fluid loss.
4. Mount the caliper in a soft-jawed vise and clamp lightly. Do not tighten the vise too much or the caliper will become distorted.
5. Work the dust boot out with your fingers.
6. Use a small pointed *wooden* or *plastic* stick to work the piston seal out of the groove in the bore. Discard the seal.

CAUTION: *Using a screwdriver or other metal tool could scratch the piston bore.*

7. Using the same wooden or plastic stick, press the outer bushings out of the housing. Discard the old bushings in the same manner. Discard them as well.
8. Clean all parts in denatured alcohol or brake fluid. Blow out all bores and passages with compressed air.
9. Inspect the piston and bore for scoring or pitting. Replace the piston if necessary. Bores with light scratches or corrosion may be cleaned with crocus cloth. Bores with deep scratches

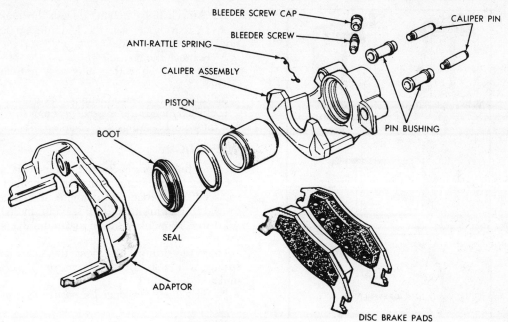

BLEEDER SCREW CAP

ANTI-RATTLE SPRING

BLEEDER SCREW

CALIPER PIN

CALIPER ASSEMBLY

PISTON

BOOT

PIN BUSHING

SEAL

ADAPTOR

DISC BRAKE PADS

Exploded view of brake caliper

may be honed if you do not increase the bore diameter more than 0.002 in. Replace the housing if the bore must be enlarged beyond this.

NOTE: *Black stains are caused by piston seals and are harmless.*

10. If the bore had to be honed, clean its grooves with a stiff, non-metallic rotary brush. Clean the bore twice by flushing it out with brake fluid and drying it with a soft, lint-free cloth.

Caliper assembly is as follows:

1. Clamp the caliper in a soft-jawed vise; do not overtighten.

2. Dip a new piston seal in brake fluid or the lubricant supplied with the rebuilding kit. Position the new seal in one area of its groove and gently work it into place with clean fingers, so that it is correctly seated. Do not use an old seal.

3. Coat a new boot with brake fluid or lubricant (as above), leaving a generous amount inside.

4. Insert the boot in the caliper and work it into the groove, using your fingers only. The boot will snap into place once it is correctly positioned. Run your forefinger around the inside of the boot to make sure that it is correctly seated.

5. Install the bleed screw in its hole and plug the fluid inlet on the caliper.

6. Coat the piston with brake fluid or lubricant. Spread the boot with your fingers and work the piston into the boot.

7. Depress the piston; this will force the boot

into its groove on the piston. Remove the plug and bottom the piston in the bore.

8. Compress the flanges of new guide pin bushings and work them into place by pressing *in* on the bushings with your fingertips, until they are seated. Make sure that the flanges cover the housing evenly on all sides.

9. Install the caliper on the car as previously outlined.

REAR DRUM BRAKES

Brake Drums

REMOVAL AND INSTALLATION

1. Remove the plug from the brake shoe adjusting hole.

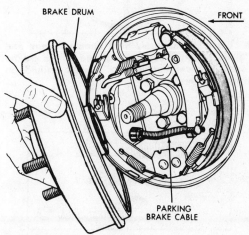

BRAKE DRUM

FRONT

PARKING
BRAKE CABLE

Remove the brake drum

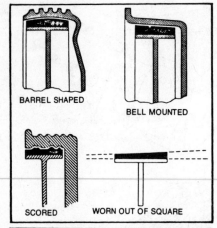

BARREL SHAPED

BELL MOUNTED

SCORED

WORN OUT OF SQUARE

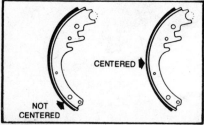

CENTERED

NOT CENTERED

Improperly worn linings are cause for concern only if braking is unstable and noise is objectionable. Compare the lining and drum wear pattern, the drum being more important, since the drum shapes the wear of the shoe

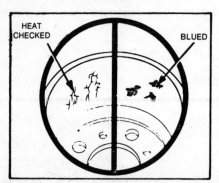

HEAT CHECKED

BLUED

A "blued" or severely heat checked drum and "blued", charred or heavily glazed linings are the result of overheating. The brakes should be checked immediately

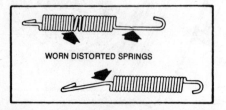

WORN DISTORTED SPRINGS

Check for weak or distorted retracting springs

2. Using a brake spoon, release the brake shoes by moving the star wheel adjuster up (left side) or down (right side).

3. Remove the grease cap.

4. Remove the cotter pin, lock nut and washer.

5. Remove the brake drum and bearings.

6. Installation is the reverse of removal. Adjust the wheel bearings (see Chapter 1).

INSPECTION

Measure the drum run-out and diameter. If not according to specifications the drum should be replaced. The variation in diameter should not exceed 0.0025 in. in 30° or 0.0035 in. in 360°. All drums show markings of maximum diameter.

Once the drum is off, clean the shoes and springs with a stiff brush to remove the accumulated brake dust.

NOTE: *Avoid prolonged exposure to brake dust.*

Grease on the shoes can be removed with alcohol or fine sandpaper.

After cleaning, examine the brake shoes for glazed, oily, loose, cracked or improperly worn linings. Light glazing is common and can be removed with fine sandpaper. Linings that are worn improperly or below 1/16" above rivet heads or brake shoe should be replaced. The NHSTA advises states with inspection programs to fail vehicles with brake linings less than 1/32". A good "eyeball" test is to replace the linings when the thickness is the same as or less than the thickness of the metal backing plate (shoe).

Wheel cylinders are a vital part of the brake system and should be inspected carefully. Gently pull back the rubber boots; if any fluid is visible, it's time to replace or rebuild the wheel cylinders. Boots that are distorted, cracked or otherwise damaged, also point to the need for service. Check the flexible brake lines for cracks, chafing or wear.

Check the brake shoe retracting and hold-down springs; they should not be worn or distorted. Be sure that the adjuster mechanism moves freely. The points on the backing plate where the shoes slide should be shiny and free of rust. Rust in these areas suggests that the brake shoes are not moving properly.

Brake Shoes

REMOVAL AND INSTALLATION

NOTE: *If you are not throughly familiar with the procedures involved in brake replacement, disassemble and assemble one side at a time, leaving the other wheel intact, as a reference.*

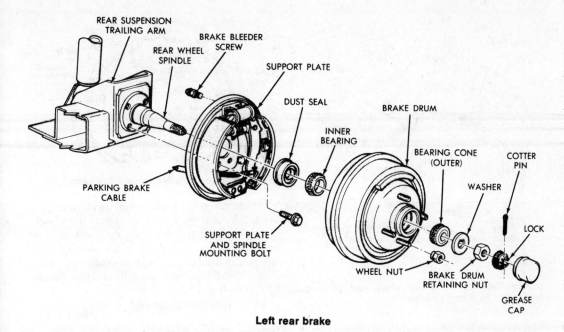

Left rear brake

1. Remove the brake drum. See the procedure earlier in this chapter.

2. Unhook the parking brake cable from the secondary (trailing) shoe.

3. Remove the shoe-to-anchor springs (retracting springs). They can be gripped and unhooked with a pair of pliers.

4. Remove the shoe hold down springs: compress them slightly and slide them off of the hold down pins.

5. Remove the adjuster screw assembly by spreading the shoes apart. The adjuster nut must be fully backed off.

6. Raise the parking brake lever. Pull the secondary (trailing) shoe away from the backing plate so pull-back spring tension is released.

7. Remove the secondary (trailing) shoe and disengage the spring end from the backing plate.

8. Raise the primary (leading) shoe to release spring tension. Remove the shoe and disengage the spring end from the backing plate.

9. Inspect the brakes (see procedures under Brake Drum Inspection).

10. Lubricate the six shoe contact areas on the brake backing plate and the web end of the brake shoe which contacts the anchor plate. Use a multi-purpose lubricant or a high temperature brake grease made for the purpose.

11. Chrysler recommends that the rear wheel bearings be cleaned and repacked whenever the brakes are renewed. Be sure to install a new bearing seal.

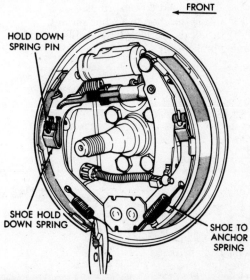

Left rear brake shoes and springs installed

The shoe-to-anchor springs can be removed with pliers

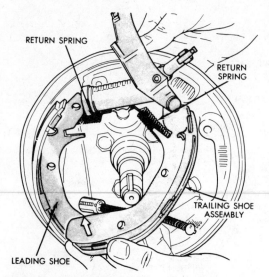

Remove the trailing brake shoe and parking brake lever by lifting upward

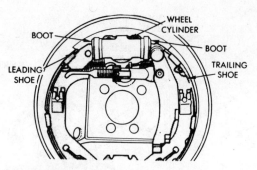

Wheel cylinder installed on backing plate.

12. With the leading shoe return spring in position on the shoe, install the shoe at the same time as you engage the return spring in the end support.

13. Position the end of the shoe under the anchor.

14. With the trailing shoe return spring in position, install the shoe at the same time as you engage the spring in the support (backing plate).

15. Position the end of the shoe under the anchor.

16. Spread the shoes and install the adjuster screw assembly making sure that the forked end that enters the shoe is curved down.

17. Insert the shoe hold down spring pins and install the hold down springs.

18. Install the shoe-to-anchor springs.

19. Install the parking brake cable onto the parking brake lever.

20. Replace the brake drum and tighten the nut to 240–300 in. lbs. while rotating the wheel.

21. Back off the nut enough to release the bearing preload and position the locknut with one pair of slots aligned with the cotter pin hole.

22. Install the cotter pin. The end play should be 0.001–0.003 in.

23. Install the grease cap.

Wheel Cylinders

REMOVAL AND INSTALLATION

1. Raise and support the car.

2. Remove the brake drums.

3. Visually inspect the wheel cylinder boots for signs of excessive leakage. A slight amount of leakage is normal, but excessive leakage will necessitate boot replacement. Replace any boots that are torn or broken.

4. In case of a leak, also remove the brake shoes and check for contamination.

5. Disconnect and plug the brake line.

6. Unbolt and remove the wheel cylinder.

7. Installation is the reverse of removal. Bleed the brakes.

OVERHAUL

1. Pry the boots away from the cylinder and remove the boots and piston as an assembly.

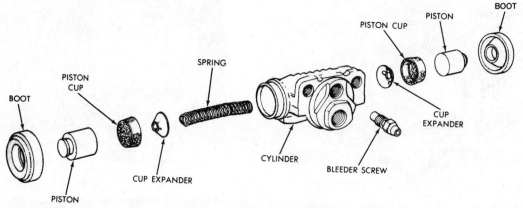

Exploded view of wheel cylinder

2. Disengage the boot from the piston.

3. Slide the piston into the cylinder bore and press inward to remove the other boot and piston. Also remove the spring with it the cup expanders.

4. Wash all parts (except rubber parts) in clean brake fluid and dry thoroughly. Do not use a rag; lint will adhere to the bore.

5. Inspect the cylinder bores. Light scoring can usually be cleaned up with crocus cloth. Black stains are caused by the piston cups and are no cause of concern. Bad scoring or pitting means that the wheel cylinder should be replaced.

6. Dip the pistons and new cups in clean brake fluid prior to assembly.

7. Coat the wheel cylinder bore with clean brake fluid.

8. Install the expansion spring with the cup expanders.

9. Install the cups in each end of the cylinder with the open ends facing each other.

10. Assemble new boots on the piston and slide them into the cylinder bore.

11. Press the boot over the wheel cylinder until seated.

12. Install the wheel cylinder.

PARKING BRAKE

ADJUSTMENT

The cable operated parking brake is adjusted at the equalizer (connector) under the car.

1. Adjust the service brakes.

2. Release the parking brake lever and back off the parking brake cable until there is slack in the cable.

3. Clean and lubricate the adjuster threads.

4. Use a brake spoon to turn the starwheel adjuster until there is light shoe-to-drum contact. Back off the starwheel until the wheel rotates freely with no brake drag.

5. Tighten the parking brake adjustment until a slight drag is felt while rotating the wheels.

6. Loosen the cable adjusting nut until both rear wheels can be rotated freely, then back the cable adjuster nut off 2 full turns.

7. Test the parking brake. The rear wheels should rotate freely without dragging.

Front Brake Cable

REMOVAL AND INSTALLATION

1. Raise and support the car.

2. Disconnect the brake cable from the connector.

3. Force the cable housing and attaching clip forward out of the body crossmember.

4. Fold back the left front edge of the floor covering and pry the rubber grommet out of the hole in the dash or from the floor pan.

5. Remove the cable-to-floor pan clip.

6. Engage the parking brake and work the cable out of the clevis linkage.

7. Force the upper end of the cable housing out of the pedal bracket.

8. Work the cable and housing assembly out of the floor pan.

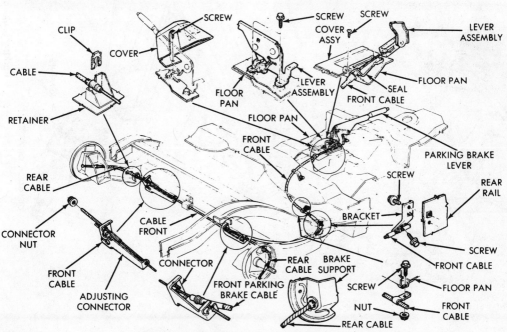

Parking brake cables—all except pickup models

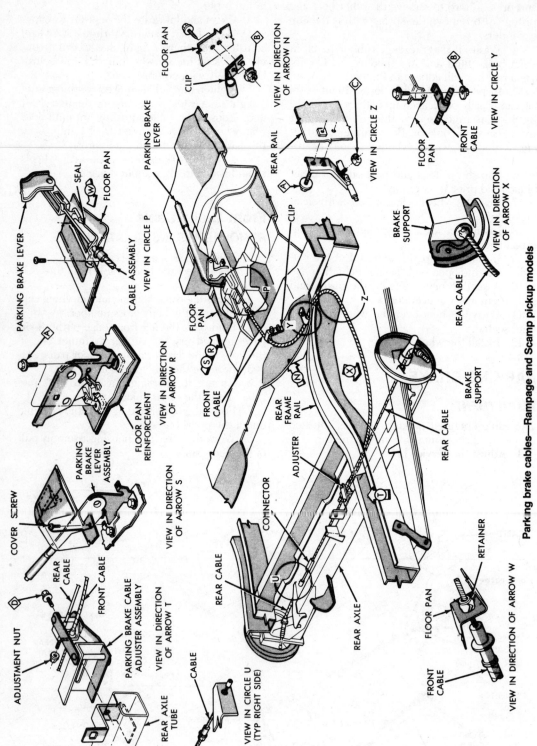

FLOOR PAN

CLIP

VIEW IN DIRECTION OF ARROW N

PARKING BRAKE LEVER

VIEW IN CIRCLE Z

REAR RAIL

FLOOR PAN

FRONT CABLE

VIEW IN CIRCLE Y

SEAL

FLOOR PAN

PARKING BRAKE LEVER

CABLE ASSEMBLY

VIEW IN CIRCLE P

BRAKE SUPPORT

VIEW IN DIRECTION OF ARROW X

REAR CABLE

PARKING BRAKE LEVER

FLOOR PAN

VIEW IN DIRECTION OF ARROW R

FLOOR PAN REINFORCEMENT

PARKING BRAKE LEVER ASSEMBLY

FRONT CABLE

REAR FRAME RAIL

ADJUSTER

BRAKE SUPPORT

REAR CABLE

VIEW IN DIRECTION OF ARROW S

COVER SCREW

REAR CABLE

FRONT CABLE

PARKING BRAKE CABLE ADJUSTER ASSEMBLY

VIEW IN DIRECTION OF ARROW T

ADJUSTMENT NUT

CONNECTOR

REAR CABLE

REAR AXLE

FLOOR PAN

FRONT CABLE

RETAINER

VIEW IN DIRECTION OF ARROW W

REAR AXLE TUBE

CABLE

VIEW IN CIRCLE U (TYP RIGHT SIDE)

Parking brake cables—Rampage and Scamp pickup models

9. Installation is the reverse of removal. Adjust the parking and service brakes and test the operation of both.

Rear Brake Cable
REMOVAL AND INSTALLATION

1. Raise and support the car.
2. Remove the rear wheels.
3. Disconnect the brake cable from the connector.
4. Remove the retaining clip from the rear cable bracket.
5. Remove the brake drum.
6. Remove the brake shoe return springs.
7. Remove the brake shoe retaining springs.
8. Remove the brake shoe strut and spring and disconnect the cable from the operating arm.
9. Compress the retainers on the end of the brake cable housing and remove the cable.
10. Installation is the reverse of removal. Adjust the service and parking brakes and test the operation of both.

Body and Trim

9

EXTERIOR

Doors

REMOVAL AND INSTALLATION

1. Disconnect the door light wiring harness on models equipped.
2. Remove the door opening check strap.
3. Support the door in the opened position. Use special tool C4614 or C4716 (depending on the size of the hinge pin) and remove the lower hinge pin. Insert special tool C4741 in place of the pin.
4. Remove the upper hinge pin using the suitable special tool. Remove the lower alignment tool and remove the door.
5. Grind a chamfer on the hinge pins to make installation easier.
6. Install the door into the opening using alignment tools C4741 in place of the hinge pins.
7. Use a small hammer and drive in the upper hinge pin from the bottom. Drive in the lower hinge pin from the top.

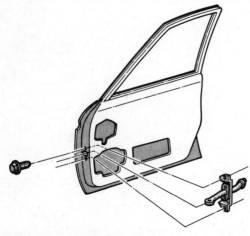

Removing/installing door check

8. Install the door check strap and reconnect the wiring harness on models so equipped.

ADJUSTMENT

The door hinges are welded to both the door panels and the door pillar. Fore and aft, up and down adjustments may be accomplished by bending the hinges using a special tool C4736. Before bending the hinges, check for correct engagement of the door striker plate. Check hinge pin fit and condition and check for proper weatherstrip installation.

Bend the hinges as follows:
1. Examine the door fit to determine which direction is necessary to bend the hinge for correct alignment.
2. Place the adjusting tool C4736 in position on the hinge to be corrected. The tool must be slipped completely over the hinge to prevent damage to the tool or the hinge.
3. Slowly apply pressure to bend the hinge. Check frequently until correct alignment is achieved.

Door Striker

The door latch should engage the striker squarely. The door should not rise up or down on the striker as it is closed. After the striker is adjusted the door should fit flush with the adjoining sheet metal.

ADJUSTMENT

1. Mark the location of the striker for reference.
2. Loosen the striker attaching screws.
3. Move the striker to the desired location and tighten the mounting screws.
4. Check alignment, readjust if necessary.

Door Latch

On late models, the outer latch can be replaced without removing the door trim panel.

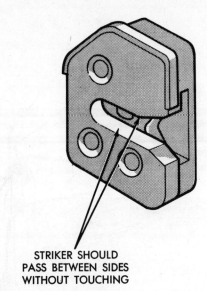

STRIKER SHOULD
PASS BETWEEN SIDES
WITHOUT TOUCHING

Outside latch assembly

The various links will hold the inner latch in position while the outer latch is removed. A thin punch can be used to align the inner latch while the outer latch is installed.

REMOVAL AND INSTALLATION

1. Raise the door glass to the full up position.
2. Remove the door trim panel and plastic weathershield.
3. Remove the push rod link, the remote control link, the outside handle link and the key cylinder link from the latch connectors.
4. Remove the latch attaching screws. Remove the outside and inside halves of the latch assembly.
5. Install in the reverse order.

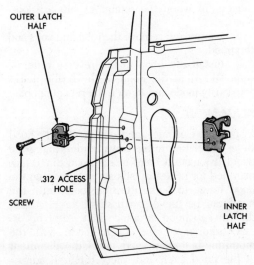

Door latch installation

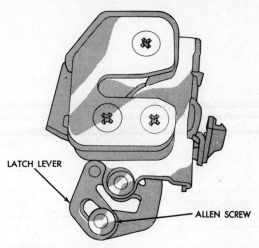

LATCH LEVER

ALLEN SCREW

Door latch adjustment

ADJUSTMENT

NOTE: *Door panel removal may be necessary for access to provide full adjustment range.*

1. Insert a 5/32 in. Allen wrench through the access hole provided in the door face and loosen the Allen screw.
2. Move the Allen wrench and screw upwards in the slot to the position required. Tighten the Allen screw to 30 in. lbs.
3. Check the position of the outside door handle for flush appearance to the door panel. Check the operation of the latch. Readjust the latch as required.

Lock Cylinder
REMOVAL AND INSTALLATION

1. Raise the window glass to the full up position.

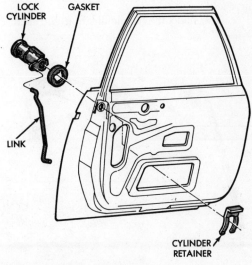

LOCK CYLINDER GASKET
LINK
CYLINDER RETAINER

Door lock cylinder installation

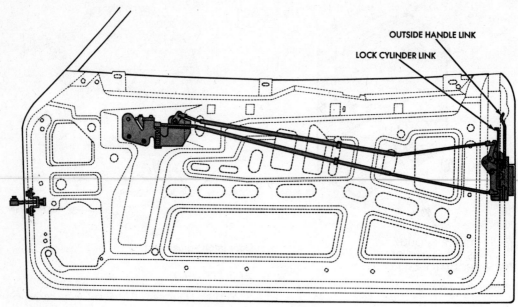

OUTSIDE HANDLE LINK

LOCK CYLINDER LINK

Typical door lock system

2. Remove the door trim panel and plastic air shield.

3. Disconnect the remote link from the lock cylinder lever.

4. Remove the horseshoe retaining clip from the cylinder lock groove. Remove the retainer and the lock cylinder.

5. Install the lock cylinder in the reverse order of removal.

Outside Door Handle
REMOVAL AND INSTALLATION

1. Raise the door glass to the full up position

2. Remove the door trim panel and plastic air shield.

3. Disconnect the handle link from the latch.

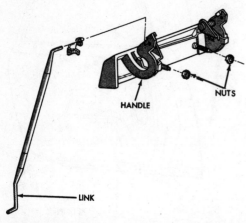

HANDLE

NUTS

LINK

Outside door handle

4. Remove the nuts that attach the handle to the door panel. Lift the handle and link from the door.

5. Install the door handle in the reverse order of removal.

Hood
REMOVAL AND INSTALLATION

1. Mark the hinge outline on the inside of the hood for reinstallation reference.

2. Place a protective padded covering over the windshield and fender ends in case the hood slides out of your grasp when the hinges are disconnected. Place a block of wood below each rear corner of the hood to prevent sudden rear movement when the retaining bolts are loosened.

3. Loosen and remove the retaining bolts and the hood.

4. Install the hood in the reverse order of removal. Align the hood to the scribe marks previously made and tighten the retaining bolts.

ALIGNMENT

Inspect the clearances and alignment of the hood slides in relation to the cowl, fenders and grille panel. Elongated holes in the hood hinges are provided for necessary adjustments. Loosen the hood hinge to hood attaching bolts until the hood can be moved with slight force. Adjust the cowl to hood clearance first. After necessary adjustment has been made and the mounting bolts tightened, check the alignment of the hood latch and safety catch. If adjustment is necessary, loosen the mounting bolts and slide the latch to the required position. Retighten the mounting bolts.

Windshield

NOTE: *The windshield is mounted with butyl tape, special tools and materials are required for installation.*

REMOVAL AND INSTALLATION

1. Cover all areas around the windshield to prevent damage to the finish.

2. Remove the windshield wiper arm and blade assemblies. Remove the windshield mouldings that interfere with windshield replacement.

3. Use an electric knife (Miller Tool No. 4386 or the equivalent) and cut the existing butyl tape as close as possible to the mounting flange of the windshield frame. Remove the windshield.

4. Remove all remaining adhesive from the mounting flange with naphtha or comparable solvent.

CAUTION: *Follow the warnings on the solvent can.*

5. Apply butyl primer (Chrys. No. 3500883 or the equivalent) on the mounting flange and butyl tape remnants.

6. Start at either side of the windshield body opening and apply the butyl tape to the frame, with the tapered edge of the tape facing the reveal surface.

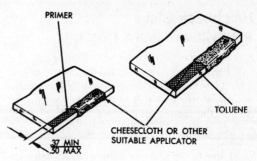
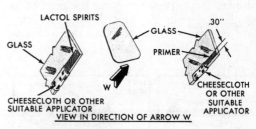

Cleaning glass surface

Primer application to glass

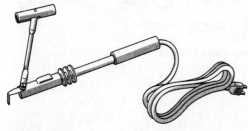

Electric knife

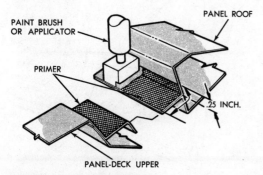

Cleaning metal frame surface

7. Cut off the excess tape and butt joint the ends. Apply sufficient pressure to ensure a good seal.

8. Clean the bonding surfaces of the windshield glass with clean cheesecloth moistened with Super-Kleen (Chrys. No. 4026030 or equivalent). Wipe off immediately with another piece of clean cheesecloth.

9. Apply butyl glass primer to the entire bonding surface of the windshield glass, both the inside surface and the edges. Allow the primer to dry for five minutes.

10. Locate the windshield in the center of the opening and make contact with the tape. Place spacers at the bottom of the glass between the glass edge and body opening. Locate one spacer on each side of the glass, over the site of the original spacer. Select spacers, or combination of spacers that will ensure a snug fit between the glass edge and frame while keeping the glass centered.

11. Use maximum hand pressure to push the glass down against the tape.

12. Inspect the bond. If the contact between the glass and tape is poor, repeat maximum hand pressure. The bond should be .25 in. or greater.

13. Check the spacers to make sure they are in the proper location.

14. Water test the seal. Repair any leaks with secondary sealer application.

15. Install any trim molding and the wiper arm and blade assemblies.

Hatchback Glass

REMOVAL AND INSTALLATION

1. Remove the locking strip center cap and pull the locking strip from the groove.

2. Carefully push the glass out of the weatherstrip, starting at one corner and continuing around the glass until it is free from the weatherstrip. Remove the weatherstrip from the hatch frame.

3. Install the glass into the weatherstrip. Install cord between the glass and weatherstrip lip.

4. Place the glass into position in the frame opening. Apply pressure against the glass while an assistant pulls the cord through the window opening which will locate the weatherstripping lip over the frame.

5. Inspect for complete sealing of the weatherstrip around the frame.

6. Install the locking strip starting at the bottom center. Install the center locking cap.

INTERIOR

Door Panels

REMOVAL AND INSTALLATION

1. Remove the inside door handle and bezel trim.

2. Remove the arm rest and window handle crank.

3. If equipped with a remote door miror, remove the retaining trim nut.

4. Use a wide prying device and unclip the panel retainers from the door. Remove the panel, and plastic shield.

5. Install the weather shield and door panel in the reverse order of removal.

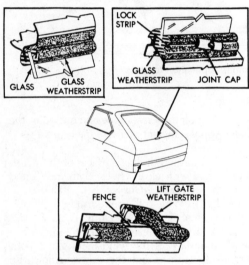

Lift-gate weatherstrips

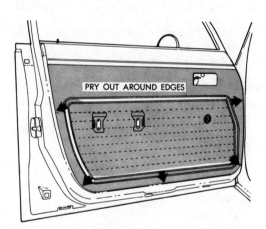

Trim panel removal

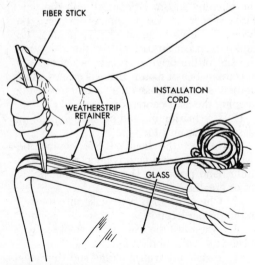

Cord installation

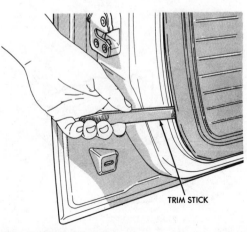

Disengage trim panel

Front Door Glass and Regulator
REMOVAL AND INSTALLATION

1. To remove the window glass: Remove the door panel and weathershield.

2. Remove the glass stops and stabilizers.

3. Lower the window until the lift channel fasteners are visible. Remove the fasteners and disengage the glass from the lift channel. Remove the glass through the belt (upper) opening. Install the glass in the reverse order.

4. To remove the window regulator: Remove the door panel and weathershield.

5. Secure the window in full up position.

6. Carefully drive out the center pin of the mounting rivets with a punch, then drill out the rivets with a suitable drill.

7. Disengage the regulator arm from the lift plate and remove the regulator through the access opening.

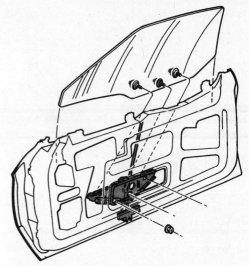

Typical glass fastener locations

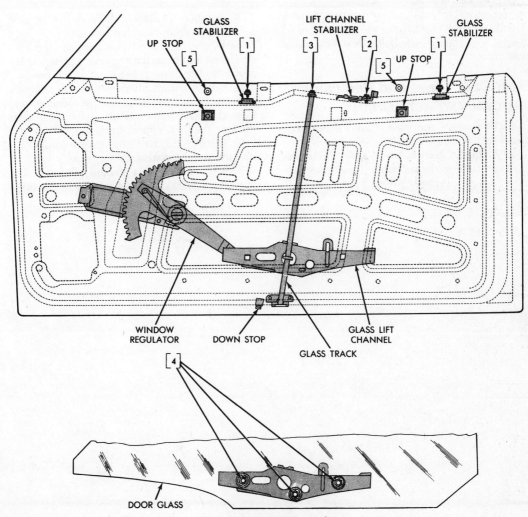

Typical glass system on door

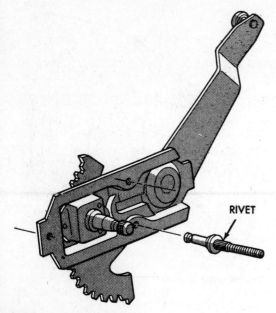

RIVET

Typical window regulator

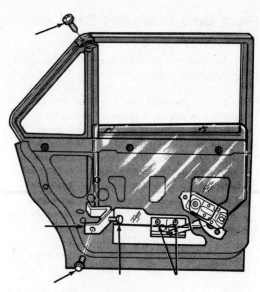

Rear door glass removal points

8. Install the regulator in the reverse order. Secure with suitable size bolts, lockwashers and nuts.

Rear Door Glass and Regulator
REMOVAL AND INSTALLATION

1. To remove the glass: Remove the door panel and weathershield.

2. Align the glass fasteners with the access hole and remove the fasteners. Lower the window glass after removing the lift fasteners.

3. Remove the lower division bar bracket screws and remove the bar bracket.

4. Disengage the division bar from the window glass and from the stationary glass and remove the bar through the main access hole.

5. Remove the stationary glass by applying a forward force to disengage the window seal from the door frame. Remove the door glass through the belt (upper) opening.

6. Install the glass in the reverse order. Install the weatherseal and door panel.

7. To remove the regulator: Refer to the previous front door regulator servicing section.

Troubleshooting
10

This section is designed to aid in the quick, accurate diagnosis of automotive problems. While automotive repairs can be made by many people, accurate troubleshooting is a rare skill for the amateur and professional alike.

In its simplest state, troubleshooting is an exercise in logic. It is essential to realize that an automobile is really composed of a series of systems. Some of these systems are interrelated; others are not. Automobiles operate within a framework of logical rules and physical laws, and the key to troubleshooting is a good understanding of all the automotive systems.

This section breaks the car or truck down into its component systems, allowing the problem to be isolated. The charts and diagnostic road maps list the most common problems and the most probable causes of trouble. Obviously it would be impossible to list every possible problem that could happen along with every possible cause, but it will locate MOST problems and eliminate a lot of unnecessary guesswork. The systematic format will locate problems within a given system, but, because many automotive systems are interrelated, the solution to your particular problem may be found in a number of systems on the car or truck.

USING THE TROUBLESHOOTING CHARTS

This book contains all of the specific information that the average do-it-yourself mechanic needs to repair and maintain his or her car or truck. The troubleshooting charts are designed to be used in conjunction with the specific procedures and information in the text. For instance, troubleshooting a point-type ignition system is fairly standard for all models, but you may be directed to the text to find procedures for troubleshooting an individual type of electronic ignition. You will also have to refer to the specification charts throughout the book for specifications applicable to your car or truck.

TOOLS AND EQUIPMENT

The tools illustrated in Chapter 1 (plus two more diagnostic pieces) will be adequate to troubleshoot most problems. The two other tools needed are a voltmeter and an ohmmeter. These can be purchased separately or in combination, known as a VOM meter.

In the event that other tools are required, they will be noted in the procedures.

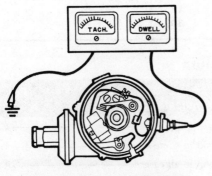

Tach-dwell hooked-up to distributor

Troubleshooting Engine Problems

See Chapters 2, 3, 4 for more information and service procedures.

Index to Systems

System	To Test	Group
Battery	Engine need not be running	1
Starting system	Engine need not be running	2
Primary electrical system	Engine need not be running	3
Secondary electrical system	Engine need not be running	4
Fuel system	Engine need not be running	5
Engine compression	Engine need not be running	6
Engine vacuum	Engine must be running	7
Secondary electrical system	Engine must be running	8
Valve train	Engine must be running	9
Exhaust system	Engine must be running	10
Cooling system	Engine must be running	11
Engine lubrication	Engine must be running	12

Index to Problems

Problem: Symptom	Begin at Specific Diagnosis, Number ___
Engine Won't Start:	
Starter doesn't turn	1.1, 2.1
Starter turns, engine doesn't	2.1
Starter turns engine very slowly	1.1, 2.4
Starter turns engine normally	3.1, 4.1
Starter turns engine very quickly	6.1
Engine fires intermittently	4.1
Engine fires consistently	5.1, 6.1
Engine Runs Poorly:	
Hard starting	3.1, 4.1, 5.1, 8.1
Rough idle	4.1, 5.1, 8.1
Stalling	3.1, 4.1, 5.1, 8.1
Engine dies at high speeds	4.1, 5.1
Hesitation (on acceleration from standing stop)	5.1, 8.1
Poor pickup	4.1, 5.1, 8.1
Lack of power	3.1, 4.1, 5.1, 8.1
Backfire through the carburetor	4.1, 8.1, 9.1
Backfire through the exhaust	4.1, 8.1, 9.1
Blue exhaust gases	6.1, 7.1
Black exhaust gases	5.1
Running on (after the ignition is shut off)	3.1, 8.1
Susceptible to moisture	4.1
Engine misfires under load	4.1, 7.1, 8.4, 9.1
Engine misfires at speed	4.1, 8.4
Engine misfires at idle	3.1, 4.1, 5.1, 7.1, 8.4

Sample Section

Test and Procedure	Results and Indications	Proceed to
4.1—Check for spark: Hold each spark plug wire approximately ¼" from ground with gloves or a heavy, dry rag. Crank the engine and observe the spark.	If no spark is evident:	4.2
	If spark is good in some cases:	4.3
	If spark is good in all cases:	4.6

Specific Diagnosis

This section is arranged so that following each test, instructions are given to proceed to another, until a problem is diagnosed.

Section 1—Battery

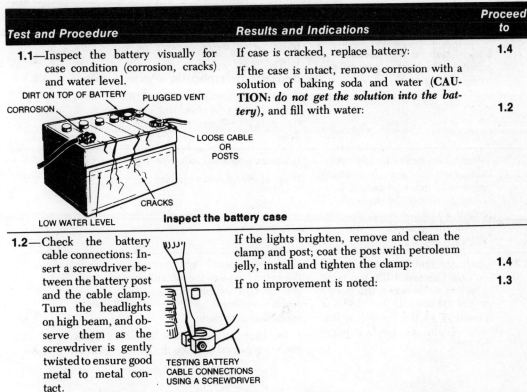

Test and Procedure	Results and Indications	Proceed to
1.1—Inspect the battery visually for case condition (corrosion, cracks) and water level.	If case is cracked, replace battery:	**1.4**
	If the case is intact, remove corrosion with a solution of baking soda and water (**CAUTION**: *do not get the solution into the battery*), and fill with water:	**1.2**

DIRT ON TOP OF BATTERY   PLUGGED VENT
CORROSION
LOOSE CABLE OR POSTS
CRACKS
LOW WATER LEVEL
Inspect the battery case

Test and Procedure	Results and Indications	Proceed to
1.2—Check the battery cable connections: Insert a screwdriver between the battery post and the cable clamp. Turn the headlights on high beam, and observe them as the screwdriver is gently twisted to ensure good metal to metal contact.	If the lights brighten, remove and clean the clamp and post; coat the post with petroleum jelly, install and tighten the clamp:	**1.4**
	If no improvement is noted:	**1.3**

TESTING BATTERY CABLE CONNECTIONS USING A SCREWDRIVER

Test and Procedure	Results and Indications	Proceed to
1.3—Test the state of charge of the battery using an individual cell tester or hydrometer.	If indicated, charge the battery. **NOTE**: *If no obvious reason exists for the low state of charge (i.e., battery age, prolonged storage), proceed to:*	**1.4**

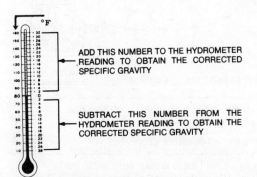

°F

ADD THIS NUMBER TO THE HYDROMETER READING TO OBTAIN THE CORRECTED SPECIFIC GRAVITY

SUBTRACT THIS NUMBER FROM THE HYDROMETER READING TO OBTAIN THE CORRECTED SPECIFIC GRAVITY

Specific Gravity (@ 80° F.)

Minimum	Battery Charge
1.260	100% Charged
1.230	75% Charged
1.200	50% Charged
1.170	25% Charged
1.140	Very Little Power Left
1.110	Completely Discharged

The effects of temperature on battery specific gravity (left) and amount of battery charge in relation to specific gravity (right)

Test and Procedure	Results and Indications	Proceed to
1.4—Visually inspect battery cables for cracking, bad connection to ground, or bad connection to starter.	If necessary, tighten connections or replace the cables:	**2.1**

Section 2—Starting System
See Chapter 3 for service procedures

Test and Procedure	Results and Indications	Proceed to
Note: Tests in Group 2 are performed with coil high tension lead disconnected to prevent accidental starting.		
2.1—Test the starter motor and solenoid: Connect a jumper from the battery post of the solenoid (or relay) to the starter post of the solenoid (or relay).	If starter turns the engine normally:	2.2
	If the starter buzzes, or turns the engine very slowly:	2.4
	If no response, replace the solenoid (or relay).	3.1
	If the starter turns, but the engine doesn't, ensure that the flywheel ring gear is intact. If the gear is undamaged, replace the starter drive.	3.1
2.2—Determine whether ignition override switches are functioning properly (clutch start switch, neutral safety switch), by connecting a jumper across the switch(es), and turning the ignition switch to "start".	If starter operates, adjust or replace switch:	3.1
	If the starter doesn't operate:	2.3
2.3—Check the ignition switch "start" position: Connect a 12V test lamp or voltmeter between the starter post of the solenoid (or relay) and ground. Turn the ignition switch to the "start" position, and jiggle the key.	If the lamp doesn't light or the meter needle doesn't move when the switch is turned, check the ignition switch for loose connections, cracked insulation, or broken wires. Repair or replace as necessary:	3.1
	If the lamp flickers or needle moves when the key is jiggled, replace the ignition switch.	3.3

Checking the ignition switch "start" position

STARTER RELAY
(IF EQUIPPED)

2.4—Remove and bench test the starter, according to specifications in the engine electrical section.	If the starter does not meet specifications, repair or replace as needed:	3.1
	If the starter is operating properly:	2.5
2.5—Determine whether the engine can turn freely: Remove the spark plugs, and check for water in the cylinders. Check for water on the dipstick, or oil in the radiator. Attempt to turn the engine using an 18" flex drive and socket on the crankshaft pulley nut or bolt.	If the engine will turn freely only with the spark plugs out, and hydrostatic lock (water in the cylinders) is ruled out, check valve timing:	9.2
	If engine will not turn freely, and it is known that the clutch and transmission are free, the engine must be disassembled for further evaluation:	Chapter 3

Section 3—Primary Electrical System

Test and Procedure	Results and Indications	Proceed to
3.1—Check the ignition switch "on" position: Connect a jumper wire between the distributor side of the coil and ground, and a 12V test lamp between the switch side of the coil and ground. Remove the high tension lead from the coil. Turn the ignition switch on and jiggle the key.	If the lamp lights:	**3.2**
	If the lamp flickers when the key is jiggled, replace the ignition switch:	**3.3**
	If the lamp doesn't light, check for loose or open connections. If none are found, remove the ignition switch and check for continuity. If the switch is faulty, replace it:	**3.3**

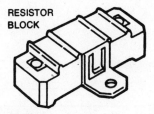

Checking the ignition switch "on" position

3.2—Check the ballast resistor or resistance wire for an open circuit, using an ohmmeter. See Chapter 3 for specific tests.	Replace the resistor or resistance wire if the resistance is zero. **NOTE:** *Some ignition systems have no ballast resistor.*	**3.3**

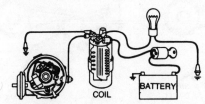

Two types of resistors

3.3—On point-type ignition systems, visually inspect the breaker points for burning, pitting or excessive wear. Gray coloring of the point contact surfaces is normal. Rotate the crankshaft until the contact heel rests on a high point of the distributor cam and adjust the point gap to specifications. On electronic ignition models, remove the distributor cap and visually inspect the armature. Ensure that the armature pin is in place, and that the armature is on tight and rotates when the engine is cranked. Make sure there are no cracks, chips or rounded edges on the armature.	If the breaker points are intact, clean the contact surfaces with fine emery cloth, and adjust the point gap to specifications. If the points are worn, replace them. On electronic systems, replace any parts which appear defective. If condition persists:	**3.4**

Test and Procedure	Results and Indications	Proceed to
3.4—On point-type ignition systems, connect a dwell-meter between the distributor primary lead and ground. Crank the engine and observe the point dwell angle. On electronic ignition systems, conduct a stator (magnetic pickup assembly) test. See Chapter 3.	On point-type systems, adjust the dwell angle if necessary. **NOTE:** *Increasing the point gap decreases the dwell angle and vice-versa.*	**3.6**
	If the dwell meter shows little or no reading;	**3.5**
	On electronic ignition systems, if the stator is bad, replace the stator. If the stator is good, proceed to the other tests in Chapter 3.	

WIDE GAP   NARROW GAP

CLOSE   OPEN

NORMAL DWELL   INSUFFICIENT DWELL   EXCESSIVE DWELL

SMALL DWELL   LARGE DWELL

Dwell is a function of point gap

3.5—On the point-type ignition systems, check the condenser for short: connect an ohmeter across the condenser body and the pigtail lead.	If any reading other than infinite is noted, replace the condenser	**3.6**

OHMMETER

Checking the condenser for short

3.6—Test the coil primary resistance: On point-type ignition systems, connect an ohmmeter across the coil primary terminals, and read the resistance on the low scale. Note whether an external ballast resistor or resistance wire is used. On electronic ignition systems, test the coil primary resistance as in Chapter 3.	Point-type ignition coils utilizing ballast resistors or resistance wires should have approximately 1.0 ohms resistance. Coils with internal resistors should have approximately 4.0 ohms resistance. If values far from the above are noted, replace the coil.	**4.1**

OHMMETER

Check the coil primary resistance

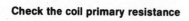

Section 4—Secondary Electrical System
See Chapters 2–3 for service procedures

Test and Procedure	Results and Indications	Proceed to
4.1—Check for spark: Hold each spark plug wire approximately ¼″ from ground with gloves or a heavy, dry rag. Crank the engine, and observe the spark.	If no spark is evident:	**4.2**
	If spark is good in some cylinders:	**4.3**
	If spark is good in all cylinders:	**4.6**

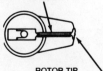

Check for spark at the plugs

4.2—Check for spark at the coil high tension lead: Remove the coil high tension lead from the distributor and position it approximately ¼″ from ground. Crank the engine and observe spark. **CAUTION: *This test should not be performed on engines equipped with electronic ignition.***	If the spark is good and consistent:	**4.3**
	If the spark is good but intermittent, test the primary electrical system starting at 3.3:	**3.3**
	If the spark is weak or non-existent, replace the coil high tension lead, clean and tighten all connections and retest. If no improvement is noted:	**4.4**
4.3—Visually inspect the distributor cap and rotor for burned or corroded contacts, cracks, carbon tracks, or moisture. Also check the fit of the rotor on the distributor shaft (where applicable).	If moisture is present, dry thoroughly, and retest per 4.1:	**4.1**
	If burned or excessively corroded contacts, cracks, or carbon tracks are noted, replace the defective part(s) and retest per 4.1:	**4.1**
	If the rotor and cap appear intact, or are only slightly corroded, clean the contacts thoroughly (including the cap towers and spark plug wire ends) and retest per 4.1:	
	If the spark is good in all cases:	**4.6**
	If the spark is poor in all cases:	**4.5**

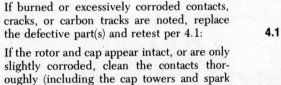

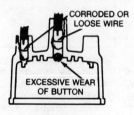

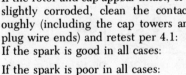

Inspect the distributor cap and rotor

Test and Procedure	Results and Indications	Proceed to
4.4—Check the coil secondary resistance: On point-type systems connect an ohmmeter across the distributor side of the coil and the coil tower. Read the resistance on the high scale of the ohmmeter. On electronic ignition systems, see Chapter 3 for specific tests.	The resistance of a satisfactory coil should be between 4,000 and 10,000 ohms. If resistance is considerably higher (i.e., 40,000 ohms) replace the coil and retest per 4.1. **NOTE:** *This does not apply to high performance coils.*	

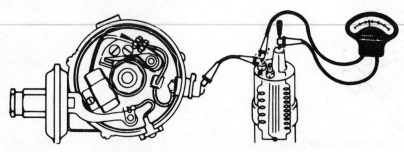

Testing the coil secondary resistance

4.5—Visually inspect the spark plug wires for cracking or brittleness. Ensure that no two wires are positioned so as to cause induction firing (adjacent and parallel). Remove each wire, one by one, and check resistance with an ohmmeter.	Replace any cracked or brittle wires. If any of the wires are defective, replace the entire set. Replace any wires with excessive resistance (over $8000\,\Omega$ per foot for suppression wire), and separate any wires that might cause induction firing.	**4.6**

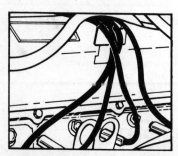

Misfiring can be the result of spark plug leads to adjacent, consecutively firing cylinders running parallel and too close together

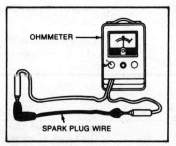

On point-type ignition systems, check the spark plug wires as shown. On electronic ignitions, do not remove the wire from the distributor cap terminal; instead, test through the cap

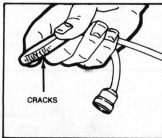

Spark plug wires can be checked visually by bending them in a loop over your finger. This will reveal any cracks, burned or broken insulation. Any wire with cracked insulation should be replaced

4.6—Remove the spark plugs, noting the cylinders from which they were removed, and evaluate according to the color photos in the middle of this book.	See following.	**See following.**

Test and Procedure	Results and Indications	Proceed to
4.7—Examine the location of all the plugs.	The following diagrams illustrate some of the conditions that the location of plugs will reveal.	4.8

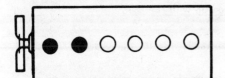

Two adjacent plugs are fouled in a 6-cylinder engine, 4-cylinder engine or either bank of a V-8. This is probably due to a blown head gasket between the two cylinders

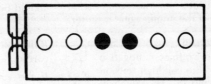

The two center plugs in a 6-cylinder engine are fouled. Raw fuel may be "boiled" out of the carburetor into the intake manifold after the engine is shut-off. Stop-start driving can also foul the center plugs, due to overly rich mixture. Proper float level, a new float needle and seat or use of an insulating spacer may help this problem

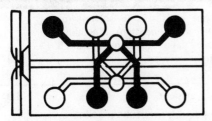

An unbalanced carburetor is indicated. Following the fuel flow on this particular design shows that the cylinders fed by the right-hand barrel are fouled from overly rich mixture, while the cylinders fed by the left-hand barrel are normal

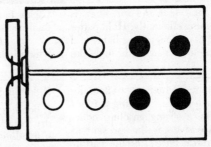

If the four rear plugs are overheated, a cooling system problem is suggested. A thorough cleaning of the cooling system may restore coolant circulation and cure the problem

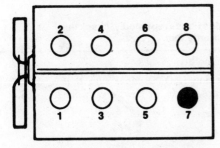

Finding one plug overheated may indicate an intake manifold leak near the affected cylinder. If the overheated plug is the second of two adjacent, consecutively firing plugs, it could be the result of ignition cross-firing. Separating the leads to these two plugs will eliminate cross-fire

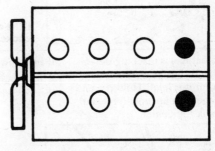

Occasionally, the two rear plugs in large, lightly used V-8's will become oil fouled. High oil consumption and smoky exhaust may also be noticed. It is probably due to plugged oil drain holes in the rear of the cylinder head, causing oil to be sucked in around the valve stems. This usually occurs in the rear cylinders first, because the engine slants that way

Test and Procedure	Results and Indications	Proceed to
4.8—Determine the static ignition timing. Using the crankshaft pulley timing marks as a guide, locate top dead center on the compression stroke of the number one cylinder.	The rotor should be pointing toward the No. 1 tower in the distributor cap, and, on electronic ignitions, the armature spoke for that cylinder should be lined up with the stator.	**4.8**
4.9—Check coil polarity: Connect a voltmeter negative lead to the coil high tension lead, and the positive lead to ground (**NOTE:** *Reverse the hook-up for positive ground systems*). Crank the engine momentarily. **Checking coil polarity**	If the voltmeter reads up-scale, the polarity is correct: If the voltmeter reads down-scale, reverse the coil polarity (switch the primary leads):	**5.1** **5.1**

Section 5—Fuel System
See Chapter 4 for service procedures

Test and Procedure	Results and Indications	Proceed to
5.1—Determine that the air filter is functioning efficiently: Hold paper elements up to a strong light, and attempt to see light through the filter.	Clean permanent air filters in solvent (or manufacturer's recommendation), and allow to dry. Replace paper elements through which light cannot be seen:	**5.2**
5.2—Determine whether a flooding condition exists: Flooding is identified by a strong gasoline odor, and excessive gasoline present in the throttle bore(s) of the carburetor. **If the engine floods repeatedly, check the choke butterfly flap**	If flooding is not evident: If flooding is evident, permit the gasoline to dry for a few moments and restart. If flooding doesn't recur: If flooding is persistent:	**5.3** **5.7** **5.5**
5.3—Check that fuel is reaching the carburetor: Detach the fuel line at the carburetor inlet. Hold the end of the line in a cup (not styrofoam), and crank the engine. **Check the fuel pump by disconnecting the output line (fuel pump-to-carburetor) at the carburetor and operating the starter briefly**	If fuel flows smoothly: If fuel doesn't flow (**NOTE:** *Make sure that there is fuel in the tank*), or flows erratically:	**5.7** **5.4**

Test and Procedure	Results and Indications	Proceed to
5.4—Test the fuel pump: Disconnect all fuel lines from the fuel pump. Hold a finger over the input fitting, crank the engine (with electric pump, turn the ignition or pump on); and feel for suction.	If suction is evident, blow out the fuel line to the tank with low pressure compressed air until bubbling is heard from the fuel filler neck. Also blow out the carburetor fuel line (both ends disconnected):	**5.7**
	If no suction is evident, replace or repair the fuel pump:	**5.7**
	NOTE: *Repeated oil fouling of the spark plugs, or a no-start condition, could be the result of a ruptured vacuum booster pump diaphragm, through which oil or gasoline is being drawn into the intake manifold (where applicable).*	
5.5—Occasionally, small specks of dirt will clog the small jets and orifices in the carburetor. With the engine cold, hold a flat piece of wood or similar material over the carburetor, where possible, and crank the engine.	If the engine starts, but runs roughly the engine is probably not run enough. If the engine won't start:	**5.9**
5.6—Check the needle and seat: Tap the carburetor in the area of the needle and seat.	If flooding stops, a gasoline additive (e.g., Gumout) will often cure the problem:	**5.7**
	If flooding continues, check the fuel pump for excessive pressure at the carburetor (according to specifications). If the pressure is normal, the needle and seat must be removed and checked, and/or the float level adjusted:	**5.7**
5.7—Test the accelerator pump by looking into the throttle bores while operating the throttle.	If the accelerator pump appears to be operating normally:	**5.8**
	If the accelerator pump is not operating, the pump must be reconditioned. Where possible, service the pump with the carburetor(s) installed on the engine. If necessary, remove the carburetor. Prior to removal:	**5.8**

Check for gas at the carburetor by looking down the carburetor throat while someone moves the accelerator

Test and Procedure	Results and Indications	Proceed to
5.8—Determine whether the carburetor main fuel system is functioning: Spray a commercial starting fluid into the carburetor while attempting to start the engine.	If the engine starts, runs for a few seconds, and dies:	**5.9**
	If the engine doesn't start:	**6.1**

Test and Procedure	Results and Indications	Proceed to
5.9—Uncommon fuel system malfunctions: See below:	If the problem is solved: If the problem remains, remove and recondition the carburetor.	6.1

Condition	Indication	Test	Prevailing Weather Conditions	Remedy
Vapor lock	Engine will not restart shortly after running.	Cool the components of the fuel system until the engine starts. Vapor lock can be cured faster by draping a wet cloth over a mechanical fuel pump.	Hot to very hot	Ensure that the exhaust manifold heat control valve is operating. Check with the vehicle manufacturer for the recommended solution to vapor lock on the model in question.
Carburetor icing	Engine will not idle, stalls at low speeds.	Visually inspect the throttle plate area of the throttle bores for frost.	High humidity, 32–40° F.	Ensure that the exhaust manifold heat control valve is operating, and that the intake manifold heat riser is not blocked.
Water in the fuel	Engine sputters and stalls; may not start.	Pump a small amount of fuel into a glass jar. Allow to stand, and inspect for droplets or a layer of water.	High humidity, extreme temperature changes.	For droplets, use one or two cans of commercial gas line anti-freeze. For a layer of water, the tank must be drained, and the fuel lines blown out with compressed air.

Section 6—Engine Compression
See Chapter 3 for service procedures

6.1—Test engine compression: Remove all spark plugs. Block the throttle wide open. Insert a compression gauge into a spark plug port, crank the engine to obtain the maximum reading, and record.	If compression is within limits on all cylinders: If gauge reading is extremely low on all cylinders: If gauge reading is low on one or two cylinders: (If gauge readings are identical and low on two or more adjacent cylinders, the head gasket must be replaced.)	7.1 6.2 6.2

Checking compression

6.2—Test engine compression (wet): Squirt approximately 30 cc. of engine oil into each cylinder, and retest per 6.1.	If the readings improve, worn or cracked rings or broken pistons are indicated: If the readings do not improve, burned or excessively carboned valves or a jumped timing chain are indicated: NOTE: *A jumped timing chain is often indicated by difficult cranking.*	See Chapter 3 7.1

Section 7—Engine Vacuum
See Chapter 3 for service procedures

Test and Procedure	Results and Indications	Proceed to
7.1—Attach a vacuum gauge to the intake manifold beyond the throttle plate. Start the engine, and observe the action of the needle over the range of engine speeds.	See below.	**See below**

INDICATION: normal engine in good condition

Proceed to: 8.1

Normal engine
Gauge reading: steady, from 17–22 in./Hg.

INDICATION: sticking valves or ignition miss

Proceed to: 9.1, 8.3

Sticking valves
Gauge reading: intermittent fluctuation at idle

INDICATION: late ignition or valve timing, low compression, stuck throttle valve, leaking carburetor or manifold gasket

Proceed to: 6.1

Incorrect valve timing
Gauge reading: low (10–15 in./Hg) but steady

INDICATION: improper carburetor adjustment or minor intake leak.

Proceed to: 7.2

Carburetor requires adjustment
Gauge reading: drifting needle

INDICATION: ignition miss, blown cylinder head gasket, leaking valve or weak valve spring

Proceed to: 8.3, 6.1

Blown head gasket
Gauge reading: needle fluctuates as engine speed increases

INDICATION: burnt valve or faulty valve clearance. Needle will fall when defective valve operates

Proceed to: 9.1

Burnt or leaking valves
Gauge reading: steady needle, but drops regularly

INDICATION: choked muffler, excessive back pressure in system

Proceed to: 10.1

Clogged exhaust system
Gauge reading: gradual drop in reading at idle

INDICATION: worn valve guides

Proceed to: 9.1

Worn valve guides
Gauge reading: needle vibrates excessively at idle, but steadies as engine speed increases

White pointer = steady gauge hand

Black pointer = fluctuating gauge hand

Test and Procedure	Results and Indications	Proceed to
7.2—Attach a vacuum gauge per 7.1, and test for an intake manifold leak. Squirt a small amount of oil around the intake manifold gaskets, carburetor gaskets, plugs and fittings. Observe the action of the vacuum gauge.	If the reading improves, replace the indicated gasket, or seal the indicated fitting or plug:	**8.1**
	If the reading remains low:	**7.3**
7.3—Test all vacuum hoses and accessories for leaks as described in 7.2. Also check the carburetor body (dashpots, automatic choke mechanism, throttle shafts) for leaks in the same manner.	If the reading improves, service or replace the offending part(s):	**8.1**
	If the reading remains low:	**6.1**

Section 8—Secondary Electrical System
See Chapter 2 for service procedures

Test and Procedure	Results and Indications	Proceed to
8.1—Remove the distributor cap and check to make sure that the rotor turns when the engine is cranked. Visually inspect the distributor components.	Clean, tighten or replace any components which appear defective.	**8.2**
8.2—Connect a timing light (per manufacturer's recommendation) and check the dynamic ignition timing. Disconnect and plug the vacuum hose(s) to the distributor if specified, start the engine, and observe the timing marks at the specified engine speed.	If the timing is not correct, adjust to specifications by rotating the distributor in the engine: (Advance timing by rotating distributor opposite normal direction of rotor rotation, retard timing by rotating distributor in same direction as rotor rotation.)	**8.3**
8.3—Check the operation of the distributor advance mechanism(s): To test the mechanical advance, disconnect the vacuum lines from the distributor advance unit and observe the timing marks with a timing light as the engine speed is increased from idle. If the mark moves smoothly, without hesitation, it may be assumed that the mechanical advance is functioning properly. To test vacuum advance and/or retard systems, alternately crimp and release the vacuum line, and observe the timing mark for movement. If movement is noted, the system is operating.	If the systems are functioning:	**8.4**
	If the systems are not functioning, remove the distributor, and test on a distributor tester:	**8.4**
8.4—Locate an ignition miss: With the engine running, remove each spark plug wire, one at a time, until one is found that doesn't cause the engine to roughen and slow down.	When the missing cylinder is identified:	**4.1**

CHILTON'S
AUTO BODY
REPAIR TIPS

Tools and Materials • Step-by-Step Illustrated Procedures
How To Repair Dents, Scratches and Rust Holes
Spray Painting and Refinishing Tips

With a little practice, basic body repair procedures can be mastered by any do-it-yourself mechanic. The step-by-step repairs shown here can be applied to almost any type of auto body repair.

TOOLS & MATERIALS

You may already have basic tools, such as hammers and electric drills. Other tools unique to body repair — body hammers, grinding attachments, sanding blocks, dent puller, half-round plastic file and plastic spreaders — are relatively inexpensive and can be obtained wherever auto parts or auto body repair parts are sold. Portable air compressors and paint spray guns can be purchased or rented.

Auto Body Repair Kits

The best and most often used products are available to the do-it-yourselfer in kit form, from major manufacturers of auto body repair products. The same manufacturers also merchandise the individual products for use by pros.

Kits are available to make a wide variety of repairs, including holes, dents and scratches and fiberglass, and offer the advantage of buying the materials you'll need for the job. There is little waste or chance of materials going bad from not being used. Many kits may also contain basic body-working tools such as body files, sanding blocks and spreaders. Check the contents of the kit before buying your tools.

BODY REPAIR TIPS

Safety

Many of the products associated with auto body repair and refinishing contain toxic chemicals. Read all labels before opening containers and store them in a safe place and manner.

• Wear eye protection (safety goggles) when using power tools or when performing any operation that involves the removal of any type of material.

• Wear lung protection (disposable mask or respirator) when grinding, sanding or painting.

Sanding

1 Sand off paint before using a dent puller. When using a non-adhesive sanding disc, cover the back of the disc with an overlapping layer or two of masking tape and trim the edges. The disc will last considerably longer.

2 Use the circular motion of the sanding disc to grind *into* the edge of the repair. Grinding or sanding away from the jagged edge will only tear the sandpaper.

3 Use the palm of your hand flat on the panel to detect high and low spots. Do not use your fingertips. Slide your hand slowly back and forth.

WORKING WITH BODY FILLER

Mixing The Filler

Cleanliness and proper mixing and application are extremely important. Use a clean piece of plastic or glass or a disposable artist's palette to mix body filler.

1 Allow plenty of time and follow directions. No useful purpose will be served by adding more hardener to make it cure (set-up) faster. Less hardener means more curing time, but the mixture dries harder; more hardener means less curing time but a softer mixture.

2 Both the hardener and the filler should be thoroughly kneaded or stirred before mixing. Hardener should be a solid paste and dispense like thin toothpaste. Body filler should be smooth, and free of lumps or thick spots.

Getting the proper amount of hardener in the filler is the trickiest part of preparing the filler. Use the same amount of hardener in cold or warm weather. For contour filler (thick coats), a bead of hardener twice the diameter of the filler is about right. There's about a 15% margin on either side, but, if in doubt use less hardener.

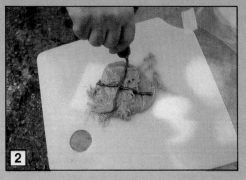

3 Mix the body filler and hardener by wiping across the mixing surface, picking the mixture up and wiping it again. Colder weather requires longer mixing times. Do not mix in a circular motion; this will trap air bubbles which will become holes in the cured filler.

Applying The Filler

1 For best results, filler should not be applied over ¼″ thick.

Apply the filler in several coats. Build it up to above the level of the repair surface so that it can be sanded or grated down.

The first coat of filler must be pressed on with a firm wiping motion.

Apply the filler in one direction only. Working the filler back and forth will either pull it off the metal or trap air bubbles.

REPAIRING DENTS

Before you start, take a few minutes to study the damaged area. Try to visualize the shape of the panel before it was damaged. If the damage is on the left fender, look at the right fender and use it as a guide. If there is access to the panel from behind, you can reshape it with a body hammer. If not, you'll have to use a dent puller. Go slowly and work the metal a little at a time. Get the panel as straight as possible before applying filler.

1 This dent is typical of one that can be pulled out or hammered out from behind. Remove the headlight cover, headlight assembly and turn signal housing.

2 Drill a series of holes ½ the size of the end of the dent puller along the stress line. Make some trial pulls and assess the results. If necessary, drill more holes and try again. Do not hurry.

3 If possible, use a body hammer and block to shape the metal back to its original contours. Get the metal back as close to its original shape as possible. Don't depend on body filler to fill dents.

4 Using an 80-grit grinding disc on an electric drill, grind the paint from the surrounding area down to bare metal. Use a new grinding pad to prevent heat buildup that will warp metal.

5 The area should look like this when you're finished grinding. Knock the drill holes in and tape over small openings to keep plastic filler out.

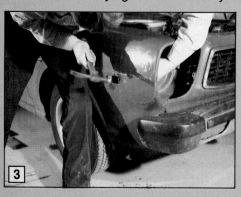

6 Mix the body filler (see Body Repair Tips). Spread the body filler evenly over the entire area (see Body Repair Tips). Be sure to cover the area completely.

7 Let the body filler dry until the surface can just be scratched with your fingernail. Knock the high spots from the body filler with a body file ("Cheesegrater"). Check frequently with the palm of your hand for high and low spots.

8 Check to be sure that trim pieces that will be installed later will fit exactly. Sand the area with 40-grit paper.

9 If you wind up with low spots, you may have to apply another layer of filler.

10 Knock the high spots off with 40-grit paper. When you are satisfied with the contours of the repair, apply a thin coat of filler to cover pin holes and scratches.

11 Block sand the area with 40-grit paper to a smooth finish. Pay particular attention to body lines and ridges that must be well-defined.

12 Sand the area with 400 paper and then finish with a scuff pad. The finished repair is ready for priming and painting (see Painting Tips).

Materials and photos courtesy of Ritt Jones Auto Body, Prospect Park, PA.

REPAIRING RUST HOLES

There are many ways to repair rust holes. The fiberglass cloth kit shown here is one of the most cost efficient for the owner because it provides a strong repair that resists cracking and moisture and is relatively easy to use. It can be used on large and small holes (with or without backing) and can be applied over contoured areas. Remember, however, that short of replacing an entire panel, no repair is a guarantee that the rust will not return.

1 Remove any trim that will be in the way. Clean away all loose debris. Cut away all the rusted metal. But be sure to leave enough metal to retain the contour or body shape.

2 Grind away all traces of rust with a 24-grit grinding disc. Be sure to grind back 3-4 inches from the edge of the hole down to bare metal and be sure all traces of paint, primer and rust are removed.

3 Block sand the area with 80 or 100 grit sandpaper to get a clear, shiny surface and feathered paint edge. Tap the edges of the hole inward with a ball peen hammer.

4 If you are going to use release film, cut a piece about 2-3" larger than the area you have sanded. Place the film over the repair and mark the sanded area on the film. Avoid any unnecessary wrinkling of the film.

5 Cut 2 pieces of fiberglass matte to match the shape of the repair. One piece should be about 1" smaller than the sanded area and the second piece should be 1" smaller than the first. Mix enough filler and hardener to saturate the fiberglass material (see Body Repair Tips).

6 Lay the release sheet on a flat surface and spread an even layer of filler, large enough to cover the repair. Lay the smaller piece of fiberglass cloth in the center of the sheet and spread another layer of filler over the fiberglass cloth. Repeat the operation for the larger piece of cloth.

7 Place the repair material over the repair area, with the release film facing outward. Use a spreader and work from the center outward to smooth the material, following the body contours. Be sure to remove all air bubbles.

8 Wait until the repair has dried tack-free and peel off the release sheet. The ideal working temperature is 60°-90° F. Cooler or warmer temperatures or high humidity may require additional curing time. Wait longer, if in doubt.

9 Sand and feather-edge the entire area. The initial sanding can be done with a sanding disc on an electric drill if care is used. Finish the sanding with a block sander. Low spots can be filled with body filler; this may require several applications.

10 When the filler can just be scratched with a fingernail, knock the high spots down with a body file and smooth the entire area with 80-grit. Feather the filled areas into the surrounding areas.

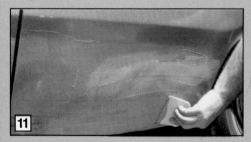

11 When the area is sanded smooth, mix some topcoat and hardener and apply it directly with a spreader. This will give a smooth finish and prevent the glass matte from showing through the paint.

12 Block sand the topcoat smooth with finishing sandpaper (200 grit), and 400 grit. The repair is ready for masking, priming and painting (see Painting Tips).

Materials and photos courtesy Marson Corporation, Chelsea, Massachusetts

PAINTING TIPS

Preparation

1 SANDING — Use a 400 or 600 grit wet or dry sandpaper. Wet-sand the area with a ¼ sheet of sandpaper soaked in clean water. Keep the paper wet while sanding. Sand the area until the repaired area tapers into the original finish.

2 CLEANING — Wash the area to be painted thoroughly with water and a clean rag. Rinse it thoroughly and wipe the surface dry until you're sure it's completely free of dirt, dust, fingerprints, wax, detergent or other foreign matter.

3 MASKING — Protect any areas you don't want to overspray by covering them with masking tape and newspaper. Be careful not get fingerprints on the area to be painted.

4 PRIMING — All exposed metal should be primed before painting. Primer protects the metal and provides an excellent surface for paint adhesion. When the primer is dry, wet-sand the area again with 600 grit wet-sandpaper. Clean the area again after sanding.

Painting Techniques

P aint applied from either a spray gun or a spray can (for small areas) will provide good results. Experiment on an old piece of metal to get the right combination before you begin painting.

SPRAYING VISCOSITY (SPRAY GUN ONLY) — Paint should be thinned to spraying viscosity according to the directions on the can. Use only the recommended thinner or reducer and the same amount of reduction regardless of temperature.

AIR PRESSURE (SPRAY GUN ONLY) — This is extremely important. Be sure you are using the proper recommended pressure.

TEMPERATURE — The surface to be painted should be approximately the same temperature as the surrounding air. Applying warm paint to a cold surface, or vice versa, will completely upset the paint characteristics.

THICKNESS — Spray with smooth strokes. In general, the thicker the coat of paint, the longer the drying time. Apply several thin coats about 30 seconds apart. The paint should remain wet long enough to flow out and no longer; heavier coats will only produce sags or wrinkles. Spray a light (fog) coat, followed by heavier color coats.

DISTANCE — The ideal spraying distance is 8″-12″ from the gun or can to the surface. Shorter distances will produce ripples, while greater distances will result in orange peel, dry film and poor color match and loss of material due to overspray.

OVERLAPPING — The gun or can should be kept at right angles to the surface at all times. Work to a wet edge at an even speed, using a 50% overlap and direct the center of the spray at the lower or nearest edge of the previous stroke.

RUBBING OUT (BLENDING) FRESH PAINT — Let the paint dry thoroughly. Runs or imperfections can be sanded out, primed and repainted.

Don't be in too big a hurry to remove the masking. This only produces paint ridges. When the finish has dried for at least a week, apply a small amount of fine grade rubbing compound with a clean, wet cloth. Use lots of water and blend the new paint with the surrounding area.

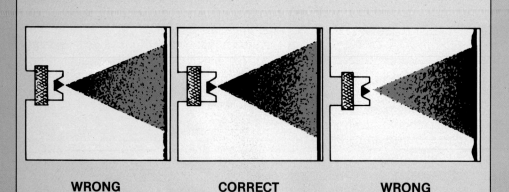

WRONG	CORRECT	WRONG
Thin coat. Stroke too fast, not enough overlap, gun too far away.	Medium coat. Proper distance, good stroke, proper overlap.	Heavy coat. Stroke too slow, too much overlap, gun too close.

Section 9—Valve Train
See Chapter 3 for service procedures

Test and Procedure	Results and Indications	Proceed to
9.1—Evaluate the valve train: Remove the valve cover, and ensure that the valves are adjusted to specifications. A mechanic's stethoscope may be used to aid in the diagnosis of the valve train. By pushing the probe on or near push rods or rockers, valve noise often can be isolated. A timing light also may be used to diagnose valve problems. Connect the light according to manufacturer's recommendations, and start the engine. Vary the firing moment of the light by increasing the engine speed (and therefore the ignition advance), and moving the trigger from cylinder to cylinder. Observe the movement of each valve.	Sticking valves or erratic valve train motion can be observed with the timing light. The cylinder head must be disassembled for repairs.	**See Chapter 3**
9.2—Check the valve timing: Locate top dead center of the No. 1 piston, and install a degree wheel or tape on the crankshaft pulley or damper with zero corresponding to an index mark on the engine. Rotate the crankshaft in its direction of rotation, and observe the opening of the No. 1 cylinder intake valve. The opening should correspond with the correct mark on the degree wheel according to specifications.	If the timing is not correct, the timing cover must be removed for further investigation.	**See Chapter 3**

Section 10—Exhaust System

Test and Procedure	Results and Indications	Proceed to
10.1—Determine whether the exhaust manifold heat control valve is operating: Operate the valve by hand to determine whether it is free to move. If the valve is free, run the engine to operating temperature and observe the action of the valve, to ensure that it is opening.	If the valve sticks, spray it with a suitable solvent, open and close the valve to free it, and retest. If the valve functions properly: If the valve does not free, or does not operate, replace the valve:	10.2 10.2
10.2—Ensure that there are no exhaust restrictions: Visually inspect the exhaust system for kinks, dents, or crushing. Also note that gases are flowing freely from the tailpipe at all engine speeds, indicating no restriction in the muffler or resonator.	Replace any damaged portion of the system:	11.1

Section 11—Cooling System
See Chapter 3 for service procedures

Test and Procedure	Results and Indications	Proceed to
11.1—Visually inspect the fan belt for glazing, cracks, and fraying, and replace if necessary. Tighten the belt so that the longest span has approximately ½″ play at its midpoint under thumb pressure (see Chapter 1).	Replace or tighten the fan belt as necessary:	**11.2**

Checking belt tension

11.2—Check the fluid level of the cooling system.	If full or slightly low, fill as necessary:	**11.5**
	If extremely low:	**11.3**
11.3—Visually inspect the external portions of the cooling system (radiator, radiator hoses, thermostat elbow, water pump seals, heater hoses, etc.) for leaks. If none are found, pressurize the cooling system to 14–15 psi.	If cooling system holds the pressure:	**11.5**
	If cooling system loses pressure rapidly, reinspect external parts of the system for leaks under pressure. If none are found, check dipstick for coolant in crankcase. If no coolant is present, but pressure loss continues:	**11.4**
	If coolant is evident in crankcase, remove cylinder head(s), and check gasket(s). If gaskets are intact, block and cylinder head(s) should be checked for cracks or holes.	
	If the gasket(s) is blown, replace, and purge the crankcase of coolant:	**12.6**
	NOTE: *Occasionally, due to atmospheric and driving conditions, condensation of water can occur in the crankcase. This causes the oil to appear milky white. To remedy, run the engine until hot, and change the oil and oil filter.*	
11.4—Check for combustion leaks into the cooling system: Pressurize the cooling system as above. Start the engine, and observe the pressure gauge. If the needle fluctuates, remove each spark plug wire, one at a time, noting which cylinder(s) reduce or eliminate the fluctuation.	Cylinders which reduce or eliminate the fluctuation, when the spark plug wire is removed, are leaking into the cooling system. Replace the head gasket on the affected cylinder bank(s).	

Pressurizing the cooling system

Test and Procedure	Results and Indications	Proceed to
11.5—Check the radiator pressure cap: Attach a radiator pressure tester to the radiator cap (wet the seal prior to installation). Quickly pump up the pressure, noting the point at which the cap releases.	If the cap releases within ± 1 psi of the specified rating, it is operating properly:	**11.6**
	If the cap releases at more than ± 1 psi of the specified rating, it should be replaced:	**11.6**

Checking radiator pressure cap

Test and Procedure	Results and Indications	Proceed to
11.6—Test the thermostat: Start the engine cold, remove the radiator cap, and insert a thermometer into the radiator. Allow the engine to idle. After a short while, there will be a sudden, rapid increase in coolant temperature. The temperature at which this sharp rise stops is the thermostat opening temperature.	If the thermostat opens at or about the specified temperature:	**11.7**
	If the temperature doesn't increase: (If the temperature increases slowly and gradually, replace the thermostat.)	**11.7**
11.7—Check the water pump: Remove the thermostat elbow and the thermostat, disconnect the coil high tension lead (to prevent starting), and crank the engine momentarily.	If coolant flows, replace the thermostat and retest per 11.6:	**11.6**
	If coolant doesn't flow, reverse flush the cooling system to alleviate any blockage that might exist. If system is not blocked, and coolant will not flow, replace the water pump.	

Section 12—Lubrication
See Chapter 3 for service procedures

Test and Procedure	Results and Indications	Proceed to
12.1—Check the oil pressure gauge or warning light: If the gauge shows low pressure, or the light is on for no obvious reason, remove the oil pressure sender. Install an accurate oil pressure gauge and run the engine momentarily.	If oil pressure builds normally, run engine for a few moments to determine that it is functioning normally, and replace the sender.	—
	If the pressure remains low:	**12.2**
	If the pressure surges:	**12.3**
	If the oil pressure is zero:	**12.3**
12.2—Visually inspect the oil: If the oil is watery or very thin, milky, or foamy, replace the oil and oil filter.	If the oil is normal:	**12.3**
	If after replacing oil the pressure remains low:	**12.3**
	If after replacing oil the pressure becomes normal:	—

Test and Procedure	Results and Indications	Proceed to
12.3—Inspect the oil pressure relief valve and spring, to ensure that it is not sticking or stuck. Remove and thoroughly clean the valve, spring, and the valve body.	If the oil pressure improves: If no improvement is noted:	— **12.4**
12.4—Check to ensure that the oil pump is not cavitating (sucking air instead of oil): See that the crankcase is neither over nor underfull, and that the pickup in the sump is in the proper position and free from sludge.	Fill or drain the crankcase to the proper capacity, and clean the pickup screen in solvent if necessary. If no improvement is noted:	**12.5**
12.5—Inspect the oil pump drive and the oil pump:	If the pump drive or the oil pump appear to be defective, service as necessary and retest per 12.1: If the pump drive and pump appear to be operating normally, the engine should be disassembled to determine where blockage exists:	**12.1** **See Chapter 3**
12.6—Purge the engine of ethylene glycol coolant: Completely drain the crankcase and the oil filter. Obtain a commercial butyl cellosolve base solvent, designated for this purpose, and follow the instructions precisely. Following this, install a new oil filter and refill the crankcase with the proper weight oil. The next oil and filter change should follow shortly thereafter (1000 miles).		

TROUBLESHOOTING EMISSION CONTROL SYSTEMS

See Chapter 4 for procedures applicable to individual emission control systems used on specific combinations of engine/transmission/model.

TROUBLESHOOTING THE CARBURETOR
See Chapter 4 for service procedures

Carburetor problems cannot be effectively isolated unless all other engine systems (particularly ignition and emission) are functioning properly and the engine is properly tuned.

Condition	Possible Cause
Engine cranks, but does not start	1. Improper starting procedure 2. No fuel in tank 3. Clogged fuel line or filter 4. Defective fuel pump 5. Choke valve not closing properly 6. Engine flooded 7. Choke valve not unloading 8. Throttle linkage not making full travel 9. Stuck needle or float 10. Leaking float needle or seat 11. Improper float adjustment
Engine stalls	1. Improperly adjusted idle speed or mixture **Engine hot** 2. Improperly adjusted dashpot 3. Defective or improperly adjusted solenoid 4. Incorrect fuel level in fuel bowl 5. Fuel pump pressure too high 6. Leaking float needle seat 7. Secondary throttle valve stuck open 8. Air or fuel leaks 9. Idle air bleeds plugged or missing 10. Idle passages plugged **Engine Cold** 11. Incorrectly adjusted choke 12. Improperly adjusted fast idle speed 13. Air leaks 14. Plugged idle or idle air passages 15. Stuck choke valve or binding linkage 16. Stuck secondary throttle valves 17. Engine flooding—high fuel level 18. Leaking or misaligned float
Engine hesitates on acceleration	1. Clogged fuel filter 2. Leaking fuel pump diaphragm 3. Low fuel pump pressure 4. Secondary throttle valves stuck, bent or misadjusted 5. Sticking or binding air valve 6. Defective accelerator pump 7. Vacuum leaks 8. Clogged air filter 9. Incorrect choke adjustment (engine cold)
Engine feels sluggish or flat on acceleration	1. Improperly adjusted idle speed or mixture 2. Clogged fuel filter 3. Defective accelerator pump 4. Dirty, plugged or incorrect main metering jets 5. Bent or sticking main metering rods 6. Sticking throttle valves 7. Stuck heat riser 8. Binding or stuck air valve 9. Dirty, plugged or incorrect secondary jets 10. Bent or sticking secondary metering rods. 11. Throttle body or manifold heat passages plugged 12. Improperly adjusted choke or choke vacuum break.
Carburetor floods	1. Defective fuel pump. Pressure too high. 2. Stuck choke valve 3. Dirty, worn or damaged float or needle valve/seat 4. Incorrect float/fuel level 5. Leaking float bowl

Condition	Possible Cause
Engine idles roughly and stalls	1. Incorrect idle speed 2. Clogged fuel filter 3. Dirt in fuel system or carburetor 4. Loose carburetor screws or attaching bolts 5. Broken carburetor gaskets 6. Air leaks 7. Dirty carburetor 8. Worn idle mixture needles 9. Throttle valves stuck open 10. Incorrectly adjusted float or fuel level 11. Clogged air filter
Engine runs unevenly or surges	1. Defective fuel pump 2. Dirty or clogged fuel filter 3. Plugged, loose or incorrect main metering jets or rods 4. Air leaks 5. Bent or sticking main metering rods 6. Stuck power piston 7. Incorrect float adjustment 8. Incorrect idle speed or mixture 9. Dirty or plugged idle system passages 10. Hard, brittle or broken gaskets 11. Loose attaching or mounting screws 12. Stuck or misaligned secondary throttle valves
Poor fuel economy	1. Poor driving habits 2. Stuck choke valve 3. Binding choke linkage 4. Stuck heat riser 5. Incorrect idle mixture 6. Defective accelerator pump 7. Air leaks 8. Plugged, loose or incorrect main metering jets 9. Improperly adjusted float or fuel level 10. Bent, misaligned or fuel-clogged float 11. Leaking float needle seat 12. Fuel leak 13. Accelerator pump discharge ball not seating properly 14. Incorrect main jets
Engine lacks high speed performance or power	1. Incorrect throttle linkage adjustment 2. Stuck or binding power piston 3. Defective accelerator pump 4. Air leaks 5. Incorrect float setting or fuel level 6. Dirty, plugged, worn or incorrect main metering jets or rods 7. Binding or sticking air valve 8. Brittle or cracked gaskets 9. Bent, incorrect or improperly adjusted secondary metering rods 10. Clogged fuel filter 11. Clogged air filter 12. Defective fuel pump

TROUBLESHOOTING FUEL INJECTION PROBLEMS

Each fuel injection system has its own unique components and test procedures, for which it is impossible to generalize. Refer to Chapter 4 of this Repair & Tune-Up Guide for specific test and repair procedures, if the vehicle is equipped with fuel injection.

TROUBLESHOOTING ELECTRICAL PROBLEMS

See Chapter 5 for service procedures

For any electrical system to operate, it must make a complete circuit. This simply means that the power flow from the battery must make a complete circle. When an electrical component is operating, power flows from the battery to the component, passes through the component causing it to perform its function (lighting a light bulb), and then returns to the battery through the ground of the circuit. This ground is usually (but not always) the metal part of the car or truck on which the electrical component is mounted.

Perhaps the easiest way to visualize this is to think of connecting a light bulb with two wires attached to it to the battery. If one of the two wires attached to the light bulb were attached to the negative post of the battery and the other were attached to the positive post of the battery, you would have a complete circuit. Current from the battery would flow to the light bulb, causing it to light, and return to the negative post of the battery.

The normal automotive circuit differs from this simple example in two ways. First, instead of having a return wire from the bulb to the battery, the light bulb returns the current to the battery through the chassis of the vehicle. Since the negative battery cable is attached to the chassis and the chassis is made of electrically conductive metal, the chassis of the vehicle can serve as a ground wire to complete the circuit. Secondly, most automotive circuits contain switches to turn components on and off as required.

Every complete circuit from a power source must include a component which is using the power from the power source. If you were to disconnect the light bulb from the wires and touch the two wires together (don't do this) the power supply wire to the component would be grounded before the normal ground connection for the circuit.

Because grounding a wire from a power source makes a complete circuit—less the required component to use the power—this phenomenon is called a short circuit. Common causes are: broken insulation (exposing the metal wire to a metal part of the car or truck), or a shorted switch.

Some electrical components which require a large amount of current to operate also have a relay in their circuit. Since these circuits carry a large amount of current, the thickness of the wire in the circuit (gauge size) is also greater. If this large wire were connected from the component to the control switch on the instrument panel, and then back to the component, a voltage drop would occur in the circuit. To prevent this potential drop in voltage, an electromagnetic switch (relay) is used. The large wires in the circuit are connected from the battery to one side of the relay, and from the opposite side of the relay to the component. The relay is normally open, preventing current from passing through the circuit. An additional, smaller, wire is connected from the relay to the control switch for the circuit. When the control switch is turned on, it grounds the smaller wire from the relay and completes the circuit. This closes the relay and allows current to flow from the battery to the component. The horn, headlight, and starter circuits are three which use relays.

It is possible for larger surges of current to pass through the electrical system of your car or truck. If this surge of current were to reach an electrical component, it could burn it out. To prevent this, fuses, circuit breakers or fusible links are connected into the current supply wires of most of the major electrical systems. When an electrical current of excessive power passes through the component's fuse, the fuse blows out and breaks the circuit, saving the component from destruction.

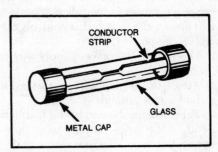

Typical automotive fuse

A circuit breaker is basically a self-repairing fuse. The circuit breaker opens the circuit the same way a fuse does. However, when either the short is removed from the circuit or the surge subsides, the circuit breaker resets itself and does not have to be replaced as a fuse does.

A fuse link is a wire that acts as a fuse. It is normally connected between the starter relay and the main wiring harness. This connection is usually under the hood. The fuse link (if installed) protects all the

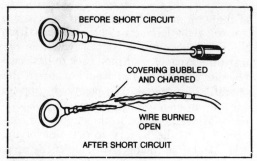

BEFORE SHORT CIRCUIT

COVERING BUBBLED
AND CHARRED

WIRE BURNED
OPEN

AFTER SHORT CIRCUIT

Most fusible links show a charred, melted insulation when they burn out

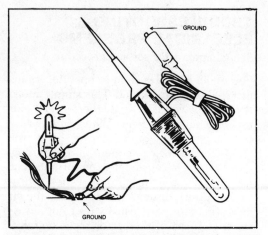

GROUND

GROUND

The test light will show the presence of current when touched to a hot wire and grounded at the other end

chassis electrical components, and is the probable cause of trouble when none of the electrical components function, unless the battery is disconnected or dead.

Electrical problems generally fall into one of three areas:

1. The component that is not functioning is not receiving current.

2. The component itself is not functioning.

3. The component is not properly grounded.

The electrical system can be checked with a test light and a jumper wire. A test light is a device that looks like a pointed screwdriver with a wire attached to it and has a light bulb in its handle. A jumper wire is a piece of insulated wire with an alligator clip attached to each end.

If a component is not working, you must follow a systematic plan to determine which of the three causes is the villain.

1. Turn on the switch that controls the inoperable component.

2. Disconnect the power supply wire from the component.

3. Attach the ground wire on the test light to a good metal ground.

4. Touch the probe end of the test light to the end of the power supply wire that was disconnected from the component. If the component is receiving current, the test light will go on.

NOTE: *Some components work only when the ignition switch is turned on.*

If the test light does not go on, then the problem is in the circuit between the battery and the component. This includes all the switches, fuses, and relays in the system. Follow the wire that runs back to the battery. The problem is an open circuit between the

battery and the component. If the fuse is blown and, when replaced, immediately blows again, there is a short circuit in the system which must be located and repaired. If there is a switch in the system, bypass it with a jumper wire. This is done by connecting one end of the jumper wire to the power supply wire into the switch and the other end of the jumper wire to the wire coming out of the switch. If the test light lights with the jumper wire installed, the switch or whatever was bypassed is defective.

NOTE: *Never substitute the jumper wire for the component, since it is required to use the power from the power source.*

5. If the bulb in the test light goes on, then the current is getting to the component that is not working. This eliminates the first of the three possible causes. Connect the power supply wire and connect a jumper wire from the component to a good metal ground. Do this with the switch which controls the component turned on, and also the ignition switch turned on if it is required for the component to work. If the component works with the jumper wire installed, then it has a bad ground. This is usually caused by the metal area on which the component mounts to the chassis being coated with some type of foreign matter.

6. If neither test located the source of the trouble, then the component itself is defective. Remember that for any electrical system to work, all connections must be clean and tight.

Troubleshooting Basic Turn Signal and Flasher Problems
See Chapter 5 for service procedures

Most problems in the turn signals or flasher system can be reduced to defective flashers or bulbs, which are easily replaced. Occasionally, the turn signal switch will prove defective.

F = Front   R = Rear   ● = Lights off   ○ = Lights on

Condition		Possible Cause
Turn signals light, but do not flash	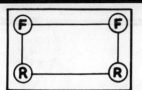	Defective flasher
No turn signals light on either side	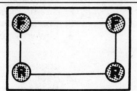	Blown fuse. Replace if defective. Defective flasher. Check by substitution. Open circuit, short circuit or poor ground.
Both turn signals on one side don't work	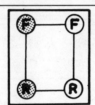	Bad bulbs. Bad ground in both (or either) housings.
One turn signal light on one side doesn't work	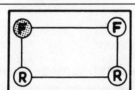	Defective bulb. Corrosion in socket. Clean contacts. Poor ground at socket.
Turn signal flashes too fast or too slowly		Check any bulb on the side flashing too fast. A heavy-duty bulb is probably installed in place of a regular bulb. Check the bulb flashing too slowly. A standard bulb was probably installed in place of a heavy-duty bulb. Loose connections or corrosion at the bulb socket.
Indicator lights don't work in either direction	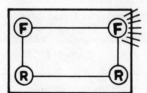	Check if the turn signals are working. Check the dash indicator lights. Check the flasher by substitution.
One indicator light doesn't light		On systems with one dash indicator: See if the lights work on the same side. Often the filaments have been reversed in systems combining stoplights with tail-lights and turn signals. Check the flasher by substitution. On systems with two indicators: Check the bulbs on the same side. Check the indicator light bulb. Check the flasher by substitution.

Troubleshooting Lighting Problems
See Chapter 5 for service procedures

Condition	Possible Cause
One or more lights don't work, but others do	1. Defective bulb(s) 2. Blown fuse(s) 3. Dirty fuse clips or light sockets 4. Poor ground circuit
Lights burn out quickly	1. Incorrect voltage regulator setting or defective regulator 2. Poor battery/alternator connections
Lights go dim	1. Low/discharged battery 2. Alternator not charging 3. Corroded sockets or connections 4. Low voltage output
Lights flicker	1. Loose connection 2. Poor ground. (Run ground wire from light housing to frame) 3. Circuit breaker operating (short circuit)
Lights "flare"—Some flare is normal on acceleration—If excessive, see "Lights Burn Out Quickly"	High voltage setting
Lights glare—approaching drivers are blinded	1. Lights adjusted too high 2. Rear springs or shocks sagging 3. Rear tires soft

Troubleshooting Dash Gauge Problems

Most problems can be traced to a defective sending unit or faulty wiring. Occasionally, the gauge itself is at fault. See Chapter 5 for service procedures.

Condition	Possible Cause
COOLANT TEMPERATURE GAUGE	
Gauge reads erratically or not at all	1. Loose or dirty connections 2. Defective sending unit. 3. Defective gauge. To test a bi-metal gauge, remove the wire from the sending unit. Ground the wire for an instant. If the gauge registers, replace the sending unit. To test a magnetic gauge, disconnect the wire at the sending unit. With ignition ON gauge should register COLD. Ground the wire; gauge should register HOT.
AMMETER GAUGE—TURN HEADLIGHTS ON (DO NOT START ENGINE). NOTE REACTION	
Ammeter shows charge Ammeter shows discharge Ammeter does not move	1. Connections reversed on gauge 2. Ammeter is OK 3. Loose connections or faulty wiring 4. Defective gauge

Condition	Possible Cause

OIL PRESSURE GAUGE

Gauge does not register or is inaccurate	1. On mechanical gauge, Bourdon tube may be bent or kinked.
	2. Low oil pressure. Remove sending unit. Idle the engine briefly. If no oil flows from sending unit hole, problem is in engine.
	3. Defective gauge. Remove the wire from the sending unit and ground it for an instant with the ignition ON. A good gauge will go to the top of the scale.
	4. Defective wiring. Check the wiring to the gauge. If it's OK and the gauge doesn't register when grounded, replace the gauge.
	5. Defective sending unit.

ALL GAUGES

All gauges do not operate	1. Blown fuse
	2. Defective instrument regulator
All gauges read low or erratically	3. Defective or dirty instrument voltage regulator
All gauges pegged	4. Loss of ground between instrument voltage regulator and frame
	5. Defective instrument regulator

WARNING LIGHTS

Light(s) do not come on when ignition is ON, but engine is not started	1. Defective bulb
	2. Defective wire
	3. Defective sending unit. Disconnect the wire from the sending unit and ground it. Replace the sending unit if the light comes on with the ignition ON.
Light comes on with engine running	4. Problem in individual system
	5. Defective sending unit

Troubleshooting Clutch Problems

It is false economy to replace individual clutch components. The pressure plate, clutch plate and throwout bearing should be replaced as a set, and the flywheel face inspected, whenever the clutch is overhauled. See Chapter 6 for service procedures.

Condition	Possible Cause
Clutch chatter	1. Grease on driven plate (disc) facing
	2. Binding clutch linkage or cable
	3. Loose, damaged facings on driven plate (disc)
	4. Engine mounts loose
	5. Incorrect height adjustment of pressure plate release levers
	6. Clutch housing or housing to transmission adapter misalignment
	7. Loose driven plate hub
Clutch grabbing	1. Oil, grease on driven plate (disc) facing
	2. Broken pressure plate
	3. Warped or binding driven plate. Driven plate binding on clutch shaft
Clutch slips	1. Lack of lubrication in clutch linkage or cable (linkage or cable binds, causes incomplete engagement)
	2. Incorrect pedal, or linkage adjustment
	3. Broken pressure plate springs
	4. Weak pressure plate springs
	5. Grease on driven plate facings (disc)

Troubleshooting Clutch Problems (cont.)

Condition	Possible Cause
Incomplete clutch release	1. Incorrect pedal or linkage adjustment or linkage or cable binding 2. Incorrect height adjustment on pressure plate release levers 3. Loose, broken facings on driven plate (disc) 4. Bent, dished, warped driven plate caused by overheating
Grinding, whirring grating noise when pedal is depressed	1. Worn or defective throwout bearing 2. Starter drive teeth contacting flywheel ring gear teeth. Look for milled or polished teeth on ring gear.
Squeal, howl, trumpeting noise when pedal is being released (occurs during first inch to inch and one-half of pedal travel)	Pilot bushing worn or lack of lubricant. If bushing appears OK, polish bushing with emery cloth, soak lube wick in oil, lube bushing with oil, apply film of chassis grease to clutch shaft pilot hub, reassemble. NOTE: Bushing wear may be due to misalignment of clutch housing or housing to transmission adapter
Vibration or clutch pedal pulsation with clutch disengaged (pedal fully depressed)	1. Worn or defective engine transmission mounts 2. Flywheel run out. (Flywheel run out at face not to exceed 0.005") 3. Damaged or defective clutch components

Troubleshooting Manual Transmission Problems
See Chapter 6 for service procedures

Condition	Possible Cause
Transmission jumps out of gear	1. Misalignment of transmission case or clutch housing. 2. Worn pilot bearing in crankshaft. 3. Bent transmission shaft. 4. Worn high speed sliding gear. 5. Worn teeth or end-play in clutch shaft. 6. Insufficient spring tension on shifter rail plunger. 7. Bent or loose shifter fork. 8. Gears not engaging completely. 9. Loose or worn bearings on clutch shaft or mainshaft. 10. Worn gear teeth. 11. Worn or damaged detent balls.
Transmission sticks in gear	1. Clutch not releasing fully. 2. Burred or battered teeth on clutch shaft, or sliding sleeve. 3. Burred or battered transmission mainshaft. 4. Frozen synchronizing clutch. 5. Stuck shifter rail plunger. 6. Gearshift lever twisting and binding shifter rail. 7. Battered teeth on high speed sliding gear or on sleeve. 8. Improper lubrication, or lack of lubrication. 9. Corroded transmission parts. 10. Defective mainshaft pilot bearing. 11. Locked gear bearings will give same effect as stuck in gear.
Transmission gears will not synchronize	1. Binding pilot bearing on mainshaft, will synchronize in high gear only. 2. Clutch not releasing fully. 3. Detent spring weak or broken. 4. Weak or broken springs under balls in sliding gear sleeve. 5. Binding bearing on clutch shaft, or binding countershaft. 6. Binding pilot bearing in crankshaft. 7. Badly worn gear teeth. 8. Improper lubrication. 9. Constant mesh gear not turning freely on transmission mainshaft. Will synchronize in that gear only.

Condition	Possible Cause
Gears spinning when shifting into gear from neutral	1. Clutch not releasing fully. 2. In some cases an extremely light lubricant in transmission will cause gears to continue to spin for a short time after clutch is released. 3. Binding pilot bearing in crankshaft.
Transmission noisy in all gears	1. Insufficient lubricant, or improper lubricant. 2. Worn countergear bearings. 3. Worn or damaged main drive gear or countergear. 4. Damaged main drive gear or mainshaft bearings. 5. Worn or damaged countergear anti-lash plate.
Transmission noisy in neutral only	1. Damaged main drive gear bearing. 2. Damaged or loose mainshaft pilot bearing. 3. Worn or damaged countergear anti-lash plate. 4. Worn countergear bearings.
Transmission noisy in one gear only	1. Damaged or worn constant mesh gears. 2. Worn or damaged countergear bearings. 3. Damaged or worn synchronizer.
Transmission noisy in reverse only	1. Worn or damaged reverse idler gear or idler bushing. 2. Worn or damaged mainshaft reverse gear. 3. Worn or damaged reverse countergear. 4. Damaged shift mechanism.

TROUBLESHOOTING AUTOMATIC TRANSMISSION PROBLEMS

Keeping alert to changes in the operating characteristics of the transmission (changing shift points, noises, etc.) can prevent small problems from becoming large ones. If the problem cannot be traced to loose bolts, fluid level, misadjusted linkage, clogged filters or similar problems, you should probably seek professional service.

Transmission Fluid Indications

The appearance and odor of the transmission fluid can give valuable clues to the overall condition of the transmission. Always note the appearance of the fluid when you check the fluid level or change the fluid. Rub a small amount of fluid between your fingers to feel for grit and smell the fluid on the dipstick.

If the fluid appears:	It indicates:
Clear and red colored	Normal operation
Discolored (extremely dark red or brownish) or smells burned	Band or clutch pack failure, usually caused by an overheated transmission. Hauling very heavy loads with insufficient power or failure to change the fluid often result in overheating. Do not confuse this appearance with newer fluids that have a darker red color and a strong odor (though not a burned odor).
Foamy or aerated (light in color and full of bubbles)	1. The level is too high (gear train is churning oil) 2. An internal air leak (air is mixing with the fluid). Have the transmission checked professionally.
Solid residue in the fluid	Defective bands, clutch pack or bearings. Bits of band material or metal abrasives are clinging to the dipstick. Have the transmission checked professionally.
Varnish coating on the dipstick	The transmission fluid is overheating

TROUBLESHOOTING DRIVE AXLE PROBLEMS

First, determine when the noise is most noticeable.

Drive Noise: Produced under vehicle acceleration.

Coast Noise: Produced while coasting with a closed throttle.

Float Noise: Occurs while maintaining constant speed (just enough to keep speed constant) on a level road.

External Noise Elimination

It is advisable to make a thorough road test to determine whether the noise originates in the rear axle or whether it originates from the tires, engine, transmission, wheel bearings or road surface. Noise originating from other places cannot be corrected by servicing the rear axle.

ROAD NOISE

Brick or rough surfaced concrete roads produce noises that seem to come from the rear axle. Road noise is usually identical in Drive or Coast and driving on a different type of road will tell whether the road is the problem.

TIRE NOISE

Tire noise can be mistaken as rear axle noise, even though the tires on the front are at fault. Snow tread and mud tread tires or tires worn unevenly will frequently cause vibrations which seem to originate elsewhere; *temporarily, and for test purposes only,* inflate the tires to 40–50 lbs. This will significantly alter the noise produced by the tires, but will not alter noise from the rear axle. Noises from the rear axle will normally cease at speeds below 30 mph on coast, while tire noise will continue at lower tone as speed is decreased. The rear axle noise will usually change from drive conditions to coast conditions, while tire noise will not. Do not forget to lower the tire pressure to normal after the test is complete.

ENGINE/TRANSMISSION NOISE

Determine at what speed the noise is most pronounced, then stop in a quiet place. With the transmission in Neutral, run the engine through speeds corresponding to road speeds where the noise was noticed. Noises produced with the vehicle standing still are coming from the engine or transmission.

FRONT WHEEL BEARINGS

Front wheel bearing noises, sometimes confused with rear axle noises, will not change when comparing drive and coast conditions. While holding the speed steady, lightly apply the footbrake. This will often cause wheel bearing noise to lessen, as some of the weight is taken off the bearing. Front wheel bearings are easily checked by jacking up the wheels and spinning the wheels. Shaking the wheels will also determine if the wheel bearings are excessively loose.

REAR AXLE NOISES

Eliminating other possible sources can narrow the cause to the rear axle, which normally produces noise from worn gears or bearings. Gear noises tend to peak in a narrow speed range, while bearing noises will usually vary in pitch with engine speeds.

Noise Diagnosis

The Noise Is:	Most Probably Produced By:
1. Identical under Drive or Coast	Road surface, tires or front wheel bearings
2. Different depending on road surface	Road surface or tires
3. Lower as speed is lowered	Tires
4. Similar when standing or moving	Engine or transmission
5. A vibration	Unbalanced tires, rear wheel bearing, unbalanced driveshaft or worn U-joint
6. A knock or click about every two tire revolutions	Rear wheel bearing
7. Most pronounced on turns	Damaged differential gears
8. A steady low-pitched whirring or scraping, starting at low speeds	Damaged or worn pinion bearing
9. A chattering vibration on turns	Wrong differential lubricant or worn clutch plates (limited slip rear axle)
10. Noticed only in Drive, Coast or Float conditions	Worn ring gear and/or pinion gear

Troubleshooting Steering & Suspension Problems

Condition	Possible Cause
Hard steering (wheel is hard to turn)	1. Improper tire pressure 2. Loose or glazed pump drive belt 3. Low or incorrect fluid 4. Loose, bent or poorly lubricated front end parts 5. Improper front end alignment (excessive caster) 6. Bind in steering column or linkage 7. Kinked hydraulic hose 8. Air in hydraulic system 9. Low pump output or leaks in system 10. Obstruction in lines 11. Pump valves sticking or out of adjustment 12. Incorrect wheel alignment
Loose steering (too much play in steering wheel)	1. Loose wheel bearings 2. Faulty shocks 3. Worn linkage or suspension components 4. Loose steering gear mounting or linkage points 5. Steering mechanism worn or improperly adjusted 6. Valve spool improperly adjusted 7. Worn ball joints, tie-rod ends, etc.
Veers or wanders (pulls to one side with hands off steering wheel)	1. Improper tire pressure 2. Improper front end alignment 3. Dragging or improperly adjusted brakes 4. Bent frame 5. Improper rear end alignment 6. Faulty shocks or springs 7. Loose or bent front end components 8. Play in Pitman arm 9. Steering gear mountings loose 10. Loose wheel bearings 11. Binding Pitman arm 12. Spool valve sticking or improperly adjusted 13. Worn ball joints
Wheel oscillation or vibration transmitted through steering wheel	1. Low or uneven tire pressure 2. Loose wheel bearings 3. Improper front end alignment 4. Bent spindle 5. Worn, bent or broken front end components 6. Tires out of round or out of balance 7. Excessive lateral runout in disc brake rotor 8. Loose or bent shock absorber or strut
Noises (see also "Troubleshooting Drive Axle Problems")	1. Loose belts 2. Low fluid, air in system 3. Foreign matter in system 4. Improper lubrication 5. Interference or chafing in linkage 6. Steering gear mountings loose 7. Incorrect adjustment or wear in gear box 8. Faulty valves or wear in pump 9. Kinked hydraulic lines 10. Worn wheel bearings
Poor return of steering	1. Over-inflated tires 2. Improperly aligned front end (excessive caster) 3. Binding in steering column 4. No lubrication in front end 5. Steering gear adjusted too tight
Uneven tire wear (see "How To Read Tire Wear")	1. Incorrect tire pressure 2. Improperly aligned front end 3. Tires out-of-balance 4. Bent or worn suspension parts

HOW TO READ TIRE WEAR

The way your tires wear is a good indicator of other parts of the suspension. Abnormal wear patterns are often caused by the need for simple tire maintenance, or for front end alignment.

Excessive wear at the center of the tread indicates that the air pressure in the tire is consistently too high. The tire is riding on the center of the tread and wearing it prematurely. Occasionally, this wear pattern can result from outrageously wide tires on narrow rims. The cure for this is to replace either the tires or the wheels.

This type of wear usually results from consistent under-inflation. When a tire is under-inflated, there is too much contact with the road by the outer treads, which wear prematurely. When this type of wear occurs, and the tire pressure is known to be consistently correct, a bent or worn steering component or the need for wheel alignment could be indicated.

Feathering is a condition when the edge of each tread rib develops a slightly rounded edge on one side and a sharp edge on the other. By running your hand over the tire, you can usually feel the sharper edges before you'll be able to see them. The most common causes of feathering are incorrect toe-in setting or deteriorated bushings in the front suspension.

When an inner or outer rib wears faster than the rest of the tire, the need for wheel alignment is indicated. There is excessive camber in the front suspension, causing the wheel to lean too much putting excessive load on one side of the tire. Misalignment could also be due to sagging springs, worn ball joints, or worn control arm bushings. Be sure the vehicle is loaded the way it's normally driven when you have the wheels aligned.

Cups or scalloped dips appearing around the edge of the tread almost always indicate worn (sometimes bent) suspension parts. Adjustment of wheel alignment alone will seldom cure the problem. Any worn component that connects the wheel to the suspension can cause this type of wear. Occasionally, wheels that are out of balance will wear like this, but wheel imbalance usually shows up as bald spots between the outside edges and center of the tread.

Second-rib wear is usually found only in radial tires, and appears where the steel belts end in relation to the tread. It can be kept to a minimum by paying careful attention to tire pressure and frequently rotating the tires. This is often considered normal wear but excessive amounts indicate that the tires are too wide for the wheels.

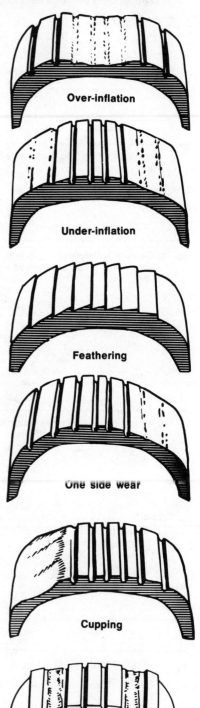

Over-inflation

Under-inflation

Feathering

One side wear

Cupping

Second-rib wear

Troubleshooting Disc Brake Problems

Condition	Possible Cause
Noise—groan—brake noise emanating when slowly releasing brakes (creep-groan)	Not detrimental to function of disc brakes—no corrective action required. (This noise may be eliminated by slightly increasing or decreasing brake pedal efforts.)
Rattle—brake noise or rattle emanating at low speeds on rough roads, (front wheels only).	1. Shoe anti-rattle spring missing or not properly positioned. 2. Excessive clearance between shoe and caliper. 3. Soft or broken caliper seals. 4. Deformed or misaligned disc. 5. Loose caliper.
Scraping	1. Mounting bolts too long. 2. Loose wheel bearings. 3. Bent, loose, or misaligned splash shield.
Front brakes heat up during driving and fail to release	1. Operator riding brake pedal. 2. Stop light switch improperly adjusted. 3. Sticking pedal linkage. 4. Frozen or seized piston. 5. Residual pressure valve in master cylinder. 6. Power brake malfunction. 7. Proportioning valve malfunction.
Leaky brake caliper	1. Damaged or worn caliper piston seal. 2. Scores or corrosion on surface of cylinder bore.
Grabbing or uneven brake action—Brakes pull to one side	1. Causes listed under "Brakes Pull". 2. Power brake malfunction. 3. Low fluid level in master cylinder. 4. Air in hydraulic system. 5. Brake fluid, oil or grease on linings. 6. Unmatched linings. 7. Distorted brake pads. 8. Frozen or seized pistons. 9. Incorrect tire pressure. 10. Front end out of alignment. 11. Broken rear spring. 12. Brake caliper pistons sticking. 13. Restricted hose or line. 14. Caliper not in proper alignment to braking disc. 15. Stuck or malfunctioning metering valve. 16. Soft or broken caliper seals. 17. Loose caliper.
Brake pedal can be depressed without braking effect	1. Air in hydraulic system or improper bleeding procedure. 2. Leak past primary cup in master cylinder. 3. Leak in system. 4. Rear brakes out of adjustment. 5. Bleeder screw open.
Excessive pedal travel	1. Air, leak, or insufficient fluid in system or caliper. 2. Warped or excessively tapered shoe and lining assembly. 3. Excessive disc runout. 4. Rear brake adjustment required. 5. Loose wheel bearing adjustment. 6. Damaged caliper piston seal. 7. Improper brake fluid (boil). 8. Power brake malfunction. 9. Weak or soft hoses.

Troubleshooting Disc Brake Problems (cont.)

Condition	Possible Cause
Brake roughness or chatter (pedal pumping)	1. Excessive thickness variation of braking disc. 2. Excessive lateral runout of braking disc. 3. Rear brake drums out-of-round. 4. Excessive front bearing clearance.
Excessive pedal effort	1. Brake fluid, oil or grease on linings. 2. Incorrect lining. 3. Frozen or seized pistons. 4. Power brake malfunction. 5. Kinked or collapsed hose or line. 6. Stuck metering valve. 7. Scored caliper or master cylinder bore. 8. Seized caliper pistons.
Brake pedal fades (pedal travel increases with foot on brake)	1. Rough master cylinder or caliper bore. 2. Loose or broken hydraulic lines/connections. 3. Air in hydraulic system. 4. Fluid level low. 5. Weak or soft hoses. 6. Inferior quality brake shoes or fluid. 7. Worn master cylinder piston cups or seals.

Troubleshooting Drum Brakes

Condition	Possible Cause
Pedal goes to floor	1. Fluid low in reservoir. 2. Air in hydraulic system. 3. Improperly adjusted brake. 4. Leaking wheel cylinders. 5. Loose or broken brake lines. 6. Leaking or worn master cylinder. 7. Excessively worn brake lining.
Spongy brake pedal	1. Air in hydraulic system. 2. Improper brake fluid (low boiling point). 3. Excessively worn or cracked brake drums. 4. Broken pedal pivot bushing.
Brakes pulling	1. Contaminated lining. 2. Front end out of alignment. 3. Incorrect brake adjustment. 4. Unmatched brake lining. 5. Brake drums out of round. 6. Brake shoes distorted. 7. Restricted brake hose or line. 8. Broken rear spring. 9. Worn brake linings. 10. Uneven lining wear. 11. Glazed brake lining. 12. Excessive brake lining dust. 13. Heat spotted brake drums. 14. Weak brake return springs. 15. Faulty automatic adjusters. 16. Low or incorrect tire pressure.

Condition	Possible Cause
Squealing brakes	1. Glazed brake lining. 2. Saturated brake lining. 3. Weak or broken brake shoe retaining spring. 4. Broken or weak brake shoe return spring. 5. Incorrect brake lining. 6. Distorted brake shoes. 7. Bent support plate. 8. Dust in brakes or scored brake drums. 9. Linings worn below limit. 10. Uneven brake lining wear. 11. Heat spotted brake drums.
Chirping brakes	1. Out of round drum or eccentric axle flange pilot.
Dragging brakes	1. Incorrect wheel or parking brake adjustment. 2. Parking brakes engaged or improperly adjusted. 3. Weak or broken brake shoe return spring. 4. Brake pedal binding. 5. Master cylinder cup sticking. 6. Obstructed master cylinder relief port. 7. Saturated brake lining. 8. Bent or out of round brake drum. 9. Contaminated or improper brake fluid. 10. Sticking wheel cylinder pistons. 11. Driver riding brake pedal. 12. Defective proportioning valve. 13. Insufficient brake shoe lubricant.
Hard pedal	1. Brake booster inoperative. 2. Incorrect brake lining. 3. Restricted brake line or hose. 4. Frozen brake pedal linkage. 5. Stuck wheel cylinder. 6. Binding pedal linkage. 7. Faulty proportioning valve.
Wheel locks	1. Contaminated brake lining. 2. Loose or torn brake lining. 3. Wheel cylinder cups sticking. 4. Incorrect wheel bearing adjustment. 5. Faulty proportioning valve.
Brakes fade (high speed)	1. Incorrect lining. 2. Overheated brake drums. 3. Incorrect brake fluid (low boiling temperature). 4. Saturated brake lining. 5. Leak in hydraulic system. 6. Faulty automatic adjusters.
Pedal pulsates	1. Bent or out of round brake drum.
Brake chatter and shoe knock	1. Out of round brake drum. 2. Loose support plate. 3. Bent support plate. 4. Distorted brake shoes. 5. Machine grooves in contact face of brake drum (Shoe Knock). 6. Contaminated brake lining. 7. Missing or loose components. 8. Incorrect lining material. 9. Out-of-round brake drums. 10. Heat spotted or scored brake drums. 11. Out-of-balance wheels.

Troubleshooting Drum Brakes (cont.)

Condition	Possible Cause
Brakes do not self adjust	1. Adjuster screw frozen in thread. 2. Adjuster screw corroded at thrust washer. 3. Adjuster lever does not engage star wheel. 4. Adjuster installed on wrong wheel.
Brake light glows	1. Leak in the hydraulic system. 2. Air in the system. 3. Improperly adjusted master cylinder pushrod. 4. Uneven lining wear. 5. Failure to center combination valve or proportioning valve.

Mechanic's Data

General Conversion Table

Multiply By	To Convert	To	
		LENGTH	
2.54	Inches	Centimeters	.3937
25.4	Inches	Millimeters	.03937
30.48	Feet	Centimeters	.0328
.304	Feet	Meters	3.28
.914	Yards	Meters	1.094
1.609	Miles	Kilometers	.621
		VOLUME	
.473	Pints	Liters	2.11
.946	Quarts	Liters	1.06
3.785	Gallons	Liters	.264
.016	Cubic inches	Liters	61.02
16.39	Cubic inches	Cubic cms.	.061
28.3	Cubic feet	Liters	.0353
		MASS (Weight)	
28.35	Ounces	Grams	.035
.4536	Pounds	Kilograms	2.20
—	To obtain	From	Multiply by

Multiply By	To Convert	To	
		AREA	
.645	Square inches	Square cms.	.155
.836	Square yds.	Square meters	1.196
		FORCE	
4.448	Pounds	Newtons	.225
.138	Ft./lbs.	Kilogram/meters	7.23
1.36	Ft./lbs.	Newton-meters	.737
.112	In./lbs.	Newton-meters	8.844
		PRESSURE	
.068	Psi	Atmospheres	14.7
6.89	Psi	Kilopascals	.145
		OTHER	
1.104	Horsepower (DIN)	Horsepower (SAE)	.9861
.746	Horsepower (SAE)	Kilowatts (KW)	1.34
1.60	Mph	Km/h	.625
.425	Mpg	Km/1	2.35
—	To obtain	From	Multiply by

Tap Drill Sizes

National Coarse or U.S.S.

Screw & Tap Size	Threads Per Inch	Use Drill Number
No. 5	40	.39
No. 6	32	.36
No. 8	32	.29
No. 10	24	.25
No. 12	24	.17
1/4	20	8
5/16	18	.F
3/8	16	5/16
7/16	14	.U
1/2	13	27/64
9/16	12	31/64
5/8	11	17/32
3/4	10	21/32
7/8	9	49/64

National Coarse or U.S.S.

Screw & Tap Size	Threads Per Inch	Use Drill Number
1	8	7/8
1 1/8	7	63/64
1 1/4	7	1 7/64
1 1/2	6	1 11/32

National Fine or S.A.E.

Screw & Tap Size	Threads Per Inch	Use Drill Number
No. 5	44	.37
No. 6	40	.33
No. 8	36	.29
No. 10	32	.21

National Fine or S.A.E.

Screw & Tap Size	Threads Per Inch	Use Drill Number
No. 12	28	.15
1/4	28	3
6/16	24	1
3/8	24	.Q
7/16	20	.W
1/2	20	29/64
9/16	18	33/64
5/8	18	37/64
3/4	16	11/16
7/8	14	13/16
1 1/8	12	1 3/64
1 1/4	12	1 11/64
1 1/2	12	1 27/64

Drill Sizes In Decimal Equivalents

Inch	Decimal	Wire	mm
1/64	.0156		.39
	.0157		.4
	.0160	78	
	.0165		.42
	.0173		.44
	.0177		.45
	.0180	77	
	.0181		.46
	.0189		.48
	.0197		.5
	.0200	76	
	.0210	75	
	.0217		.55
	.0225	74	
	.0236		.6
	.0240	73	
	.0250	72	
	.0256		.65
	.0260	71	
	.0276		.7
	.0280	70	
	.0292	69	
	.0295		.75
	.0310	68	
1/32	.0312		.79
	.0315		.8
	.0320	67	
	.0330	66	
	.0335		.85
	.0350	65	
	.0354		.9
	.0360	64	
	.0370	63	
	.0374		.95
	.0380	62	
	.0390	61	
	.0394		1.0
	.0400	60	
	.0410	59	
	.0413		1.05
	.0420	58	
	.0430	57	
	.0433		1.1
	.0453		1.15
3/64	.0465	56	
	.0469		1.19
	.0472		1.2
	.0492		1.25
	.0512		1.3
	.0520	55	
	.0531		1.35
	.0550	54	
	.0551		1.4
	.0571		1.45
	.0591		1.5
	.0595	53	
	.0610		1.55
1/16	.0625		1.59
	.0630		1.6
	.0635	52	
	.0650		1.65
	.0669		1.7
	.0670	51	
	.0689		1.75
	.0700	50	
	.0709		1.8
	.0728		1.85

Inch	Decimal	Wire	mm
	.0730	49	
	.0748		1.9
	.0760	48	
	.0768		1.95
5/64	.0781		1.98
	.0785	47	
	.0787		2.0
	.0807		2.05
	.0810	46	
	.0820	45	
	.0827		2.1
	.0846		2.15
	.0860	44	
	.0866		2.2
	.0886		2.25
	.0890	43	
	.0906		2.3
	.0925		2.35
	.0935	42	
3/32	.0938		2.38
	.0945		2.4
	.0960	41	
	.0965		2.45
	.0980	40	
	.0981		2.5
	.0995	39	
	.1015	38	
	.1024		2.6
	.1040	37	
	.1063		2.7
	.1065	36	
	.1083		2.75
7/64	.1094		2.77
	.1100	35	
	.1102		2.8
	.1110	34	
	.1130	33	
	.1142		2.9
	.1160	32	
	.1181		3.0
	.1200	31	
	.1220		3.1
1/8	.1250		3.17
	.1260		3.2
	.1280		3.25
	.1285	30	
	.1299		3.3
	.1339		3.4
	.1360	29	
	.1378		3.5
	.1405	28	
9/64	.1406		3.57
	.1417		3.6
	.1440	27	
	.1457		3.7
	.1470	26	
	.1476		3.75
	.1495	25	
	.1496		3.8
	.1520	24	
	.1535		3.9
	.1540	23	
5/32	.1562		3.96
	.1570	22	
	.1575		4.0
	.1590	21	
	.1610	20	

Inch	Decimal	Wire & Letter	mm
	.1614		4.1
	.1654		4.2
	.1660	19	
	.1673		4.25
	.1693		4.3
	.1695	18	
11/64	.1719		4.36
	.1730	17	
	.1732		4.4
	.1770	16	
	.1772		4.5
	.1800	15	
	.1811		4.6
	.1820	14	
	.1850	13	
	.1850		4.7
	.1870		4.75
3/16	.1875		4.76
	.1890		4.8
	.1890	12	
	.1910	11	
	.1929		4.9
	.1935	10	
	.1960	9	
	.1969		5.0
	.1990	8	
	.2008		5.1
	.2010	7	
13/64	.2031		5.16
	.2040	6	
	.2047		5.2
	.2055	5	
	.2067		5.25
	.2087		5.3
	.2090	4	
	.2126		5.4
	.2130	3	
	.2165		5.5
7/32	.2188		5.55
	.2205		5.6
	.2210	2	
	.2244		5.7
	.2264		5.75
	.2280	1	
	.2283		5.8
	.2323		5.9
	.2340	A	
15/64	.2344		5.95
	.2362		6.0
	.2380	B	
	.2402		6.1
	.2420	C	
	.2441		6.2
	.2460	D	
	.2461		6.25
	.2480		6.3
1/4	.2500	E	6.35
	.2520		6.
	.2559		6.5
	.2570	F	
	.2598		6.6
	.2610	G	
	.2638		6.7
17/64	.2656		6.74
	.2657		6.75
	.2660	H	
	.2677		6.8

Inch	Decimal	Letter	mm
	.2717		6.9
	.2720	I	
	.2756		7.0
	.2770	J	
	.2795		7.1
	.2810	K	
9/32	.2812		7.14
	.2835		7.2
	.2854		7.25
	.2874		7.3
	.2900	L	
	.2913		7.4
	.2950	M	
	.2953		7.5
19/64	.2969		7.54
	.2992		7.6
	.3020	N	
	.3031		7.7
	.3051		7.75
	.3071		7.8
	.3110		7.9
5/16	.3125		7.93
	.3150		8.0
	.3160	O	
	.3189		8.1
	.3228		8.2
	.3230	P	
	.3248		8.25
	.3268		8.3
21/64	.3281		8.33
	.3307		8.4
	.3320	Q	
	.3346		8.5
	.3386		8.6
	.3390	R	
	.3425		8.7
11/32	.3438		8.73
	.3445		8.75
	.3465		8.8
	.3480	S	
	.3504		8.9
	.3543		9.0
	.3580	T	
	.3583		9.1
23/64	.3594		9.12
	.3622		9.2
	.3642		9.25
	.3661		9.3
	.3680	U	
	.3701		9.4
	.3740		9.5
3/8	.3750		9.52
	.3770	V	
	.3780		9.6
	.3819		9.7
	.3839		9.75
	.3858		9.8
	.3860	W	
	.3898		9.9
25/64	.3906		9.92
	.3937		10.0
	.3970	X	
	.4040	Y	
13/32	.4062		10.31
	.4130	Z	
	.4134		10.5
27/64	.4219		10.71

Inch	Decimal	mm
	.4331	11.0
7/16	.4375	11.11
	.4528	11.5
29/64	.4531	11.51
15/32	.4688	11.90
	.4724	12.0
31/64	.4844	12.30
	.4921	12.5
1/2	.5000	12.70
	.5118	13.0
33/64	.5156	13.09
17/32	.5312	13.49
	.5315	13.5
35/64	.5469	13.89
	.5512	14.0
9/16	.5625	14.28
	.5709	14.5
37/64	.5781	14.68
	.5906	15.0
19/32	.5938	15.08
39/64	.6094	15.47
	.6102	15.5
5/8	.6250	15.87
	.6299	16.0
41/64	.6406	16.27
	.6496	16.5
21/32	.6562	16.66
	.6693	17.0
43/64	.6719	17.06
11/16	.6875	17.46
	.6890	17.5
45/64	.7031	17.85
	.7087	18.0
23/32	.7188	18.25
	.7283	18.5
47/64	.7344	18.65
	.7480	19.0
3/4	.7500	19.05
49/64	.7656	19.44
	.7677	19.5
25/32	.7812	19.84
	.7874	20.0
51/64	.7969	20.24
	.8071	20.5
13/16	.8125	20.63
	.8268	21.0
53/64	.8281	21.03
27/32	.8438	21.43
	.8465	21.5
55/64	.8594	21.82
	.8661	22.0
7/8	.8750	22.22
	.8858	22.5
57/64	.8906	22.62
	.9055	23.0
29/32	.9062	23.01
59/64	.9219	23.41
	.9252	23.5
15/16	.9375	23.81
	.9449	24.0
61/64	.9531	24.2
	.9646	24.5
31/32	.9688	24.6
	.9843	25.0
63/64	.9844	25.0
1	1.0000	25.4

Index

Chilton's Repair & Tune-Up Guides

The Complete line covers domestic cars, imports, trucks, vans, RV's and 4-wheel drive vehicles.

RTUG Title	Part No.	RTUG Title	Part No.
AMC 1975-82	7199	**Corvair 1960-69**	6691
Covers all U.S. and Canadian models		Covers all U.S. and Canadian models	
Aspen/Volare 1976-80	6637	**Corvette 1953-62**	6576
Covers all U.S. and Canadian models		Covers all U.S. and Canadian models	
Audi 1970-73	5902	**Corvette 1963-84**	6843
Covers all U.S. and Canadian models.		Covers all U.S. and Canadian models	
Audi 4000/5000 1978-81	7028	**Cutlass 1970-85**	6933
Covers all U.S. and Canadian models including turbocharged and diesel engines		Covers all U.S. and Canadian models	
Barracuda/Challenger 1965-72	5807	**Dart/Demon 1968-76**	6324
Covers all U.S. and Canadian models		Covers all U.S. and Canadian models	
Blazer/Jimmy 1969-82	6931	**Datsun 1961-72**	5790
Covers all U.S. and Canadian 2- and 4-wheel drive models, including diesel engines		Covers all U.S. and Canadian models of Nissan Patrol; 1500, 1600 and 2000 sports cars; Pick-Ups; 410, 411, 510, 1200 and 240Z	
BMW 1970-82	6844		
Covers U.S. and Canadian models		**Datsun 1973-80 Spanish**	7083
Buick/Olds/Pontiac 1975-85	7308	**Datsun/Nissan F-10, 310, Stanza, Pulsar 1977-86**	7196
Covers all U.S. and Canadian full size rear wheel drive models		Covers all U.S. and Canadian models	
Cadillac 1967-84	7462	**Datsun/Nissan Pick-Ups 1970-84**	6816
Covers all U.S. and Canadian rear wheel drive models		Covers all U.S and Canadian models	
Camaro 1967-81	6735	**Datsun/Nissan Z & ZX 1970-86**	6932
Covers all U.S. and Canadian models		Covers all U.S. and Canadian models	
Camaro 1982-85	7317	**Datsun/Nissan 1200, 210, Sentra 1973-86**	7197
Covers all U.S. and Canadian models		Covers all U.S. and Canadian models	
Capri 1970-77	6695	**Datsun/Nissan 200SX, 510, 610, 710, 810, Maxima 1973-84**	7170
Covers all U.S. and Canadian models		Covers all U.S. and Canadian models	
Caravan/Voyager 1984-85	7482	**Dodge 1968-77**	6554
Covers all U.S. and Canadian models		Covers all U.S. and Canadian models	
Century/Regal 1975-85	7307	**Dodge Charger 1967-70**	6486
Covers all U.S. and Canadian rear wheel drive models, including turbocharged engines		Covers all U.S. and Canadian models	
		Dodge/Plymouth Trucks 1967-84	7459
Champ/Arrow/Sapporo 1978-83	7041	Covers all $^1/_2$, $^3/_4$, and 1 ton 2- and 4-wheel drive U.S. and Canadian models, including diesel engines	
Covers all U.S. and Canadian models			
Chevette/1000 1976-86	6836	**Dodge/Plymouth Vans 1967-84**	6934
Covers all U.S. and Canadian models		Covers all $^1/_2$, $^3/_4$, and 1 ton U.S. and Canadian models of vans, cutaways and motor home chassis	
Chevrolet 1968-85	7135		
Covers all U.S. and Canadian models			
Chevrolet 1968-79 Spanish	7082	**D-50/Arrow Pick-Up 1979-81**	7032
Chevrolet/GMC Pick-Ups 1970-82 Spanish	7468	Covers all U.S. and Canadian models	
		Fairlane/Torino 1962-75	6320
Chevrolet/GMC Pick-Ups and Suburban 1970-86	6936	Covers all U.S. and Canadian models	
Covers all U.S. and Canadian $^1/_2$, $^3/_4$ and 1 ton models, including 4-wheel drive and diesel engines		**Fairmont/Zephyr 1978-83**	6965
		Covers all U.S. and Canadian models	
		Fiat 1969-81	7042
		Covers all U.S. and Canadian models	
Chevrolet LUV 1972-81	6815	**Fiesta 1978-80**	6846
Covers all U.S. and Canadian models		Covers all U.S. and Canadian models	
Chevrolet Mid-Size 1964-86	6840	**Firebird 1967-81**	5996
Covers all U.S. and Canadian models of 1964-77 Chevelle, Malibu and Malibu SS; 1974-77 Laguna; 1978-85 Malibu; 1970-86 Monte Carlo; 1964-84 El Camino, including diesel engines		Covers all U.S. and Canadian models	
		Firebird 1982-85	7345
		Covers all U.S. and Canadian models	
		Ford 1968-79 Spanish	7084
		Ford Bronco 1966-83	7140
Chevrolet Nova 1986	7658	Covers all U.S. and Canadian models	
Covers all U.S. and Canadian models		**Ford Bronco II 1984**	7408
Chevy/GMC Vans 1967-84	6930	Covers all U.S. and Canadian models	
Covers all U.S. and Canadian models of $^1/_2$, $^3/_4$, and 1 ton vans, cutaways, and motor home chassis, including diesel engines		**Ford Courier 1972-82**	6983
		Covers all U.S. and Canadian models	
		Ford/Mercury Front Wheel Drive 1981-85	7055
		Covers all U.S. and Canadian models Escort, EXP, Tempo, Lynx, LN-7 and Topaz	
Chevy S-10 Blazer/GMC S-15 Jimmy 1982-85	7383		
Covers all U.S. and Canadian models		**Ford/Mercury/Lincoln 1968-85**	6842
Chevy S-10/GMC S-15 Pick-Ups 1982-85	7310	Covers all U.S. and Canadian models of FORD Country Sedan, Country Squire, Crown Victoria, Custom, Custom 500, Galaxie 500, LTD through 1982, Ranch Wagon, and XL; MERCURY Colony Park, Commuter, Marquis through 1982, Gran Marquis, Monterey and Park Lane; LINCOLN Continental and Towne Car	
Covers all U.S. and Canadian models			
Chevy II/Nova 1962-79	6841		
Covers all U.S. and Canadian models			
Chrysler K- and E-Car 1981-85	7163		
Covers all U.S. and Canadian front wheel drive models			
Colt/Challenger/Vista/Conquest 1971-85	7037		
Covers all U.S. and Canadian models		**Ford/Mercury/Lincoln Mid-Size 1971-85**	6696
Corolla/Carina/Tercel/Starlet 1970-85	7036	Covers all U.S. and Canadian models of FORD Elite, 1983-85 LTD, 1977-79 LTD II, Ranchero, Torino, Gran Torino, 1977-85 Thunderbird; MERCURY 1972-85 Cougar,	
Covers all U.S. and Canadian models			
Corona/Cressida/Crown/Mk.II/Camry/Van 1970-84	7044		
Covers all U.S. and Canadian models			

continued on next page

RTUG Title	Part No.
1983-85 Marquis, Montego, 1980-85 XR-7; LINCOLN 1982-85 Continental, 1984-85 Mark VII, 1978-80 Versailles	
Ford Pick-Ups 1965-86 Covers all $1/2$, $3/4$ and 1 ton, 2- and 4-wheel drive U.S. and Canadian pick-up, chassis cab and camper models, including diesel engines	6913
Ford Pick-Ups 1965-82 Spanish	7469
Ford Ranger 1983-84 Covers all U.S. and Canadian models	7338
Ford Vans 1961-86 Covers all U.S. and Canadian $1/2$, $3/4$ and 1 ton van and cutaway chassis models, including diesel engines	6849
GM A-Body 1982-85 Covers all front wheel drive U.S. and Canadian models of BUICK Century, CHEVROLET Celebrity, OLDSMOBILE Cutlass Ciera and PONTIAC 6000	7309
GM C-Body 1985 Covers all front wheel drive U.S. and Canadian models of BUICK Electra Park Avenue and Electra T-Type, CADILLAC Fleetwood and deVille, OLDSMOBILE 98 Regency and Regency Brougham	7587
GM J-Car 1982-85 Covers all U.S. and Canadian models of BUICK Skyhawk, CHEVROLET Cavalier, CADILLAC Cimarron, OLDSMOBILE Firenza and PONTIAC 2000 and Sunbird	7059
GM N-Body 1985-86 Covers all U.S. and Canadian models of front wheel drive BUICK Somerset and Skylark, OLDSMOBILE Calais, and PONTIAC Grand Am	7657
GM X-Body 1980-85 Covers all U.S. and Canadian models of BUICK Skylark, CHEVROLET Citation, OLDS-MOBILE Omega and PONTIAC Phoenix	7049
GM Subcompact 1971-80 Covers all U.S. and Canadian models of BUICK Skyhawk (1975-80), CHEVROLET Vega and Monza, OLDSMOBILE Starfire, and PONTIAC Astre and 1975-80 Sunbird	6935
Granada/Monarch 1975-82 Covers all U.S. and Canadian models	6937
Honda 1973-84 Covers all U.S. and Canadian models	6980
International Scout 1967-73 Covers all U.S. and Canadian models	5912
Jeep 1945-87 Covers all U.S. and Canadian CJ-2A, CJ-3A, CJ-3B, CJ-5, CJ-6, CJ-7, Scrambler and Wrangler models	6817
Jeep Wagoneer, Commando, Cherokee, Truck 1957-86 Covers all U.S. and Canadian models of Wagoneer, Cherokee, Grand Wagoneer, Jeepster, Jeepster Commando, J-100, J-200, J-300, J-10, J20, FC-150 and FC-170	6739
Laser/Daytona 1984-85 Covers all U.S. and Canadian models	7563
Maverick/Comet 1970-77 Covers all U.S. and Canadian models	6634
Mazda 1971-84 Covers all U.S. and Canadian models of RX-2, RX-3, RX-4, 808, 1300, 1600, Cosmo, GLC and 626	6981
Mazda Pick-Ups 1972-86 Covers all U.S. and Canadian models	7659
Mercedes-Benz 1959-70 Covers all U.S. and Canadian models	6065
Mereceds-Benz 1968-73 Covers all U.S. and Canadian models	5907

RTUG Title	Part No.
Mercedes-Benz 1974-84 Covers all U.S. and Canadian models	6809
Mitsubishi, Cordia, Tredla, Starion, Galant 1983-85 Covers all U.S. and Canadian models	7583
MG 1961-81 Covers all U.S. and Canadian models	6780
Mustang/Capri/Merkur 1979-85 Covers all U.S. and Canadian models	6963
Mustang/Cougar 1965-73 Covers all U.S. and Canadian models	6542
Mustang II 1974-78 Covers all U.S. and Canadian models	6812
Omni/Horizon/Rampage 1978-84 Covers all U.S. and Canadian models of DODGE omni, Miser, 024, Charger 2.2; PLYMOUTH Horizon, Miser, TC3, TC3 Tourismo; Rampage	6845
Opel 1971-75 Covers all U.S. and Canadian models	6575
Peugeot 1970-74 Covers all U.S. and Canadian models	5982
Pinto/Bobcat 1971-80 Covers all U.S. and Canadian models	7027
Plymouth 1968-76 Covers all U.S. and Canadian models	6552
Pontiac Fiero 1984-85 Covers all U.S. and Canadian models	7571
Pontiac Mid-Size 1974-83 Covers all U.S. and Canadian models of Ventura, Grand Am, LeMans, Grand LeMans, GTO, Phoenix, and Grand Prix	7346
Porsche 924/928 1976-81 Covers all U.S. and Canadian models	7048
Renault 1975-85 Covers all U.S. and Canadian models	7165
Roadrunner/Satellite/Belvedere/GTX 1968-73 Covers all U.S. and Canadian models	5821
RX-7 1979-81 Covers all U.S. and Canadian models	7031
SAAB 99 1969-75 Covers all U.S. and Canadian models	5988
SAAB 900 1979-85 Covers all U.S. and Canadian models	7572
Snowmobiles 1976-80 Covers Arctic Cat, John Deere, Kawasaki, Polaris, Ski-Doo and Yamaha	6978
Subaru 1970-84 Covers all U.S. and Canadian models	6982
Tempest/GTO/LeMans 1968-73 Covers all U.S. and Canadian models	5905
Toyota 1966-70 Covers all U.S. and Canadian models of Corona, MkII, Corolla, Crown, Land Cruiser, Stout and Hi-Lux	5795
Toyota 1970-79 Spanish	7467
Toyota Celica/Supra 1971-85 Covers all U.S. and Canadian models	7043
Toyota Trucks 1970-85 Covers all U.S. and Canadian models of pick-ups, Land Cruiser and 4Runner	7035
Valiant/Duster 1968-76 Covers all U.S. and Canadian models	6326
Volvo 1956-69 Covers all U.S. and Canadian models	6529
Volvo 1970-83 Covers all U.S. and Canadian models	7040
VW Front Wheel Drive 1974-85 Covers all U.S. and Canadian models	6962
VW 1949-71 Covers all U.S. and Canadian models	5796
VW 1970-79 Spanish	7081
VW 1970-81 Covers all U.S. and Canadian Beetles, Karmann Ghia, Fastback, Squareback, Vans, 411 and 412	6837

Chilton's Repair & Tune-Up Guides are available at your local retailer or by mailing a check or money order for **$12.50** plus **$2.25** to cover postage and handling to:

**Chilton Book Company
Dept. DM
Radnor, PA 19089**

NOTE: When ordering be sure to include your name & address, book part No. & title.